ITALY
IN THE MAKING
January 1st 1848 TO *No*

By

G. F.-H. & J. BERKELEY

CAMBRIDGE
AT THE UNIVERSITY PRESS
1940
REPRINTED
1968

CAMBRIDGE UNIVERSITY PRESS
Cambridge, New York, Melbourne, Madrid, Cape Town, Singapore,
São Paulo, Delhi, Dubai, Tokyo, Mexico City

Cambridge University Press
The Edinburgh Building, Cambridge CB2 8RU, UK

Published in the United States of America by Cambridge University Press, New York

www.cambridge.org
Information on this title: www.cambridge.org/9780521158657

First published 1940
Reprinted 1968
First paperback edition 2010

A catalogue record for this publication is available from the British Library

Library of Congress Catalogue Card Number: 33-7256

ISBN 978-0-521-07429-2 Hardback
ISBN 978-0-521-15865-7 Paperback

Additional resources for this publication at www.cambridge.org/9780521158657

ITALY

IN THE MAKING

January 1*st* 1848 TO *November* 16*th* 1848

The truth, the whole truth,
and nothing but the truth,
—with the help of God.

CONTENTS

MAPS & PLANS

The following maps are available for download from
www.cambridge.org/9780521158657

General map of the campaign in Upper Italy in the year
1848.

The Field of Custoza. Position of the contending armies
late on July 25th, the fourth day.

PREFACE

The third volume of *Italy in the Making* deals with the year 1848 up to November 24th. This seems a very short space of time to fill a whole volume, but it cannot be fully described in less. It is the period when all the eight small nations of Italy come to the crisis of their fate. It is the stage of rebellion and war when the Risorgimento makes a fresh start.

Almost every episode during this adventurous year has been more or less a subject of controversy; and sometimes our views must differ from those of the earlier English school. But such instances are often attributable to the fact that thousands of fresh documents are now available; and usually our conclusions approximate to those of the more modern Italian historians. In Italy the writers of the present day admittedly have reached a very different stage from those of the nineteenth century. In any case, however, we give detailed references with specimen extracts, and the documents must speak for themselves.

We should like to record our gratitude once more to Commendatore Menghini, for so many years chief of the Biblioteca del Risorgimento in Rome—a never-failing friend and a shrewd critic; also to Commendatore Re, Director of the Real' Archivio di Stato, for valuable and friendly advice and assistance; to Monsignor Mercati Prefect of the Vatican Archives; to Commendatore Dorini Director of the State Archives in Florence; to Professor Gross the kindly and courteous Chief of the Haus-Hof-Staatsarchiv in Vienna.

In addition to many friends already mentioned in our previous volumes, we wish to convey our thanks to the Director and Staff of the Regio Istituto di Storia patria in Rome; also to Conte Buraggi Director of the State Archives of Piedmont; to the Vizconde de Mamblas of the Spanish Foreign Office and to Senhor D. S. Morcuenda Chief of the

Archivio General, Ministerio de Estado, Madrid; also to the Director of the Archives des Affaires Etrangères in Paris, and to the officials of the Record Office in London. Finally our warm thanks are due to Prince Louis-Alphonse de Bourbon-Siciles for kindly showing us his grandfather's Memoir of the Neapolitan revolution, and various family letters; and for many interesting and intimate reminiscences of the court of Naples. Also to Colonel P. R. Worrall, C.B.E., D.S.O., M.C., for his great kindness in so generously placing at our disposal the military knowledge and experience obtained during his distinguished career.

G. F.-H. B.
J. B.

January 29 1940

AUTHORITIES CONSULTED

A. *PUBLISHED SOURCES*

I. GENERAL

(not relating especially to any one state, nor to
the war in Lombardo-Venetia)

ANZILOTTI = ANZILOTTI. *Gioberti.* 1922.

Archivio triennale = *Archivio triennale delle cose d' Italia dall' avveni-
mento di Pio IX all' abbandono di Venezia.* 3 vols. 1851.

ASHLEY = ASHLEY. *Life of Lord Palmerston.* 2 vols. 1876.

BALBO = BALBO, Conte CESARE. *Delle speranze d'Italia.* 2nd ed.
1844.

BALBO, *Sommario* = BALBO, Conte CESARE. *Sommario della storia
d' Italia.* Popular ed. 1933.

BELL = BELL, E. C. *Lord Palmerston.* 2 vols. 1936.

BERTI = BERTI. *Vincenzo Gioberti.* 1881.

BEUST = BEUST, Count VON. *Memoirs of;* trans. by Baron H. de
Worms. 2 vols. 1887.

BIANCHI, *Stor. doc.* = BIANCHI, N. *Storia documentata della diplo-
mazia europea in Italia dall' anno 1814 all' anno 1861.* 8 vols.
Vols. V and VI, 1869.

BONGHI = BONGHI, RUGGIERO. *Vita e tempi di Valentino Pasini.*
1867.

BOUILLET = BOUILLET, M. N. *Dictionnaire d'histoire et de géographie.*
1908.

Camb. Mod. Hist. XI = *Cambridge Modern History.* Vol. XI. "The
growth of Nationalities." 1909.

CANTÙ = CANTÙ, CESARE. *Cronistoria.* 3 vols. 1872 *et seq.*

Carte segrete = *Carte segrete ed atti ufficiali della polizia austriaca in
Italia.* 3 vols. 1851–8.

CASTELLI = CASTELLI, MICHELANGELO. *Ricordi* (1847–75), editi per
cura di L. Chiala. 1888.

CASTELLI, *Carteggio* = CASTELLI, MICHELANGELO. *Carteggio politico,*
edito per cura di L. Chiala. 2 vols. 1890–2.

CECIL = CECIL, ALGERNON. *Metternich.* 1931.

Civiltà Cattolica = *Civiltà Cattolica, La.* 1879. BALLERINI, Article
"Pio IX e Carlo Alberto".

Civiltà Cattolica causa = *Civiltà Cattolica, La.* BALLERINI, Article
"La causa nazionale". 1898.

COPPI = COPPI, A. *Annali d' Italia dall' anno 1814.* n.d.

D'AZEGLIO, *Correspondance* = D'AZEGLIO, MASSIMO. *Correspondance politique.* 1867.

D'AZEGLIO, *Lettere* = D'AZEGLIO, MASSIMO. *Lettere a sua moglie.* 1876.

D'AZEGLIO, *Proposta* = D'AZEGLIO, MASSIMO. *Proposta di un programma per l' opinione nazionale.* 1847.

D'AZEGLIO, *Raccolta* = D'AZEGLIO, MASSIMO. *Raccolta degli scritti politici.* 1850.

D'AZEGLIO, *Ricordi* = D'AZEGLIO, MASSIMO. *I miei Ricordi.* New ed. 1910.

D'AZEGLIO, *a Torelli* = D'AZEGLIO, MASSIMO. *Lettere a Giuseppe Torelli.* 2nd ed. 1870.

DEBIDOUR = DEBIDOUR. *Histoire diplomatique d'Europe.* Vol. II. 1871.

DE GUICHEN = DE GUICHEN, Vicomte. *Les grandes questions Européennes et la diplomatie des puissances sous la seconde république française.* Tome I. October 1847 au 1er mai 1848. 1925.

Diz. del Risorg. = *Dizionario del Risorgimento nazionale.* 4 vols.; one of events and three of persons, the last of which has still to appear.

Encyc. Brit. = *Encyclopaedia Britannica.* Various articles.

FARINI, *Epist.* = FARINI, LUIGI CARLO. *Epistolario,* per cura di Luigi Rava. 1914.

FICQUELMONT = FICQUELMONT, Graf. *Lord Palmerston, l'Angleterre et le Continent.* 2 vols. 1852–53.

FISHER = FISHER, Rt. Hon. H. A. L. *A History of Europe.* 1938.

GARIBALDI = *Garibaldi, Giuseppe, Autobiography of.* Authorised translation by A. Werner. Vol. I, 1807–49. 1889.

GIOBERTI = GIOBERTI, VINCENZO. *Prolegomeni del Primato.* 1846.

GIUSTI = GIUSTI, GIUSEPPE. *Memorie inedite,* edite per cura di F. Martini. 1890.

GOOCH = GOOCH, G. P. *Later Correspondence of Lord John Russell.* Vol. II. 1926.

GORI = GORI, AGOSTINO. *Storia della rivoluzione italiana durante il periodo delle riforme* (1846 al 14 Marzo 1848). 1897.

GREER = GREER, DONALD. *L'Angleterre, la France et la Révolution de 1848. Le troisième ministère de Lord Palmerston au Foreign Office* (1846–51). 1925.

GUALTERIO = GUALTERIO, F. A. *Gli ultimi rivolgimenti italiani. Memorie storiche.* 6 vols. 1850–1.

GUIZOT = GUIZOT, FRANÇOIS. *Mémoires pour servir à l'histoire de mon temps.* 8 vols. 1850.

HERMAN = HERMAN, ARTHUR. *Metternich.* 1932.

HILLEBRAND = HILLEBRAND. *Geschichte Frankreichs von der Thronbesteigung Louis Philipps bis zum Fall Napoleon III.* Vol. III. 1879.

BOLTON KING = KING, BOLTON. *History of Italian Unity.* 2 vols. 1889.

BOLTON KING, *Mazzini* = KING, BOLTON. *Mazzini.* Everyman ed. 1919.

KOCH = KOCH, JULIUS. *Deutsche Geschichte.* Band IV. Sammlung Goschen. 1924.

LA CECILIA = LA CECILIA, GIOVANNI. *Memorie storico-politiche dal 1820 al 1876.* 1876.

LA FARINA = LA FARINA, GIUSEPPE. *Storia d' Italia dal 1815 al 1850.* Vol. II. 2nd ed. 1861.

LAVALLE e PEREGRO = LAVALLE e PEREGRO. *I misteri repubblicani e la Ditta Brofferio, Cattaneo, Cernuschi e Ferrari.* 1851. A pamphlet.

LEMMI = LEMMI, FRANCESCO. *Il Risorgimento (Guida bibliografica).* 1936. For Lemmi *v.* also under Piedmont.

LE ROY BEAULIEU = LE ROY BEAULIEU. *Les Catholiques libéraux de 1830 jusqu'à nos jours.* 1885.

LOEVINSON = LOEVINSON, ERMANNO. *Giuseppe Garibaldi e la sua legione nello Stato Romano 1848–49.* 2 vols. 1904.

London Corr. = *Correspondence respecting the Affairs of Italy,* 1846–49. 4 vols. 1849.

LÜTZOW = LÜTZOW, Count. *Bohemia.* 1895.

LUZIO = LUZIO, A. *Profili biografici e bozzetti storici.* 1927. For Luzio *v.* also under Piedmont.

MARIO = MARIO, JESSIE WHITE. *The Birth of Modern Italy.* 1909.

MARRIOTT = MARRIOTT, Sir J. A. R. *Makers of Modern Italy.* 1931.

MARTINENGO = MARTINENGO CAESARESCO, Countess Evelyn. *Italian Characters.* 1890.

MASI = MASI, ERNESTO. *Il Risorgimento italiano.* 2 vols. 1917.

MASI, *Nell' Ottocento* = MASI, ERNESTO. *Nell' Ottocento.* 1922.

MASI, *Risorg. nei libri* = MASI, ERNESTO. *Il Risorgimento nei libri.* 1911.

MASI, *Fra libri e ricordi* = MASI, ERNESTO. *Fra libri e ricordi.* 1887. *V.* also *Cambridge Modern History,* vol. XI: "Italy and the Revolution." 1909.

MASSARI = MASSARI, G. *Le Opere inedite di Vincenzo Gioberti.* Vols. IX and X. 1861.

MAZZINI, A.E. = MAZZINI, GIUSEPPE. *Scritti editi ed inediti,* edizione diretta dal autore. (A.E. = Author's Edition.) *Proemi,* vols. I–VIII, written by Mazzini. Ditto, vols. IX–XII, by AURELIO SAFFI. 12 vols. 1861–89.

MAZZINI, E.N. = MAZZINI, GIUSEPPE. *Scritti editi ed inediti.* Edizione Nazionale a cura di Mario Menghini. 1906 *et seq.*

MENGHINI = MENGHINI, MARIO. *La Giovane Italia.* 1902.

METTERNICH = METTERNICH, Fürst CLEMENS VON. *Aus Metternichs nachgelassenen Papieren.* Vol. VII; edited by Adolf von Klinkowström. 1883.

METTERNICH, *Mémoires* = METTERNICH, Fürst CLEMENS VON. *Mémoires*. French ed. 2nd ed. 1880. *V.* also under Cecil, Herman and Srbik.

MINGHETTI = MINGHETTI, MARCO. *I miei Ricordi.* 3 vols. 4th ed. 1899.

Nuovo Atlante = *Nuovo Atlante.* 1820.

OECHSLI = OECHSLI. *History of Switzerland from 1499 to 1914.* 1922. *V.* also *Cambridge Modern History,* vol. XI. 1909.

ORSI = ORSI, PIETRO. *Histoire de l'Italie moderne.* French trans. by Bergmann. 1911.

ORSINI = ORSINI, FELICE. *Memoirs and Adventures.* English trans. by Carbonel. 1857.

PROTOCOLLO = *Protocollo della Giovine Italia.* Appendix to the National Edition of Mazzini's works. 6 vols. 1915–22.

QUINTAVALLI = QUINTAVALLI, F. *Storia dell' unità italiana.* 1926.

RANALLI = RANALLI, F. *Le Istorie italiane dal 1846 al 1854.* Vol. I. 1858.

Rass. stor. = *Rassegna storica del Risorgimento.* The organ of the Società nazionale per la storia del Risorgimento. Various dates.

RAULICH = RAULICH, ITALO. Storia del Risorgimento politico d' Italia. 1923.

RAVIOLI, C. *La campagna del Veneto del 1848.* 1883.

Revue des deux Mondes = *Revue des deux Mondes.* 1923. Article "L'Italie libérée".

RICCIARDI = RICCIARDI, G. N. *Cenni storici intorno agli ultimi casi d' Italia.* 1849.

RINAUDO = RINAUDO, COSTANZO. *Il Risorgimento italiano.* Vol. I. 1911.

Risorgimento = *Il Risorgimento.* The review, predecessor of the *Rassegna storica.* Various dates.

Riv. Ital. = *Rivista italiana.* Nuova serie. Vol. II. 1927.

ROSI = ROSI, M. *Storia contemporanea d' Italia.* 1922.

SILVA = SILVA, PIETRO. *La Monarchia di Luglio e l' Italia.* 1917.

SRBIK = SRBIK, HEINRICH RITTER VON. *Metternich der Staatsmann und der Mensch.* 2 vols. 1925.

STERN = STERN. *Geschichte Europas seit den Vorträgen von 1815 bis zum Frankfurter Frieden von 1871.* Vols. IV, V, VI, VII. 1916.

STILLMAN = STILLMAN. *The Union of Italy.* 1899.

THAYER = THAYER, WILLIAM ROSCOE. *The Dawn of Italian Independence.* 2 vols. 1894.

THUREAU-DANGIN = THUREAU-DANGIN. *Histoire de la monarchie de Juillet.* 8 vols. 1884–92.

TIVARONI, *Ital. Sett.* = TIVARONI, CARLO. *Italia Settentrionale,* being vol. I of his *Italia durante la dominazione austriaca. V.* vol. II of *Italy in the Making* for a complete description of Tivaroni's work. 1892.

TIVARONI, *Ital. Cent.* = TIVARONI, CARLO. *Italia Centrale,* being vol. II of *Italia durante la dominazione austriaca.* 1893.

TIVARONI, *Ital. Merid.* = TIVARONI, CARLO. *Italia Meridionale.*
Vol. III of *Italia durante la dominazione austriaca.* 1894.
TREVELYAN, *Roman Republic* = TREVELYAN, G. M., *Garibaldi and the Defence of the Roman Republic.*
VANUCCI = VANUCCI, ATTO. *I Martiri della libertà italiana.* 1860.
Vita italiana = Volume called *La Vita italiana nel Risorgimento 1846–49* in the series of *La Vita italiana*, volume of historical essays. 1898–1901.

II. THE VARIOUS ITALIAN STATES

LOMBARDO-VENETIA

BELGIOJOSO = BELGIOJOSO, Principessa DI. *L'Austria e la rivoluzione italiana.* 1847.
BIANCHI-GIOVINI = BIANCHI-GIOVINI. *L'Austria in Italia.* 1847.
CASATI, ANT. = CASATI, ANTONIO. *Milano ed i principi di Savoia.* 1853.
CASATI, CARLO = CASATI, Dr CARLO. *Nuove rivelazioni sui fatti di Milano nel 1847–48.* 2 vols. 1888.
CATTANEO = CATTANEO, CARLO. *L' Insurrezione di Milano.* 1849.
CORRENTI = CORRENTI, CESARE. *L' Austria e l' Italia.* 1847.
CORRENTI, *Scritti* = CORRENTI, CESARE. *Scritti scelti*, per cura di L. Masserana. 2 vols. 1891.
GASPARRINI = GASPARRINI, LUISA. "I partiti politici a Milano dopo le Cinque Giornate", *Rass. Stor.* 1927, p. 29 *et seq.*
GLI ULTIMI FATTI. *Gli ultimi tristissimi fatti narrati dal Comitato di pubblica difesa.* August 16th, 1848.
HELFERT = HELFERT, Freiherr VON. *Geschichte der Österreichischen Revolution.* Vols. I and II. 1907 and 1909.
HELFERT, *Mailand* = HELFERT, Freiherr VON. *Mailand und der lombardische Zustand.* 1858.
HELFERT, *Casati* = HELFERT, Freiherr VON. "Casati und Pillersdorf." *Archiv für Österreichische Geschichte.* Einundneunziger Band. No date.
OTTOLINI = OTTOLINI, VITTORE. *La Rivoluzione lombarda del 1848 e 1849.* 1887.
PALLAVICINO = PALLAVICINO. *Memorie* pubblicate per cura della moglie. 2 vols. 1892–5.
SANDONÀ = SANDONÀ, AUGUSTO. "Il preludio delle cinque giornate di Milano", in *Rivista d' Italia*, January–February. 1927.
SANDONÀ, *Regno Lombardo* = SANDONÀ, AUGUSTO. *Il regno lombardo-veneto, 1814–59.* 1912.
TORELLI = TORELLI, LUIGI. *Pensieri di un anonimo lombardo.* 1846.
TREVELYAN = TREVELYAN, G. M. *Manin and the Venetian Revolution of 1848.* 1923.

NAPLES AND SICILY

AMARI = AMARI, M. *La Sicile et les Bourbons*. Paris, 1849. *V.* also under Palmieri.

ARCUNO = ARCUNO, IRMA. *Il regno delle due Sicilie nei rapporti con lo Stato Pontificio*. 1933.

Atti (Naples) = *Atti e documenti del processo di maestà per gli avvenimenti del 15 Maggio in Napoli*. Torino, 1851.

BELTRANO-SCALIA = BELTRANO-SCALIA, M. *Memorie storiche della rivoluzione di Sicilia, 1848–49*. 2 vols. 1933.

CALVI = CALVI, P. *Memorie storiche e critiche della rivoluzione Siciliana*. 1851.

CHIARAMONTE = CHIARAMONTE, S. *Il Programma del 1848 e i partiti politici in Sicilia dal 1830 al 1861*. 1901.

COLLETTA = COLLETTA, P. *Storia del reame di Napoli*. Vol. II. Popular ed. 1861.

COPPOLA = COPPOLA, A. *La vita di Giuseppa La Masa*. 1919.

Corr. (Naples). *Correspondence respecting Naples and Sicily, 1848 and 1849*. 1849.

CRISPI = CRISPI, FRANCESCO. *La Sicilia e la rivoluzione*. Essay in *La Vita italiana*. Vol. *Il Risorgimento* (1846–49).

D'ANCONA = D'ANCONA, A. *Carteggio di Michele Amari*. Vol. II. 1896.

D'AYALA = D'AYALA, MARIANO. *Vita del Re di Napoli (Ferdinand II)*. 1856.

DE CESARE = DE CESARE, RAFFAELLO. *La fine di un regno. Dal 1855 al 1860*. 1895.

GUARDIONE = GUARDIONE, F. *Il dominio dei Borboni in Sicilia*. 2 vols. 1907.

GUARDIONE, *Sicilia* = GUARDIONE, F. *La Sicilia, 1795–1860*. 1907.

IMBRIANI = IMBRIANI, VITTORIA. *Lettere e documenti del 1848. Alessandro Poerio e Venezia*. 1884.

LA CECILIA = LA CECILIA, G. *Memorie storico-politiche dal 1820 al 1876*. Vol. II. 1877.

LA FARINA = LA FARINA, GIUSEPPE. *Storia d' Italia dal 1815 al 1850*. 2nd ed. Vol. II. 1861.

LA FARINA, *Sicilia* = LA FARINA, G. *Storia documentata della rivoluzione della Sicilia*. 2 vols. 1851.

LA FARINA, *Epistolario* = LA FARINA, G. *Epistolario raccolto e pubblicato da Ausonio Franchi*. Vol. I. 1869.

LA MASA = LA MASA, GIUSEPPE. *Documenti della rivoluzione Siciliana nel 1847–49*. 2 vols. 1851.

LEOPARDI = LEOPARDI, PIERSILVESTRO. *Narrazioni storiche con documenti relativi alla reazione Napolitana*. 1856.

LIBERTINI and PALADINO = LIBERTINI, G. and PALADINO, G. *Storia della Sicilia*. 1933.

MAAG = MAAG, DR ALBERT. *Geschichte der Schweizertruppen in Neapolitanischen Diensten* 1825–61. 1909.

MASSARI = MASSARI, G. *I casi di Napoli.* 1849.

NISCO = NISCO, Barone N. *Gli ultimi trentasei anni del Reame di Napoli.* Vol. II. 1890.

NISCO, *Storia* = NISCO, Barone N. *Storia d' Italia dall'* 1814 *al* 1880. Vol. III. 1885.

NISCO, *Ferdinando II* = NISCO, Barone N. *Ferdinando II ed il suo regno.* 1884.

NITTI = NITTI. *Sui moti di Napoli in* 1848. In *La Vita italiana.* Vol. *Il Risorgimento,* 1848–49.

PALADINO = PALADINO, G. *Il* 15 *Maggio del* 1848 *in Napoli.* 1921.

PALADINO, *La Rivoluzione* = PALADINO, G. *La rivoluzione Napolitana nel* 1848. 1914. *V.* also under Libertini.

PALMIERI = PALMIERI. *Saggio storico e politico sulla costituzione del Regno di Sicilia.* Preface by Michele Amari. 1847.

PEPE = PEPE, Generale GUGLIELMO. *L' Italia nel* 1847, 1848, 1849. 1850.

PEPE, *Narrative* = PEPE, General GUGLIELMO. *A Narrative of the Political and Military Events which took place in* 1820 *and* 1821. 1821.

PETRUCELLI = PETRUCELLI, F. *La rivoluzione di Napoli nel* 1848. Ricordi di Ferdinando Petrucelli. 1850.

RICCIARDI = RICCIARDI, GIUSEPPE. *Cenni storici intorno agli ultimi casi d' Italia.* 1849.

ROSSI, *Storia* = ROSSI, G. G. *Storia dei rivolgimenti politici delle Due Sicilie dal* 1847 *al* 1850. 1851–2.

SANSONE = SANSONE, A. *La Sicilia nella storia del Risorgimento italiano.*

SETTEMBRINI = SETTEMBRINI, L. *Ricordanze della mia vita.* 1879.

THE PAPAL STATE

Acta = *Acta Pii Papae IX.* The religious encyclicals etc. of Pius IX.

AMIGUES = AMIGUES, JULES. *L'état romain depuis* 1815 *jusqu'à nos jours.* 1862.

Atti = *Atti del Sommo Pontefice Pio IX.* The civil proclamations, notifications etc. of Pius IX.

BALAN = BALAN, PIETRO. *Pio IX, la chiesa e la rivoluzione.* 2 vols. 1898.

BALLERINI = BALLERINI, P. RAFFAELLO. *Les premières pages du pontificat du Pape Pie IX.* 1909.

BAUDRILLART = BAUDRILLART, Mgr. *Dictionnaire d'histoire et géographie ecclésiastique.* Vol. I. 1912.

BONI = BONI, DE. *Congiura di Roma.* 1848.

CALDERARI = CALDERARI, ANGELO. *Il 15 e 16 Novembre 1848, ovvero Risposta a L. C. Farini, autore dello "Stato Romano".* 1850.

Cath. Encyc. = *Catholic Encyclopaedia, The.* Pius IX. Vol. XII. n.d.

CERRO = CERRO, EMILIO. *Cospirazioni romane.* 1899.

Civiltà Cattolica = *Civiltà Cattolica, La.* 1879. BALLERINI. Article "Pio Nono e Carlo Alberto".

CORBOLI BUSSI. *V.* under Manno.

COSTA = COSTA, NINO. *Quel che vidi e quel che intesi,* a cura di Giorgia Guerrazzi Costa. 1927. *V.* also under Rossetti.

CRETINEAU-JOLY = CRETINEAU-JOLY. *L'Église romaine en face de la révolution.* 1859.

DEBIDOUR, *Rapports* = DEBIDOUR. *Histoire des rapports de l'église avec l'état en France de 1789 à 1870.* 1898.

FALDELLA = FALDELLA, G. *Massimo d'Azeglio e Diomede Pantaleoni.* 1888.

FARINI, L. C. *Lo stato romano dal anno 1815 al 1850.* 4 vols. Vol. II. 1850.

FERRARI = FERRARI, RINA. *Il Principe di Canino e il suo processo.* 1926.

GABUSSI = GABUSSI, G. *Memorie della rivoluzione degli stati romani.* 3 vols. 1851.

GALEOTTI = GALEOTTI. *Della sovranità e del governo temporale dei Papi.* 1847.

GALLETTI = GALLETTI, GIUSEPPE. *Memorie intorno ai fatti accaduti in Roma nel 1848 e 1849.* 1863.

GAMS = GAMS. *Geschichte der Kirche Christi im XIX. Jahrhundert.* 1854–56.

GENNARELLI = GENNARELLI, A. *La Corte di Roma.* 1866.

GENTILI = GENTILI, FERDINANDA. "La Lega Doganale." Article in *Rassegna storica del Risorgimento.* 1914.

GIOVAGNOLI = GIOVAGNOLI, R. *Pellegrino Rossi e la rivoluzione Romana.* 3 vols. 1898–1911.

GIOVAGNOLI, *Ciceruacchio* = GIOVAGNOLI, R. *Ciceruacchio e Don Pirlone.* 1894.

HERGENRÖTHER = HERGENRÖTHER, Cardinal. *Histoire de l'église.* French trans. by the Abbé Bélet. 1892.

JOHNSON = JOHNSON, Rev. HUMPHREY. *The Papacy and the Kingdom of Italy.* 1926.

JOHNSTON = JOHNSTON, R. M. *The Roman Theocracy and the Republic* (1846–49). 1901.

LEDERMANN = LEDERMANN, LAZLO. *Pellegrino Rossi, l'homme et l'économiste.* 1929.

MAGUIRE = MAGUIRE. *Rome, its Ruler and its Institutions.* 1857.

MANNO = MANNO, A. *L'opinione religiosa e conservatrice in Italia dal 1830 al 1850 ricercata nella corrispondenza di Monsignor Giovanni Corboli Bussi.* 1910.

MASI, *Vescovo* = MASI, E. *Il Vescovo d'Imola*, in *La Vita italiana nel Risorgimento*. Serie II. Vol. I. n.d.

MONTI = MONTI, A. *Pio IX e il Risorgimento italiano*. 1928.

MORONI = MORONI, GAETANO. *Dizionario di erudizione ecclesiastica*. Vol. LIII. 1851.

PASOLINI = PASOLINI, G. *Memorie raccolte dal suo figlio*, 1815–76. 2 vols. 4th ed. 1915.

PASOLINI, *Eng.* = PASOLINI, G. The preceding, translated and abridged by the Countess of Dalhousie. 1885.

PASOLINI, *Carteggio* = PASOLINI, G. *Carteggio con Marco Minghetti*, ed. by Count Guido Pasolini. Vol. I. 1924.

PELCZAR = PELCZAR, Mgr. JOSEF. *Pio IX e il suo Pontificato*. Italian trans. 3 vols. 1909.

SAFFI = SAFFI, AURELIO. *Storia di Roma*. (Vol. II of *Ricordi e scritti*.) 1893.

RIVES = RIVES, LUIS GARCIA. *La republica Romana de 1849*. 1932.

Rivista d' Italia. *Rivista d' Italia*, 1898. D. G. *Rivelazioni sulla uccisione di Pellegrino Rossi*.

ROSSETTI = ROSSETTI, OLIVIA AGRESTI. *Giovanni Costa, his life, work and times*. 1907.

SILVAGNI = SILVAGNI, DAVID. *La Corte e la società Romana nei secoli XVIII e XIX*. Vol. III. 1885.

SODERINI = SODERINI, Conte EDUARDO. *Il Pontificato di Leone XIII*. 3 vols. Vol. I. 1932.

SPADA = SPADA, GIUSEPPE. *Storia della rivoluzione di Roma*. 3 vols. 1868–69.

TROCCHI = TROCCHI, DINO. *Pio IX e la rivoluzione romana*. 1934.

VERCESI = VERCESI, ERNESTO. *Pio IX*. 1930.

WARD = WARD, WILFRED. *Life of Cardinal Wiseman*. 2 vols. 1897.

WARD, Mgr. BERNARD = WARD, Monsignor BERNARD. *Sequel to Catholic Emancipation*. 2 vols. 1915.

PIEDMONT

ALBERTI = ALBERTI, MARIO DEGLI. *La politica estera di Piemonte sotto Carlo Alberto secondo il carteggio diplomatico del Conte Bertone di Sambuy*. 1835–46. *Biblioteca storica del Risorgimento italiano*. 1914–19. Vol. III.

BARANTE = BARANTE, Baron DE. *Souvenirs*. Vol. IV. 1894.

BERSEZIO = BERSEZIO, VITTORIO. *Il Regno di Vittorio Emmanuele II*. 2 vols. 2nd ed. 1895.

BIANCHI, *Curiosità* = BIANCHI, N. *Curiosità e ricerche di storia subalpina*. 8 vols. 1874–81.

BIANCHI, *Stor. doc. V.* under GENERAL.

BOSIO = BOSIO, FERDINANDO. *Il Marchese Pes di Villamarina*. 1877.

BROFFERIO = BROFFERIO, ANGELO. *Storia di Piemonte*. 3 parts. 1849–51.
CIBRARIO = CIBRARIO, L. *La vie et la mort du roi Charles Albert*. 1861.
COLOMBO = COLOMBO, A. *Dalle riforme allo statuto di Carlo Alberto*. 1924.
COSTA DE BEAUREGARD = COSTA DE BEAUREGARD. *Les dernières années du roi Charles Albert*. 1890.
D'AZEGLIO, COSTANZA = D'AZEGLIO, COSTANZA. *Souvenirs historiques*. 1884.
LEMMI = LEMMI, FRANCESCO. *La politica estera di Carlo Alberto*. 1928.
LUZIO = LUZIO, A. *Carlo Alberto e Mazzini*. 1923.
MATTER = MATTER, PAUL. *Cavour et l'unité italienne*. 3 vols. 1922.
MONTI, GIOV. = MONTI, ANT. *La giovinezza di Vittorio Emanuele II*. 1939.
ODERICI = ODERICI. *Il Conte Cibrario ed i tempi suoi*. 1872.
PREDARI = PREDARI, F. *I primi vagiti della libertà in Piemonte*. 1860.
REVEL = REVEL, GENOVA DI. *Dal 1847 al 1855*. 1891.
RICOTTI = RICOTTI, E. *Della vita e degli scritti del conte Cesare Balbo*. 1856.
RINIERI = RINIERI, I. *Lo statuto e il giuramento del re Carlo Alberto*. 1899.
RODOLICO = RODOLICO, NICCOLÒ. *Carlo Alberto Principe di Carignano*. 1930.
RODOLICO, CARLO ALBERTO = RODOLICO, NICCOLÒ. *Carlo Alberto negli anni di regno, 1831–1843*. 1936.
SALATA = SALATA, FRANCESCO. *Carlo Alberto inedito*. 1931.
SALICE = SALICE, A. *Vita di Re Carlo Alberto il magnanime*. 1867.
THAYER = THAYER, WILLIAM ROSCOE. *Life and Times of Cavour*. 1911.
VIDAL = VIDAL, C. *Charles Albert et le Risorgimento*. 1827.
WHYTE = WHYTE, Rev. Dr A. J. *Early life and letters of Cavour*. Vol. I. 1925.

TUSCANY, PARMA AND MODENA

BALDASSERONI = BALDASSERONI, G. *Leopoldo II e suoi tempi*. 1871.
BIANCHI, *Ducati* = BIANCHI, N. *I Ducati estensi dall' anno 1815 al 1850*. 1852.
CAPPONI = CAPPONI, Marchese GINO. *Lettere*. 1886.
CAPPONI, *Carteggio* = CAPPONI, GINO. *Carteggio. Lettere di Gino Capponi e di altri a lui*. A Carrarese. 2 vols. 1883. *V*. also under Tabarrini.
GALVANI = GALVANI, C. *Memorie storiche intorno la vita di S. A. R. Francesco IV*. 4 vols. 1847.
GIUSTI = GIUSTI, GIUSEPPE. *Memorie inedite*, per cura di Ferdinando Martini. 1890.

GUERRAZZI = GUERRAZZI, D. *Apologia*. 1851.
GUERRAZZI, *Memorie* = GUERRAZZI, D. *Memorie*. 1849.
HANCOCK = HANCOCK, W. K. *Ricasoli and the Risorgimento in Tuscany*. 1926.
HUTTON = HUTTON, EDWARD. *Florence and the Cities of Northern Tuscany*. 1907.
MARTINI = MARTINI, FERDINANDO. *Il '48 nella Toscana*.
MONTANELLI = MONTANELLI, GIUSEPPE. *Memorie sull' Italia*. 2 vols. 2nd ed. 1880.
RICASOLI = RICASOLI, Barone BETTINO. *Lettere e documenti*, pubblicati per cura di M. Tabarrini e A. Gotti. 1887.
TABARRINI = TABARRINI, M. *Gino Capponi; i suoi tempi, i suoi studi, i suoi amici*. 1899.
TOMMASEO = TOMMASEO, N. and CAPPONI, G. *Carteggio inedito dal 1833 al 1874*, per cura di T. del Lungo e P. Prunas. 3 vols. Vol. II (1837–49). 1914.
ZOBI = ZOBI, A. *Storia civile della Toscana*. 5 vols. 1850–52.

THE WAR IN LOMBARDO-VENETIA

BALDINI = BALDINI, ALBERTO. *La guerra del 1848–49*. 1930.
BENEDEK = *Benedek's nachgelassene Papiere*, herausgegeben von H. Friedjung. 1901.
CARLO, ALBERTO. *V. Memorie inedite*.
CESARI = CESARI, CESARE. *Corpi volontari italiani dal 1848 al 1870*. 1921.
D'AZEGLIO, MASSIMO. *V. Succinta relazione*.
DE LAUGIER = DE LAUGIER. *Le milizie toscane nella guerra di Lombardia del 1848*.
DELLA ROCCA = DELLA ROCCA, Generale ENRICO. *Autobiografia di un veterano*. 1897.
DURANDO = DURANDO, Generale GIOVANNI. *Schiarimenti sulla condotta del generale Giovanni Durando comandante le truppe pontificie nel Veneto, scritti da lui medesimo*. 1848.
FABRIS = FABRIS, Colonnello CECILIO. *Gli avvenimenti militari del 1848 e 1849*. 1904.
FEA = FEA, PIETRO. *Storia dei Bersaglieri*. 1879.
Feldzug = *Der Feldzug der österreichischen Armee in Italien in 1848*. Four parts, bound together. 1852.
HILLEPRANDT = HILLEPRANDT, ANTON EDLEN VON. *Der Feldzug in Oberitalien im Jahre 1848*. With volume of maps. 1867.
HÜBNER = HÜBNER, Comte DE. *Une année de ma vie, 1848–9*. 1891.
KUNZ = KUNZ, HERMANN. *Die Feldzüge des Feldmarschalls Radetzky in Oberitalien 1848 und 1849*. 1890.
LUMBROSO. *V. Memorie inedite*.
MARZI = MARZI, DEMETRIO. *Altre notizie intorno alla campagna Toscana del 1848 in Lombardia*. 1909.

Memorie inedite = *Memorie inedite di Carlo Alberto, Re di Sardegna sul* 1848. Ed. with an introduction by A. Lumbroso. 1936.

MEYER OTT = *Die kriegerischen Ereignisse in Italien im Jahre* 1848. 1848. Attributed to Meyer Ott, a Swiss. *V*. also *Military events.*

Military events = *Military events in Italy in* 1848–9, trans. from the German by the Earl of Ellesmere. 1851. *V*. Meyer Ott, of whose book this is a translation.

MONTECCHI = MONTECCHI, MATTIA, segretario del Generale Costante Ferrari. *Divisione Ferrari.* 1850.

MONTÙ = MONTÙ, Generale. *Storia della artiglieria italiana.* Part II, Vol. III. 1935.

OVIDI = OVIDI, E. *Roma e i Romani nelle campagne del* 1848–9. 1903.

PEPE. *V*. under Naples and Sicily.

PIMODAN = PIMODAN, le Marquis DE. *Souvenirs.* Vol. I. 1891.

PINELLI = PINELLI, Maggiore FERDINANDO. *Storia militare del Piemonte.* 1854–5.

RADETZKY, *Briefe* = *Briefe des Feldmarschalls Radetzky an seine Tochter Friederike* 1847–57. 1892.

RADETZKY, *Denkschriften* = *Denkschriften militarisch-politischen Inhalts des k.k. österreichischen Feldmarschalls Radetzky.* 1858.

RADETZKY, *Leben* = *Leben des k.k. österreichischen Feldmarschalls Radetzky. Biografische Skizze nach den eigenen Dictaten und der Correspondenz des Feldmarschalls, von einem österreichischen Veteranen* (General Heller). 1858.

REVEL = REVEL, GENOVA DI. *Dal 1847 al 1855.* 1891.

ROMANO = ROMANO, UN. *Roma e Venezia. Ricordi storici.* 1895.

SCHÖNFELD = SCHÖNFELD, KARL Graf. *Erinnerungen eines Ordonnanzoffiziers Radetzky.* 1904.

SCHÖNHALS = SCHÖNHALS, Feld-Marschall KARL VON. *Erinnerungen eines österreichischen Veteranen aus dem italienischen Krieg der Jahre 1848 und 1849.* 2 vols. 1852.

Studie = *Studie über den Feldzug des F.M. Graf von Radetzky,* 1848. 1907.

Succinta relazione = *Succinta relazione delle operazioni del Generale Durando.* 1848. Massimo Azeglio (*sic*).

TOSI = TOSI, RAFFAELLO. *Da Venezia a Mentana.* 1910.

ULLOA = ULLOA, Général. *Guerre de l'indépendance italienne en 1848–9.* 1859.

Un ufficiale Piemontese. Memorie ed osservazioni, 1850. *V*. under *Memorie inedite.*

WELDEN = WELDEN, LUDWIG Freiherr VON, k.k. Feldzeugmeister. *Episoden aus meinem Leben.* 1853.

WILLISEN = WILLISEN, General W. VON. *Der italienische Feldzug des Jahres 1848.* 1849.

WOLF-SCHNEIDER = WOLF-SCHNEIDER VON ARNO, Oberst OSKAR. *Der Feldherr Radetzky.* 1834.

III. NEWSPAPERS

Newspapers were still in their infancy in 1848; the following are some of the most important that we have consulted.

ROME.   *Bilancia.* Moderate, edited by Professor Orioli.
          Contemporaneo, by the year 1848 had become extreme under Sterbini's guidance.
          Diario di Roma. Official.
          Don Pirlone. Comic, extremist.
          Epoca. Succeeded the *Bilancia* in 1848.
          La Pallade. Popular, humorous.
          La Rivista. Moderate, literary.

BOLOGNA.   *Il Felsineo.* Moderate.

FLORENCE.   *L'Alba.* Mazzinian.
          La Patria. Moderate.

LEGHORN.   *Corriere mercantile.* News.

MILAN.   *L'Italia del Popolo.* Mazzini's paper.

TURIN.   *Concordia.* Founded by Valerio. Democratic. Liberty first, then independence.
          Corriere mercantile. Genoese. Even more anti-Austrian than the *Concordia*.
          Opinione. Giacomo Durando's paper. Surprisingly moderate in view of his opinions.
          Risorgimento. Cavour's newspaper.

B. *UNPUBLISHED SOURCES*

LONDON. RECORD OFFICE. Foreign Office papers. (Ref. in text F.O. Reports of the British Ministers in Naples and Turin in 1848. England had no Minister in Rome. The greater part of these were published as a Blue Book in 1850 (*v.* Published Sources, *London Corr.*), but the originals are worthy of the attention of the student because they include certain details not mentioned in the printed version. It is true probably that no facts of any importance have been left out, but a great deal of human interest in the form of shrewd comment on persons and events was necessarily omitted as being too personal in the year 1850.

ROME. VATICAN ARCHIVES. *Fondo Spada.* A collection of printed and unprinted material made by the Roman banker Spada for his *Storia della Rivoluzione di Roma.* These documents are essential for Roman history during this period.

ARCHIVIO DI STATO. Reference in text, *Rome Arch.*

The *Archivio Politico* contains hundreds of interesting and necessary documents for the war of 1848.

The *Processo Rossi.* This is the procès-verbal of the trial resulting from the murder of Pellegrino Rossi; in 16 MS. volumes. It is chiefly valuable for the insight thrown by the immense mass of evidence on the life of all classes in Rome at the time; and it includes many curious revelations as to the underworld of the city.

REGIO ISTITUTO DI STORIA PATRIA. This now includes the *Archivio del Risorgimento.* We have drawn on it chiefly for the *Carte Pentini*; namely, notes for a memoir left by Monsignor Pentini who was Sostituto to the Ministero dell' Interno in Pellegrino Rossi's government. Some of these have been published.

Another very interesting and impartial set of reports are those of the Comte Liederkerke, Dutch Minister to the Holy See.

Finally, an interesting item in these Archives is an attested copy of the Diary of the Rev. Matthew Drake Babington, English chaplain at Messina during the bombardment. It gives an independent description of that event which differs in some respects from that of the British consul. Reference in the text for all these, *Rome, Reg. Ist.*

VIENNA. HAUS HOF STAATS ARCHIV. Reference in text, *H.H.S.A.*

We have consulted these great Archives mainly for the interesting series of reports from Count Lützow, Ambassador to the Holy See; for those from Count Buol von Schauenstein, Envoy and Plenipotentiary to the Court of Turin; and for those from Prince Felix Schwarzenberg, Minister to Naples. Also for the reports of Graf Ficquelmont on the Milanese situation in January and February 1848. Among these documents there are a number of letters of instruction from Metternich to his envoys, of which the most illuminating are perhaps those to Lützow to whom he wrote as a personal friend—as Lützow also was of Pius IX.

These instructions show that Metternich—who has been generally believed to have used the Revolution as a cover for fresh aggression, in reality was only trying himself to weather the storm.

From London there are despatches concerned with the Hummelauer mission; and they throw some sidelights on Palmerston's methods. But the most interesting for the present work are Graf Buol's reports of his talks with Charles Albert; some of them have Metternich's own comments scrawled across them. For instance, on February 8th, 1848, Buol writes: "Comment nous cacher plus longtemps que Charles Albert est devenu notre ennemi le plus implacable?" And Metternich has scrawled on it: "Est-ce aujourd'hui que nous en fesons (*sic*) la découverte?"

PARIS. ARCHIVES DES AFFAIRES ETRANGÈRES. Reference in text, *Paris Aff. Etr.* These splendid Archives contain valuable reports of the French Ambassador to the Holy See, and of the French Ministers to the courts of Turin and Naples.

MADRID. MINISTERIO DE ESTADO. Chiefly useful for the impartial account of the days of revolution in Rome. We were unable to return to them owing to the Civil War.

TURIN. REALE ARCHIVIO DI STATO. Reference in the text, *Turin Arch.* Important chiefly for the reports of the Piedmontese representatives in Rome, Vienna and Naples. Of these, perhaps the most interesting are the reports of Marchese Balestrino and Conte Colobiano, Ministers to the Court of Naples. As to the happenings of "May 15th" in Naples, and the subsequent press-campaign against Ferdinand, Colobiano wrote a long description overwhelmingly in favour of the King; as to the bombardment of Messina, he evidently had a very low opinion of the Sicilians and especially of their "squadri" or volunteers.

FLORENCE. THE STATE ARCHIVES OF TUSCANY. Reference in the text, *Florence Arch.* Documents from Rome, Turin, Naples; but the most interesting are those from Rome. The Tuscan minister Bargagli was on intimate terms with Pius IX; his despatches have especial value for the Allocution and for their detached account of the negotiations for the League of Italian States.

RELAZIONE OF THE PRINCE OF AQUILA. A MS. account of the early months of 1848 in Naples, written down some years afterwards by Louis, Count of Aquila, brother of Ferdinand II of Naples, and very kindly shown to us by his grandson, Prince Louis de Bourbon-Siciles.

PRELIMINARY

SITUATION ON JANUARY 1ST, 1848

I

At the beginning of the year 1848 the two principal factors in the situation were the influence of Pope Pius IX, now rather on the wane, and the still-invincible Austrian army.

By this date, all the small Italian nations except Naples were on the verge of an outbreak against Austrian domination. But to state this alone is to state nothing. What made the outlook so ominous was the fact that on the continent of Europe almost every civilised people was on the verge of an outbreak. During the coming eighteen months there would be bloodshed in nearly all the capitals: in Paris, Vienna, Berlin, Budapest, Prague, Warsaw and others; and —up and down Italy—in Rome, Milan, Venice, Naples, and Palermo, as well as in most of the secondary towns. For all the different types of revolution, whether national, racial, social or political, their crises seemed to have arrived simultaneously. Very soon insurgent nationalism would cause Czechs and Poles and Hungarians to rise against Germans and Russians; Croats against Hungarians; and Italians against Austrians. At the same time, racially there were three great upheavals, the Pan-German, the Pan-Slav and the Pan-Italian. Thirdly, in some countries the strife was social, such as the rising of the Polish serfs against their landlords. And lastly, as to Liberalism, there hardly existed a civilised nation in which progressive leaders were not claiming freer forms of government.

The above summary is not written with a view to dramatic effect, but because it governs the whole situation. The Revolution was about to break its bounds; and the wide-spread anarchy which would result was not fully realised by any of the men in authority except Metternich. In Italy, however, there was one counterbalancing hope: that this world-upheaval would offer a wonderful chance of winning her freedom; and this possibility was clearly understood by most educated Italians. But, inevitably, it would be an opportunity of very short duration; and that fact was realised by hardly anyone, except, probably, King Charles Albert.

Among Italian nationalists the leader was still His Holiness Pope Pius IX. It was now a year and a half since, as newly-elected Pope, he had stepped voluntarily into the arena, and had declared that the old order of things could no longer continue. His great act of amnesty to political offenders had been received with almost unimaginable gratitude.

It was felt that here was a ruler who was ready to make sacrifices for the general good; and after each fresh concession immense crowds came to thank him with tears of gratitude, and knelt in their thousands to receive his blessing. Gradually they had set him up as their national leader in a war of liberation against Austria. Many of them failed to perceive that although he believed in free institutions and in uniting Italy, he was, first of all, a devoted priest. To risk the status of the Holy See was unthinkable; and thus he was torn between the two greatest calls that a man can hear,[1] his patriotism and his religion.

Now, by the beginning of the year 1848, he had granted almost all that it was possible for a Pope to concede. And although to thousands of people he was still their beloved Pio Nono, he knew that he was at the parting of the ways. The crowds did not mean to let him come to a halt in his

---

[1] He would refuse to become a constitutional sovereign and thereby submit his will to that of the people. But he had set up a Consulta or consultative assembly, and hoped thus to get good work done for his state. As to the problem of unifying Italy, he was opposed to the Mazzinian plan of union by fusion, but he had tried to carry out the scheme of Gioberti, a federation of the Italian states, whereby the separate identity of the Temporal Power could be preserved.

career of concession. When he had tried to modify their New Year's Day demonstration, they had shown signs of anger. They were under the sway of the mob leaders, and those leaders meant to drive him on from point to point until they had compelled him to declare war and excommunicate the Austrians. They were determined that their war of liberation should also be proclaimed a Holy War.

Naturally Pius had no intention of excommunicating the Austrian soldiers or of declaring war against anyone unless in self-defence. His state was guaranteed by all the Great Powers of Europe.

Looking back on the scene after ninety years, certainly most of us will agree that if the Pope was thus debarred from declaring war, that fact also debarred him from having a state at all. But in 1848 such ideas as this did not exist. The Papal State had been solemnly re-established by all the World Powers in 1815, only thirty-three years earlier. It was absolutely safe, and Pius must have felt himself treated with outrageous ingratitude, if not by the people, at all events by the popular leaders. As long as he had concessions to make, they had fawned on him; but now they were raising his own people against him; and several of these were men who, but for his amnesty, would still have been in exile or even in prison.[2]

The question remained: if war broke out, what did he intend to do? Perhaps his position is best illustrated by his

[2] In a despatch of January 15th, 1848, Count Lützow, the Austrian ambassador, described a very interesting interview with Pius: " Je m'apercevais qu'il voit et qu'il redoute les nuages qui couvrent l'horizon de l'avenir. Des exclamations telles que 'Que ferons-nous? Que deviendrons-nous?' Lui échappèrent à diverses reprises. Il convint avec moi qu'il ne Lui restait plus rien à concéder à ses sujets, et qu'il ne tenait qu'à eux de profiter des avantages qu'Il leur avait accordés et largement distribués. Sa Sainteté me parla avec peine de l'ingratitude avec laquelle tous les sacrifices qu'Il a portés ont été recompensés. Sa Sainteté se plaignait amèrement de ne pas avoir été compris...." Vienna H.H.S.A., Rome, 1848.

well-known interview with Professor Montanelli of Pisa University. Montanelli[3] was a lecturer—a bearded, excitable little man, an intellectual and rather a visionary, but honest and self-sacrificing. In the course of a short stay in Rome he succeeded in obtaining an interview with Pius. During such interviews Pius nearly always made a favourable impression; at the age of fifty-six he had still his share of good looks, and of course would never lose his air of breeding and his gentle sense of fun; but on this occasion he seemed to be rather weary. The interview lasted nearly two hours and was certainly more important and more dramatic than either of them realised at the time.[4]

Pius spoke with surprising frankness: evidently he wanted to make an end of the vast misunderstanding. After complaining several times of the constant misuse that was made of his name, he told Montanelli that he knew that a war of independence was inevitable: that, as an Italian, he wanted to see the foreign invaders driven out of his country, but that as Pope—as the universal Father—he could never declare a war of independence against Austria.

"But", said Montanelli, "when all Italy is seething with warlike enthusiasm; when Lombardy rises and calls upon the young men from every part of Italy to come to her rescue, will not the Italian populations of the State of Your Holiness want to take their share in the effort?"

"I see that too", said Pius; "I see that it will be impossible to restrain them.... They will go."

Strange as it may seem, these words came as a revelation to Montanelli. He, like all the rest of Italy, had pictured the Pope as leading a military and religious crusade against the Austrians. Now the true situation dawned upon him: that the Papal State was not a national but an international institution: that it could not declare war unless it were invaded: that Pius would let his young men go—for, indeed, he could

[3] *V. Italy in the Making*, II, 128.
[4] Montanelli, *Memorie*, II, 56.

not possibly prevent them even if he had ever wanted to do so. But that was all. Anyone interested in the Revolution can imagine the fearful disappointment to an enthusiast such as Montanelli. In his splendid vision of the future it seemed now as if the principal figure had vanished.

All depended on keeping his "great Pius" in the movement.

He continues: "I was convinced that for Italy, which was without political or moral unity, and was emerging from slavery without any well-defined principles of freedom, the name of Pius standing above all the transitory chaos of revolution, constituted the force which was acting as an impulse to some men, as a restraint to others and a bond of union for all: and that if we should be deprived of his prestige before we became ordered as a national entity, we ran the risk of breaking up into small and powerless factions...." And so great was his distress that he threw himself on his knees and, with tears, entreated Pius not to abandon Italy.

This interview shows us that Pius IX had foreseen the coming crisis: his sympathies were with his young men but his religious duty was with the Holy See—and within five months of that day his hegemony of the Italian national movement was to be one of the chief developments of the year 1848.

II

The Austrian army in Italy, about which Pope Pius IX and Professor Montanelli were talking, was undoubtedly one of the best in Europe at that day, and at the same time one of the most peculiar. To obtain a vivid perception of it we need only read the following list of the units and their nationalities.[5]

[5] Our chief authorities for the Austrian army are the *Feldzug*, Hilleprandt, Kunz, Heller, Fabris, Meyer Ott, Radetzky's writings; the memoirs or letters left by various officers (such as Schönhals, Benedek, Pimodan, etc., etc.). For other names *v.* the Bibliography.

STAFF

Commander-in-Chief	Field-Marshal Count Radetzky
Chief of General Staff	Field-Marshal Hess[6]
First Adjutant-General	Field-Marshal Carl Schönhals

FIRST ARMY CORPS

Commanding Officer	Field-Marshal Count E. Wratislaw
Chief of Staff	Lieut.-Colonel von Nagy
Adjutant of Army Corps	Major von Woyciechowski

WEIGELSPERG'S DIVISION (H.Q. Milan)

Maurer Brigade (Milan)

	*B.	S.	G.	
2nd Regt Ottochaner Borderers, 1st Batt.	1	.	.	Croats
3rd Regt Oguliner Borderers, 1st Batt.	1	.	.	Croats
Kaiser Jägers, 11th Batt.	1	.	.	Italians
44th Regt Archduke Albert's Infantry, 3rd Batt.	1	.	.	Italians

Gyulai Brigade (Magenta)

Kaiser Jägers, 2nd Batt.	1	.	.	Tyrolese (Aust.)
Kaiser Jägers, 3rd Batt.	1	.	.	Tyrolese (Aust.)
Kaiser Jägers, 4th Batt.	1	.	.	Tyrolese (Ital.)
43rd Regt Geppert Infantry, 3rd Batt.	1	.	.	Italians
Horse Battery, No. 1	.	.	6	

Schaafgotsche Brigade (Milan)

Regt Sardinia (re-named Radetzky) Hussars	.	8	.	Hungarians
Horse Battery, No. 3	.	.	6	

WISSIAK'S DIVISION (H.Q. Milan)

Wohlgemuth Brigade (Milan)

1st Regt Kaiser Infantry, 1st and 2nd Batts.	2	.	.	Moravians
21st Regt Paumgarten Infantry, 1st and 2nd Batts.	2	.	.	Bohemians
Field Battery, No. 2	.	.	6	

* B. = Battalions; S. = Squadrons; G. = Guns.
The battalions were roughly 1000 strong, with six companies each:
the squadrons about 180 strong; and the batteries about 150 men with
six guns. *Feldzug*, 1, 6. Fabris, 1, 203.

[6] Hess did not arrive until May 12th after the battle of Santa
Lucia. Before that the Chief of Staff had been Colonel Johann
Wratislaw, an officer of less standing; Radetzky's chief adviser had
been Schönhals, who was much disappointed at the arrival of Hess.

Clam Brigade (Milan)

	B.	S.	G.	
18th Regt Reisinger Infantry, 1st and 2nd Batts.	2	.	.	Bohemians
33rd Regt Gyulai Infantry, 1st and 2nd Batts.	2	.	.	Hungarians
Field Battery, No. 1	.	.	6	

SCHWARZENBERG'S DIVISION (H.Q. Brescia)

Schönhals Brigade (Cremona)

	B.	S.	G.	
18th Regt Archduke Albert Infantry, 1st and 2nd Batts.	2	.	.	Italians
51st Regt Rukawina Infantry, 1st and 2nd Batts.	2	.	.	Hungarians
23rd Regt Ceccopieri Infantry, 3rd Batt.	1	.	.	Italians
Field Battery, No. 7	.	.	6	

Archduke Sigismund Brigade (Bergamo)

	B.	S.	G.	
4th Regt Szluiner Borderers, 1st Batt.	1	.	.	Croats
17th Regt Hohenlohe Infantry, 1st and 2nd Batts.	2	.	.	Gorizian Istrians
38th Regt Haugwitz Infantry, 3rd Batt.	1	.	.	Italians
45th Regt Archduke Sigismund's Infantry, 1st Batt.	1	.	.	Italians
Field Battery, No. 9	.	.	6	

WOCHER'S DIVISION (H.Q. Milan)

Strassoldo Brigade (Saronno)

	B.	S.	G.	
5th Regt Warasdiner Kreuzer Borderers, 1st Batt.	1	.	.	Croats
8th Regt Gradiscaner Borderers, 1st Batt.	1	.	.	Slovaks
7th Regt Prohaska Infantry, 1st and 2nd Batts.	2	.	.	Carinthians
10th Batt. Feld-Jägers	1	.	.	Austrians
Field Battery, No. 3	.	.	6	

Rath Brigade (Milan)

	B.	S.	G.	
43rd Regt Geppert Infantry, 1st and 2nd Batts.	2	.	.	Italians
Freysauff Grenadiers (from 33rd, 52nd and 61st Regts)	1	.	.	Hungarians
D'Anthon Grenadiers (from 38th, 43rd and 45th Regts)	1	.	.	Italians
Field Battery, No. 8	.	.	6	

Archduke Ernst Brigade (Lodi)

	B.	S.	G.	
4th Regt Imperial Uhlans	.	6	.	Galician Poles
2nd Regt Bavarian Dragoons	.	6	.	Austrians
Horse Battery, No. 4	.	.	6	

Artillery reserve

	B.	S.	G.
One battery, No. 1	.	.	6
One rocket battery, No. 1	.	.	6
Total of First Army Corps	35	20	66

SECOND ARMY CORPS

Commanding Officer	Field-Marshal Baron D'Aspre
Chief of Staff	Major von Schmerling
Adjutant to Army Corps	Major Taude

WIMPFFEN'S DIVISION (H.Q. Padua)

Lichtenstein Brigade (Padua)

	B.	S.	G.	
6th Regt Warasdiner S. Georger Borderers, 1st Batt.	1	.	.	Croats
9th Regt Peterwardiner Borderers, 1st Batt.	1	.	.	Slovaks
Feld-Jägers, 8th Batt.	1	.	.	Italians
Feld-Jägers, 9th Batt.	1	.	.	Austrians
Mounted Battery, No. 2	.	.	6	

Prince William Taxis Brigade (Vicenza)

27th Regt Piret Infantry, 1st and 2nd Batts.	2	.	.	Styrians
52nd Regt Archduke Franz Karl Infantry, 1st and 2nd Batts.	2	.	.	Hungarians
Field Battery, No. 4	.	.	6	

LUDOLF'S DIVISION (Treviso)

Auer Brigade (Udine)

10th Regt 1st Banal Borderers, 1st Batt.	1	.	.	Croats
11th Regt 2nd Banal Borderers, 1st Batt.	1	.	.	Croats
16th Regt Zanini Infantry, 3rd Batt.	1	.	.	Italians
26th Regt Archduke Ferdinand d'Este Infantry, 3rd Batt.	1	.	.	Italians

Culoz Brigade (Venice)

13th Regt Wimpffen Infantry, 3rd Batt.	1	.	.	Italians
47th Regt Kinsky Infantry, 1st and 2nd Batts.	2	.	.	Styrians
Angelmayer Grenadiers (from 16th and 26th Regts)	1	.	.	Italians
5th Garrison Batt.	1	.	.	Italians

PRINCE HANNIBAL TAXIS DIVISION (H.Q. Verona)

Boccalari Brigade (Verona)

32nd Regt Archduke Franz d'Este Infantry, 1st and 2nd Batts.	2	.	.	Hungarians
38th Regt Haugwitz Infantry, 1st and 2nd Batts.	2	.	.	Italians
6th Garrison Batt.	1	.	.	Italians
Pioneers (four companies)	.	.	.	
Field Battery, No. 5	.	.	6	

Nugent Brigade (Verona)

	B.	S.	G.	
7th Regt Brooder Borderers, 1st Batt.	1	.	.	Slovaks
45th Regt Archduke Sigismund's Infantry, 3rd Batt.	1	.	.	Italians
48th Regt Archduke Ernst Infantry, 1st and 2nd Batts.	2	.	.	Italians
Field Battery, No. 6	.	.	6	

Simbschen Brigade (Verona)

7th Hussar Regt Reuss	.	8	.	Hungarians
4th Cavalry Regt Windischgratz	.	8	.	Bohemian-Moravians
Horse Battery, No. 5	.	.	6	

Artillery reserve

One battery, No. 2	.	.	6
One rocket battery, No. 2	.	.	6
Total of Second Army Corps	26	16	42

About 70,000 men in all: 61,000 infantry; 5000 cavalry; 108 guns

What a strange state of things in a garrison town, to hear perhaps four or five different languages in the streets! It must have tended to add to the difficulties of the officers, just as it did during the Great War.[7] But at the same time we shall find counterbalancing factors which made Radetzky's army one of the best in Europe.

The history of the Austrian military service has been traced, through the wars against Frederick the Great, to feudal days when Vienna was an outpost of Europe against the Turks. But in the present work we need only go back forty years to the period of desperate reorganisation against Napoleon; and since 1831 Field-Marshal Radetzky had been in command. It was mainly he who had taken the conscripts of all these various races and had formed them into what seems a rather strange army—for it was an entity apart from

[7] In 1918 a British officer told one of the present writers that several days earlier he had captured a batch of Austrians at the Asiago plateau and that around him he heard nine languages being spoken at the same moment: English, French, Italian, German, Hungarian, Czech, Polish, Rumanian (and one other now forgotten), and that this did not make for efficiency, especially as the men had had no regular ration for over twenty-four hours!

nationality: it was a soldier-organisation in which loyalty to the Kaiser was the watchword, and courage the universal *culte*; a splendid military machine, aristocratic and yet professional, hard as Bessemer steel, but, alas, employed in holding down the Italian population; and necessarily, in time of war, prepared to treat their villages as foreign territory.[8]

In 1848, however, the language differences were a more serious difficulty than ever heretofore, because each language represented a separate patriotism and a separate nationality. It was a danger which had long ago been foreseen by Radetzky. In December 1834 he had written on the subject of forming one national army:

We possess various provinces which never could be transformed into military countries because no trust can be placed in their loyalty. To this category belong Italy, and perhaps also Poland. Moreover we have other provinces over which we have not full control, such as Hungary and Siebenbergen; in them our Imperial Master could only obtain a few recruits to bring his depleted Hungarian regiments up to strength. How can we hope that these countries will adopt the military system of the hereditary dominions? And what results from such abuses? The German provinces have had to bear the burden alone, and thus are punished instead of being rewarded for their genuine loyalty and self-sacrifice. And unfortunately this is still the case. The German is called up at eighteen years of age. He serves fourteen years and then, after the expiration of his enlistment, he is liable for duty in the Landwehr for a further thirteen years—that is to say, until his 45th year. On the other hand the Italians and Tyrolese serve for only eight years and are then free from all further duty; while the Hungarian depends entirely on the discretion of his State. How can there exist any conformity here?[9]

[8] A specimen of Radetzky's views on politics: speaking of Prussia he said, "To hit Napoleon she worked out her system at that time. Since his overthrow everything has gone out of its course; nowadays instead of the true soldier-spirit we deal out everywhere nothing but political humbug (*Schwindel*), just as formerly religious fanaticism. God alone knows when the folly of men will come to an end. I fear it will not be until there arises some great conqueror who will make the peoples tremble for their independence." Radetzky, *Denkschriften*, p. 538.   [9] Radetzky, *ibid.* p. 539.

During this campaign of 1848 the growth of nationality actually proved a drawback on the field of battle. It accounts for the fact that, after each battle, in the Austrian casualty-lists there are about 25% returned as "missing". Thus among the Tyrolese Jägers, for instance, there were often episodes of splendid heroism by the German-speaking Tyrolese who feared Piedmontese aggression, strangely accompanied by the defection of a score or two of their comrades who were Italians in speech and sentiment. The overwhelming majority of the "missing" were Italians, and, as they were conscripts, no one could blame them for refusing to shoot down their Piedmontese neighbours.

The greatest mistake made by Radetzky was to have left so many Italian regiments and their depots in Italy.[10] When the revolution broke out he had no less than twenty Italian battalions in Lombardo-Venetia—nearly 20,000 men; and, very naturally, within the first fortnight, about four-fifths of them had departed. Besides these there were ten battalions and one cavalry regiment serving at various stations in Austria.[11]

So much for the difficulties of Radetzky's army; and now for the elements which account for its exceptional efficiency.

Firstly their organisation. In days before the Great War, Kaiser Wilhelm II once observed that the Austrian Empire reminded him of a wall built of large blocks of stone held together by very good cement: the good cement was the German element in the population. This is a simile which we might apply equally well to Radetzky's army; as also the contemporary belief in Austrian powers of administration. Radetzky's military organisation must have been one of the best in Europe. It made the Piedmontese H.Q. seem like amateurs.

Secondly, the quality of the rank and file: his men were splendid raw material. This had always accounted for

[10] He would have replied that he could not carry out his work with fewer men. For years he had been saying that he required 150,000, but this demand was outside the scope of Austrian finances.

[11] *Archivio triennale*, I, 266.

Austrian power of recuperation—the fact that she had a reserve of fine hardy populations to her hand.[12] At that moment, for instance, she had in Italy several splendid battalions of Tyrolese Kaiser Jägers—mountaineers and marksmen, the grandsons of the men who fought against Napoleon under Andreas Hofer; also, perhaps equally good, six battalions of Croat light infantry; and best unit of all, Colonel Kopal's magnificent 10th Jägers who were German-Austrians—not Tyrolese; they won renown in almost every engagement. As for cavalry, there were the Hungarians—the Radetzky and the Reuss-Kotritz Hussars; the Polish Uhlans; the Czech Chevaux-legers and other regiments less well known.

Among these young men of fighting races their old General had been able to nurture a wonderful *esprit-de-corps*. And, by a strange paradox, the aim of their training was to disassociate the soldiers as far as possible from their native land. They were enlisted for fourteen years,[13] and at the end of that period they often re-engaged themselves; so that many of them had no real home except in the army. They became hard professional soldiers and good N.C.O.s. As for the officers: "They had no other nationality save that of the sword and sash, whose membership bound them to one another in one single loyalty and in one single language of honour and duty."[14] Thus in each regiment there might be officers of all the different races in the Empire, and of some from outside; the latter were often those who belonged to conquered nations and felt that they could not honourably take service at home. "To claim that an officer should understand the native language of his men would have entailed an entire dissolution of the army and its being reduced to the

[12] In 1859 when Napoleon III was about to attack Austria he made the above observation to a friend, and instanced the fact that when the allies invaded France in 1814 it was the Austrian army which had the finest men in its ranks.

[13] Hilleprandt, p. 9.

[14] This description was written in 1850 by Meyer Ott, a Swiss writer who knew some of the officers on either side. Meyer Ott, p. 29.

level of a civic guard. But each officer could make himself understood through his N.C.O.s, of whom a sufficient proportion had been trained in the men's native language and also in German. In every regiment, too, there was a certain number of officers of its own nationality so that, in case of need, there was always a way for direct communication between officers and men."[15]

What was the mentality of the officers? It varied. Some were foreigners—and surely they might have fought in a better cause! There was young Count Pimodan, for instance, the son of a Legitimist French noble who had left France in 1830. Pimodan said afterwards that he had enjoyed this campaign; he was serving the Empire, as was suitable for a Pimodan; and under that beautiful Italian sky the fighting on either side was carried on as befitted gentlemen. For such views there was no excuse during the nineteenth century. Far sadder was the case of those belonging to conquered nations. The greatest of these was Field-Marshal Count Nugent of Westmeath, one of the thousands of Irish exiles who maintained their military tradition in Austria.[16]

[15] Meyer Ott, pp. 29-30.
[16] A good list of them up to the end of the Napoleonic wars is to be found in the *Journal of the Royal Society of Antiquaries* for September 14th, 1926. In it Colonel Cavanagh publishes the names of all those who became Knights of the Imperial Military Order of Maria Theresa.
    Another who won fame in 1848 was Colonel Baron Kavanagh. He was killed during the attack on Vicenza on June 10th (*v.* p. 313). According to Pimodan's *Memoirs* (p. 246), when Kavanagh heard the first boom of the guns that morning, he laughed and said: "I must carry on to-day, so that my wife may see my name in the bulletin of the battle." He simply threw away his life while leading his men, as we know from the descriptions of Pimodan and from the Austrian *Feldzug* (II, 33). And he is still remembered. In the Heeresmuseum in Vienna his portrait and his medals are to be seen in one of the principal cases, near the relics of Radetzky, of Nugent, Kopal and others. He was dark, with deep blue eyes, a slightly sunken oval face and a typically Irish complexion. It will be remembered that Pimodan also sacrificed his life to a Legitimist cause—that of the Pope in 1860.

But even among those who were Austrian subjects many must have felt the call of racial patriotism: of the Polish provinces; of Hungary; of Bohemia; or most of all of Lombardo-Venetia. There was, for instance, the young Hungarian Count Schönfeldt, who dreamed of a glorious career in Imperial service at the head of his loyal Magyar troopers. The tone among the older men was of feudal loyalty to the Kaiser; many of them were nobles, doubtless with their sixteen quarterings and their splendid physique. In spite of all this feudalism, however, what strikes the student as the distinctive characteristic of Radetzky's army is the fact that it was manned and led by trained professional soldiers. Its plans left little to chance; its blows were delivered with overwhelming force, and its orders were carried out like clockwork by the units engaged.[17]

One black truth unfortunately cannot be omitted: on occasion it would strike without mercy. Witness the slaughtering of the villagers of Melegnano and of Castelnuovo, to prevent a general rising.

The man who has received the credit for the success of the Austrian army and its previous preparation is Radetzky. Small wonder—in the year 1848 he was a veteran of eighty-one years, who had learnt his profession in wars against Napoleon: a young Staff Officer at Marengo, Divisional-General at Wagram and Chief of Staff at Leipzig. He had seventeen campaigns to his credit, seven wounds and had seen nine horses shot under him. And now in 1848, as the revolution spread far and wide throughout Austria, it was realised by both officers and men that the life of the Empire depended on their standing firm. Its last stronghold was in the fortified lines of Marshal Radetzky: "In deinem Lager liegt Österreich."

The life which he had led had left its mark. He had a

---

[17] We state this boldly because we are following the opinions of various professional authorities, notably those of General Willisen in his course of lectures to the Prussian staff officers.

surprisingly vigorous body; a rather bull-dog, weather-beaten face and a jovial smile, with a fairly hard expression underneath it. Undoubtedly he must have possessed an extraordinary power of carrying men with him. As an example we will quote the following description which is one of many by eye-witnesses;[18] it was written by Count Leopold Kolowrat. He was in Milan on March 12th, 1849, and was dining with Radetzky and his staff when news arrived that Charles Albert had terminated the armistice. This meant fresh war and suffering and hardship for everyone. Nevertheless no sooner was dinner over than they heard the crash of military music, and, one after another, five different regimental bands marched from various quarters to salute the Field-Marshal, each accompanied by scores of men, until the courtyard was full.

The Field-Marshal betook himself, just as he was, with uncovered head, down among the men in the courtyard, accompanied by us all. To describe that scene I must allow myself an unfettered pen. All the soldiers thronged round the Marshal, kissed his hand and were happy if they could only reach the hem of his coat; and they filled the air with their shouts of *Vivat, Evviva, Eljen, Zivio, Vater Radetzky!*[19] He went round among his men and talked to one and another, now in German, now in Polish, now in Italian, Bohemian or Slav. For each one of them he had a word or two of friendliness, or sometimes just a pat on the men's shoulder or cheek. So moving was it all to see that there wasn't a dry eye among us. No one who has not witnessed such a scene of enthusiasm can form any idea of it. The rapid result of the ensuing campaign must have converted the unbelievers, and shown them what kind of spirit there dwells in the Austrian army.[20]

[18] For instance: "In his dealings with the soldiers he had a way of his own; and the reverence and love of the men for him bordered on the unbelievable." Von Ravelsberg, *Feldmarschall Radetzky*, p. 45. Heller said that probably no Austrian commander except the Archduke Charles had ever been so much beloved by his men. Heller, *Graf Radetzky*, p. 437. This is one of the most moderate statements out of many.

[19] The cheers of the German, Italian, Hungarian and Croat soldiers for "Father" Radetzky.

[20] Kolowrat, *Meine Erinnerungen*, II, 66.

Chapter I

JANUARY AND FEBRUARY 1848. THE PROVINCES UNDER AUSTRIAN RULE

In Metternich's Italy, at the beginning of the year of revolution, 1848, the seven leading Italian states might be classified under two categories.

I. The four territories in which the people could not expect to achieve any results by peaceful agitation; where, consequently, their chief hope lay in methods of violence. These were the Lombardo-Venetian kingdom which was under the direct rule of the Austrian Emperor; and the two Duchies (Parma and Modena) now freshly garrisoned by Austrian troops and bound to the Empire by treaties which reduced them almost to vassalage.[1] The kingdom of Naples and Sicily was in a similar position in so far as it was under the rule of an absolute king, but its risings have very little relation to the unification of Italy. It stands apart. The Neapolitan insurgents were merely Liberals in rebellion against their own king; and the Sicilians were patriotic islanders raging to be free from Naples.

II. Distinct from these we have three other units which in 1848 were known as the reforming states—the Papacy, Piedmont and Tuscany. In these three little nations the Liberal advance was in full progress, and all three of them were overflowing with enthusiasm and gratitude for the reforms recently granted by their respective rulers.

Over these Liberalised governments Metternich could maintain his domination only indirectly, by means of his

---

[1] Austria had thus extended her military power right across the centre of Italy, and the Italian progressives were consequently in a state of great anxiety as to what her next move might be; in Florence the Tuscan government lived in daily fear of an invasion.

ambassadors. These representatives, however, were a far more effective authority than is usually realised.[2] In each of the small states there was an Austrian diplomat who regarded himself as "fighting his corner" for the Empire. They were there to keep the puppet on his throne, and if he granted any popular concessions they treated him as a coward who was giving way. In cases of difficulty they could always get the support of the Russian and Prussian ambassadors.

Undoubtedly the danger to European peace lay in those states in which all concessions were refused. It will be best to begin by examining the condition of the provinces directly under Austrian rule, because it was this domination of Italians by Germans which was the chief, in fact the root-cause of the movement for the unification of Italy.

In the principal towns of Lombardy and Venetia the popular agitation had been in full swing for two or three months. Its strongest centre was Milan (population 156,326,[3] exclusive of certain suburbs), and its avowed aim was to oust the Austrians. At first the task seemed impossible. In that town there was a garrison of men of all arms under Marshal Radetzky. The importance, therefore, of this agitation during January and February lies in the fact that it aroused the Milanese to such a pitch of fury that, contrary to all human probability, they were able to achieve the famous "Five Glorious Days", March 18th to 22nd, 1848.

The difficulties of the Milanese were threefold: first they were divided among themselves; the nobles, for instance, headed by the Podestà, Count Casati, rather tended to consort with the Piedmontese nobles. Other Milanese, mostly of the

[2] Count Lützow in Rome, Count Buol in Turin, Baron Neurath in Florence and Prince Felix Schwarzenberg in Naples. The only exception to the above remarks was Count Lützow who had been many years in Rome and showed a rather touching consideration for his friend Pope Pius IX (v. Vienna Docts; also Cantù, II, 773).
[3] The figure used by Radetzky when allotting his soldiers to their garrisons. Vienna H.H.S.A. Staatskanzlei, Provinzen Lombardo-Venezia, No. 23, 1847–8.

poorer class, were Mazzinians—republicans; and some, headed by Carlo Cattaneo, were republican-federalist.[4] Undoubtedly their chief bonds of union were, on the one hand, hatred of Austria, and on the other, the universal enthusiasm for Pius IX. We may note that to cry *Viva Pio Nono*, or to inscribe these words on a wall, were actually tabulated by the police as a seditious offence. Secondly, their money supply was not on a satisfactory basis; and thirdly, they had very few arms. The rich men, though usually ready to subscribe for patriotic purposes, considered, naturally enough, that the moment to buy arms had not yet come.

Nevertheless the citizens were full of patriotic and revolutionary enterprise,[5] and, as long as they were fighting against Austria, they could unite like one man.

On January 1st, 1848, was initiated their now-famous anti-smoking campaign. This scheme, copied from the Boston tea-party,[6] was to abstain from tobacco and from the game of lotto, and thereby to diminish the profits of the Austrian customs and excise. The story of what happened is well known. On January 1st the town was full of good Milanese citizens who meant to put an end to all smoking. "Wherever a cigar was to be seen, their cry was *Fuori! Fuori!*" says the Austrian historian Helfert. Those who refused to obey were mobbed. Before long the police were compelled to interfere, and during one of these street rows Count Casati, the Podestà, was arrested by mistake and taken to the police-station. He was not kept there long, but this affair aroused great indignation, especially as the police had arrested various

[4] For Cattaneo's federalism *v.* Cantù, II, 675, 794.

[5] "La population de Milan était comme emportée par une vaste conspiration sans qu'il y eut de conspirateurs. La ville agissait comme un seul homme; les projets les plus bizarres étaient adoptés sur-le-champ par toute la population." *L'Insurrection de Milan en 1848*, p. 28, par Carlo Cattaneo, Paris 1849 (the French edition of his work).

[6] Ottolini, p. 26, gives the originating document in full; *v.* also Cantù, II, 769.

other perfectly innocent people. However by nightfall the town was quiet.

It is admitted that on this day, January 1st, the rioting was partly due to provocation on the part of the Austrians. Their soldiers and especially the N.C.O.s had marched boldly along the Corso puffing the smoke from their mouths in the faces of the indignant populace.[7] Indeed, according to their own accounts, Count Gustav Neipperg[8] had strolled up and down in front of the Scala for a whole hour, enjoying an excellent cigar. So says the Austrian account; but, according to the Italian version, in the end it was knocked down his throat.[9]

On January 3rd there occurred the conflict which has passed into history as *I Lutti di Lombardia*, "the Mourning of Lombardy".[10]

For a moment let us look at these matters from the soldiers' point of view.

Undoubtedly they were in a very difficult position. Their duty was to support the police in preventing acts of aggression. They could not possibly help themselves. They were conscripts. During the next two months there were many regrettable doings in Milan; but surely the people most to blame are the Austrian government which refused all Liberal concessions.

[7] Cattaneo (French ed.), p. 33; Ottolini, p. 30.
[8] He was the son of the Archduchess Marie Louise (Napoleon's widow) by her second husband Count Neipperg.
[9] Carlo Casati says he was arm-in-arm with Mr Castle, an English phrenologist.
[10] For the *Lutti di Lombardia* our Italian authorities mainly consist in descriptions by eye-witnesses—about a dozen in all: Cesare Cantù, Carlo Cattaneo, Gabrio Casati, Antonio Casati, Ottolini and the many companions whom he quotes, Visconti Venosta, and Dr Carlo Casati who also quotes many eye-witnesses and gives documents.

For the Austrian side we have relied on letters in the Vienna Archives from Ficquelmont and Radetzky; on the various letters of Austrian officers in Italian histories; on Schönhals and Hübner.

On both sides there are excellent general histories such as Tivaroni, Rosi, the *Feldzug*, Helfert, etc.

On January 3rd both sides began the day in a state of irritation. Torresani, the Chief of Police, had issued an order warning the public that if there were any interference with smoking, the armed men would use force.

The strife began almost at once, and each side accuses the other of having begun it. According to the Italian accounts, even during the morning hours the Austrian soldiers were supplied with cigars and primed with brandy and went out into the streets to provoke the populace; they wanted to break the anti-smoking campaign. On the Austrian side, Graf Ficquelmont, then adviser to the Viceroy, reported to Metternich that the soldiers went out in batches of not more than three; that they were hooted at and insulted for smoking; that, as the crowds increased, they gathered together in groups of a dozen or more: that at last the stones began to fly, and the soldiers, claiming to act in self-defence, attacked the unarmed populace with swords and bayonets.[11] Whatever may be the truth, it seems probable that up to midday, honours were even, so to speak. But Helfert tells us that after midday the Austrian soldiers went out "into the streets, many of them N.C.O.s, fine strong figures who did not look at all like allowing themselves to be made fun of", and that "they paraded the streets in batches of ten or twelve with cigars in their mouths; and some of them with a lit cigar at each corner of his mouth[12] and blew smoke into the faces of the agitators, and drew their weapons at those who interfered". We may note that the Comte de Flahault, French Ambassador at Vienna, blames Radetzky for having left the matter in the hands of privates and N.C.O.s.[13]

At about half-past five the fighting began. The dragoons (at first on foot we think) attacked the unarmed crowds.

[11] Vienna H.H.S.A. Staatskanzlei, Provinzen Lombardo-Venezia 23, Briefwechsel mit Ficquelmont, No. 89, January 14th, 1848. Cantù gives a letter purporting to be written by the Viceroy: v. Cronistoria, II, 770.   [12] Helfert, p. 127. He does not give his authority.
[13] Vienna H.H.S.A. ibid. Letter of Flahault to Metternich docketed with the above. Cantù, ibid.

According to Helfert, the soldiers had orders to clear the streets. They only used swords or bayonets, but evidently they meant to give the townspeople a lesson, because some of the fugitives were pursued into their houses and stabbed. There were sixty-four casualties, of whom five died.[14] Some idea may be formed of the wounds inflicted, by a glance at the following specimens from a list of sixty.

Name	Age	Profession	Observations
Pirola, Antonio	14	Armourer's boy	Two serious wounds; one a sword-cut on the head; the other a bayonet wound on the left shoulder
Invernizzi, Vicenzo	60	Property-owner and silk-merchant	Two bayonet wounds in the throat; in danger of dying

They killed an old man of seventy-four, one Carlo Manganini, a Counsellor of Appeal. He received four sword-cuts on his head and two on his right arm. Evidently the men were "seeing red", for they overlooked the fact that this old septuagenarian was a pro-Austrian; moreover they wounded a woman and a little girl only four years old.

Radetzky confined his men to barracks for the next five days. It seems evident that if there existed any Austrian plan for provoking and crushing the anti-smoking movement, neither he nor Ficquelmont had anything to say to it. It must have been hatched by junior officers and N.C.O.s. In the Vienna Archives there are a series of confidential documents which throw some new light on the *Lutti*; notably an angry letter written on January 4th by Radetzky to Ficquelmont in which he says:

Your Excellency, in a letter kindly addressed to me yesterday evening, expressed the opinion that our soldiers, by smoking

---

[14] Tivaroni, *Ital. Sett.* p. 415, gives these totals. Gori, p. 388, says sixty; Ottolini, who was in Milan, says sixty-one. Consul-General Dawkins says five dead and about sixty wounded. *London Corr.* Pt II, January 6th and 11th, 1848.

cigars in the streets had provoked the unrest of the last two days. I must hereby most emphatically repudiate the suggestion.... Against whom are these aggressions directed? Against the State revenue; against an article of ordinary use which is manufactured only by the State! and in these circumstances, am I to issue an order forbidding the soldiers to smoke cigars openly, merely because the Jokey Clubb (*sic*) has decreed it?...[15]

In this private letter to Ficquelmont the old Field-Marshal wrote a page or more of fulminations which seem to show that he had not planned any traps for the Milanese, and Ficquelmont's confidential despatch to Metternich of January 4th shows that no such idea had occurred to him.[16] He was rather horrified at the doings of the previous day. In reality he was in favour of concessions, and on the 5th he persuaded the Viceroy to issue a soothing proclamation,[17] which was regarded by some of his co-nationalists as abandoning the army.

This day of suffering most certainly marks a step forward towards freedom. Henceforward there was "a river of blood" between Italians and Austrians; and the *Lutti di Lombardia* became magnificent propaganda, especially in the able hands of the experienced leader of agitation, Massimo d'Azeglio.[18]

[15] Vienna H.H.S.A. Staatskanzlei, Provinzen Lombardo-Venezia 23, Briefwechsel mit Ficquelmont, No. 11.

[16] In it he says that he hates the cigar-smoking and other causes of bitterness. His chief fear is lest "we should be driven to the kind of measures which would be odious", a sentence underlined by Metternich, with the words "Ganz wahr".

[17] To be found in *Archivio triennale*, 1, Doc. 145.

[18] *I Lutti di Lombardia*, Firenze, 1848, by Massimo d'Azeglio. D'Azeglio's celebrated pamphlet begins in the following words: "A great iniquity has been committed in Milan. The greatest iniquity that could be conceived by a human mind; taking the lives of men who are unarmed; therefore it is cowardice; of men attacked unaware; therefore it is treachery; of men neither indicted nor condemned by law; therefore it is oppression, and oppression carried out by obscure assassins against men who could not get at their

All Italy was bitterly incensed, and throughout Lombardo-Venetia the agitation soon became general and furious; but here we can only briefly describe its chief phases. In a general way during these months the names accepted by all classes as being those of the national leaders, are Pius IX, Charles Albert and Leopold II (of Tuscany). The clergy was now so strongly national that the *Corso Porta Romana* was renamed the *Corso Pio Nono* after Pius IX, and on March 15th an Austrian order appeared at Vienna forbidding the rank and file to go to confession to any but army chaplains, because the Italian clergy, with a few exceptions, are among "our most open and dangerous enemies".[19]

At the same time Charles Albert was generally spoken of as "the King" and those of the nobles who believed in Piedmont sent various envoys, Count Martini, Count d'Adda and others to Turin to appeal to him. Unfortunately these appeals did not win the approval of the republicans; and certainly no one can deny that although their party included some of the most patriotic and self-sacrificing of the citizens, they were not a very satisfactory element in the situation. They failed to perceive that the only chance of winning freedom was by means of the Piedmontese army. They were more in sympathy with the disaffected republicans of Genoa, and after the fall of Louis Philippe they looked for support to the French Republic and to Mazzini.[20]

Thus the methods of violence were coming nearer and nearer to a crisis, but meanwhile the old organised political agitation by the richer classes had not been abandoned.

slayers, and therefore could not possibly have tried to provoke them; of men who on the contrary were deliberately provoked so that a cry from them, an exclamation or a whistle-call might be made a pretext for their death. Therefore—to sum up—cowardice, treachery, oppression, and fraud."

[19] Ficquelmont in a letter written from Vienna on May 3rd says: "Le clergé s'est mis partout à la tête de l'insurrection." Vienna H.H.S.A. Staatskanzlei, Provinzen Lombardo-Venezia 23, Briefwechsel mit Ficquelmont, 1848.

[20] Carlo Cattaneo (French edition), p. 25.

Between January 3rd and March 17th there were no less than ten or eleven political documents drawn up and presented or published, on one side or the other. On the Milanese side there were signed protests and petitions from the *Congrega* of the Municipality, from the leading citizens, from the *Congrega Provinciale* and other bodies;[21] on the Austrian side there were proclamations and manifestos from the Emperor, from Radetzky and from the authorities in Milan. It is generally agreed that the Austrian government might have allayed discontent by granting some form of Home Rule to Lombardo-Venetia, or separately to Lombardy and Venetia. So far from trying this experiment, on February 22nd the government published an imperial rescript which had arrived on November 24th, but had been prudently withheld. In order to restore public tranquillity throughout the whole of Lombardo-Venetia it promulgated forms of summary procedure. Among various other clauses it established a special Commission to deal with cases of high treason, of disturbing public order, of raising rebellion and of serious offences against the peace. The trial was to begin on the spot and to be completed within fourteen days, and those found guilty were to be liable to the death sentence without any right of appeal or recommendation to mercy (Clause 9).

Nevertheless for the time being all the citizens of Milan were united like one man for resistance. The Austrians were pursued and badgered in every way imaginable. Among the higher classes, their officers were socially boycotted; duels took place; Count Borromeo sent back the Order of the Golden Fleece "which is now covered with blood".[22] And every fresh clash with the soldiers or police was followed by furious reports in the now free Press of the reforming states; especially the newspapers of Turin, of Genoa, of Bologna and of Rome.

[21] Perhaps the fullest account of them is to be found in *Nuove Rivelazioni sui fatti di Milano*, II, by Dr Carlo Casati.
[22] Ottolini, p. 42.

In Venetia the chief heroes of the agitation are Manin, the lawyer-patriot, and Tommaseo, the Dalmatian man of letters. Manin was a man with business connections, and Tommaseo, in addition to his political connections, was in touch with the Pope and clergy. The policy of these two patriots was to pile protests and petitions onto the Austrian bureaucracy until it could no longer carry on government without granting concessions. All was to be done within the limits of the law. Throughout the story of these two men it is only fair to remind ourselves of the great sacrifice that they were making. Tommaseo was giving up all that he symbolised by the words, "my beloved solitude": Manin, a prosperous man, was risking not only his own happiness but that of his wife and family.

We have already described Tommaseo's speech to the Ateneo (Athenaeum) in Venice[23] on December 3rd, 1847. On January 14th, 1848, he sent it to Vienna, together with a demand for a more national government, for representative deputies and for freedom of the Press. On this same day a deputy named Count Morosini read to the *Congregazione Provinciale* a document of Manin's, making similar demands, and arguing that Lombardo-Venetia had a right to claim them under the Emperor's Patent of 1815. On January 5th Manin presented to the *Congregazione Centrale* of Venetia his now famous list of sixteen points amounting definitely to a claim for complete Home Rule. These were followed by protests from Tommaseo, and by others from Verona and elsewhere.

It had been a good fortnight's work, since December 20th. Agitation was spreading throughout the State. The authorities could no longer keep their eyes shut. They had already warned Manin; on January 18th they arrested him and also Tommaseo on a charge of stirring up and inflaming the public mind.

[23] *Italy in the Making*, II, 256–7 and notes. The Venetian agitation has already been described in English and far more perfectly than can be attempted here by Professor G. M. Trevelyan: *v. Manin and the Venetian Revolution of* 1848.

During the first half of March Manin was tried behind closed doors. He was prepared, of course, to plead that his actions were within the law; and he was acquitted. But that did not imply that he would be released. The Austrian police did not mean to let him return to his agitation. Outside the prison walls, however, the case was arousing immense sympathy; it was one of the influences which during the first ten weeks of 1848 were nerving Venice for the coming months of heroic resistance. The siege of Venice was at hand.

Meanwhile throughout the provinces of Venetia the movement was spreading. There were collisions with the soldiers in Vicenza, Padua and Treviso. In Padua there was fighting on February 5th, over the anti-smoking campaign, and on the 8th it developed into a battle outside the Caffè Pedrocchi—townsmen and students against soldiers; stones and pistols against swords and muskets, with the university bells "clanging the storm". The losses were one student killed and six seriously wounded; the Austrian losses are not stated.

Chapter II

JANUARY AND FEBRUARY 1848: THE THREE "REFORMING STATES"

I

Let us now make a short review of the three "reforming states"—the Papacy, Piedmont and Tuscany. Naturally it will include a survey of the Piedmontese army, the only force which the Italians had to set against Radetzky.

In the Papal State Pius' Consulta had been considered a great concession by all genuine Moderates. But the crowds were in the hands of the extremists, and the extremists did not mean to make any compromise with the Holy See. They intended to push Pius further and further until they had won a completely democratic form of government.[1] After that the Mazzinians dreamed of winning republics.

By this time, however, the Consulta was actually in being. It is interesting because it represents the regime which might have been set up in Rome in normal times. Pius regarded it as the most Liberal constitution possible for the State of the Church. It was a purely consultative assembly, but had the valuable right of making suggestions. It was composed largely of country gentry and others of the educated classes. As an example of its methods we may note that Count Pasolini—the same Pasolini who had been Pius' friend before the Conclave—was now a Consultore and called upon to make a general study of:

The carrying out of hydraulic and provincial works.

Properties and direct taxes.

---

[1] This was strongly the opinion of Count Lützow, Austrian ambassador to the Holy See, who recurs to it continually in his letters to Metternich. Vienna H.H.S.A., Rome, January and February, 1848.

The governmental and administrative ordering of the state.
The sea-ports of the state.
The Tiber Commission (*Presidenza delle Ripe*).
During its short life the Consulta really seems to have worked very well. Indeed it must have done so, for its doings win the warm approval of Gabussi, the republican historian.[2] He says that the Consultori began by suggesting military reforms;[3] they then abolished the existing system of industrial money prizes, and substituted a public exhibition of arts and crafts; suggested a commission for reviewing the accounts passed before 1847; abolished monopolies with regard to the cloth for the troops' uniforms and substituted competitive public tenders; settled on the introduction of the same monetary system that existed in France and Piedmont; abolished the monopoly of diligences; instituted infant asylums in Ferrara, Bologna, Imola, Genzano, Rome and elsewhere; and made special studies and reports on the various subjects before them. This seems a good record for an assembly which was merely consultative and only remained in existence for three and a half months.

In peace time Pius' Consulta would have done good work; but in 1848 the Roman public was occupied only with its own complete unreadiness for war against Austria, and was calling daily for military training and money.

In armament it was entirely unprepared. We may note that this question had been raised by the Circolo Romano, a club which was becoming the guiding influence in Rome. On January 10th its members had laid before the Consulta a report which asserted in plain terms that the State was in danger owing to the military advance of Austria; that Parma

---

[2] The Consultori were so active as to win the disapproval of Lützow who declared that they were arrogating to themselves the rights of a legislative assembly. Vienna H.H.S.A., Rome, No. 10A, January 30th, 1848.

[3] This suggestion came from the Circolo Romano, and was due to the news of the conflicts in Milan between the citizens and the Austrian garrison (January 3rd).

was already invaded; that the repressive government of Modena relied upon Austrian bayonets; that Ferrara was not yet free; and that, from Vienna, new regiments were being continually ordered into Italy. At the same time the report showed that the Papal forces were entirely lacking in material, training and discipline—both the Army and the Civic Guard.

In reply, the Consultori freely admitted that they had no military experience and recommended that a general and several other officers should be invited from abroad, preferably from Piedmont, to reorganise the army and to give advice to the Minister of War and to the Consulta itself. These sensible views were put into practice; a layman (for the first time on record) was appointed Minister of Arms, namely Prince Gabrielli, an old soldier with the reputation of being severe and honest; and several senior officers were invited from Piedmont to direct the reorganisation. It is worth noting that in this manner the Piedmontese government was allowed to appoint its officers to the highest commands in the Papal army; and shortly afterwards, the Tuscan government, too, applied for Piedmontese instructors. In fact, Charles Albert was laying his train of preparation, not only in Lombardo-Venetia but also throughout the rest of Italy.

At the same time the Consulta voted an increase of the forces, and the organisation of a reserve.

It was not long before these Piedmontese officers received their official appointments. Their commanding officer was to be General Giovanni Durando, brother of General Giacomo Durando, the author of *Nazionalità italiana*. Giovanni Durando had begun life in the Guards, but after the troubles of 1821 had gone into exile, and for twelve years had served with distinction in the armies of Spain and Portugal.[4] He was

---

[4] Born at Mondori 1804; died in Florence 1869. Began as an officer in the Guards; 1827, transferred to the Cacciatori di Savoia; 1831, promoted Lieutenant; retired; served three months in Belgian army; obtained a Captaincy in Portugal under Don Pedro; 1833, wounded in right arm at Oporto; 1834, wounded and obtained Military Cross at Aspiceira; at defence of Lisbon had right arm

joined by Count Casanova; and also unofficially by Marchese Massimo d'Azeglio, by Conte Michelini and others. It will be remembered that during the previous year these Piedmontese officers had already secured for themselves an influential position in Rome among the Liberals, and even among the extremists. One of their best friends was that life-long rebel and patriot, Conte Terenzio Mamiani della Rovere (lately pardoned by Pius), who was a great admirer of Piedmont, and who, says Gori, instilled a similar admiration among his friends, especially Minghetti and Farini. This circle often met at the house of Dr Pantaleoni, a well-known doctor who was a fearless exponent of d'Azeglio's ideas.

Undoubtedly it was necessary to get officers from outside to train the Papal army; and the only Italians available were the Piedmontese. But there was some danger[5] in allotting to them these high commands, because all their loyalty centred round Charles Albert. Pius did not mean to declare war; but if war broke out, naturally these officers would want to fight; and—whatever the difficulties of the Papal government—at the sound of the first shot they would do their best to rally every Papal soldier to the Piedmontese army.

II

Next of the reforming states was Piedmont, the bilingual little realm of nearly five million inhabitants under its King Charles Albert.

broken and was promoted Major; then served as Major in Spanish army (Christina's); after distinguishing himself in four or five engagements was rewarded with the Cross of St Ferdinand and the rank of Brigadier-General. In 1843 returned to Piedmont; in 1848 started out again to be the General in charge of the training of the Papal army.

[5] Lützow was not unnaturally annoyed and suspicious at these plans for the army. But he reports on February 10th that Cardinal Bofondi, the Papal Secretary of State, had told him that the Papal troops were so much demoralised that some reorganisation was absolutely necessary. Vienna H.H.S.A., Rome, No. 17 B, 1848.

This is the sub-Alpine land, and here we get the breeze of the mountains which puts life into a people.

It is from the north, most undoubtedly, that the modern Kingdom of Italy was made. This fact is no longer so apparent; because when the great task was accomplished the old realm of the Savoys passed away. Inevitably Rome was the capital of the new nation. No one on earth could imagine a united Italy of which the capital was not Rome; but that does not alter the fact that it was northerners— nearly all Piedmontese—who made it.

The characteristic which more than any other differentiated this people from the rest was undoubtedly their possessing more commonsense.[6] In every enterprise they kept the main end in view, and were persevering in following it, and realised the necessity of organisation. In 1848 they were still rather undeveloped; their social inequalities for instance had the disadvantage of shutting out middle-class men and boycotting Liberals, but at all events they also kept out the street orators of the revolution; such men as Sterbini, Canino, Ciceruacchio could not have flourished in Turin. In that city there was order, and loyalty to their king. In this volume he is the leading character and it is necessary to picture him as he appeared during that last fateful year of his life.

Charles Albert was now forty-nine years of age; he was tall and pale and prematurely grey in hair and moustache; not very handsome in face but unmistakably a man of good breeding; still active in body and enthusiastic in mind, but profoundly sad.[7]

[6] Cf. the opinion given by Baron André to Guizot. Speaking of the advance of Liberalism in Piedmont he said that the situation "n'est point dans les conditions du reste de l'Italie. Le peuple est plein de bon sens; l'administration régulière et paternelle." Paris, Aff. Etr., No. 320, Sardaigne, January 4th, 1848.

[7] For a previous description and authorities, *v. Italy in the Making,* I and II. For criticism of Charles Albert as a Commander-in-Chief, *v.* chapter VII.

Physically a delicate man[8] and mentally over-religious, from regarding life as a mission he had reached the point of seeing special interpositions of Providence even in trivial matters; as, for instance, when his horse fell without crushing him. Nevertheless owing to his method of life he was prepared for hardship in war;[9] and in battle he was an example to everyone.

Ever since 1821 religion had been his refuge from attacks to which he could make no reply. During his best years of patriotic work, he had been entirely misunderstood by his own people, and compelled to constant concealment before the Austrians, usually a target for either one side or the other. Friends who remembered his youth knew that he had once been a careless young cavalry subaltern, rather too impatient and given to laughing at others; but now his features were always impassive, and his temperament was betrayed only by the changing brightness in his eyes.[10] In

[8] The following is an entirely impartial description of him by an enemy who did not know him. "The traveller who got out of his carriage and presented himself to me was a very tall man, slightly bent, pale in face, of high forehead with hair rather thin above the temples. He introduced himself as the Count de Bars (sic). On the whole he seemed to be downcast, but he had the bearing of a man of refined breeding...." This description was written to Radetzky by General Thurn about a Piedmontese colonel who applied to him for leave to drive through the Austrian lines during the night after the battle of Novara. He was struck by this colonel's appearance, but never suspected that he was interviewing the conquered King on his way to exile in Portugal. V. Salata, p. 435.

[9] After the ovations to him on November 3rd and 4th he was ill for a week: "à la suite des fêtes qui ont accompagné son retour de Turin, la toux l'a repris et on a dû le saigner trois fois dans la journée d'hier." "Sa constitution est visiblement alterée et...il aggrave son mal en s'obstinant à ne prendre aucun soin de sa personne. Un triduo se fait à ce moment"—prayers in church; and in the night there appeared hand-written on the walls "Priez pour la santé du Roi". Paris, Aff. Etr., No. 320, Sardaigne, M. Burgoing to Guizot, December 7th and 8th, 1847.

[10] Cibrario, p. 23; Rodolico, Carlo Alberto, p. 6.

1848 he must have known that he was very near the crisis of his mission.

For he regarded this as his mission; to lead all Italy in a war of liberation against the Austrians: and he believed that his own life was to be the price of freedom.[11]

For us students, however, it is important to remember that *Italia farà da sè* was not merely a patriotic hope; it was also a policy. It meant that while others believed that Italy was not strong enough to drive out the Austrians without a foreign ally, Charles Albert hoped that if he declared war, the rest of Italy would flock to his standard, and a foreign alliance would not be necessary. The story of these two years was destined to prove that Italy was not yet sufficiently united to carry out his idea. Cavour learned and realised this before 1849, and spent the next ten years in building up a Piedmontese position outside Italy, together with a French alliance for the war of 1859.

The period between January 1st and March 24th, 1848, can be divided into three phases: (1) war policy and preparation; (2) an interruption to settle the constitutional question; (3) war policy resumed.

During these twelve weeks before the outbreak of hostilities Charles Albert was torn in two directions almost every day, between the recklessness of his own patriotic Liberals and the sullen anger of Metternich and of his representative at Turin, Count Buol. By his reforms of October 29th, 1847, Charles

[11] On many occasions he said or wrote words expressing this belief, and those who knew him best had no doubt about its genuineness.
"L'entreprise terminée avec la grâce de Dieu, ce ne sera pas moi qui régnerait" disait Charles Albert. "Beaucoup hésitait à ajouter foi à ces paroles. Et moi je les crois parfaitement sincères..." (Cibrario, p. 121). "He believed that he was fated and called by God to the future redemption of Italy, though at the price of himself becoming its victim" (Della Rocca, I, 79). Minghetti who was on his staff in 1848 was greatly touched at seeing that he regarded his supreme sacrifice as already accomplished. *V.* Rodolico, II, 7 *et seq.* and for our authorities on Charles Albert *v. Italy in the Making*, I and II.

Albert had freed the Press, and now it was openly and persistently attacking Austria.[12] The *Concordia* (Lorenzo Valerio), the *Opinione* and others in Turin, and the *Corriere Mercantile* in Genoa were preaching rebellion in Lombardo-Venetia; and after each resulting street-fight they proclaimed the iniquity of Austrian rule. On the other hand, day after day, Count Buol poured in a volume of formal complaints often supported by both Russia and Prussia. Between these conflicting torrents it is greatly to Charles Albert's credit that he succeeded in maintaining a surprising degree of dignity and independence. And now at length we notice that beneath the formal surface of diplomatic politeness there appears from time to time a glimpse of the human spirit which had been compelled to live self-restrained and suppressed during twenty-seven years. Evidently at last Charles Albert is beginning to raise his head. His interview with Count Buol on January 19th, 1848, is an instance of what we mean.[13]

At that interview Buol had come to complain, for the third or fourth time, about a revolutionary article in the very first number of Lorenzo Valerio's paper, the *Concordia*. The Censor who had passed that number had already been reprimanded, but, by Metternich's direction, Buol now asked for his punishment. At first Charles Albert ignored the request, but then he said: "I too have been odiously libelled at Milan by one of your subjects. It goes back to an event in the year 1821. At that time there appeared under the eyes of your government a statement that I had been in communication with General Bubna, and even that I had been to see him, which was absolutely untrue."

In reply Buol hastened to plead "his complete ignorance about an event now passed for over a quarter of a century".

---

[12] The principal papers were: the *Gazzetta Piemontese*, official; the *Opinione*, Giacomo Durando, Reform; the *Concordia*, editor, Lorenzo Valerio an ex-Mazzinian: he advocates first a Constitution and then war; the *Risorgimento*—the paper of Cavour, Balbo, Roberto d' Azeglio and others.

[13] Vienna H.H.S.A. Turin, No. 8A, 1848, Buol's despatch of January 21st.

He did not remember the episode of 1821; but the King replied with quiet resentment: "Well, I remember it, just as if it had happened yesterday." It was a reply full of meaning. He knew that it would go straight to Metternich. They both knew that the year 1821 brought back a hundred untold memories besides this libellous newspaper article; memories of poor Santarosa; of a kingdom almost lost; of an oath enforced on him by Austria; of the miserable days in Spain. And this reply to Metternich's request was duly delivered to him in the next despatch.

Nowadays Charles Albert was no longer in the Slough of Despond; when Buol renewed his complaints about the Press stirring up rebellion, and meaningly begged the King to "keep a watch on this unfortunate tendency which tries to rouse quarrels between neighbours", Charles Albert interrupted him in the midst of his sentence. "I cannot prevent my subjects from talking", he said, "and I cannot impose sympathies upon them." Well might Buol complain that throughout this interview the King had not spoken a single sentence which showed a desire to stand well with Austria.

It was a pity that the Italians in general could not be made aware of his changing attitude towards Metternich, because many of them still regarded him as half-hearted in their cause.

At this juncture there occurs an episode which has become famous, partly because it heralds the first dramatic moment in the life of the great Cavour.

Hitherto Charles Albert had always said that he would never grant a Constitution. He believed that it would open the door to political intrigues and shake discipline. "For war you require soldiers, not lawyers," he said to Roberto d' Azeglio.[14] Early in February 1848 news arrived that the citizens of Genoa who (at heart still republicans) were among the most radical of Charles Albert's subjects, had organised a petition with 20,000 signatures asking him to expel the Jesuits and establish the Civic Guard. On the arrival of their

[14] G. Briano, *Roberto d' Azeglio*, p. 54, Turin, 1861.

deputation Charles Albert refused to receive it, and ordered the deputies to go back to Genoa. It was probably the wisest thing to do; but this rather curt refusal aroused some sympathy for them among the leading Piedmontese journalists, and on that same evening a meeting was held attended by the representatives of the five leading newspapers, and presided over by the Marchese Roberto d' Azeglio.[15]

At that meeting Lorenzo Valerio, founder of the *Concordia*, an able man but one who rather liked to figure as the Caius Gracchus of the democracy, proposed that they should all support the Genoese demands, both as to the Jesuits and as to the *Guardia Civica*; and Brofferio, a Radical, speaking for the *Messaggero Torinese* duly seconded his motion. So far, therefore, the meeting had proceeded entirely to their satisfaction —in the hands of proved democrats. But then suddenly there rose Count Camillo Cavour, the son of an out-and-out Conservative aristocrat, and he began to speak for the *Risorgimento* newspaper. He said that fundamental changes were necessary and that, instead of supporting the demands of the Genoese, he proposed that they should make straight for their goal and ask the King for a constitutional regime at once. This was indeed taking the wind out of the democratic sails, and Valerio refused to accept it; but Brofferio agreed to it, and before long he was followed by Roberto d' Azeglio, by Giacomo Durando[16] and all the others present.

When the minutes of the meeting were reported to Charles Albert he was very angry, especially with the "rebel" Cavour, and refused to allow the news to be published. In a talk with Roberto d' Azeglio in which he spoke his mind with surprising freedom, he pointed out that it was not yet the moment to strike. All Italy was seething with divisions and his own army was not strong enough to face Radetzky single-

[15] Elder brother of Massimo d' Azeglio. He was a strong Liberal.
[16] Brother of General Giovanni Durando. All the above scene is described by Briano who was there with Cavour to represent the *Risorgimento*; *v*. Briano, *Roberto d' Azeglio*, p. 57.

handed. To set up a Constitution would only open the way to debates which would weaken the government and endanger discipline. "Remember, Marchese d' Azeglio", concluded the King, "that I want the freedom of Italy just as you do, and for that very reason I will never grant a Constitution to my people." As we know there was also another reason—a grief always present to his mind—the promise exacted from him by Metternich after his debacle in 1821.

Thus the setting up of a Constitution involved a definite rupture with the Austrian Empire. Nevertheless it was now only a matter of time, for Cavour's motion had convinced the most go-ahead men of its necessity. And this demand for a Parliament became the initial step forward in the great Piedmontese crusade against Austria. Very suitably its prime mover was Cavour.

III

In Tuscany, third among the reforming states, governmental authority had almost broken down. In September 1847 the Grand Duke had appointed Ridolfi to be his Minister. But several towns were disposed to go their own way. Leghorn (Livorno) for instance was a turbulent sea-port filled with extremists headed by Guerrazzi. The Grand Duke himself was torn in opposite directions between the veiled threats of Metternich, who claimed his allegiance as an Austrian Grand Duke, and his own sympathetic desire to figure as a broad-minded Italian prince.

On January 6th Guerrazzi raised a great demonstration at Leghorn calling for arms, announcing the approach of an Austrian invasion, and accusing the government of treachery.

For the moment Ridolfi was able to maintain his authority. The Civic Guard stood by him; and on the 9th he had Guerrazzi and his leaders arrested.

But in Florence[17] the Liberals were displeased at Guerrazzi's

[17] *London Corr.* II, January 9th and 14th; February 2nd.

arrest. Riots ensued, both there and at Leghorn, and this time the Civic Guard did not stand by Ridolfi.

Meanwhile the Grand Duke, encouraged by England to proceed with Liberal measures in despite of Metternich, appointed (on January 3rd) a Commission of five Moderates under Gino Capponi to draw up a scheme of reform for the Press and the Consulta. It was hoped that these reforms would satisfy the Liberals and stave off the demand for a Constitution; but, as we shall see, popular opinion was being inflamed daily by news from Sicily and Milan, so that this last moderate attempt was doomed to failure. But, for the moment, we must leave Tuscany.

It will be seen that during the month of January 1848 all three of the reforming states were on the verge of demanding a Constitution.

IV. THE PIEDMONTESE ARMY WHICH FOUGHT AGAINST THE AUSTRIANS IN 1848

Ever since Charles Albert's accession to the throne, his chief care and the centre of his secret hopes had been the army. He had an "instinctive love for arms", says General Montù, the historian of the Italian artillery. He had begun his career by serving for six months in a cavalry regiment under Napoleon; later, as the heir-presumptive, he had been O.C. of the Piedmontese Artillery; and in 1822 had distinguished himself during the French expedition in Spain at the taking of the Trocadero. It will be remembered that after that engagement the French Grenadiers of the 6th Regiment voted him their honorary Corporal—the same honour which the 3rd Zouaves were destined to bestow on his son Victor Emmanuel in 1859 after Palestro.

As king, he embarked at once on his scheme of army reform. The minister responsible was Villamarina, who had served in the Piedmontese and Austrian campaigns against Napoleon. Together these two undoubtedly produced a wonderfully good army in that small divided nation. The population numbered only 4,368,972, without the 450,000 in Sardinia which in those days was exempt from conscription —although these islanders have since then provided some of the hardiest units in time of war. By 1848 they had done a great work.[18] They had taken a service whose finest traditions made it feudal and reactionary in tone, and had converted it into the army which, under Cavour, could be trained by the Crimean campaign for the wars of 1859 and 1860, and would eventually imbue with its own sentiment and even its own songs, the whole national army of Modern Italy; just as Charles Albert's newly-granted Statuto was destined, only twenty-two years later, to become the Italian Parliament in Rome.

Nevertheless in 1848 the war (like every other war) soon showed up various points of weakness, especially in the existing system of conscription. The army was recruited on a two-fold system: (1) *Ordinanza*: voluntary enlistment under which the men served for eight years on end, and then were free from all further service. These men were the pick of the army, real professional soldiers, but they appear to have been very few in number. At the outbreak of war there were only 8000 of them with the colours, which seems to show that they came in at the rate of about 1000 a year. (2) *Provinciali*. By far the greater number of the men were conscripts drawn by lot as *provinciali*; this meant that, at the start, they only served for fourteen months on end, and then were dismissed; but they were liable to be called on during the following sixteen years; from the ages of twenty to twenty-eight they could be called up to fill the ranks whenever necessary; they were on the active list. And from the ages of twenty-eight to thirty-six they could be called up (in time of war) to form a

[18] This sketch of the army is taken from Fabris, Pinelli, Lumbroso, Tivaroni (*Ital. Sett.* pp. 205 *et seq.*), Montù, and all the hundred or more *Rapporti*, official reports for this campaign; also from Memoirs, etc., etc.

reserve. Thus about 8500 *Provinciali* recruits[19] came in each year, and nearly 1000 *Ordinanza*.

The Bersaglieri underwent two years of training and the mounted arms three.

In January 1848 Charles Albert had 8000 *Ordinanza* men to hand, but he could not call up any more of them because, once demobilised, *Ordinanza* men were free from further service. Of the *Provinciali* he must have had about 8500 of the 1827 class, namely boys of twenty years, but they were absolutely raw recruits. He had also 8500 of the 1826 class whom he had kept with the colours in case of emergency. This ought to have given him 25,000 men in all. And naturally there were some extras; his numbers are estimated at 30,000.

By February he had called up the youngest class of the back-levies (1825). This must have brought him at least another 7000.

On March 2nd he called up the 1824, 1823, and 1822 classes. This may have given him a total on paper of about 56,000 men, but many of them did not arrive until after the troops had started for the war.

On March 26th therefore his infantry regiments were only just over 2000 strong; or about 680 men per battalion. Thus, before the battle of Goito (April 8th) most probably he had only about 45,000 men of all arms in the field, over and above the last-joined recruits. And some thousands more of the *Provinciali* were still on the way.

But on March 23rd, when he declared war, he called up the two remaining classes, 1821 and 1820. These did not reach him until April 25th or even later; but they must have raised his numbers in the field to about 60,000 Piedmontese, excluding all his allies.[20] There were twenty infantry regiments

[19] Fabris, 1, 66, says 8500, but perhaps that refers only to the first year. Tivaroni, *op. cit.* p. 205, says 7000; he may have been thinking of the older classes called up, and apparently they did not produce even that number.

[20] We have not succeeded in finding the actual Official returns, but they have been dealt with in detail by all the leading authorities.

each of about 2550 men, which gives at least 800 men per battalion; and these figures remained approximately accurate during the campaign. In the squadrons there were 90 men, in the batteries about 160.

This system has been bitterly criticised. It is said that the only satisfactory soldiers were those of the *Ordinanza*, and the most recent classes of *Provinciali*. In the case of the others, their soldiering had been learnt in only fourteen months and since then it had not been refreshed; and now some of them were married men with families. Promis adds that there were only 35 *Ordinanza* men per company, nearly all of them used up as N.C.O.s. Obviously these criticisms would hardly apply at all to cavalry or artillery, but even so they are very serious. Still there is something to be said for a system which produced an active field-force of about 60,000 men, all under twenty-eight years of age; and left another eight classes to be called up as a reserve. Later on, the government summoned the men of 29, 30 and 31 years of age and formed a reserve about 19,000 strong—which was considered "a great effort for Piedmont".

In such a situation the point which above all others strikes a reader is that anything like haste was to be dreaded. Given time and care—a month or two for instance—these battalions would soon settle down to their routine work; but anything like a hurried mobilisation would be most unfortunate, because the majority of the new arrivals would not yet have found their place, and consequently would be at sixes and sevens with each other.

We must not omit a new and extremely serviceable corps of light infantry which had been started under Charles Albert's patronage—the celebrated Bersaglieri—the soldiers who are well known to foreigners on account of their plumes of cocks' feathers. It had been originally proposed in 1836

V. Fabris, I, 66, 74, 222, 228, 267, 286 n., 315, 324; II, 13 *et seq.* Tivaroni, *op. cit.* pp. 152, 205, 213. Baldini, p. 42 *et seq.* Hille- prandt, p. 50. Pinelli, III, 296.

by the Marchese Alessandro La Marmora, then an enthusiastic young captain in the Grenadier Guards. His idea was to have a corps armed with rifled carbines, and consisting of men specially trained in marksmanship, in gymnastics and in "the greatest possible mobility in manœuvring";[21] also in working in extended order and scouting. Its physical and educational standards were to be higher than those of other corps. In 1836 one battalion was raised consisting of two companies; in 1843 it was increased to four companies; in 1848 at the outbreak of war the total strength was raised to two battalions. But the real unit of the Bersaglieri was the company—nominally 200 strong; a Bersaglieri company was supposed to be able to go anywhere and do anything. They were numbered straightaway from Number One to the last raised, regardless of battalions.

This was the beginning of the celebrated corps which in 1910 consisted of twelve regiments of four battalions each. And when we look back on the last hundred years we may well join the Duce in saying: "What a glorious record!"

The Piedmontese cavalry has earned far more favourable reports than the infantry. Salasco, Prince Ferdinand, and other superior officers do not hesitate to tell us that their regiments were superior to the Austrians, who were considered among the best in Europe. The Piedmontese reports admit that in reconnaissance and other cavalry work their squadrons were not so well trained, but they claim that their troopers rode better; and that they had taken at once to the lance—a new weapon.[22]

[21] The Bersaglieri manœuvred at the double. They were picked men, 70% of them *ordinanza* and the remainder trained for two years instead of fourteen months: *v. Storia dei Bersaglieri*, by Pietro Fea, Firenze, 1879.

[22] Prince Ferdinand says that his men were stronger; that the thrust of their lance was fatal; that in a fight of cavalry against cavalry below Volta, the Genova and Savoia Regiments had charged eight hostile squadrons and defeated them completely. He says the Austrians halted to fire (*Rapporti*, 1, 283). Prince Ferdinand's

Best of all was the Artillery. This had been the weapon on which Charles Albert had bestowed special interest, and undoubtedly it did him credit. A Piedmontese battery consisted of six guns (usually eight-pounders) and two howitzers; with 150 men. Villamarina had only allowed one battery to a brigade: this was not a liberal allowance—one battery to 4000 infantry. The Austrians allowed in their First Army Corps six guns to 3000 men, and in their Second Corps one battery to 3500. But the Piedmontese had three batteries of sixteen-pounders;[23] and certainly were more than satisfied with their artillery work during the whole campaign.

The remaining services were almost non-existent. Even the Engineers, though good, numbered only about forty or fifty men per division. The Commissariat and Supply Service was mainly entrusted to the Lombard government, which paid large sums to contractors; but the drivers were all civilians, and towards the end of the campaign the food did not arrive. Indeed some of it did not even start.[24] During the last crucial days of fighting in the torrid-zone heat, Prince Ferdinand in his official report tells us that throughout his division the distributions could not be made oftener than once in two days. In fact during that disastrous fortnight between July 23rd and August 5th, there were only six or seven

report has been considered one of the best by military experts. His position placed him above personal rivalries, and at the same time left him a freer hand than if he had been heir-apparent. Evidently he was endowed with exceptional military talents. About the cavalry, even Pinelli can say that it was more alive than the infantry because the superior officers and N.C.O.s were younger.

[23] The Piedmontese pound weighed about $\frac{1}{3}$ of a kilogram, or $\frac{11}{15}$ of an English pound.

[24] *Rapporti*, I, 288. *V.* also report of Giustiniani, Chief of Staff to the First Division (*ibid.* p. 174). Della Rocca says in his *Ricordi* that in his division the Commissariat was not always so bad, but that it was on the days of the longest marches or heaviest fighting that it failed to arrive. *V.* also report of Ferrere, O.C. Second Division (*ibid.* pp. 202, 211); also of Broglia, O.C. Third Division (*ibid.* p. 220) and of Somis his Chief of Staff (*ibid.* p. 228).

distributions of rations. Similar reports were sent in from all the other divisions.

The doctors, ambulances and hospital service were all entirely insufficient. When the army started, there were only eighteen vehicles. By the middle of June, 5 % of the men were sick; and by the middle of July, 10 %. According to Somis, the hospitals were very well managed, but the ambulance service was disgraceful.

Such an army necessarily depended on the adaptability of the officers and N.C.O.s. It must have added greatly to the difficulties of the situation that so many of the N.C.O.s were men recently promoted.[25] As to the officers, it is very hard indeed to form a certain opinion.

In the official reports and memoirs, a British student will often find descriptions and criticisms which remind him of those of the British army at the beginning of the Boer war. The Piedmontese army was one formed on the old ideas— the officers all gentlemen, and most of the men of poorer class. And officers of this type are undoubtedly splendid raw material, but like steel, they require sharpening. After a long period of peace the professional element is not sufficiently developed; that, at all events, was said of the British officers in the years 1899–1901. It is a type which develops heroes in the field, but is satisfied with amateur knowledge elsewhere, and consequently it is the senior officers who are the least efficient. The subalterns and even the captains have less need of professional knowledge.[26]

[25] Speaking of the difficulties of an infantry captain if his men got out of hand, General Salasco wrote in his report: "What use is force against passive resistance of 150 to 200 peasants or workmen, most of whom are married and have children?" As to the officers, *v.* Minghetti, II, 4.

[26] Prince Ferdinand said in his report: "Except Bes and the Colonel of the Pinerolo Brigade and a few majors, all the superior officers of my division were bad. Any good thing that we did was

It is a remarkable fact that in the Austrian army the converse was true. Although most of the senior officers were men with the feudal sixteen quarterings, they evidently maintained a standard of professional efficiency for which the Piedmontese staff could show no equivalent.

This difference between the amateur and the professional is clearly revealed by a comparison of their respective plans of initiative—a point which is emphasised very strongly by Lumbroso.[27] We need only compare the tentative, unsystematized initiatives at Santa Lucia or after the fall of Vicenza, with the sudden overwhelming blows struck by Radetzky at Curtatone, Vicenza and Custoza; in his case everything worked like a huge machine.

Who was to blame? Charles Albert was Commander-in-Chief, but naturally he required with him some strong driving professional soldier to define everyone's duty and see it carried out punctually: to do the work which Kitchener did for Roberts during the Boer war. But as yet there was no such strong professional organiser among his senior officers; men such as Fanti or Cialdini were not yet sufficiently senior. The right commanders were still to seek as well as the right method.

Perhaps the person really to be blamed was Villamarina. Undoubtedly his system of training had included too much parade-ground work; manœuvres were held only every second year; and his officers had gained very little useful experience.

The staff officers of 1848 were almost as general a target for abuse as they were in England in the year 1917; but it seems inevitable that they should be selected for blame after every unsuccessful campaign. Among Charles Albert's senior officers there were some who had begun their career under Napoleon;

due to some captains, to many subalterns, and above all to our men who were of the right breed." *V.* also Pinelli, II, 196–7, but it must be remembered that Pinelli, evidently grieving over the defeat, takes a very adverse view of everything and everybody except Bava.

[27] Lumbroso, pp. 23–5.

but there were none who had served in his wars with a higher rank than that of captain. The best of them, military opinion agrees, was General Baron Bava. Bava[28] was an infantry officer aged fifty-seven, with a fine military record as a Napoleonic soldier of fortune. He was the son of middle-class parents which perhaps made him popular with the public, but was not a point in his favour with some of the élite of that day. At the outbreak of war he was in command of the First Army Corps; and during this campaign of 1848, owing to his greater experience, he gravitated gradually into the position of Commander-in-Chief, and during the final retreat virtually took over the sole command from Charles Albert. The chief criticism pointed at him is that he did everyone's work himself; but this was often inevitable.

The next of Charles Albert's advisers was General Count Franzini,[29] the Minister of War, an ex-artillery officer of sixty. He is described as an honest and able man, and very severe—Pinelli says hot-tempered. Count Lumbroso tells us that he retired rather than contradict Charles Albert. Undoubtedly it was a very bad system to have the Minister of War at H.Q. as well as the Chief of Staff and Bava; one man made plans for another to carry out; hence recriminations.

[28] Born in 1790 in Piedmont, the son of a goldsmith; in appearance tall and athletic. When the French overran Piedmont, his father entered him in the College of St Cyr in 1802; he passed out in 1805 and became an N.C.O. in the Grande Armée. 1806 and 1807, served in the Prussian and Polish campaigns. 1808, promoted 2nd Lieutenant; served at siege of Saragossa and elsewhere. 1809, wounded in Portugal and taken to England a prisoner, but, with some companions, seized a schooner and escaped to France. 1811, in command of a mobile column fighting against Spanish guerrillas; rewarded with Legion of Honour. 1814, fought as Captain in the Peninsular War. 1814, returned home and served as Captain in the Piedmontese army; rewarded with Cross of S. Maurizio for gallantry at Grenoble. During the long peace he was promoted: 1830, Colonel; 1832, Major-General; 1838, Lieut.-General; 1843, created Baron. In 1848 he was given command of the First Army Corps.
[29] He had served for five years in Napoleon's armies. Fabris, 1, 225, 233.

General Conte di Salasco was Chief of Staff. No one denies that he was honest and knowledgeable, but according to Lumbroso he was a man of detail and red tape;[30] and according to Della Rocca, without military initiative or intuition. Certainly the H.Q. staff work seems to have been extremely inefficient. Orders took hours to reach their destination; Della Rocca remarks that it was natural that Charles Albert, whose whole soul was in the cause of independence, must accompany the army in order to inspire both officers and men with his enthusiasm; but that he required at his side a Chief of Staff who was bold, intelligent and well-informed, master of the mind and heart of his sovereign, just as was Berthier in the early campaigns of Napoleon. Unfortunately no such Chief of Staff was to be found.

General Count de Sonnaz, as second in order of seniority, was in command of the Second Army Corps. By birth he was one of the old Savoyard nobility whose traditional loyalty had made the wonderful fortunes of the House of Savoy. De Sonnaz was now sixty-one,[31] a kindly wizened little veteran. He had begun his career in 1813 as a volunteer in Napoleon's Life Guards; had been promoted subaltern and received the Legion of Honour for an act of gallantry; and, says Fabris,

[30] Della Rocca, *Autobiografia*, I, 169. "The Chief of Staff was General Salasco, and next in command Colonel Cossato, both cultivated, honest men and lovers of discipline; but unfortunately without military initiative or intuition. The Minister of War, Franzini, who accompanied the army, was certainly the best soldier of the three; but he was not given directing authority, but merely a consultative vote." Della Rocca wrote this in 1893 when he was 86 years of age. *V.* also the opinion of Minghetti, *Ricordi*, II, 4, 5; Pinelli, p. 206 *et seq.*; Lumbroso, p. 116 *et seq.*

[31] Born 1787, died 1867. Fought as a volunteer at the battles of Dresden, Kulm and Leipzig; at Hanau won the Legion of Honour for saving the life of a colonel. In 1813 he was present at La Rothière; during the night he was commanding the escort of Napoleon's carriage and repulsed a raid by Cossacks. After the fall of Napoleon he returned to Piedmont and pursued his career in the Piedmontese army. Fabris, I, 237. Also Pinelli, II, 206, and Lumbroso, p. 146.

had always retained that good-natured, affectionate manner which bound to one another the officers and the men in the Napoleonic army like members of one family. If any thought him over-affable to subordinates, it was forgiven on account of his genuine kindness. And "great energy, great experience of men and long habit of handling troops made up for it, if he had any lack of knowledge of the highest commands in the army". Unfortunately he made a disastrous end to this campaign.

It is noticeable that in 1849 Charles Albert appointed a foreigner, Chrzanowski, to command. This may have been due to a belief that there were jealousies among his own officers, but more probably perhaps to a feeling that in 1848 none of them had seemed quite of the calibre necessary for so extremely difficult an enterprise.[32]

The following military opinion of General Del Bono perhaps confirms the paucity of able commanders: "I consider Ferdinand...the only general of first-class ability possessed by Piedmont, in his time." But Prince Ferdinand was only twenty-six in 1848.

To summarise the situation, therefore, at the beginning of 1848.

The nationalist agitation had spread from Rome all over Northern Italy. It had reached Florence and the other Tuscan towns; even Austrian-ruled Lombardo-Venetia was seething with it; meanwhile Charles Albert and his advisers

[32] "At G.H.Q. there were no officers of first-class ability" (Minghetti, *Ricordi*, p. 5). Minghetti was a barrister and one of the ablest in Italy, attached to the Staff during the war. *V.* also Pinelli, II, 196; Lumbroso, p. 146; and the reports of many of the officers.

For a table giving the names and numbers of the Piedmontese army which advanced into Lombardy at the end of March, *v.* p. 49. For opinions on Salasco, *v.* Lumbroso, p. 117; Fabris, I, 239; Minghetti, II, 4; Della Rocca, I, 169; Costa de Beauregard, p. 146; Pinelli, III, 205. For Franzini, *v.* Fabris, I, 234–6; Della Rocca, I, 170. For Bava, Lumbroso, p. 121 *et seq.*; Fabris, I, 234–6; also Pinelli and many other authorities.

were in full tide of preparation. But the three reforming states[33] possessed no military force except the Piedmontese army. And that army was by no means strong enough to cope with the Austrians, as long as the political situation remained normal.

Thus for the time being the circle of small princes remained intact. The bomb-shell destined to break up their ring was to come from the most unexpected quarter—from the island of Sicily.

THE SARDINIAN ARMY DURING THE CAMPAIGN OF 1848*

(This table of Pinelli's is dated April 25th. The strength of all the units was afterwards increased. *V.* comment at the end of the list of totals.)

Commander-in-Chief	H.M. King Charles Albert
Chief of Staff	General di Salasco
Sub-Chief of Staff	Colonel di Cossato
Minister of War	Major-General Franzini
G.O.C. Artillery	Ferdinand Duke of Genoa
G.O.C. Engineers	Major-General Chiodo
O.C. Bersaglieri	Colonel Alessandro Lamarmora

FIRST ARMY CORPS

General Officer Commanding	Lieutenant-General Bava
Chief of Staff	Colonel Lagrange

FIRST DIVISION (d'Arvillars)

Aosta Brigade (Sommariva)	B.	C.	S.	G.	M.†
5th Regt Infantry	3	.	.	.	1992
6th Regt Infantry	3	.	.	.	1983

* Pinelli. Vol. III, 294–5.
† B. = Battalions; C. = Companies; S. = Squadrons; G. = Guns; M. = Men.

[33] Naples had a well-equipped army; but "the Kingdom of the Two Sicilies" was so far south that it had little share in the anti-Austrian movement. Its organisation was better than is commonly supposed. It had been reorganised by Nugent during the years 1822–5. One of the frequent jibes hurled at it by revolutionary writers was the number of its Field-Marshals; but the same jibe might have been pointed at the Austrian army: in it, to be a Field-Marshal was the usual rank for a Divisional General.

Regina Brigade (Trotti)	B.	C.	S.	G.	M.
9th Regt Infantry	3	.	.	.	1971
10th Regt Infantry	3	.	.	.	1974
Real Navi	1	.	.	.	287
Bersaglieri	.	1	.	.	183
Regt Aosta Cavalry	.	.	6	.	534
Engineers	.	1	.	.	207
6th and 8th Field Batteries	.	.	.	16	338

SECOND DIVISION (Di Ferrere)
Casale Brigade (Passalacqua)

	B.	C.	S.	G.	M.
11th Regt Infantry	3	.	.	.	2071
12th Regt Infantry	3	.	.	.	1974

Acqui Brigade (Villafaletto)

	B.	C.	S.	G.	M.
17th Regt Infantry	3	.	.	.	1971
18th Regt Infantry	3	.	.	.	1946
Regt Nizza Cavalry	.	.	6	.	547
2nd and 3rd Field Batteries	.	.	.	16	327
Carbineers	.	.	½	.	50
Transport	.	.	.	.	40
Totals	25	2	12½	32	18395

SECOND ARMY CORPS

General Officer Commanding   Lieutenant-General de Sonnaz
Chief of Staff   Colonel Carderina

THIRD DIVISION (Broglia)
Savoia Brigade (D'Ussillon)

	B.	C.	S.	G.	M.
1st Regt Infantry	3	.	.	.	1896
2nd Regt Infantry	3	.	.	.	1879

*Composite Brigade (Conti)

	B.	C.	S.	G.	M.
16th Regt Infantry	3	.	.	.	1932
Parma Contingent	1	.	.	.	865
Bersaglieri	.	2	.	.	325
Regt. Novara Cavalry	.	.	6	.	563
7th Field Batt. and 2nd Siege Batt.	.	.	.	16	322
Engineers	.	1	.	.	204

FOURTH DIVISION (Federici)
Piemonte Brigade (Bes)

	B.	C.	S.	G.	M.
3rd Regt Infantry	3	.	.	.	1976
4th Regt Infantry	3	.	.	.	1988

Pinerolo Brigade (Manno)

	B.	C.	S.	G.	M.
13th Regt Infantry	3	.	.	.	1949
14th Regt Infantry	3	.	.	.	1972
Regt Piemonte Reale Cavalry	.	.	6	.	497
1st and 4th Field Batteries	.	.	.	16	331
Carbineers	.	.	½	.	48
Transport	.	.	.	.	200
Totals	22	3	12½	32	16947

* Formerly the Savona Brigade; but its second Infantry Regt, the 15th, had been left behind in Savoy on garrison duty. When joined by the contingents from the Duchies it became the Mista or Composite Brigade.

RESERVE DIVISION

General Officer Commanding	H.R.H. The Duke of Savoy
Chief of Staff	Colonel Morozzo della Rocca

	B.	C.	S.	G.	M.
Guards Brigade (Biscaretti)					
1st Regt Grenadiers	3	.	.	.	1674
2nd Regt Grenadiers	3	.	.	.	1682
Cuneo Brigade (D'Aviernoz)					
7th Regt Infantry	3	.	.	.	1980
8th Regt Infantry	3	.	.	.	1938
Cavalry Brigade (Sala)					
Regt. Genova Cavalry	.	.	6	.	485
Regt. Savoy Cavalry	.	.	6	.	514
1st and 2nd Mounted Battery, and 1st siege Battery	.	.	.	24	517
Engineers	.	½	.	.	102
Carbineers	.	.	½	.	38
Transport etc.					50
Totals	12	½	12½	24	8980

TROOPS ATTACHED TO G,H.Q.

	B.	C.	S.	G.	M.
Officers of various ranks	.	.	.	.	26
Carbineers	.	.	3	.	280
Engineers	.	1	.	.	208
Bersaglieri	.	1	.	.	163
Transport	.	.	.	.	14
Bridging train	.	.	.	.	240
Totals	.	2	3	.	931

RECAPITULATION

	B.	C.	S.	G.	M.
1st Corps	25	2	12½	32	18395
2nd Corps	22	3	12½	32	16947
Reserve Division	12	½	12½	24	8980
G.H.Q.	.	2	3	.	931
Totals	59	7½	40½	88	45253

The above figures are those before the 1821 and 1820 classes had joined up. When they arrived the total strength rose to about 60,000, and the following are the figures given by Baldini (p. 217):

B.	S.	G.
65	36	120

Baldini's cavalry squadrons omit the Carbineers. And the reason for his far higher total of guns is that three heavy batteries were brought up for the siege of Peschiera; and also one extra field battery.

The infantry of the old Piedmontese army consisted of ten brigades, each of two regiments. Each regiment consisted of three battalions, each of four companies.

Chapter III

THE SICILIAN RISING

The Sicilian outbreak initiates the period of Constitutions; indeed it became the spark which presently set half of Europe ablaze.

It is a very strange chance that the first great victory in the Risorgimento should have been initiated by the population which was least of any concerned in the movement. When the islanders of Sicily flew to arms, they were thinking only of winning their freedom from Naples. What resulted was that King Ferdinand II granted a Constitution to Naples as well as Sicily, and that this compelled all the other Italian monarchs to follow his example.

The Kingdom of "The Two Sicilies" contained some 8,000,000 souls—about 6,000,000 in Naples and 2,000,000 in Sicily; but owing to their mutual hatred these two southern units neutralised each other's importance. They had very little influence on the Risorgimento.[1]

The Sicilians had only one great enthusiasm—to free their island from the hated Neapolitans. Once free, they meant to re-erect the Constitution of 1812 enjoyed under the English. *Per contra*, the Neapolitans' first aim was to maintain their hold on Sicily; apart from the Sicilian question, however, some of the townsmen and middle classes were Liberals and wanted to set up in Naples the Neapolitan Constitution of 1820 sworn by King Ferdinand I, but forbidden by the Austrians.

Thus the King could do no right. The Congress of Vienna had left him in an impossible position. If he granted a Constitution to Naples, he would be courting an Austrian invasion. If he granted Home Rule to Sicily, he would have

[1] *V. Italy in the Making*, II, 268.

to face the fury of the Neapolitans, all strong Unionists. Any concession on either side of the straits would almost certainly lead to disaster. He himself (Ferdinand II, 1830–58) happened to be a convinced Bourbon Conservative, so that, before the end of his reign, his repressions of Sicily had earned him the soubriquet of "Bomba", and his disposal of the Liberal Constitution had won him the title of "the thrice-perjured King of Naples". Yet, one is sometimes tempted to ask oneself: What was there for him to do?[2]

In neither of his two countries was there any real desire for the Risorgimento. To them, those northern ideas—the call for freedom from Austria, and for Italian unity—were of little practical concern. The Neapolitan Liberals were asking for their own Constitution of 1820; the Sicilians for their own Constitution of 1812;[3] and they hated each other.[4]

The beautiful island of Sicily and its political wrongs have already been described at some length in volume II of this work.[5] We may remember that during the Napoleonic interregnum the Sicilians had remained faithful to King Ferdinand I; but no sooner had the fear of Napoleon departed than Ferdinand I returned to Naples and presently proceeded to abolish or Neapolitanise all distinctively Sicilian institutions; before long there was no separate Constitution, no navy, no army and no national flag.

In 1820 the Sicilians rose in rebellion and succeeded in

[2] *V.* Appendix A. He said this himself. In his private letter dated January 28th, 1848, to his friend the Czar he stated all this situation and ended: "Le Roi se voit donc dans l'impossibilité d'écarter les dangers dont il est menacé." This was perfectly true. Vienna Staats-Arch. Neapel, 1848, fasz. 74.

[3] The Constitution of 1812 was the Sicilian battle-cry; the least that they would accept: but it contained a House of Peers, and presently there arose a small extremist party which wanted something more democratic: but it was the Constitution of 1812 that was voted. La Masa, I, 178.

[4] *London Corr.* Naples and Sicily, September 28th, 1848. British Consul at Catania. *V.* also Amari and other Sicilian writers.

[5] *Italy in the Making*, II, ch. xx, and elsewhere.

winning the right to vote themselves a separate Parliament; but as soon as the Neapolitan troops were allowed into their forts, the Parliament at Naples cynically repudiated the agreement. This breach of faith was the more remarkable in that it was carried out by the Liberals of Naples—the party which had just claimed and set up for itself the Constitution of 1820—in fact, the same Liberal party which in the very same year stigmatised forever Ferdinand I and his successors as "the perjured King of Naples".

Thus not only was it a case of hereditary cat-and-dog hatred, but during the Napoleonic wars they had, as it were, taken opposite sides—Sicily under the British fleet, and Naples under Napoleon. During this period the Sicilians had imbibed certain British ideas. Their ancient Constitution, which dated back to their Norman conquest[6] and recalled their glorious struggle for freedom at the time of the Vespers, had been modernised under English influence. After having been for centuries feudal in character and guided by the nobles, it had now become comparatively democratic and was the pride of the people. It was known as the Constitution of 1812. It had been the work of the English admiral Lord William Bentinck and, in consequence, he was beloved throughout the island. So true is this that, according to Gualterio, in 1815 the Sicilians would have been content to remain as they were, an island state under British protection.[7] Numerically their population would have been fifth among the Italian states. Before Lord William Bentinck departed in 1815 he obtained for the Sicilians a promise from old King Ferdinand I that the existing Sicilian privileges should remain untouched. Ever since then this promise had been regarded as virtually a British guarantee of the existing Constitution.

And here we get the fatal catch in the deadlock. The Sicilians were struggling not merely for self-government in a general sense; they wanted nothing else on earth but their

[6] Gualterio, IV, 176.   [7] *Ibid.* pp. 184–6.

beloved Constitution of 1812. This demand meant complete separation from Naples; for that Constitution of 1812 guaranteed to them that if the King should ever return to Naples he was to make Sicily a separate kingdom[8] under his son; or, if he left Sicily without permission of their Parliament, the Sicilians might elect a new King.

A compromise, therefore, had become almost impossible. Ferdinand might be willing to go as far as in him lay, or as far as Minto suggested, on the road to Home Rule, but he could hardly agree to a Constitution which would enable the Sicilians to elect a rival King.[9]

In Sicily the risings may be classified as real genuine war-of-the-people. Throughout the rest of Italy there was nothing comparable to them. As their movement was not republican, the nobles could be good Sicilians and so could many of the priests. And thus Metternich lived to see that even a small people, if united by a genuine sense of injustice, is not a negligible quantity. It was they who poignarded his system. And it was the strangest outcome of his policy that the first decisive blow in a world-wide contest of principle should have been struck by these islanders who had no real interest in the Risorgimento.

In volume II of *Italy in the Making* we related how the young La Masa had left the city of Florence and his *fidanzata*, the daughter of the Duke of Bevilacqua, in order to go and become a leader of rebellion in his native island.[10]

We have seen that he was in touch with Montanelli in

[8] *V.* Constitution of the Kingdom of Sicily 1812. Section relating to the succession to the throne, Clauses VI and VIII respectively. To be found in *London Corr.* Naples and Sicily.

[9] In July 1848 the Sicilians invited Charles Albert's second son to be their King. This would have been dangerous for Naples.

[10] "Biondo era e bello e di gentil aspetto", he was fair-haired and beautiful and of winning aspect. La Masa has been described by the incomparable line in which Dante pictured Manfred. As he had been long out of Sicily there was a certain mystery about him for the first day or two. *V.* Torrearsa, *Ricordi*, p. 110.

Florence, and with the Liberals in Rome, notably with the Piedmontese group, and also with Lord Minto and General Sir Frederick Adam (vol. II, p. 313). But as matters turned out these Liberal connections were of little advantage to his enterprise. The rising was purely Sicilian, and—a piece of daring bravado, hitherto unknown—it was publicly announced beforehand. It will always be remembered as the *Sfida a giorno fisso*, the challenge to battle on a day previously fixed.[11] The revolutionists actually issued a proclamation on January 10th announcing a rising for January 12th, 1848, the King's birthday. This is surely unique in the history of rebellions.

On the morning of January 12th in Palermo the guns were firing salutes and the soldiers were in the squares for the birthday parade. Some insurgents had been brought in secretly during the night, and the streets were crammed with people wondering whether there would be any excitement or not; but no one thought of action. It seemed as if the rising had missed fire. Suddenly from within the crowd there came a shout of *All' armi!* This hero was a young man called Pietro Amedeo—before nightfall he had given his life for his cause. At the same time, in the Piazza Vigliena (now Quattrocanti) two priests raised their crucifixes and called the people to arms in the name of God; and in the Piazza Fieravecchia (now Piazza della Rivoluzione) the lead was given by a young lawyer called Paternostro. In answer to these appeals a few armed men appeared. And at another point La Masa stepped into the street with a shout of *Viva Pio Nono, Viva l'Italia*, and raised a tricolour handkerchief on the end of a stick. Several men followed him, but when it was seen how few of the rebels had arms, the crowd quickly dispersed; the shops were

[11] Owing to the reports from the British consuls at Palermo and Messina British ships of war had actually been sent to both these ports to protect British interests in the event of an outbreak on January 12th. Torrearsa says the writer of this proclamation was a young man called Francesco Bagnasco.

barred; the streets became empty and the one or two dozen insurgents were left to face the authorities.

By prompt action they would have been crushed. But with wonderful courage they continued calling upon the people to rise, while the church bells clanged out above them *a stormo*. And before long, various small bands were formed of armed men and boys, who slipped about rapidly from one point to another. They had no real plan, and on the first day did not attempt barricades, but they attacked four or five Neapolitan patrols, and by nightfall the troops had lost ten men killed and the insurgents only two.[12]

That evening the leaders fixed their headquarters in the Piazza Fieravecchia.

January 13th. The leaders must have been profoundly thankful that they had not been raided during the night. The troops could easily have suppressed the rebels during the first two days. But the Neapolitan Lord Lieutenant, General De Majo and the officer-in-command, General Vial, were not on very good terms, and seem to have imagined that they were face to face with a rising on a large scale and helped by the English.[13] They thought it wiser to stand on the defensive and make sure of the four most important points in the town; so they garrisoned the Royal Palace (bastions and guns), the Castello, the barracks of San Giacomo (four guns), and the Noviziato. From their positions inside the town they could sweep the two long straight streets which lie like a great cross through the centre of Palermo: while outside the walls were the forts of Castellamare, the Molo and others. Thus for the next five days from the 13th to the 18th they kept up intermittent artillery fire, sufficient to force foreign residents to take refuge on board H.M.S. *Bulldog*, but without doing any great

[12] They cannot have created any great excitement, as the consul at Palermo thought the rising was at an end. *V.* La Masa, *Documenti della rivoluzione siciliana*, p. 51 *et seq.*, who gives a vivid account. He says there were only fifty-eight muskets in all on the first day (p. 58).
[13] Tivaroni, p. 304; Gori, p. 401.

damage in the town except for one shell which burnt the Monte di Pietà.

During the night the Sicilians had succeeded in bringing in sixty peasants from outside, so that they now had 300 men armed with muskets and 300 with scythes or pikes.[14] From this semi-equipped force, La Masa tells us, they sent patrols right and left through the city to keep up the hearts of their friends and, before evening, they had succeeded in cutting to pieces a contingent of fifty-two of the much-loathed police.

January 14th. There was rather a lull in the fighting because the troops were expecting reinforcements and the Sicilians were short of ammunition. Hitherto they had had only shotgun ammunition, but now they succeeded in manufacturing a little powder besides what they had brought in from outside. On this day[15] they called together twenty-six leading citizens at the Piazza Fieravecchia and formed four directing committees: those for Public Food Supply, for War, for Finance and for Intelligence. On these Committees we find some of the names that have lived in Italian history, such as La Masa, Stabile, and especially Admiral Ruggiero Settimo, a fine old veteran who had fought for Sicilian freedom in 1820 and was now over seventy years of age.

On January 15th there was fighting at various points, and the insurgents took the Prefecture of Police: but during the night the Neapolitan reinforcements arrived—the Count of Aquila, who was a younger brother of the King, with a fleet of five steamships and four corvettes, bearing 8000[16] men and two batteries under General de Sauget.

These new troops seemed to bring an absolutely overwhelming accretion of strength to the Regulars. In reality, however, had the insurgents known it, their arrival was not

---

[14] La Masa, I, 66; La Farina, *Storia*, II, 117.

[15] Gori, p. 401 and Tivaroni, p. 304; also *London Corr.* Naples and Sicily, p. 64.

[16] La Farina (p. 118) says 5000.

entirely a misfortune. Though a Bourbon, the Count of Aquila was a man of Liberal sympathies,[17] and he very soon perceived that repression was useless. After a visit of only two nights he returned, on the 17th, to Naples bearing a report from de Sauget, in which both these officers expressed their opinion that this was not, as had been supposed, merely a local disturbance in Palermo, but a national uprising of the whole of Sicily with which it was necessary to negotiate. On receipt of this news from his brother, King Ferdinand realised that it was wisest to treat at once, and he proceeded to do so; but his first proposals could not arrive at Palermo until the 21st. Meanwhile of course the fighting had continued.

Nevertheless it is a point to note that it was owing to his prompt acquiescence in the suggestion of his brother, the Count of Aquila, that the Neapolitan ships never bombarded Palermo.[18]

[17] The Count of Aquila, youngest brother of the Bourbon-Siciles family, was a good Royalist and loyal to his brother, but from his earliest youth had been pursuing a keen and successful career in the navy. He was now a captain; and his experience of life had given him Liberal ideas. While he was in Brazil he had even received an invitation from Garibaldi to come and accept a command in the Argentine forces. From 1848 onwards he became perhaps the most sensible of the advisers of King Ferdinand, who seems to have appreciated his gifts and character though afraid of his political views.

He left a *Relation* describing the chief events in his lifetime; an exceedingly interesting MS. which the present writers have had the privilege of reading by the kind permission of Prince Louis de Bourbon-Siciles, the Count of Aquila's grandson. His order that Palermo should not be bombarded is confirmed by Mr Lyon, an Englishman who was there. *V. London Corr.* Naples and Sicily, p. 41.

[18] This is stated, not only by the Count of Aquila himself, but also by Prince Schwarzenberg the Austrian ambassador: although personally he disliked Aquila. *V.* Schwarzenberg's despatch of January 21st, 1848. Vienna H.H.S.A. No. 6B, Rapports, Expéditions, Varia, 1848. It is also confirmed by Mr Lyon, *v.* note 17. Also by the Marquis Pareto, Piedmontese ambassador in Rome, who reported that " on the 18th of this month the Count of Aquila returned to Naples to obtain from the King new and more precise

The 16th was evidently a day of stress. The Committees were done for. Out of over thirty names on the list, only nine turned up at H.Q. But these were ready for any sacrifice. Among them were old Ruggiero Settimo, Mariano Stabile and La Masa. A rebel attack on the Palazzo delle Finanze failed, but the insurgents discovered a cannon with which they played on the royalists in Toledo; a Neapolitan attack on the Porta Maqueda was repulsed after three hours of hard fighting, from 2 to 5 p.m. The troops lost a gun and some prisoners. It was during this struggle that the Sicilian brigand Scordato earned great glory. On this day several Consuls headed by the British representative offered themselves as mediators, but the rebel leader Mariano Stabile simply replied: "Sicily means to recover her ancient liberties."

January 17th. By now the people were better armed. They attacked the troops, took the San Zita barracks, making 300 prisoners; and cut off the water supply from the Palazzo Reale and Quattro Venti. From this day onwards it is no longer "the bands" who are fighting: it is "Il Popolo".

The miraculous story of these sixteen days is too lengthy to be pursued in detail. The fighting continued until the 26th, but except on occasions the losses cannot have been very serious.

On the 21st King Ferdinand's proposals duly arrived; but they were refused. The rebel Pretore of Palermo replied that the people would not stop fighting until they could meet together in their own Parliament at Palermo.

The 25th was another great day of success for the people. It was *Siciliani all' armi!* And these citizens, short in stature, but sturdy and active and united like brothers, attacked and took several of the most important fortified buildings. At 2 a.m. that night their ammunition ran short; but, by then, the Neapolitan generals had decided to retire. The infantry

instructions as to their method of operations; in as much as the city of Palermo was entirely in the hands of the insurgents, and the method proposed by the officer in command of the expedition was to bombard it, an extremity to which His Royal Highness would not agree without knowing the intentions of the King". Turin Arch., Lettere Ministri, Roma, January 20th, 1848.

was played out after fourteen nights of strain, and the artillery could not be used to bombard the town "without arousing protests from the British and other consuls".[19]

So far the townsmen had only lost 100 killed and 200 wounded, but the losses of the troops must have been far higher.

On January 29th the army, still nearly 11,000 strong, was embarked for Naples.[20]

On the same day King Ferdinand granted a Constitution to both his realms. By that grant he hoped to save Sicily for the Crown and simultaneously to conciliate Naples; moreover he left an opening for Sicily to come into the new Constitution, by negotiation. But the Sicilians refused to accept any Constitution except that of 1812.

At the same time they published a statement which defined their position with regard to the Risorgimento. It amounted more or less to saying: "It is no use to try to persuade us to coalesce with Naples in order to win a united Italy, because we should only come into a united Italy on a federal basis, and as a separate unit from Naples." This reply would constitute an answer to the Neapolitan Liberals as well as to the Conservatives. On the outbreak of war against Austria the Sicilians' fear of the Neapolitans prevented their joining Charles Albert, but they sent a company of a hundred men under La Masa to show their good will.

Thus their marvellous effort had proved victorious. After thirty-two years Sicily was free. A fortnight later not a Neapolitan unit remained in Sicily except—unfortunately a very important exception—the garrison about 4000 strong

[19] These words are attributed to General Vial.

[20] The men were exhausted for want of sleep and by strain. Unfortunately this was afterwards felt to have been an ignominious retirement. In their hurry that evening some of them shot their horses and spiked their guns, although the rebels in pursuit were only a thousand strong. It is said that this accounts for the revengeful spirit afterwards displayed by the Neapolitan soldiers at the bombardment of Messina and elsewhere.

in the Citadel of Messina. These were days of unimaginable happiness for the patriots.

But, alas, that we should have to write it!—they were soon to learn that the moment of triumph is often a moment of danger; only too often it initiates an era of over-confidence, of controversies and of mistakes. These men were descended from Greeks—from the Greco-Sicilian stock with a dash of the Saracen; a splendid blend to unite against an invader, but unstable. Apparently they had inherited no single trait from their Norman ancestors—from that race of born organisers. Perhaps the truth was that at the end of every revolution the men who have risen to the command are those who have fought most recklessly, and these are not always men who can organise.

At all events the fact remains that during the next six months they were guilty of such an unthinkable number of errors and omissions as almost to destroy the sympathy aroused by their heroic struggle for freedom.[21]

[21] The quarrels between Sicily and Naples have no bearing on the Risorgimento except in so far as they prevented either of them from taking part in it: but, for general interest, we may say that during the next six months the Sicilians showed such lack of capacity that, by September, Ferdinand was able to reconquer them after meeting with very little opposition. During that period they refused to accept from him the most extreme grants of Home Rule offered under the aegis of Lord Minto. At the same time they formed no army for the defence of their newly-won freedom. Tivaroni tells us that for several months they continued to kill the agents of the former Neapolitan government; they offered the crown of Sicily to Charles Albert's second son, which naturally alarmed and aroused Ferdinand. They made no attempt to take the citadel of Messina, which remained a sort of bridgehead through which the Neapolitan troops could re-enter the island and take their revenge for recent humiliations. Hence the celebrated bombardment of Messina, September 8th, 1848, after which Ferdinand was nicknamed *Bomba*. By that re-conquest Ferdinand and the Neapolitan people were able to maintain their union with Sicily. But it takes two sides to make a union; and only eleven years later the Sicilians, by the help of Garibaldi and a thousand redshirts, were able to regain their freedom: a victory which heralded the fall of the Neapolitan monarchy and nationality.

Chapter IV

CONSTITUTIONS

I. THE BREAKDOWN OF METTERNICH'S SYSTEM

The triumph of the Sicilians was the beginning of a European debacle, because it meant the failure of Metternich's system all over Italy. When once Ferdinand had granted a Constitution, it would become impossible for the Pope and the Grand Duke of Tuscany to refuse Constitutions, and very difficult even for Charles Albert; and then the network of Austrian ambassadors would become ineffective, and their bureaucracy in Milan would be proclaimed an anachronism.

Metternich's ambassador in Naples, Prince Felix Schwarzenberg,[1] foresaw all this and tried hard to prevent it. He was fighting his corner for the Empire, and already he had urged Metternich to land ten thousand men on the Adriatic coast to stiffen Ferdinand's government.[2] When he heard of the granting of the Constitution, he blamed the King and his brother as cowards for giving in; in fact he used the self-same terms of abuse[3] which Buol applies to Charles Albert for granting the Statuto, but it was all to no purpose. Metternich did not want to send Austrian troops into Southern Italy.

[1] "Le Prince Felix a du talent, une grande connaissance de la situation et du nerf. Son caractère militaire tourne également en faveur de son choix", namely for the post which Hübner held in Milan. Metternich to Ficquelmont, March 1st, 1848. Vienna H.H.S.A., Kanzlei, No. 23.
[2] *V.* his despatch of October 29th, 1847. Vienna H.H.S.A., Naples, No. 45 B, 1847, Rapports, Expéditions, Varia, II, Question d'intervention.
[3] His letter of January 27th, 1848; but in that letter he had no good word for anyone. Vienna H.H.S.A., Neapel, 1848, Politische Berichte.

Hitherto it has always been believed that at this time Metternich's policy in Italy remained unalterably aggressive. His recent occupation of Ferrara, Modena, Parma and Piacenza had alarmed the Italian statesmen of that day. They regarded him almost as a tiger ready for a spring; and ever since then, their historians have tended to take the same view. But the Viennese documents convey quite a different impression. The whole tenour of Metternich's correspondence with Italy shows that while the Italians lived in daily fear of invasion, he was merely hoping that Austria might be able to ride out the storm—just as forty years earlier she had ridden out the Napoleonic storm—and still remain a great power when it was past.[4]

He had even reached the point of saying that if the Italian rulers granted Constitutions, that fact at all events released Austria from all obligation of coming to protect them.

The following episode is rather striking. At that time there existed an old secret treaty of 1815[5] which ought to have made Ferdinand perfectly secure. By its terms, the then King of Naples, Ferdinand's grandfather, had bound himself never to grant a Constitution, and in return Austria had undertaken to defend the *status quo*. Consequently during October 1847 Ferdinand had gone so far as to remind a friend of Schwarzenberg's that he was entitled to Austrian protection;[6] and now, during the last eleven days after the return of the Count of Aquila from Palermo, from January 18th to the 29th, he

---

[4] The most instructive of all his correspondence is perhaps that with Count Lützow to whom he wrote as to an old friend.

[5] This secret treaty is to be seen in the Austrian Archives, a copy being enclosed in Schwarzenberg's letter of October 29th, 1847, cited above. It was properly an annexe to the Treaty of Vienna. It must have been an important item in the political situation in 1820 and 1821. *V.* also Genoino, *Le Sicilie al tempo di Francesco I*, ch. 11.

[6] Vienna H.H.S.A. *ibid.* No. 6 D. Secret despatch of January 21st, 1848, and also despatch of March 23rd. On November 4th, 1847, Metternich had sent six good reasons against undertaking intervention. *V.* his despatch of that date, Vienna H.H.S.A. *ibid.*

again sounded Schwarzenberg as to the possibility of Austrian intervention. But after some consideration, the idea of intervention was abandoned; and abandoned for a reason which, two years earlier, would have amazed the civilised world. The pontifical government refused to allow the Austrian troops to march across its territory, and Metternich made this a reason for not sending them.[7]

It was only then that Ferdinand gave in. On January 27th there was a street demonstration estimated at 20,000 people, all shouting for a Constitution. That evening, Ferdinand called a committee of generals who told him that they could not entirely trust their troops. This statement provided a sufficient answer to Metternich, and decided the matter.

On January 29th he promised his Constitution. The deed was done. He had forestalled the revolution, but it was at the price of alienating all his best supporters from the Czar and Metternich down to Del Carretto and Monsignor Cocle. He had made this—for him—immense concession in order to save Sicily for the Crown and to stave off revolution in Naples.[8]

In Naples itself the state of public feeling is very hard to gauge. As the King rode out he was received everywhere with an unparalleled ovation. Was it for the Constitution, or was it for himself as opposed to the innovators? Probably the Constitution was received with joy only by a limited number of middle-class burghers—at all events we know that on election-day, ten weeks later, only about 2500 people troubled to vote, out of an electorate of 12,000 in the city of Naples.[9]

The bulk of the population preferred King Ferdinand's rule to any that they were likely to get from the mediocrities

[7] Vienna H.H.S.A. Neapel N.A. 36. Politische Weisungen 1847. Metternich to Schwarzenberg, Nov. 14.

[8] Del Carretto was banished from the State. Ferdinand is accused of having behaved heartlessly to him. We do not know the truth.

[9] Prince Schwarzenberg wrote to Metternich that there were only about 2000 people who really wanted the Constitution. Vienna H.H.S.A. Neapel, No. 8 B, 1848, Politische Berichte. He would be very likely to under-estimate.

of the Liberal party; and in some quarters he was greeted by the poor fishermen and artisans with shouts of *Viva il Re assoluto*! "Long live the Absolute King!"

The following is Napier's description of the scene:

On leaving the gate of the palace a great multitude surrounded their sovereign, kissing his hands and his stirrups, addressing him in the most affectionate language, and giving many touching demonstrations of gratitude and devotion. The King was deeply moved by these marks of attachment, spoke to his good people in a gracious manner and shed tears in which he was joined by all around.

In passing along the great street of Toledo, a magnificent spectacle of enthusiasm suddenly manifested itself; for the whole way was lined with ranks of carriages and crowds of the humbler orders who, with flags and ribbons of the patriotic colours and joyful cries, saluted the approach of His Majesty in a fashion of which he has hitherto had no experience, and the Neapolitan capital has not offered an example since the events of 1820.... A disorder among the poorer classes in the course of the afternoon was subdued by the National Guard without loss of life, though a disposition to pillage was manifested, and some shots had to be fired before the populace dispersed.... [10]

II

The grant of the Neapolitan Constitution marks the end of the period of reforms and the beginning of the period of Constitutions. It meant the close of the methods of agitation and the return to methods of violence. In every state there were people who argued: if the Sicilians can rout a well-equipped Neapolitan army and navy, any other of the peoples can do as much against its own government.

The triumph of Liberalism in Naples was received with indescribable joy in all the other small states. In Rome, public feeling was so much aroused that the Senate decided to forestall popular desires by organising an official celebra-

---

[10] *London Corr.* II, 63. *V.* also Paladino, *Il Quindici Maggio*, p. 8, as to the general satisfaction even in the Liberal press. The Piedmontese minister in Naples also describes the universal joy, and the tactful wearing of white favours instead of tricolours to please the King. Turin Arch., Lettere Ministri, Napoli, January 31st, 1848.

tion with a general illumination. The festivities took place on February 3rd, but there were far more badges of tricolour than of the Papal white and yellow.

Among the rulers, however, this concession of the King of Naples was received with profound misgiving, because by granting it he had placed every one of them in his own dilemma.[11] They saw at once that the wild beast, the Revolution, was loose again, and that they would all be compelled to grant Constitutions or go; so certain was this to result, that, on hearing the news from Naples, Monsignor Corboli Bussi actually foretold war with Austria, because he realised that when all the Italian states had won free assemblies, Lombardy would rise and claim one, and that it was impossible for Metternich to grant a free assembly to any part of the Empire. This prophecy was fulfilled within the next six weeks.

By now, one might say that the various Italic peoples had taken the bit in their teeth and were running away with their rulers. It was raining Constitutions, says Spada. Piedmont was the first state to follow suit. On February 9th Charles Albert issued the bases of a Constitution (Statuto) on the model of that of Louis Philippe[12] and on March 5th it was publicly proclaimed.

[11] The first-fruits of this Constitution must have been an object-lesson to Pius. On March 6th a Liberal ministry was returned to power. On March 9th there was a manifestation against the Jesuits. On March 14th there were serious disorders among the poorer classes because it was rumoured that, the Jesuits being now banished, the Liberals would proceed to expel the Carmelites and others; the common people believed that the extreme radicals were enemies of religion. Eight people were killed. *V. London Corr.* II, 163, 221-2, Napier's despatches. Also letters from all Italian courts showing the effect of Ferdinand's concessions.

Whether these measures were right or wrong, they must inevitably have alarmed Pius. Similar results occurred after the granting of the Piedmontese Constitution and on a far more important scale.

[12] *London Corr.* II. Abercromby, February 9th, encloses copy of the draft. *V.* Spada, II, ch. III, for the events in Rome during this period. For a summary of the events, *v.* Rosi, p. 188 *et seq.* Also Cibrario's description. *Charles Albert* (French edition), p. 113 *et seq.*

In Tuscany the Grand Duke Leopold had probably hoped to escape granting a Constitution, for on January 3rd he issued a *Motu Proprio* proclaiming reforms of the Press and of the Consulta; but when Charles Albert gave in, it was no longer possible for Leopold to hold out; so on February 11th he promised a Constitution which was duly sworn on February 17th.

On February 24th came the greatest news of all. Paris had risen and driven out Louis Philippe. France was again a republic. The effect of this news can hardly be realised now. It was said that in Rome one enthusiast died of joy!

Certainly the Sicilians had brought down Metternich's Italian system like a house of cards. No less than four representative Constitutions had been erected in Italy during the course of thirty-five days; and the Papal State, whose Liberalism had set the example over half of Europe, now found itself left behind the others in the race for popular governments. And finally, to crown the situation, France had declared herself a republic!

In Rome the situation was more critical than elsewhere. Such a torrent of changes was naturally far from welcome to Pius, with his intricate twofold machinery of government; he seems to have been very anxious during these weeks. Each of the great events had been greeted with fresh delight by the Mazzinians. The aims of the people were now twofold: a Constitution, and an army for war against Austria. It was only nineteen months since Pius had inaugurated his policy of reform, but already it had driven every monarch in Italy into measures which, in turn, were now necessitating still more dangerous concessions from Pius himself. As matters stood he had little left to rely on, except the gratitude of the people.

It has been suggested by Tivaroni that this moment forms the turning-point in the fall of the Temporal Power and in the movement of 1848; that it was still possible for Pius to put his foot down and stop the ding-dong competition with his neighbours. There were two alternatives: on the one hand if he granted a Constitution it would almost certainly lead him into war against Austria, because the people would have the power, and their politicians were set upon having war against Austria. But there was another alternative. He might say, "No more Liberal advance, no Constitution in the Papal State"; and then take a firm stand upon the Consulta and call the Moderates round him.

This course might have been possible if the times had been normal, as Pius had originally expected. But it could not hold its ground in the face of events such as the street fighting in Milan or the revolution in Paris. His great effort at compromise was failing. The population was in far too feverish a condition to accept it; and fresh episodes were occurring nearly every day.

On January 10th the Consulta in Rome considered the organisation of the army for safety against Austria.

On January 12th, at the church of San Carlo, before a congregation consisting of the Consulta and some of the best-known people in Rome, Padre Gavazzi preached a fiery sermon on the text *Fuori i Barbari!*, "Out with the Barbarians!"

On February 8th there was a tumult of the populace in Rome because they believed that the proposition as to artillery, duly voted by the Consulta, had been rejected by the Ministers. The streets were filled with men and women shouting: "We want an army; we want lay ministers; down with the police; Pius IX forever." This was a definite demonstration against the clerics holding any ministerial offices, and Pius must have felt hurt at the people's instantly turning his concessions against the Church.[13] Mr Petre tells us that

[13] His ministry resigned in consequence of the feeling displayed on this occasion; and Pius seems to have made three changes: in the new ministry were included Count Pasolini (Minister of Commerce) for Fine Arts, Industry and Agriculture, Francesco Sturbinetti for Public Works, and Don Miguel (or Michelangelo) Caetani, Prince of Teano, for Police. *V.* Spada, II, 37, 49.

many of the people were armed with pistols and daggers—
principally those from Romagna.

In this connection it is useful to note the opinion of
Abercromby, British Minister at Turin, as to the development
of popular liberties. Writing to Lord Palmerston on February
2nd he said:

> By the wise and moderate measures adopted by the courts of
> Turin, Florence and Rome, the people were placed in a position
> gradually to prepare themselves for the future exercise of con-
> stitutional institutions; but I am afraid that if they are suddenly
> to be entrusted with the management of such privileges, they will
> be found to be inexperienced and unprepared for the temperate
> and judicious administration of affairs.

He adds that "he much fears that there will be great
difficulty in finding persons fit to engage in such an undertaking".[14] If he said this about the northern states, what
would he not have said about Naples?

On February 10th Pius published a *Motu Proprio* which
created a great sensation and has never been forgotten. It
came from the heart. In it he introduced the phrase *Benedite
Gran Dio l' Italia!* "O Lord God, bless Italy!", and this was
taken to be a secret blessing on the war. Most certainly it was
not a blessing on the war, but it was one on his country. And
simultaneously Pius was reminding his people that so long as
the Papal State remained Papal, so long would it have protection from the rest of the Catholic world; and that therefore
its existence was a standing safeguard for all the other Italian
states. At the same time, though he did not bless the war,
undoubtedly he did bless Italy, provided she retained the
Papal State in being. Surely it is the cry of one who is afraid
of being left out of the National movement. The paragraph
in question runs as follows:

> What danger, indeed, can hang over Italy so long as a bond of
> gratitude and faith uncorrupted by violence, unites the strength of
> the peoples, the wisdom of the princes and the sanctity of their

---

[14] *London Corr.* II, 33.

rights? For Us especially—for Us as Head and Supreme Pontiff of the most holy Catholic religion—if we were unjustly assailed, is it possible that we should not find for our defence innumerable sons who would support the centre of Catholic unity as though it were their father's house? A great gift from heaven is this: one of the many gifts which He has bestowed on Italy; that a bare three million of our subjects possess two hundred million brothers of every nation and every tongue. In times very different from these, when the whole Roman world was disordered, this fact remained the salvation of Rome. Owing to it, the ruin of Italy was never complete. And this will always be her protection so long as the Apostolic See stands in her midst.

Therefore, O Lord God, bless Italy and preserve for her this most precious gift of all—her faith! Bless her with the benediction for which Thy Vicar with his head bowed to the earth is humbly entreating Thee. Bless her with the benediction that is entreated of Thee by the saints to whom she gave birth; by the Queen of the Saints who protects her; by the apostles whose glorious relics she preserves; by Thy Son, made Man, who selected Rome as the habitation of His representative on earth.

Benedite Gran Dio l' Italia! The last great appeal of one who already feels the outbreak of the storm.

On the following day there appeared on the Piazza Quirinale a crowd of about four or five thousand people to return thanks for the great *Motu Proprio*. But Pius received it "not as usual smiling, but sad and with the appearance of being ill".

He spoke some words referring to the Constitution, and at one point was interrupted by a voice calling out, "No more priests!"[15] Whereupon Pius, interrupting himself for a moment, turned towards the speaker and called out in a loud tone: "There are certain cries and certain demands which I cannot, will not, and ought not to admit"; after which he continued his discourse and bestowed his blessing on Italy.

---

[15] According to Spada the cry was "that they wanted a Constitution or something similar" (Spada, II, 47). The above words are given by Bishop Pelczar, I, 347.

Evidently he was in a state of great anxiety about the welfare of the Church during this period of change.

By now Rome was seething with agitation for a Constitution. All the other states had got one; and in Bologna there had been immense demonstrations; at the theatre, cries of *Viva la Costituzione*: but at the end of all things, the hymn of Pius IX.

It had become evident that the concession must be made. The municipality of Rome, chiefly composed of nobles and rich men, petitioned for "a government with representative forms". Even the Cardinals saw that it was inevitable, and passed it unanimously. The Conservatives were frightened, and the Moderates in a state of consternation about their reforms.

On March 10th the Recchi ministry was formed.[16]

On March 15th, 1848, was published the Statuto or fundamental statute establishing the Constitution. This was the last of Pius' great list of Liberal concessions. His work for the Risorgimento was finished when he called for a blessing on the new nation.

[16] Count Recchi's Ministry which passed the Constitution was composed of men every one of whom became well known during this period.

Chapter V

THE REVOLUTIONS

I

The larger Italian states except Lombardo-Venetia were now all in enjoyment of their free Constitutions. The Liberals had accomplished a new stage in their history. It was necessary to call a prolonged halt before proceeding to the next act of the drama: namely, that of a war against Austria.

Before any such venture could even be considered, immense and entirely fundamental changes had to be undertaken. The people, especially the peasants, had to be educated and inspired with the spirit of nationality; commerce and industry had to be stimulated. Above all, says Gabussi, each State was to have its national army; and naturally that was a reform which would require years of preparation. He adds that in Central Italy of that date the chance of raising forces for a war of liberation were virtually non-existent. In Naples "the soldiers were too much devoted to their prince for us ever to hope for their help in a war to which he would never willingly have lent his hand". In Lombardo-Venetia there was good material, but it was scattered all over the Austrian Empire. In fact, everywhere there was an immense amount to be done; for that reason, he considered, free parliaments had been an absolute necessity in each of the States, and especially in Rome. Without an assembly, nothing could have been achieved, and, even under its guidance, the work would take years.[1]

The republicans, he adds, saw this work of preparation now beginning to go forward all round them, but they remained quiet: consequently their strength was not realised.

[1] We quote Gabussi because he was a republican and therefore, on this period, much less likely to be biassed in favour of any of the existing leaders. Gabussi, I, 192.

The suddenness with which revolution crashed onto the new Constitutions can best be realised by a comparison of dates. The parliaments had been won, that is to say, promised, on the earlier dates given in our last chapter; but naturally the actual Statuti could not be proclaimed for some days later. The interval was a period of waiting and, in some cases, of reaction; in this way about a month had been spent.

The Neapolitan Constitution was proclaimed on February 11th; the Tuscan on the 17th; the Piedmontese on March 5th; the Roman not until March 17th; but already, on February 24th, the revolution had broken out in Paris, and on March 13th the people rose in Vienna; this meant chaos.

On the following morning Metternich was fleeing from the town in the last stage-coach available, with his wife and family. The whole of Europe was in a state of upheaval. For Italy the great moment had suddenly arrived, namely the triumph of the revolution in Vienna itself. Austria was shaken to her foundations, and, to crown all, Metternich was gone. The news travelled from town to town accompanied by every form of exaggeration and the people went temporarily mad. In Rome the bells were ringing from church to church and banners were raised high on each tower, while crowds poured through the streets firing arquebuses and shouting *Italia! Italia!*

In this sudden and dramatic manner the great moment had broken upon Italy long before she was ready—this incomparable chance of shaking off her oppressor once for all. His organisation was paralysed at its chief centre. The only Austrian authority left in Italy was Radetzky and his army. It remained for the small Italian states to combine and surround the old lion and tear him to pieces between them.

The following account from Cattaneo's narrative will give a good idea of the condition of Northern Italy at this time.[2]

[2] Cattaneo (1921 edition, Italian), p. 139. Cattaneo's figures are *not* always to be trusted; but he gives a vivid account of the time as he saw it.

The rising of the Lombardo-Venetian kingdom was universal. Unexpectedly and without any previous agreement, it blazed up on the same day in Venice and Milan, owing to the simultaneous arrival of the news from Paris and from Vienna. Zichy (Austrian commandant at Venice) surrendered all the forts of the lagoon and embarked for Trieste with 7000 men. The garrisons of Osopo and Palmanova[3] were disarmed, the mountaineers of Carnia and Cadore closed the roads from Austria; the Tyrol was in a state of agitation; in Trent there were only 200 soldiers to be found, and the fortress of Bressanone was without a garrison. The young men of Lecco and Bergamo, of the Valtelline and the Val Camonica occupied the passes from the Tyrol into the valleys of the Adda and the Oglio. Rocca d'Anfo in the upper valley of the Clisio had been taken. Both the sea and the Alps had been closed to the enemy. Inland, the Venetian cities, which were usually considered lukewarm in the cause of Italy, rose bravely in rebellion. Schwarzenberg, commandant of Brescia, came to terms and marched away. In Bergamo, a son of the Viceroy remained momentarily in the hands of the citizens, and then succeeded in escaping with his people. The volunteers liberated Varese, Como, and Monza[4] making prisoners of all the garrisons. At Cremona three thousand Italians deserted and surrendered six guns. Four hundred Hussars asked to be allowed to leave their colours. The forts of Pizzighettone and Piacenza were abandoned with their artillery; eight hundred Hungarians of the garrison at Parma capitulated, and the garrisons of Modena and Reggio tried to take refuge in Mantua. Columns of volunteers, in spite of Charles Albert's opposition, were arriving from Genoa, from Alessandria, from Casale, from Acqui and from Saluzzo. Tuscany, Romagna and the Kingdom of Naples were preparing for the national crusade.

The Austrian authority had depended on force; and now the force no longer existed except in the fortresses of the Quadrilateral. And even in them it had been a close call. If the people in Mantua had risen, they would have won their freedom, and perhaps changed the whole fate of the campaign.

[3] Old General Zucchi of Napoleonic fame was in this fortress serving the end of a life sentence for his share in the rebellion of 1831 (v. *Italy in the Making*, I, 95–7). The rebels freed him and made him commandant of the place; he stood a siege.

[4] The Austrian garrison at Monza cut its way out and retired on Milan.

With a population of about 30,000 it had a garrison of only about 3800, of whom about 3000 were Italians of the Haugwitz battalions. For more than a day, rebellion hung in the balance; and then the place was secured by 7000 Austrians of Wohlgemuth's Brigade, ordered thither by Radetzky at the urgent request of General Count Gorchowski, the commandant of Mantua, a Polish officer of exceptional ability.[5]

Naturally the first provincial capital to receive the news was Venice; and the second was Milan. In the case of Venice, lack of space prevents our giving more than the merest skeleton-outline of her rising; but as it has already been splendidly described by Professor G. M. Trevelyan in his *Manin* we have followed his account entirely. It seems to us that no other English version is necessary.[6]

The wonderful news of the Viennese revolution reached Venice in the evening of March 16th; and on the morning of the 17th the crowds rushed off to the Governor's house shouting *Fuori Manin e Tommaseo!* Within two hours both these patriots were free. And it was due to their release that, only five days later, Venice also became free.

At that time the Governor was Count Palffy, and the commanding officer was Lieutenant-Marshal Zichy, both Hungarians, and neither of them likely to cause a massacre of the citizens. The troops at their disposal were 7000 men, but of these 4000 were Italians. Still there remained about 3000 reliable Austrians to be dealt with; and there was one good officer, Captain Marinovich, the second-in-command of the *Arsenalotti*, or workers in the arsenal. He was not only strong but also a hard man.

[5] Fabris, I, 191 and note; Hilleprandt, pp. 37–8.
[6] *V. Manin and the Venetian Revolution of* 1848, by G. M. Trevelyan. English readers can find interesting sidelights on Professor Trevelyan's narrative in *London Corr.* II, in the letters of Mr Clinton Dawkins.

What was required was an equally strong man on the Venetian side; one who was ready not only to put his own life in the balance, but also the lives of his followers. Here was the character-role for Manin.

The first two days he spent in getting into touch with his sympathisers; and undoubtedly the best idea evolved during those days was the plan to claim a Civic Guard.

It came from Manin. After several scenes of rioting and some bloodshed, Count Palffy had appealed to him to keep order, and Manin replied that that was impossible unless he were allowed to form a Civic Guard. Palffy refused, but, under pressure from the municipality, agreed to allow 200 citizens to be armed: only a few hours later he found that Manin had armed 2000; namely, the agreed 200 equipped from the government stores, and the remaining 1800 from the shops and museums.

On the 19th and 20th a temporary reconciliation took place, owing to the news that the Emperor had accepted constitutional government in principle; but the Civic Guards were quietly occupying some of the most important tactical points, and Manin saw that such imperial promises as this gave no kind of security for the future. He spent the 21st in practical preparations; he meant to take the bull by the horns. He would attack the Arsenal, the old historic arsenal whose great gate is so well known to tourists. It was full of arms. The chief difficulty was that there were 300 Croats inside it under command of Marinovich.

This is the great moment in Manin's life. His friends thought it madness for their Civic Guards to attack the Arsenal. But Manin said: "Attack." His friends wanted various battle-cries that would appeal to the Moderates or to Piedmont. Manin chose *Viva San Marco!*, the battle-cry of the old Venetian republic. That call would arouse the whole people.

What happened on the following morning (22nd) has been brilliantly described by Professor Trevelyan and he gives the well-known picture of Manin in his white Civic Guard sash, saying good-bye to his family.

Manin thought he would never see them again; but fortune was favouring him. At nine o'clock that morning the *Arsenalotti* or arsenal workers had suddenly risen and murdered the hated Marinovich. This meant that the Austrians had lost their only efficient leader in Venice, and that 3000 *Arsenalotti* were irrevocably committed to the revolution. When Manin arrived, some of the Civic Guards had already succeeded in getting into the place on the plea of restoring order. There was very little fighting—only one man wounded, Major Boday, a brave Hungarian officer who tried to do his duty single-handed. By one o'clock Manin had the situation in hand, that is to say, his men were choosing muskets in the armoury.

By six o'clock that evening, the two Austrian governors had come to terms. The foreign troops, 3000 strong, were shipped to Trieste. There remained in Venice about 4000 Italian troops, together with 36,000 muskets and military stores of all sorts; and all the ships within the lagoon.

This was the first day of the great Venetian defence of 1848 and 1849.

Manin has been blamed for proclaiming a republic; but he made it perfectly clear that the new State was a federal republic, "one of the centres which will serve gradually to fuse our beloved Italy into one single whole".

II

We now come to the "Five Glorious Days" of Milan. It seems right to deal with this episode in some detail because it is one of those which govern the campaign, and apart from that fact, it is undoubtedly one of the most remarkable instances in history of successful street-fighting.

Milan was an active-minded business city of about 156,000 inhabitants, with perhaps 20,000 more in its suburbs. For

Milan to win its freedom was far harder than for Venice, because, as capital of Lombardo-Venetia, it was the headquarters of the whole Austrian army in Italy. In the town itself, there was a garrison of about 10,500 men:[7] nine infantry battalions, each about 1000 strong; four squadrons totalling between 600 and 700 cavalrymen; and five batteries (one mounted) of six field-guns each. There was also a force of about 900 Italian police. And finally—the most formidable consideration of all—these were under the command of Marshal Radetzky himself. His Chief-of-Staff was Colonel Count Wratislaw,[8] but his customary adviser was Field-Marshal von Schönhals, now chiefly remembered as a military writer.

Throughout the town all the strongest defensible buildings were in occupation by the Austrians.

To oppose to these regulars and their thirty field-guns, the citizens had no trained soldiers and only six or seven hundred firearms.[9] They had not the slightest chance of success. Nevertheless they possessed one advantage which, on this occasion, by some miracle, was destined to outweigh all the others; though ordinarily divided by mutually hostile political creeds, for the moment they were united in one wave of patriotic revenge.[10] Men, women and even children were seething with hatred against the Austrians.

On March 17th news arrived of the revolution in Vienna. It had taken four days to come, as the two towns were not in direct telegraphic communication, and naturally it was received with intense but half-suppressed excitement. Various consultations were held during the night, ending up with one on the morning of the 18th. At these it became evident that the two main party-divisions still persisted, and indeed were destined to govern the whole period; firstly there were the

[7] *V.* Fabris, I, 129 note, 141 note and 203: also the *Feldzug*, p. 6, Hilleprandt, p. 22. Their figures vary, especially as to cavalry.

[8] Not to be confused with Field-Marshal Wratislaw, O.C. of the First Army Corps. Hess, the celebrated Chief-of-Staff, did not arrive until May 12th, as will be remembered.

[9] Cantù, II, 798.   [10] Ottolini, p. 55.

Albertists—the more aristocratic party headed by the Podestà Conte Gabrio Casati—who believed in waiting for Charles Albert's arrival, and, as eventually became plain, in fusing Lombardy with Piedmont; secondly, the republicans, whose leaders were young men such as Correnti and Cernuschi who wanted to begin the fight at once. Between the two sections was Carlo Cattaneo, a federalist-republican.[11]

Casati was a patriot of many years' experience, whose sister had died of grief because of the imprisonment of her husband, Conte Federico Confalonieri. He was not of inspiring appearance—a wide, smooth face, clean-shaven except for his Dundreary whiskers—but he was a secret and persistent worker for the Albertist ideas. Cesare Correnti, secretary of the committee, has already been described in volume II. He was a Government employé who had produced a great deal of valuable and courageous literary propaganda. Cernuschi was a fair-haired young tradesman with a strong profile, proud of his university education; he was a republican, nicknamed "the young Robespierre" mainly on account of his clothes (a black coat, white cravat and waistcoat and a top hat!).

Besides these, there was the republican-federalist, Carlo Cattaneo. Cattaneo was a real influence in Milan, where travellers may see his statue to this day; a well-known professor at the University, and, with his aquiline features and grey-blue eyes, one of the best-looking men of the town. He was an enthusiastic patriot, but he refused to believe in any sort of violent action: "To attack the Austrians", he said, "is a task for all Italy, not for the Milanese alone."

At the various meetings it became evident that Casati too considered an armed rising hopeless. He advised waiting for Charles Albert.

[11] For the Italian side we have relied on: eye-witnesses of the events—Cantù, Antonio Casati, Gabriele Casati, Cattaneo, Dandolo, Ottolini.   Not eyewitnesses—Dr Carlo Casati, nephew of the Podestà; the general histories; Tivaroni, Masi, Rosi and others.

On the Austrian side, we have eyewitnesses: Radetzky, Schönhals, Hübner and the *Feldzug*.   Not eyewitnesses: Willisen, Helfert, Hilleprandt, Wolf Schneider von Arno, etc.

On the morning of the 18th the Austrian authorities still hoped to stave off rebellion. The two senior officials had departed for Vienna, but they had left behind, in charge, a man who inspired confidence—the Vice-Governor, Graf O'Donell. Only twelve days earlier, Ficquelmont, in a confidential report to Metternich, had said of him that he had energy and at the same time, calmness, and that he thought he would do well.[12] Evidently O'Donell, now no longer young, disliked repression, and from first to last he made every effort to prevent bloodshed. He was able to begin the day by posting up a notice announcing that the Emperor was conceding representative government. He hoped that that concession would save the situation; but nevertheless, for greater security, he prepared a message to Radetzky, asking him to occupy all the principal points in the city. Undoubtedly this occupation would have forestalled the rising; but, before despatching the message, he sent a secretary to Casati (the Podestà) and to Bellati (Provincial Delegate) to consult them on the subject. This was simple-mindedness on his part. Casati and Bellati seized their chance of stopping the order. They drove down to the Governor's palace where they found O'Donell mentally torn in two between his fear of causing fresh clashes with the soldiers, and his desire to prevent rebellion. They protested against the employment of the military arm, on the ground that it was always an immediate cause of bloodshed. O'Donell knew that this was true; so he wrote to Radetzky asking him not to allow any armed interference with the coming demonstrations unless especially called upon to do so; and, for himself, he refused to accept a company of infantry as guard of his palace. This action of Casati's saved the revolution. It prevented Radetzky from using his forces until too late.[13]

[12] Vienna H.H.S.A. 1848, Briefwechsel mit Graf Ficquelmont, March 6th (a private letter). *V*. also *London Corr*. II, 210.

[13] Dr Carlo Casati, II, 76; *v*. also *Feldzug*, I, 8; Willisen, p. 29; and Radetzky's report (of which there is an Italian translation in the *Rass. Stor.* for August 1939).

In any case, however, the time was past for concessions. The younger men were determined on action, and they had elaborated a plan. They proposed to name a deputation of their own leaders, to join it to the existing Town Council (Casati, etc.) and to get it proclaimed by the people as the Provisional Government. Meanwhile placards were posted up, claiming a Provisional Government, a free press, an elected National Assembly, a Civic Guard, and several other concessions, and calling a public meeting for three o'clock.

These demands amounted to a revolution. The question was, would they lead to an outbreak of violence? Evidently the lesser officials thought so, for Hübner tells us that by eleven o'clock, as he moved about the Governor's palace—for which O'Donell ought not to have refused a garrison—the employés were pale and *affolés de peur*: and he noticed that the sentry, a gigantic Croat, looked at him inquiringly but said nothing.[14] This man was probably one of those who died at his post an hour or two later.

The leaders had planned to hold a meeting at 3 p.m.—but to-day Vienna was a negligible quantity, and the people took command of the situation at once. At noon, a large crowd collected outside the Broletto with shouts of "To the government". Incited by Cernuschi, instead of proclaiming a new Provisional Government, they decided to take their Podestà, Gabrio Casati, and march down to the existing authority to claim the abolition of the police and the arming of the Civic Guard. It was an awkward moment for Casati. As Podestà he represented law and order. However he agreed to go with them, and very soon he and the tricolour flag were swinging along at the head of a mob some fifteen or twenty thousand strong down to the palace of the government. The church bells were ringing, says Dandolo;[15] the women on the balconies

[14] Hübner, p. 58. Apparently the sentries resisted and were killed; but the several other men of the guard were disarmed by the crowd.
[15] Dandolo, p. 33.

were waving handkerchiefs and throwing cockades: "Men to the street, women to the windows", was the cry. There were two sentries at the San Damiano bridge, posted there to guard the palace of the government, and when they saw such a confused multitude of people coming down on them, they fired their weapons into it. In a flash they were slaughtered;[16] and the crowd burst onwards disordered and quivering after its vengeance. Everything in their path was overturned; at the palace, the most secluded rooms were ransacked, papers thrown to the winds, glass and furniture smashed to atoms. In vain Casati, Fava, Borromeo, Guerrieri and all those who had most popularity and influence tried to restore calm. The councillors and the employés had fled, and in the council-room there remained only one man, O'Donell, Acting-Governor in the absence of Count Spaur. It was a bad moment for O'Donell, but in another sense, worse for Casati.

The room had been invaded by ten or more of the revolutionary leaders—Cernuschi, Guerrieri, Marco Greppi, Beretta, Taverna, Correnti, Clerici and Olofredi; and Giulio Bossi, who was present, tells us that the Vice-Governor and the Podestà "looked at each other with mutual uncertainty". All that O'Donell said was, "Oh Signor Conte!" but he must have perceived that he had been ruined. It was only three and a half hours since, as Podestà, Casati had dissuaded him from applying for any soldiers, on the plea that it would arouse disorders, and now, as Podestà, he was leading the revolutionary crowd. It was probably an expressive "Oh", for "Casati's answer was merely a sigh". This is confirmed by Bertani who says: "Casati, while at the Government palace with O'Donell, said nothing, or merely spoke in a

[16] Apparently they challenged and fired in the usual way. The names of these heroic men are not known; they were of the Paumgarten Regiment. Vice-Consul Campbell says three soldiers were killed; *London Corr.* II, 211. Ottolini says only one (Ottolini, *La rivoluzione lombarda*, p. 72); Carlo Casati says one was stabbed with a stiletto (Casati, *Nuove rivelazioni*, II, 78).

halting way; did not assert himself; decided nothing, and claimed nothing."[17] Cernuschi, however, seized this moment of invasion to present three vital decrees for signature.

(I) A National Guard was to be instituted.

(II) The police authority was to be handed over to the municipality.

(III) The existing police were to be disarmed.

Count O'Donell was a thick-set man with fairly determined aquiline features, but in von Helfert's phrase, he was "cornered". Nevertheless, according to most of the eye-witnesses, he faced the crowd well. It was only after some parleying and delay that he agreed to walk over to the window and sign the decree (written out by Casati) in view of the immense crowd below. And he took the opportunity to register his formal protest before them all. "This signature is obtained under pressure", he called out. "No matter", returned young Cernuschi. "Come what may, come it will!"[18]

The people were now free to act. Before the day was out, all citizens between the ages of twenty and sixty, not living

[17] White Mario, *Agostino Bertani and His Times*. For Bossi's description, v. *Archivio triennale*, I, Doc. 10.

[18] Most of the above is from the Italian accounts. The following is from Helfert's Austrian version: "O'Donell had withdrawn into his office, when he found himself surprised by the visit of the townspeople and assailed with demands of every sort; and there were some people among them in whose threatening fist there gleamed a knife or a dagger. [This is confirmed by Bertani.] Their first claim was a National Guard. After some resistance, O'Donell gave in. Paper and ink were brought...all these resolutions the Vice-President had to put down on paper himself and sign. 'My signature is extorted from me', called out the Graf, who felt himself cornered. 'No matter', replied they, 'Whatever is to come of it, come it will.'" Helfert, I, 329.

Dr Carlo Casati has reproduced in facsimile these decrees. They appear to be written in two different hands. The signature, "C. O'Donell, Vice-Presidente" is in slightly larger and bolder writing than the rest. One Italian writer speaks of him at that moment as "trembling", but none of his three consecutive signatures show any signs whatever of this.

by their daily work, were called upon to join the Civic Guard.

As soon as the decrees were signed, the Podestà and the crowd left the palace, taking O'Donell with them as a hostage. They intended to go back to the Broletto, but as they arrived at the Via Monte Napoleone, suddenly a shot rang out and one man fell. They had run into an Austrian picket; so, to avoid further losses, Casati turned into the Casa Vidiserti which became henceforth his headquarters.[19] This was a providential piece of good luck, for, only a few hours later, Radetzky attacked and took the Broletto, under the impression that it was still their centre of direction.

Here we get the strange anomaly that for the next four days of fighting, the only legal authority of the citizens was their Podestà, Casati, and the Municipio (such few of the Town Councillors as remained with him) with O'Donell as a hostage, all hidden in the Casa Vidiserti. They issued orders as a municipality, and clung desperately (perhaps rightly) to being a legal authority—although their legal powers were drawn from Vienna, and at the same time they had to keep two men on guard over O'Donell.[20] Finally, on the last day, March 22nd, they added some names to their list and called themselves the Provisional Government, that is to say, the

[19] Ottolini, p. 75.

[20] Helfert gives the following story; perhaps it accounts for the fact that Dr Carlo Casati rather tends to decry O'Donell: "On the 20th at about one o'clock the municipality issued a fresh summons to arms to all citizens between twenty and sixty capable of bearing them. Casati was still signing everything as Podestà, and never without the concurrence of one of the municipal assessors, for he wished 'to remain within the limits of the narrowest legality', says the Italian procès-verbal composed that day to be published in case of a reverse. To O'Donell he tried to portray himself as virtually a prisoner of the insurgents, and on one occasion, in Count Taverna's office, he led him before a picture of the Madonna and conjured him with tears—in the literal, not the figurative sense—not to believe him capable of such shameless treachery." Helfert, i, 336, and, for more detail, Helfert, *Mailand*, pp. 37–8. Evidently this is O'Donell's side of the story.

Rebels. It was a great step forward, as we shall see, when finally they discarded legality.

The populace, however, was well aware that its only chance of success lay in blocking up the streets at once. Ottolini tells us that he helped to erect the first barricade.

I and a few friends of my own age, seeing that there was nothing for us to do in the Governor's Palace, came out of the chaos and dashed off at full speed into the town, in search of a gun. We were at the San Damiano bridge, when along the road beside the Naviglio (canal) there passed a great waggon loaded with empty barrels. In half no time the crowd had unharnessed the horses and overturned the waggon across the outer entrance of the bridge. This was the first barricade; within an hour, four others were ready.[21]

The barricades were the chief weapon of the rebels during the five days. Those erected first were comparatively weak, but they hindered Radetzky's movement of troops; to carry out his orders, each unit "had to take the barricades by storm".[22] Nevertheless on this first day, every single one of the Austrian units succeeded in reaching its appointed post.[23] But on the 19th about 700 barricades were constructed—for the most part better built and stronger—and before the end of the "Five Days" they numbered between 1650 and 1700.

Radetzky, however, was not taken by surprise. Such situations had long been foreseen and provided for. From his H.Q. in the Castello he could send out, right and left, not only his infantry but his cavalry and field artillery, sweeping along the ring of bastions which surround the town, or dashing down the large streets into its centre. At the same time, he had small garrisons in all the strong buildings, such as the

---

[21] Ottolini, p. 73.

[22] *Feldzug*, p. 9; Hilleprandt, p. 21. He says that already there was a "lively" fire from the houses.

[23] *Wiener Zeitung*, based on Radetzky's report, quoted in translation in *London Corr.* III, 334.

Palazzo Reale, the Palazzo di Giustizia (Law Courts), the Palazzo Marino, the Police station, the Municipio (Town Hall) the Genio (H.Q. of the Royal Engineers), and the Palazzo del Governo (Governor's Palace) which he had to retake; also in eight or nine different barracks and police stations; and he held all the gates of the town, so as to cut off help from outside.[24]

During all this time he was receiving information from various sources—notably from a cool intelligence officer, Lieutenant Wagner, who had been sent out to walk the streets in mufti—and by about two o'clock he had formed a good working idea of what was afoot. "Now we know where we stand", he said, and gave orders[25] to Marshal Schönhals to fire the alarm-guns so that the troops should carry out their pre-arranged movements. At the same time he ordered Count Johann Huhn to go to Verona and bring back reinforcements of troops and war material. "See what you can do over there", was his final injunction.

By 3 p.m. all the *Rioni* had risen, and various strong points were being fortified—such as the great arches of the ancient Porta Nuova,[26] the same which in medieval days had been defended against the Emperor Barbarossa. Isolated soldiers or small squads were being attacked, and some of them had been killed or wounded. But during this first day, the citizens were at a disadvantage because they had nothing ready: very few arms, and those few ill-distributed: hardly any ammunition: hardly any co-ordination. They found, however, that all classes and political creeds were ready to work together, and soon arms began to appear. The noble owners of the great Poldi Pezzoli and Ubaldi collections threw their priceless specimens open to the fighting men. At the same

---

[24] Cattaneo (French ed.), p. 41. *V.* also Radetzky's official report.
[25] *Feldzug*, I, 8; Helfert, I, 329–30; Schönhals, I, 102.
[26] According to Tivaroni, this was not done until the 19th. The fortification was certainly completed on the 19th. *V.* Carlo Casati, II, 118; Tivaroni, *Ital. Sett.* p. 434.

time the chemists began to make gunpowder and guncotton with astonishing success. Soon there were "bodies of citizens armed with fowling-pieces, rifles, swords and pistols or old halberts and carrying tricolour flags...crying *Viva Pio Nono! Viva l'Italia! Viva la Repubblica!*" They passed the fire-arms from hand to hand. "Meanwhile", says the *Wiener Zeitung*, "the struggle had begun in every part of the city; the soldiers were fired upon from the windows and every kind of projectile (stones, boiling oil and water) was showered on them from the roofs."[27]

Radetzky exchanged several notes with Casati and his few Town Councillors at the Casa Vidiserti. In these he threatened to bombard the town; and consequently the Municipality under Casati issued a proclamation calling on the people to cease arming. Radetzky must have thought that he had the rebellion by the throat; towards seven o'clock he struck what he believed would be a decisive blow. He sent a large force of about a thousand Croats and Bohemians, with two guns, to surround and take the Broletto (municipal palace) which was a strong building about half-way from the Castello to the cathedral; he still believed it to be the H.Q. of the Provisional Government. It was defended by old General Lecchi, a Napoleonic veteran who was in command of 300 volunteers, but had only sixty firearms. Nevertheless it repulsed the Austrians at first and held out for four hours with great obstinacy—in fact until the gates were blown down by twelve-pounders—then after a room-to-room fight the garrison surrendered. The Austrian success, however, was barren, because the Municipal Government had long ago been moved elsewhere.

March 19th. After a night of downpour during which the

---

[27] *London Corr.*, III, p. 334. *V.* also *Feldzug*, I, 10, and Helfert, p. 330; and of course all the Italian eye-witnesses mentioned in Note 11. Willisen (p. 30) says it was about five o'clock when Radetzky ordered the attack on the Broletto. Hilleprandt says at seven (p. 32).

Austrians destroyed a good many barricades, Sunday dawned to the angry clanging of bells and the sound of artillery fire. The Austrians were attacking; they were trying to demolish the barricades which cut off their garrisons from the Castello and from each other. In the streets they moved forward slowly, firing volleys to scatter the people before making their final rush. They took a certain number of the barricades, but in most cases the young defenders had vanished right and left; and, before the more serious defences, the assailants were several times repulsed.

In the Piazza del Duomo at 5 a.m. they sent their Jägers up on to the cathedral roof from whence, amid those thousands of marble figures, they continued to fire all day on the windows and on the enemies below.[28]

On this day, Cattaneo—although he regarded rebellion as hopeless—decided to join the rebels. He was considered to possess the best brain among the republicans, and they included the pick of the young fighting leaders. Cernuschi, Correnti, Manara, Dandolo, Terzaghi were perhaps the most successful of the young heroes who spent their days dashing from point to point, everywhere arousing, directing and leading the rebels. By Cattaneo's advice the citizens' headquarters was moved from the Casa Vidiserti to the house of Count Paolo Taverna in the Via Bigli. The Casa Vidiserti would easily be noted and surrounded; but that narrow, curving Via Bigli, he tells us, was easier to barricade, and, owing to its gardens, harder for the enemy to surround.

[28] *Feldzug*, I, 11, 12, speaks highly of their marksmanship; of one in particular it says: "Oberjäger Hüpfauf was always with his rifle at the ready; and as soon as an insurgent showed at a window or tried to work at a barricade, he was brought down by his seldom-failing bullet." Helfert, I, 331, adds that Lorenz Hüpfauf received a bullet on the badge in his hat—the small silver bugle of the Jägers. He and his squad were reputed to have hit about eighty of the enemy, and he was rewarded with the gold medal for valour; but in his old age he hated the remembrance of the slaughter of innocents, and refused to have it mentioned before him. Schönhals speaks of his accounting for thirty-six Milanese.

The following description by an eye-witness gives some idea of how the barricades were erected.[29]

> As soon as they could get hold of a couple of tons of soil, they erected a barricade. The people had never seen one, but they understood them at the first glance. And it was a strange exhibition of the various social conditions of the town; for in the rich quarters they used carriages, luxurious furniture, harpsichords, beds, looking-glasses; in the business quarters barrels, bales of goods, packing cases, chairs from the cafés; in the poor quarters palliasses, anvils, benches; near the churches, seats, pulpits, confessionals; near schools, armchairs and benches; near the theatres, machinery, thrones, statues, sham trees and sham giants. Wherever possible, trees or shrubs were felled across the openings; then the whole was completed with faggots, shutters, doors, paving-stones, beer bottles and dirt. The windows were well-provided with vases, with tiles and with cobble-stones. Everything bore witness to the universal zeal of every class and condition.

On this day, some of the Austrian units began to find themselves, as it were, caught in a morass. The following is an instance of their difficulties. At one point Hauptmann Kaas undertook to clear a line of retreat. He took the first two barricades easily enough, but the third with some difficulty; at the fourth he was repulsed by a fire consisting mainly of paving-stones. Consequently he retired to the Castello for ammunition and fresh troops. Then, on his return, he captured another point, but only after a room-to-room fight. This was considered excellent work by the Austrians; but for the insurgents, what did half a dozen barricades matter, out of seventeen hundred?[30]

At one stretch of about a hundred yards, there were no less than five barricades.

On this day too Radetzky began to receive discouraging news from outside Milan. In Como, there was a rising, and Swiss help was expected; bad reports from Padua and Venice;

[29] Cantù, II, 797.
[30] *Feldzug*, I, 14, 15. Hilleprandt, p. 23, says that as soon as one barricade was demolished, another sprang up.

on the Piedmontese frontier batteries were to be seen. Hitherto he had used artillery only on barricades, but he began to fear that he would be compelled to bombard the town itself.

The 20th was destined to be the turning-point of the struggle.

During the night Radetzky had evacuated the centre of the town; henceforth he was occupying the rampart of circumvallation and the gates; thus he was preventing all ingress and egress.[31] He meant to reduce the city by starvation; but his withdrawal left the citizens much freer to carry out their surprise movements. In reality he had been compelled to withdraw the posts within the town because they were encircled and could no longer be supplied with ammunition.[32] Thus, for instance, his order to the Tyrolese was proved to have been ill-judged. At the start they had had to fight their way up to the cathedral and then, after only about twenty-four hours, they were compelled to retire, and had to storm two or three barricades to get home.

During this day the citizens made an important change. Hitherto the only established authority had been that of Casati and the Municipality; and these leaders, though good patriots, were Town Councillors whose proceedings remained too formal for street fighting. The young men were bitterly discontented and talked of proclaiming a republic or a Provisional Government. These dissensions were heartbreaking; but Cattaneo solved this difficulty by leaving Casati where he was, and creating a separate Council of War to direct the fighting. He relates how, late that night, amid all the turmoil of people rushing to and from the barricades, he named a Council of Four; himself, Terzaghi, Clerici and

[31] *London Corr.* II, 334; Willisen, p. 31; Cantù, II, 798; Helfert, I, 334; Schönhals, I, 115.

[32] According to Hilleprandt, pp. 23–4, many of Radetzky's officers thought that the only chance of success lay in an attack in force towards the Scala and Palazzo Borromeo; but the Field-Marshal refused on account of the inevitable losses.

Cernuschi.[33] Thus, henceforward, there were two separate centres of direction; first, Casati and the municipal authorities who still clung to any shred of legality; and saw plainly that, without Charles Albert's army, there would be no relieving force, and they might have to fight on until they were smashed; and secondly the young republicans of Cattaneo who probably hated Charles Albert; but at that moment were much the best directors of fighting, because they meant to drive out the Austrians or die.

At midday, Baron von Ettinghausen, Major in a Croat regiment, arrived at the Via Bigli with a flag of truce. The Municipal Commission was divided on the subject. Some of them wanted to accept a truce, in order to allow Charles Albert time to arrive. But Cattaneo, supported by his followers,[34] said that it would be impossible to withdraw their men from the barricades; moreover all Lombardy and Venetia were in arms, and the only way to end bloodshed would be for the Austrian government to withdraw the Austrian troops everywhere. Manifestly this was mere defiance. Evidently the young men had reached a stage where they wanted at any price to be fighting. The humiliation of being a subject people had eaten into their hearts. Probably von Ettinghausen understood this, for when he departed, his last words were: *Addio brava e valorosa gente.* "And this", says Cattaneo, "was the first time for thirty-four years that we heard one of our oppressors pay this well-deserved tribute to our people." The Milanese had lived under the heel of Austria; but the young men of the new generation were offering their lives so that it should be no more a reproach.

On the 21st Cattaneo's Council of War got to work. It determined to cut its way out through the ring of Austrians on the walls, and get into touch with its thousands of friends

[33] Cattaneo (French ed.), p. 49.
[34] Dr Carlo Casati, II, 134; also Cattaneo, *Ibid.* pp. 56–62. Cattaneo says that Casati wanted to accept the truce, which seems likely enough.

outside. It called upon all men with previous experience of soldiering. The defenders of the inner barricades were moved to the outer. Orders were given to attack the Comando del Genio, the Comando militare (Military H.Q.) and the San Francisco barracks.

They were all captured; and the attack on the Genio was immortalized by the heroism of a poor old hunchback named Sottocorno who pulled himself across a side street on his crutch, and sprinkled the gate with *acqua ragia*,[35] was wounded, but returned with two bundles of hay and set it on fire.

As the days went by, there were a certain number of horrible reprisals[36] carried out by the infuriated Austrian soldiers; but Hübner generously admits that there were no instances of cruelty by the Italians. After spending the whole of the "Five Days" in Milan, he assures us that the Italians are not cruel.

During the morning the foreign consuls tried to arrange for an armistice, and Radetzky agreed. But the people did not want an armistice. A great crowd gathered round the Casa Vidiserti, anxious lest their leaders should accept dishonourable terms. Cattaneo and his young republicans refused any form of armistice. It was rejected by twelve votes to three; and when Correnti went to the window to call out the news, he was greeted by the excited crowd below with a great shout of *Guerra! Guerra!*, which spread from the Via Bigli right away to the barricades.[37] It was felt that the Austrians had had their answer.

Yet, hardly were these armistice proposals defeated than Casati issued an order claiming full authority in the town, adding to his list some six new members, none of them followers of Cattaneo. He also named six directing com-

---

[35] Some form of resin.
[36] Schönhals, I, 107, says that they have been entirely exaggerated, but that some events of the sort were inevitable.
[37] Cattaneo, *Ibid.* p. 71; Helfert, I, 337; Schönhals, p. 119; and many others.

mittees—one of them for defence. This seemed very like a challenge to Cattaneo's Council of War.

At this critical moment there arrived Count Martini who had been sent off on the 18th to Turin to ask for help from Charles Albert. He brought a reply in which the King promised his help. This meant salvation! They could go on fighting with good confidence, for they knew now that they would soon be relieved.

For diplomatic reasons Charles Albert asked them to send him a formal appeal for help. Cattaneo was bitterly angry. As a republican, he wanted an appeal not merely to Charles Albert, but to all the other Italian states as well, for united national action. He hurled a jibe at Casati's supporters: "Can't you bear to be your own masters even for once in your lives?"[38] Nevertheless Casati sent off the appeal and posted up a proclamation welcoming the Piedmontese.[39]

On this last day Milan, hemmed in all round by Austrians along its walls, was beginning to starve; to meet the situation a good many moveable barricades, on wheels, were constructed in order to attack the gates, especially the Porta Tosa, and scores of small balloons were sent up with messages calling for help from the peasants outside.

The following proclamation of Cattaneo to the men on the barricades gives some idea of the conditions:

> Forward boys! The town is ours now. The enemy is retiring onto the bastions to begin his retreat. Harry him! Leave him neither truce nor rest. To-night all the gates must be unblocked; eight thousand men from the country are ready to join hands with us. The enemy asks for a truce; do not waste time in discussion. The moment has arrived when we can be rid of him for ever. *Viva l'Italia!*

This proclamation was truer than he knew. Radetzky had just begun to think of retirement. His news was bad; Parma

---

[38] Tivaroni, *Ital. Sett.* p. 441.

[39] Apparently this appeal did not reach Charles Albert because the whole struggle was over on the following day.

and Modena had risen and set up Provisional Governments: in Piacenza and Crema there had been fighting; his General, Strassoldo, who was in Varese watching the Swiss frontier, reported that armed bands were moving, and General Maurer who was at Magenta watching the Piedmontese frontier, reported that Piedmontese troops were assembling at Novara. At any moment Charles Albert might cross the Ticino.

Radetzky sent orders to Strassoldo and Maurer to join him at Milan, and they arrived on the following day.

Radetzky's men were dead-beat and rain-soaked. At 2 p.m. he held a Council of War, and the Austrian staff decided to evacuate Milan. He regarded a Piedmontese invasion as certain, and he knew that the whole northern half of the peninsula was in arms, so he wisely decided to retire into the Quadrilateral, and there to concentrate around him every remaining Austrian soldier in Italy.[40]

Meanwhile, at long last, the insurgents had arrived at an agreement. Casati declared his Municipio to be the Provisional Government; that is to say, no longer a remnant of the Viennese administration, but a new rebel authority; no doubt he hoped to hand it over to Charles Albert. Now that he was a rebel, however, Cattaneo and his friends were ready to work under him. Their Council of War was amalgamated with Casati's Committee of Defence. Now at last they had a genuine rebel government.

And there we must leave them. That morning they attacked three city gates, and with their wheel barricades they succeeded in rushing the Porta Tosa. Milan was open to the outside world.

[40] "Am 21. Marz abends fasste der Feldmarschall den grossen klaren ganzen Entschluss; Preisgabe der Lombardei, Rückzug ins Festungsviereck, dort Versammlung, Konsolidierung seines ganzen Heeres, dann erst zum Schlag ausholen." Wolf Schneider von Arno, *Der Feldherr Radetzky*, p. 61, the latest authority on the subject. Also Willisen, p. 33. Hilleprandt says that the first intention was only to evacuate Lombardy up to the Adda; to secure his communications; and then come back reinforced to attack Milan. Hilleprandt, p. 27.

At nine o'clock on that dark night, Radetzky's men emerged from the Castello. They were exhausted after fighting five days and nights in the cold rain, says Schönhals, and they took five hours to get clear of the town. Nevertheless they were able to retire with all the method of a regular army. They felt that perhaps they were not far ahead of the Piedmontese. The work of their advance- and of their rear-guard, the convoy of their women and wounded[41] had all been carefully thought out, and the most important points along their way were already occupied.

The Austrians were gone. It had been a marvellous achievement.

[41] Losses. In spite of their few firearms, and miserable shortness of ammunition, the citizens had succeeded in accounting for at least 602 Austrians, and probably more. Killed: 5 officers and 176 men. Wounded: 11 officers and over 230 men. Prisoners: 150 to 180. On the Milanese side there were 350 dead and about 600 wounded including priests, women and children: for, in those days of hate, there were some priests and some women who fought; and there were instances of street-boys, only ten or twelve years old, who, apparently too young to be dangerous, walked up to an Austrian soldier, and then fired a pistol point-blank at him—and paid the penalty. Helfert, I, 333; Cantù, II, 800; Hilleprandt, p. 29. Also Tivaroni, *op. cit.* p. 446.

Cattaneo estimated the Austrian losses at 4000!

For the Austrian losses we have followed Hilleprandt. But he states the Milanese losses at 424 dead, 600 wounded and 300 prisoners, and this is too high. For the Milanese losses we have followed Tivaroni and Cantù. Fabris, I, 181, has arrived at the same totals as ours.

Chapter VI

ITALIA FARÀ DA SÈ. PIEDMONT DECLARES WAR, MARCH 24TH

When Radetzky emerged out of the inferno[1] in which the Milanese republicans and Albertists had encircled him, he found a new political situation opening out all around his retiring troops; *Italia farà da sè.*

He had foreseen war against Piedmont and the rebels; but this new combination meant that all the other states in Italy would rise up against him, or make some show of doing so. Militarily, however, none of them counted for much except Naples.

The principal forces on the Italian political stage at the moment were:

I.   Radetzky and his army.
II. Charles Albert with Piedmont; followed by the lesser states.
III. Pope Pius IX: it was hoped that he would head a crusade and excommunicate Austria; but in any case, he was still the protagonist of the schemes for uniting Italy by a league or by a federation.
IV. The republicans, mainly directed by Mazzini; but their movement was destined not to take the lead in Italy until after all the others had been tried.

During this retirement the old Marshal must have felt himself lamentably uncertain as to many vital points in the situation.[2] Latterly several of his expected messengers had been intercepted by the rebels, and consequently he could

---

[1] "During six days and nights he never took off his clothes and perhaps enjoyed no hours of quiet sleep" (Schönhals, I, 112), quoted by the editor of Radetzky's letters to his daughter.

[2] *V.* Hilleprandt, p. 35 *et seq.*

not possibly tell how many outlying Austrian units had been captured, or how many Italian units had deserted to the enemy. Everything around him was in a state of see-saw, including even Vienna. But he had taken a definite decision; he meant to get onto firm ground inside the Quadrilateral. With that aim in view he could retire his First Corps (Wratislaw's) from Lombardy to join his Second Corps (D'Aspre's) in Venetia. These would form a central main body on which all the smaller scattered units could direct their march. Soon he would know how he stood; he would restore communications with Vienna; get supplies and perhaps reinforcements from there. And from his positions in the almost impregnable Quadrilateral, he could defend Lombardy indirectly; as long as he held those strongholds in force, the Piedmontese army would never be safe anywhere east of the Ticino.[3]

Henceforth he must prepare himself for a regular military campaign, so he was resigning the Austrian authority in Lombardy, but only temporarily, in order to restore it permanently.[4]

His first problem was to get to the positions behind the River Mincio before Charles Albert could catch him up; but he did not hurry his men. One tragic episode marked his passage. The Milanese had seen the Austrian soldiers retiring exhausted, soaked to the skin and dazed by the noise during five sleepless nights; and they thought them incapable of

___

[3] "We are collecting our forces on the Mincio, trying to reconquer the insurgent Venetian territory, and so, when once reinforced, to advance again. We have been able to save very few of our things. In haste, from your Father." Radetzky to his daughter Fritzi, March 30th, 1848 (*Radetzky Briefe*, p. 77).

[4] Military opinion has justified Radetzky's retirement. Speaking about a commander in this difficulty, Willisen (p. 53) argues that it is no use his holding territory if he is too weak to strike, but that once his strength has been reassembled, the first step has been taken towards a return. The furthest point of the retirement should be the point where his strength lies. And he adds elsewhere that if a commander's place of refuge is really strong, he can defend the territory around, indirectly.

much further resistance.[5] Consequently a band of volunteers dashed out from Milan and occupied the village of Melegnano. When Radetzky arrived there on the 23rd, they tried to defend the place against him, and imprisoned his billeting officer. Radetzky naturally perceived that this must be stopped, and he gave over the village to his men for plunder. A systematic attack soon drove out the volunteers, but the unfortunate villagers paid the penalty—fifteen of them were killed and over a hundred wounded, and their houses were burnt. After this episode his march was not molested.[6]

The fact was that his men, being regular soldiers, were by now in better fettle than they seemed. Once away from the Milanese streets and out in the country, they only took a day or two to become fairly normal. In appearance they were still rather tired, and rain-sodden, but then—as one of their veterans was heard to remark—"The army looks like it always does in time of war".

Radetzky's line of march was Melegnano (March 23rd) to Lodi (night 23rd–24th) where his troops had two days' rest behind the River Adda, and were joined by various garrisons. Then[7] to Crema (26th) and by slightly longer marches to Orzinovi (27th), Manerbio (28th) and finally to Montichiari (29th) behind the River Chiese. The marches were short, as the roads and weather were fearful. Once behind the River Chiese he was able to slacken speed; during the next six days his army gradually took up defensive positions behind the

[5] Cattaneo and his friends were completely taken in by this idea. They always said and thought that if Charles Albert had rushed in headlong, he might have attacked and destroyed the Austrian army.

[6] Hilleprandt, p. 31; Ottolini, pp. 199–201; *London Corr.* II, 336, quoting *Wiener Zeitung* of April 8th, 1848.

[7] *Feldzug*, I, 41 *et seq.*; Hilleprandt, pp. 32, 35–8. Milan to Melegnano is about 16 kilometres; Melegnano to Lodi about 16; Lodi to Crema 16. Thus on the 26th he started from Crema about 48 kilometres ahead of Charles Albert's advance-guard which entered Pavia that morning. The marches to Orzinovi and Manerbio were each about 18 kilometres.

River Mincio, but it was not until April 4th that he withdrew the last of his rear-guard from Montichiari and Mendola (south-west of Lake Garda).

He was now in the foremost position of the Quadrilateral; the line running north and south, from the fortress of Peschiera to the fortress of Mantua—over 20 miles from end to end—with the River Mincio all along its front.

Meanwhile on April 2nd he had transferred his G.H.Q. to Verona, a fortified town thirteen or fourteen miles back, from whence he could reinforce any point in his line; and where he himself could size up the situation in peace. Once established and entrenched within this triangle, he would be a very difficult man to move.

Just to give an idea of the general conditions round him, we may quote the following list of places: Milan, Piacenza and Pavia had been evacuated by the Austrians when Radetzky retired; in Varese the splendid 10th Jägers, a German battalion under Colonel Kopal, had cut its way out of the town and was free. At Como the Austrian battalion of Warasdiner Borderers and some Hussars were surrounded and compelled to surrender. At Brescia, part of the Haugwitz battalion (Italian) deserted, and the remainder retired fighting; at Bergamo a battalion of Szluiner Croats and another of the Archduke Sigmund's infantry retired fighting; at Cremona three Italian battalions joined the insurgents. These are merely the principal towns in Lombardy; in Venetia almost every town had risen.[8]

Writing unofficially to his daughter on April 27th, Radetzky said:

I have lost 10,860 privates through desertion, and 13,000 through being cut off, besides which I count 360 dead and 700 wounded. Of the officers, there are 6 dead and 18 wounded; 360 cut off and two known deserters.[9]

[8] Schönhals, I, 134 *et seq.*, 164; Hilleprandt, p. 32 *et seq.*; Fabris, I, 166, 179, 185, etc.
[9] *Radetzky Briefe*, p. 80.

That left him only about 24,000 men, apart from garrisons! The Austrian army in Italy had consisted (March 18th) of about 73,000 men (full strength).

First Army Corps (Count Wratislaw): in Lombardy.

Infantry: 35 battalions; about 35,000 men.

Cavalry: 20 squadrons; about 3200 men.

Artillery: 66 guns (11 batteries); about 1650 men.

Total 39,850.

Second Army Corps (Baron D'Aspre): in Venetia.

Infantry: 26 battalions; about 26,000 men.

Cavalry: 16 squadrons: about 2560 men.

Artillery: 42 guns (7 batteries); about 1050 men.

Total 29,610.[10]

The official total of its strength is 73,000 (*Feldzug*, I, 6): so (following Hilleprandt) we may call it 70,000.

But during the first fortnight the losses had been terrific. According to official figures, which are not exactly identical with those given by Radetzky to his daughter, about 17,000 men had been cut off or become deserters, and by May 6th the ordinary casualties were about 3000 more. This would only leave him 50,000, of whom 5000 were in the Tyrol and 23,000 were required for garrisons.[11] Thus, when he settled

[10] No doubt the units were not quite up to strength, for the *Feldzug* (I, 6) gives the official strength as 73,000; Willisen (p. 27) at 65,000–70,000; and Montù (III, 263) and Hilleprandt (p. 14) at about 70,000 men, which is perhaps the most usual estimate. The latest work by the Austrian staff, Wolf Schneider von Arno, *Der Feldherr Radetzky*, gives in round figures: field force 50,000; garrisons 15,000; the corps in the Tyrol 5000. This leaves 30,000 under Radetzky's hand in Verona, but must include the garrison there (p. 67).

[11]			
	Verona	9,000 men.	Fabris gives 9000 (II, 175).
Quadrilateral			So does Hilleprandt, pp. 73, 110, etc.
garrisons	Mantua	10,400	
	Peschiera	1,500	
	Legnago	1,100	
		22,000	in garrisons of Quadrilateral. (There was also a garrison of 1000 in Ferrara.)

down in Verona to defend himself against Charles Albert, he
cannot have had more than about 22,000–24,000 men free to
strike.[12]

It is said that he was deserted by about four-fifths of his
20,000 Italians, and suffered the additional aggravation of
knowing that they would go over to the enemy and fight
against him.[13]

But he was not easily discouraged.

As already related, it was on April 2nd that he moved his
H.Q. to Verona; and in the course of his Order of the Day,
he addressed to his men the following very pregnant sentence:
"It is I, not you, who have retired before the enemy. *You*
have not been defeated and you will not be."

What a fine old soldier was Radetzky! And what a pity
that he should have taken part in this campaign!

In Piedmont the "Five Glorious Days" had brought the
enthusiasm for war to fever-heat—all the more exuberant
perhaps, because none of the younger people could remember
a real war. In this quarrel they were manifestly in the right;
it was—before Heaven—a good cause and a generous enthusiasm that drove them forth to help their fellow-Italians
to win freedom; but they had very little conception of what
war meant.

For those who believed in *Italia farà da sè* the war had
come far too soon. It was impossible for the Italian states to
make a good muster. Even the most progressive of them were
still in the throes of trying to set up a new constitution. What
they required was three or four years of leisure in which to
establish their free institutions, train their army and arrange
for combined action; but actually in Piedmont itself the old

[12] *V. Feldzug*, 1, 6, 131.
[13] When describing this event General Willisen, the Prussian
military historian, remarks with a serene and perfect simplicity:
"One can never rely on the gratitude of conquered peoples."

absolutist ministry had lasted until March 4th; thenceforth there could be no fresh government until after the elections. On March 14th Balbo's ministry took office. The new Liberal Constitution was entirely untried, and Charles Albert, although he felt the necessity of granting it, in order to have the nation at his back, rather doubted its being an efficient machine for war: "for war you require soldiers, not lawyers."

On March 18th when the "Five Days" began, Charles Albert watched the progress of the revolution with profound anxiety. Was it, or was it not, the great moment for which he had held his people in expectancy during eighteen years? Was this rebellion merely a flash in the pan, or was it about to spread throughout Lombardy and Venetia? Would the Viennese revolution develop far enough to allow him a chance of victory? For it must be remembered that, in normal times, Piedmont had no chance of victory against Austria. And in this war of 1848 her chance can hardly be said to have lasted longer than about two and a half months.

It has been made a jibe against Charles Albert that, although he had encouraged Milanese revolutionists, he did not come to help them until too late; and that by delaying eight days he allowed Radetzky to escape him. But surely this is being wise after the event. His dealings with the Milanese were as follows.

On March 19th Count Arese arrived in Turin to ask for Charles Albert's help. He had been sent off by the Milanese the day before—at the outbreak of their rebellion. Charles Albert received him, and also Count Martini and Count d' Adda who were Milanese nobles already in Turin. He seems to have temporised; no doubt he wanted to make certain that, if he declared war, he would not find the rebellion over, or perhaps even discover that he was being called upon to support a Milanese republic. Nevertheless on this same day Count Castagnetto, Charles Albert's confidential secretary, sent Martini to Milan to say that if the King's presence was required there, he would come.

On March 21st Martini arrived at Milan and presented to the Provisional Government this offer of help. The republicans wanted to refuse it, but Casati accepted it and announced to the townsmen that "our Piedmontese brothers are coming".

On March 22nd Radetzky retired defeated, and naturally enough the tone of the Milanese towards Charles Albert became rather different. The republican feeling may be described more or less as follows: We were encouraged to believe that Charles Albert would help us, but he left us to fight for our lives, and now he wants to come in as our protector—well we still require regular troops and artillery, so if he comes, he will receive the gratitude of the people. But it is his turn to do something.

On the 23rd Charles Albert had to take the vital decision about his declaration of war. To defeat Austria militarily, he required an ally; but none existed.[14] France, if she helped him, would perhaps ask for Savoy in return; Prussia sympathised with Austria; England, though friendly, disapproved of his crossing the frontier, and Russia had threatened to make it a *casus belli*. On the other hand, Piedmont was in turmoil, and all other patriots in Italy were deeply stirred. Cavour wrote his celebrated article, "The supreme hour has come for the Sardinian monarchy"; volunteers were starting for Milan; the republicans were stirring: the only uncertain element was the new constitutional government. Balbo and the other ministers were doubtful; they wanted time to prepare. But Charles Albert's own mind was now made up. During the meeting of the Council that afternoon, he carried the ministers with him by announcing that he would take all responsibility; and consequently, at dinner that evening, when Martini returned from Milan with a message accepting the royal offer of help, the King himself was able to tell him that war had already been decided.[15] "And all around him were full of

[14] This difficulty was considered serious by Costa de Beauregard, *Les dernières années*, p. 143.
[15] Della Rocca, p. 162.

confidence; they said 'No allies? It does not matter. *Italia farà da sè!'*"

At midnight the people thronged below his windows to give him an enthusiastic ovation; and then, at last, he let himself go. He received their cheers with joy and waved a tricolour flag. For this campaign his colours were to be the tricolour of Italy, with the Cross of Savoy imposed on it.

On March 24th war was declared; on the 25th his leading brigade under General Bes, perhaps his ablest brigadier, crossed the frontier at Novara, marching on Milan in the order of an advance-guard. On March 26th amid a downpour, it entered Milan in triumph between the lines of the victorious citizens. It had covered 28 miles in fourteen hours.[16]

Charles Albert was risking everything, not merely life itself, but his whole life's work, the mission of his House, the army, even the nation. All around him was in a state of flux and instability. He had to ask himself: in Vienna, would the revolution last? In Lombardy, were there many republicans? In Venetia, was there already a republic? Even at home there was this new Statuto which was not satisfactory; and behind him in France was the new republic which might do almost anything.[17] Yet he was right to move when he did. There were conditions in his favour that would never recur; notably, that all Lombardy and Venetia were in triumphant rebellion; that his army was so deeply stirred that he could hardly have prevented its marching; that the enemy's capital was paralysed; that he had a Liberal Pope at his back; that, with the influx of volunteers, his numbers would be superior temporarily to those of Radetzky.

He has never received full credit for this, his true life's

---

[16] 46·7 kilometres.

[17] Mazzini was in Paris. Casati says that the Milanese republicans were confident that the French would declare a "war of the people" and come to their assistance. Costa de Beauregard says that the Piedmontese Conservatives were extremely uneasy at the attitude of the French, and feared that armed bands might invade Savoy—as actually happened. Costa de Beauregard, pp. 152–3.

work; he held his people in leash for eighteen years and then brought them into the war at exactly the right moment. For over two months to come, up to June 10th, *Italia farà da sè* seemed possible; they had a chance of victory.

All the above-named advantages were with him in 1848, but they were all destined to be absent in 1849, when he tried to renew the contest, and so gallantly offered his life at Novara.

In any case, however, before he died, his twice-tendered challenge to Austria had singled out Piedmont as the only possible champion of Italy; during 1848 all the other states were tried and found wanting.

On March 23rd he had already launched his war proclamation, of which the following are the most salient sentences:

Peoples of Lombardy and Venetia!
The destinies of Italy are maturing. . . .
Our arms which were concentrated on your frontier when you anticipated the liberation of your glorious Milan, are now coming to offer you in the latter phases of your strife the help which a brother expects from a brother, and a friend from a friend.
We will second your just desires, confident as we are in the help of God Who is manifestly on our side; of God Who has given Pius IX to Italy;[18] of God Who by such marvellous impellings (*impulsi*) has enabled Italy to rely on her own strength (*fare da sè*). . . .

It was a fine proclamation; but it caused people all over Italy to realise that *fare da sè* meant fighting without allies; and it made the other governments suspect that the Cross of Savoy imposed on the tricolour meant Piedmont imposed on a united Italy. "This", says Signor Rosi, "proved discouraging" both to recruiting and to alliances with the other states.[19]

During these hectic days Charles Albert had lined his army, about 40,000 strong, along the frontier at various

[18] The proclamation was written by Sclopis; this reference to Pius IX did not appear in his original draft, but was inserted by Charles Albert before publication. Fabris, I, 221 and note; Cibrario (French ed.), p. 120 and note.
[19] Rosi, *Storia*, p. 197 and note.

places between Novara and Stradella. On March 25th he began his invasion of Lombardy by crossing the Ticino at two widely separated points; on his left, the advance-guard under General Bes[20] moved along the Novara-Magenta-Milan route, and reached Milan on the 26th as already described. Simultaneously the other advance-guard under General Trotti crossed the Ticino much farther south, in front of Pavia, and entered that town at 11 a.m. on the 26th. By that time Radetzky was already at Crema, nearly 30 miles distant. This brigade of Trotti's at Pavia was to cover the passage of the main body which was following close on its heels.

Of these two forces, we will deal first with that of Bes. He was received in Milan with enthusiasm, but then his difficulties began, and they were mainly political.

It was noticed as he marched into the town that, although his troops—the infantry and cavalry of the fine Piemonte and Pignerol Regiments—were loudly cheered, there were no shouts for the King. Very fortunately it had been decided that Charles Albert should not enter Milan until he could do so as a victorious leader.

Apart from the political hostilities, there were also the differences inevitable between civilians and soldiers. The Milanese citizens were overflowing with triumph and still more with impatience. For three long days since Radetzky's departure they had been awaiting the Piedmontese army. They believed that the Austrians were retiring utterly demoralised, and that their long column—27 miles long, said Cattaneo, rather absurdly[21]—including several hundreds of wounded

---

[20] Bes was O.C. of the Piemonte Brigade, one of the finest; but at that moment one regiment was absent. He had the Fourth Regiment of the Piemonte Brigade, quartered at Novara; one regiment of the Pinerolo Brigade, quartered at Turin; a regiment of Piemonte Reale Cavalry, and one battery. Lumbroso, p. 198.

[21] Cattaneo cannot have been very serious over this statement; but Willisen says that the Austrians, with their wounded, women, etc., took five hours to file out of Milan (p. 33).

and civilians, was a splendid target for attacks, and they entreated Bes not to lose this wonderful opportunity.

Bes, whose career had begun under Napoleon, probably understood that for him with 4000 men to attack Radetzky with now about 14,000 of all arms, was not so easy as they believed. Nevertheless, on the 27th he took his brigade by train to Treviglio, where he was joined by several bands of volunteers, notably that of Manara, 1000 strong; but his orders from Charles Albert did not arrive until March 30th, by which time Radetzky was at Montichiari safely behind the River Chiese. Bes then advanced and occupied Brescia, the principal town on the eastern side of Lombardy; he moved cautiously according to orders, but various bands of the Lombard volunteers, led by Manara, Torre and others, showed great enterprise. The recklessness of the "Five Days" was in their blood. Manara in particular distinguished himself by his successful dashes on Salò and Desenzano.

Thus by April 5th the Lombard volunteers, supported by Bes, had caused Radetzky to withdraw the last of his outposts behind the Mincio. In fact, the Austrian troops were now back in Venetia; so, for the moment, Lombardy could be considered free.[22]

Meanwhile, covered by Trotti's column in Pavia (the extreme right of the line), the main body of the Piedmontese army had crossed the Ticino.

On March 29th Charles Albert made his solemn entry into Pavia. Apparently his first plan was to march north-westward on Brescia, so as to join hands with Bes and cover Milan from a return by Radetzky. In fact by the 30th his advance-guard had got as far as Crema which Radetzky had evacuated only two days earlier.[23] But on the 31st his scheme was altered. He determined to continue on his southern route, and advance along the left bank of the River Po. By this time

[22] Fabris, I, 260 *et seq.*; Bes' report, *Rapporti*, II, 104 *et seq.*
[23] On the 28th, according to Hilleprandt (p. 37) who says that Bava was at Lodi on the same day.

Radetzky had abandoned the River Chiese and was settling down to his line behind the Mincio. There was no danger of his turning back, so Charles Albert moved his G.H.Q. to Cremona along the southern route, and left Bes up north in Brescia, rather isolated from the main body.

In this way he had got Bes' brigade threatening the extreme right of the Austrians, while he and his main body threatened their extreme left. Evidently he felt sure that Radetzky would not attempt any offensive against Bes. For his own main body, the southern route of advance seemed best; because, if he decided to force the Austrian lines behind the Mincio, their southern positions would be the easiest to attack; secondly because his Piedmontese would have the broad River Po on their right flank during their advance; thirdly, because it would enable Charles Albert himself to join hands with the Papal, Tuscan and Neapolitan troops which were marching up from the south to help him.

Moreover, there were political reasons. South of the Po, great events had been happening. On March 28th Piacenza had been evacuated by the Austrians; six weeks later, it gave itself to Charles Albert. Parma had been abandoned by its ruler and by its Austrian garrison; Duke Francesco V had left Modena on March 21st, after which it had been occupied by Bolognese revolutionists under Zambeccari. As events proved, these Duchies were soon to follow the lead of Piacenza.[24] It was advisable for the Piedmontese army to be in touch with all the lesser states, which in the coming campaign were to take the place of foreign allies.

These were great days in the life of Charles Albert. He had now accomplished the first stage in his mission. The whole story is like a romance. Certainly there must have been a wonderful persistence about a man who, year after year, had never abandoned his hope or permitted himself a

[24] Rosi, pp. 195–6, 205; and other general authorities.

rash step until he recognised that at last the chance of success had come. We know that already in the very first months of his reign—on April 11th, 1832—he had written to a friend:

> From all parts of Italy we hear that the hatred of Austria seems to be multiplied a hundredfold, and the wishes of all honest people are calling for us; but the moment to show ourselves has not yet arrived.[25]

And during all the intervening period, his ministers had known of his secret purpose, but they regarded it as a daydream.

But now he was riding out at the head of the army which he had made, to be the first captain of the new nation. So far all had gone well. The army had marched right across Lombardy, and was face-to-face with the Austrians; in a few days it would be superior to them in numbers. That, in itself, was a wonderful success. At the same time, too, by his decision to take the chances, he had advanced another stage on the way to hegemony for Piedmont; and that was the beginning of Italian unity.

More vital still, he had established Piedmont as a modern parliamentary nation; as a people capable of progressive work which would gradually terminate the era of spasmodic and unmilitary revolutions.

The importance of Charles Albert's decision is illustrated by a rather surprising coincidence. The artillery officer who, as a young lieutenant fired the first round in this campaign of 1848, at the first battle of Goito, was the same man who fired the very last rounds in the wars of the Risorgimento, as a General at the taking of Rome in 1870! His name was Celestino Corte.[26]

[25] Salata, *Carlo Alberto*, p. 286.   [26] Montù, p. 298.

Chapter VII

PIEDMONT VICTORIOUS AT GOITO
APRIL 8TH

In the view of the present writers, it is best to begin by pointing out that, whoever might be the "Generalissimo" or Chief Commander on the Piedmontese side was certain to be made a scapegoat in case of their defeat; and that their defeat was virtually a foregone conclusion, at all events after they were left in the lurch by the Papal and Neapolitan contingents.

This would be the case in any nation similarly placed. Here was a small people full of patriotic enthusiasm attacking a temporarily shaken world power. For the moment the prospects seemed bright. In reality they were never so bright as they seemed. Then came the heart-breaking disappointment. Naturally everyone asked: who was to blame? Inevitably, the man who was both King and Commander-in-Chief.

In our own campaigns we Britons have our scapegoats—and sometimes we have to rehabilitate them afterwards. During the Boer War, fortunately, our chief scapegoat was the War Office: but there was one week during which, if Lord Kitchener had made a Pride's Purge of that G.H.Q., many Englishmen would have said that he was right.

When Charles Albert crossed the frontier he had with him only three divisions out of the five, or 23,200 men—apart from Bes' advance-guard in Milan. According to Della Rocca and others, the intention was to advance rapidly with about 25,000 men whose number should later be brought up to 45,000 before the serious fighting began. On that day, in fulfilment of his historic promise,[1] Charles Albert was offering not only his own life and his army, but also the lives of his

---

[1] On the day of his celebrated interview with Massimo d'Azeglio. V. *Italy in the Making*, I, 210 *et seq.*

two sons; the elder, Prince Victor Emmanuel, Duke of Savoy, was in command of the so-called Reserve Division which was usually to be found in the front line; and the second, Prince Ferdinand, Duke of Genoa, was at first in command of the Artillery, but later O.C. of the Fourth Division. And certainly these princes have earned surprisingly high praise from historians, not only for their tact and courage, but for actual military knowledge. Prince Victor Emmanuel, the future King of United Italy, showed a gallant fighting spirit and was wounded at the second battle of Goito; but his younger brother Ferdinand, together with equally fine courage, displayed a very exceptional talent for war: although he was only twenty-six his report is admittedly one of the best submitted.[2]

Before a week had passed, the Piedmontese officers began to find their troubles thick upon them. The root-cause of most of their sorrows was the extraordinarily hurried mobilisation.[3] It is commonly said that Franzini asked for twelve days, and was only allowed two; and anyone who has ever been through such an experience can realise its maddening results in all departments. Men called up from their firesides were sent, not to the depot, but straight to their regiment, which was already on the march, and in which too many of the N.C.O.s were men only lately promoted. Many battalions were several days distant from the frontier; and one of Bes' regiments when it reached Milan had been on the way for a week, and had covered 96 miles.[4]

---

[2] In the opinion of two well-known authorities, Generals Nasalli-Rocca and Del Bono, Prince Ferdinand's report was actually the best of any written by officers of his rank. V. Lumbroso's edition of the *Memorie* attributed to Charles Albert, p. 155.

[3] "In 1848 no such thing existed as what we now call 'a mobilisation scheme'; nor was the personnel of a war formation arranged in time of peace. Consequently, it was necessary, as General Del Bono reminds me, to think of everything, and to proceed, during the space of a few days, to draw up a plan as to what was indispensable" (*ibid.* p. 199 note).   [4] Baldini, p. 52; Montù, III, 271.

At the same time there was the war strain on men and officers, very few of whom had seen a shot fired in anger, or ever experienced the hardships and irritations of a campaign. What surprised them most, perhaps, was the mixed character of their reception. The towns greeted them with enthusiastic cheers, but the country people, except the gentry, received them unwillingly, and often refused to provide them with supplies or even information. These unfortunate peasants remembered that the wars of Napoleon had lasted for twenty years, and were determined that no one else should start a fresh epidemic of ruin and suffering.[5] Della Rocca tells us how, on one occasion, they actually flooded a field so as to prevent his men from bivouacking there.[6]

These difficulties, however, were counterbalanced by a splendid enthusiasm among officers and men. Della Rocca says that never again did he see such cheerful determination to make the best of everything.

During all these changing scenes it is sometimes a little difficult to call up before us an exact picture of Charles Albert. Minghetti, however, who arrived in camp on May 10th, has left a vivid description of their first interview. "The King", he said, "received me that evening. He spoke to me of this enterprise as having been the dream of his life.... In person he is tall and thin; his face pale and full of sadness; his hands long and tapering. Severe in manner and full of dignity, but at the same time affable and courteous. He seemed like a Knight of the Middle Ages...it is said that owing to his

[5] "These villagers who had been afflicted not very long ago by a terrible war which lasted nearly twenty years...conceived an unutterable aversion from war and associated it with a sure triumph of the Imperialists. We called ourselves their brothers come to save them, but they regarded us as odious bringers of war and therefore of ruin and Austrian revenge", Promis' preface to the original edition of Charles Albert's *Memorie* quoted by Lumbroso, p. 190. In a note Lumbroso says that Promis is referring to the Napoleonic wars. *V.* also Bava, *Relazione*; *Rapporti*, I, 36, and other officers. Garibaldi made the same complaint (*Autobiography*, I, 281).
[6] Della Rocca, I, 167.

fervour of devotion he wears a hair-shirt and often fasts...he is marvellously intrepid in the field but irresolute and hesitating in council.''[7]

These last words remind us that for long periods of years after 1848 it was the custom to blame Charles Albert's leadership most bitterly for the loss of the campaign,[8] as if he alone were to blame. Certainly no one could suppose that Charles Albert and Bava were equal in leadership to Radetzky and Hess. But surely no sane man would expect it of them. They were pitted against what was perhaps the best staff-combination in Europe.[9] And a similar disadvantage applied to their army; it was an army of *Provinciali* in which only one-seventh of the rank and file were long-service men, opposed to an army of occupation almost entirely composed of long-service men. The new system was on trial; and we know that the only complete training for war is war itself. At the same time, however, military authority has since agreed that Bava was an officer of ability rather above the average; and undoubtedly Charles Albert was a very pains-taking worker. Therefore, against ordinary leaders of average calibre, might there not have been a very different story? Is it not rather probable that during these first two months of chaos in Vienna, Charles Albert would have kept them in play until they agreed to cede Lombardy to him? And that was all that he required. It was his parliament and the Milanese Assembly who insisted on having more.

Everyone knows that long before the war Charles Albert had been irrevocably nicknamed the *Re Tentenna*, the wavering king:[10] and after the defeat of 1848 and 1849 there

[7] Minghetti, *Ricordi*, II, 2.

[8] At the time, the officers' reports blamed almost everybody; this was natural and inevitable.

[9] Critics such as the Prussian General Willisen thought very highly of the Radetzky-Hess combination.

[10] Those who gave him this name were not aware that whenever he initiated any action favourable to the national cause he was met by a protest from the Austrian ambassador, often supported by those of Russia and Prussia. Their reports are in the Austrian archives.

were thousands of variations on this theme; but perhaps the most damning description of all is that in which Costa de Beauregard (who is quoted by Tivaroni) condemns him.

All the lacunae in his entirely speculative spirit made themselves felt. A propos of the slightest strategic movement the King engaged himself in a daedalus of pros and cons in which one became lost; one might say that, in the last analysis, the true talent of Charles Albert consisted in seeing the defects of all combinations, even of those which were especially his own.

Any reader of Costa de Beauregard's work will agree that, whether consciously or unconsciously, he has deliberately made Charles Albert the scapegoat for the defeats of the Piedmontese army. At the close of the campaign the officers in their reports blamed, not Charles Albert alone, but almost everything and everyone else as well; the training, the system of recruiting, the commissariat, and all the senior officers: Salasco, Franzini, Cossato, Della Rocca, Carderina, even the faithful Castagnetto, are usually described as good honest men, but always as entirely unequal to the situation. In the above accusation against the King, however, we have, no doubt exaggerated, a jibe very probably founded on fact.

In peace time Charles Albert was a very conscientious worker which mainly accounted for his success. We know from Cibrario that if he disagreed with a member of his Council over any point of importance, he might let the matter pass for the time being, but afterwards he would seek out that member and reason with him so as to make sure of every detail; and he always had two advisers who took opposite views. This seems to have been the method which he tried to pursue during the campaign. For advisers, he had Bava and Franzini, the Minister of War.

How far such methods are possible in war is a question for military opinion; but the truth was, and it is profoundly sad, that after all those years of work Charles Albert had embarked on a very difficult enterprise: one that was beyond his powers, and equally beyond the powers of the officers around him.

And that nevertheless the assemblies in Turin and Milan would not allow him to make peace as long as there was an Austrian soldier in the land. His service to Italy was to supply the failures which enabled others to achieve success.

Many of the descriptions of Charles Albert were written, like that of Costa de Beauregard, years after the war was over. But here is one written at the time. Early in April the Milanese Provisional Government sent a representative to the camp, and on the 15th he wrote as follows about their private interview:

> You could not believe what a profound impression was made on my mind by my talk with the King. He is a man who wishes to die; he says so openly and I believe him because his whole being both physical and moral reveals the fact. In this man, in his face, in his way of speaking, there is something at once melancholy, resigned and energetic which inspires compassion and respect.[11]

At the same time everyone was filled with admiration for his unfailing courage; and also with wonder at his physical endurance. Perhaps he had understood, more than people supposed, the importance of physical fitness in war.[12] Later on in this campaign, when others were exhausted, he would mount his horse as lightly as ever.

We now come to the problem before the Piedmontese staff: how to get Radetzky out of the Quadrilateral. His four-sided position, between his fortresses, was extraordinarily strong;

---

[11] Letter of Cesare Givelini of April 13th, 1848, now in the Milan Archives (*Archivio Bertani*, cart. II, plico III). Quoted by Rodolico, *Carlo Alberto*, p. xv. Martini, the Florentine representative at Charles Albert's camp, felt a similar impression.

[12] In books about him we often read of his "macerations" and his overwork, but fundamentally his day was planned for physical fitness: at 5.30 a.m. a ride in the country: then breakfast; chapel; work. At midday, luncheon, then work, sometimes out-of-doors. Then came dinner with the ladies, over by 6.30. Finally 9.30 to 10.30 billiards and talk with the men: but no one might smoke. *V.* Della Rocca, I, 82.

westward, facing the Piedmontese, it was defended by the line of the Mincio; on the south by the Po; on the east by the Adige; and on the north by Lake Garda and the Upper Adige. At all four corners there were strong forts: Peschiera (garrison 1500), Mantua (garrison about 10,400) on the Lombard frontier. In the rear were Verona (garrison 9000), now reinforced by Radetzky's army, and Legnago (1100) on the west of the oblong Quadrilateral.

Facing the Piedmontese was the line of the Mincio, a 20-mile stretch between Peschiera (north) and Mantua (south). Thirteen or fourteen miles behind it was Radetzky in Verona, with 32,000 men: of these he had left 12,000 defending his Mincio line, and another 5000 along the northern bank of the Adige, up towards the Alps;[13] 9000 were the normal garrison of Verona, now reinforced by 6000 more.

Inside this fortified block we may assume that Radetzky was safe. It will be remembered that in 1859 the French did not attempt to take the Quadrilateral. Napoleon III was told that to take it would cost 30,000 casualties. With his large numbers he could afford to cover it and pass it by.

But Radetzky's front line, along the Mincio, was defended by only 12,000 men.

On April 4th Charles Albert held a Council of War at Cremona; and their decisions were all-important.

Evidently it was realised that a direct attack on the Quadrilateral would be dangerous; but a fortress which cannot be taken may perhaps be starved out. Radetzky had only two lines of communication: one long, not very satisfactory line northward to the Tyrol and thence into Austria; the other, straight back eastward via Vicenza, Treviso and Venice. This second was his true line for obtaining provisions and reinforcements; but for the time being it was gone. The

[13] Hilleprandt gives 28,000 as the number Radetzky could put in the field exclusive of the garrisons which he counts at 22,000, of which 9000 were in Verona (p. 73). Perhaps this includes the 5000 who were along the left bank of the Adige towards Rivoli.

whole of Venetia, including the only piece of railway from Venice to Verona, was a hornet's nest of rebellion behind him. He was cut off from Austria; and his provisions, though the Piedmontese were not aware of the fact, were estimated only to last for another ten days.[14]

At Charles Albert's Council of War old General de Sonnaz gave rather unexpected advice. He suggested marching right round the southern flank of the Austrians and attacking them from behind, using Venice as a base; by that means they would prevent Radetzky's ever receiving reinforcements from Austria. On being reminded that such a movement would enable the Austrians to advance and fall on Lombardy or even on Piedmont itself, he replied that they would never abandon their fortresses—or if they did, so much the better.[15]

[14] Hilleprandt says that on April 18th when Radetzky had finally decided on his plan of operations, Verona was only provisioned for ten days ahead; and requisitioning was immediately taken in hand.

[15] This is the course preferred by the Prussian military writer Lieut.-General Willisen in his book published in 1868—apparently a series of military lectures on the campaign. He held that the Quadrilateral was impregnable when attacked from the west; that this was proved, not only in this campaign of 1848, but also in that of 1866. (He might have added that in 1859 Napoleon III did not attempt it.)

The way to attack it was by cutting its line of communications: but he did not believe in cutting the northern line towards Rivoli; he said that Charles Albert would have had to send so strong a force that he would have weakened his main body and that then Radetzky might have sallied out from Verona and crushed it—as he did three months later at Custoza.

Willisen believed therefore that the best course was to attack from the south; that Charles Albert should have marched right round the Austrians and made Venice his base; or else Ferrara, on the Po. He preferred Venice, and suggested that the Piedmontese, in their final position, would face northwards; their left would occupy Governolo strongly (to shut off Mantua and command the valleys of the Mincio and the Po); on their right they would have communication through Padua to Venice: to connect the two wings they would fortify a crossing of the Adige above or below Legnago.

But, he adds, more easily could they have made Ferrara their base.

In his youth De Sonnaz had been at Dresden and Leipzig, and on Napoleon's escort during his wonderful campaign of 1814. Was this advice a reminiscence of the great days? At all events it is the view approved by Pinelli, by Prince Ferdinand of Savoy, by the Prussian staff-officer Willisen, and by several historians. They claim that Charles Albert ought to have known beforehand that he could not take the Quadrilateral, and therefore should have intercepted Radetzky before he got into it;[16] or, failing that, should have started sooner on the process of starving him out. Even Tivaroni, always impartial, considers that, at the first out-break, Charles Albert should have dashed over the frontier and rescued Milan at any cost before the fighting ceased, and that thus he would have aroused all Italy to receive him as a saviour and dictator; that the original situation required a "crowned Garibaldi". And that now, on April 4th, having failed to make the dash, he should at once have made sure of starving Radetzky out. He should have pushed a few columns as far as the Mincio to hold up any Austrian sally, and mean-while his main body could make a southern detour, according to De Sonnaz' scheme.

To these views of Tivaroni and others, we can only reply: is this not wisdom after the event? On April 4th Charles Albert did not yet know for certain that he would be unable to take Verona or Mantua. And in any case the state of his army and his commissariat did not enable him to try hazardous flank marches. On one occasion the civilian drivers actually refused to cross the Mincio; and, in any case, these southern movements would not have intercepted Radetzky's northern line of communication with the Tyrol.

At Ferrara Charles Albert could have gathered round him all the forces of Central and Southern Italy—the Papal, Neapolitan and other armies, perhaps 60,000 fresh troops in all—and made a new line of communication up to Vicenza to take Radetzky in rear and cut him off from Austria. Willisen, p. 73 *et seq.*

[16] Hilleprandt takes this view, but he over-estimates Charles Albert's actual strength in the field at the time (pp. 61-2).

Even if possible, such a plan would have been insane politically. If the Piedmontese had weakened their Mincio front,
Radetzky could have sent out raiders into Lombardy and put an
end to all the war preparations in the Duchies; and as Charles
Albert had promised to be their defender, he would have been
called *Traditore* by every republican assemblage in Italy.

It is this situation which has convinced the present writers
that the Piedmontese had no real chances of success, except
during a very short period, while Radetzky was still struggling
to re-establish his communications. Once the line was re-
established, he could receive provisions and reinforcements
which would enable him to take the offensive. In normal times
he was much stronger than the Piedmontese.[17] Their success
depended on what help they received from the rest of Italy.

Charles Albert did not accept De Sonnaz' plan. Instead he
took Bava's advice: he decided to force the line of the Mincio;
to besiege Peschiera, and then to see what was feasible
against the other fortresses; and, if possible, to cut the
Austrian communications in the north. But their chief line
of communications—that through Vicenza and Venetia—he
could not attack himself; he was obliged to leave it to his
allies, the Papal and Neapolitan armies. As they numbered
about 17,000 and 40,000 respectively, they ought to have been
able to stop the Austrian relief forces, only 18,000 strong
under Nugent, from getting through that hostile country to
Verona, to rescue Radetzky.

[17] Cf. Salasco's opinion; in his report on the campaign he says:
"The Austrians did not limit themselves to the four strong places
on the Mincio and the Adige which made their position impregnable;
they entrenched and barricaded with abattis the villages nearest to
Verona" (*Rapporti*, I, 13). *V.* also Prince Ferdinand's opinion. He
says that the Piedmontese made a mistake in trusting to their Italian
allies; but that without Italian allies their enterprise was "rash,
even foolish": nevertheless they were compelled to try it, because
they had encouraged the Milanese to revolt. But they could not
expect their allies and the Venetian volunteers to hold up Nugent
for more than about three weeks, and ought to have tried to strike
their blow within that time (*Rapporti*, I, 294).

After the Council of War, Charles Albert moved his H.Q. forward to Bozzolo, only about 17 miles from the Austrian fortress of Mantua; around it were the troops of the First Army Corps (First and Second Divisions). These were the units which were to strike the first blow. And nearly 30 miles away up north, in front of Brescia, was the rest of the Fourth Division under Bes as already described.

The Reserve Division was in San Giovanni in Croce, Rivarolo, etc., reinforcing the extreme right.

On April 6th was heard the first shot of the campaign.

On the road to Mantua, Marcaria was occupied by an advance-guard consisting of a battalion, a squadron and a company of Bersaglieri; with vedettes thrown out a thousand yards in front. At 6 a.m. that day some Tyrolese Jägers crawled past the Piedmontese sentries and boldly opened fire on the sleeping troopers, while their own Uhlans dashed down the road and captured nine men and eight horses. This successful cavalry skirmish was one of the early exploits of Colonel Benedek (of the Austrian Hussars) who ended his career as Commander-in-Chief at Sadowa.

At Bozzolo Charles Albert started on his first really concerted movement, that of forcing the line of the Mincio— apparently a difficult task. He decided to attempt it by attacking its bridges at two different points; firstly and chiefly that of Goito—to be undertaken by his First Army Corps, Divisions I and II—and secondly the two bridges at Monzambano and Borghetto (opposite Valeggio) to be forced by the Second Army Corps. On April 6th he issued his orders for the movement against Goito and this was the opening engagement of the war.

The Mincio is a pleasant river flowing between flat fields and willows. At Goito its width is about two-thirds of the Thames at Reading, and the village is on its right bank, the side near to the Piedmontese; close below the church is the bridge. This stretch of the Mincio from Goito northwards to Pozzolo —an hour's march from each other—had been entrusted by

Radetzky to the brigade of General Wohlgemuth who had posted one battalion of Gradiscaner Borderers at Pozzolo (3 miles to north). But at the bridge of Goito there were all six companies of the 4th Battalion of Kaiser Jägers, splendid Tyrolese marksmen, and one of the 1st Oguliners, tall athletic Croats;[18] also half a squadron of Hussars and four guns. These were the men who fought—about 1200 infantry and a hundred gunners.[19] On the morning of April 8th they were in process of mining the bridge, and had therefore left one company of Jägers under Hauptmann Knesich in the village to protect the operation, but all the rest of the troops with their four guns were on the Austrian side of the river. In reserve at Marmirolo (nearly 5 miles) there was another company and a half, and at Marengo (about 2 miles) three and a half companies of Oguliners. Wohlgemuth had orders only to delay the enemy and prevent his crossing before the Austrians were out of reach.

There are four or five roads converging on to the Goito bridgehead, and none of them was defended against the Piedmontese;[20] but it was through Gazzoldo that Bava and Charles Albert had decided to advance to the attack.

[18] The Oguliners were soldiers of the 3rd Infantry Regiment recruited in the Croatian district of which Ogulin is the chief town.

[19] D'Arvillars, the Piedmontese General who directed the attack, said that there were 1200 Austrians against him (*Rapporti*, 1, 164). *Feldzug*, 1, 63, and Schönhals, 1, 180, say that Wohlgemuth had a company of Kaiser Jägers in the village of Goito, and the rest of the Kaiser Jäger Battalion, the 1st Oguliner Battalion, four guns and two squadrons of Hussars on the left bank.

[20] There had been a movement of the whole Piedmontese army right across the Austrian front. On April 7th the First Army Corps moved as follows: one portion of the First Division had been at Canneto and the other at Bozzolo; these two portions were to march to Gazzoldo and then move on together to attack Goito.

On their left the Second Division was to move from Canneto and occupy Pierbega and Solarolo (6 kilom.). They formed a half-moon round the bridgehead of Goito.

The Second Army Corps: the Third Division was to leave Asola and march to Castel Goffredo. The Fourth Division under Bes was to march away from Montichiari to Castiglione delle Stiviere and thence to Guidizzolo.

Lake Garda

Peschiera

R. Mincio

VERONA
Radetzky's H.Q.

Monzambano
bridge

Borghetto
bridge

Valeggio

R: Res

Volta

Guidizzolo

Pozzolo

Castel-
Goffredo
(one mile)

Massimbona

Ceresara

Marengo

Goito
bridge

Marmirolo

Piubega

Solarolo

R. Mincio

9,500 1st Div.

*From Cannetto
and Bozzolo*

Gazzoldo

MANTUA

Curtatone

Montanara

1st BATTLE of
GOITO
(April 8th)

Piedmontese
troops

Austrians

0   2   4   6

Scale of Miles

By the evening of April 7th, Bava had brought up his troops and posted them in a half-moon around Goito. Three of his columns were within striking distance.

Their northern column under Bes had marched down from Brescia as far as Guidizzolo, about 7 miles north-west of Goito.

In the centre the Second Division was at Solarolo about 4 miles west of Goito.

Bava's First Division was at Gazzoldo within 6 miles to the south-west of the Bridge of Goito; and it was this First Division (General d'Arvillars) which was to carry out the attack.

On the morning of April 8th, after a stormy night's bivouac, the men of the First Division fell in without food and the officers without maps, but they marched off full of suppressed excitement to take the place of honour in the first battle of the war. They were headed by cavalry patrols and by a company of Bersaglieri. Soon the day cleared up and no difficulties occurred until, by 8 a.m., they approached the crest of ground actually overlooking Goito. From that point they were fired on by the Jäger outposts; whereupon the Bersaglieri and a troop of cavalry who were leading the way at once advanced and charged their enemies. As a result the Jäger outposts retired, still firing, into the village by the river, to some extent covered by the shots from their own four guns on the left bank.

Bava now formed up his line of attack, deployed two battalions of the Regina Brigade on the semicircle of rising ground behind the Bersaglieri, and posted some companies of Cacciatori (Chasseurs) on either flank; and he brought up, along the Gazzoldo road, the Battaglione Reale Navi, an excellent little battalion of sailors about 300 strong with two guns, to act as supports. Finally, he formed the rest of the division in second line. There must have been about 2500 men in the firing-line and supports, and the rest of the division in rear. The attack was at once renewed by the Bersaglieri company about 150 strong, and led with great enthusiasm by Colonel Alessandro La Marmora. On this day he had the joy of commanding this new corps, founded and trained by himself, in their first action. They charged down the slope, and entered the village with a rush; but on the way La Marmora received a bullet in the mouth which incapacitated him for nearly all the rest of the campaign.

In this way the Piedmontese had entered the village very quickly, and were soon occupying it in force. But when they began to try to cross the bridge they came under a heavy fire of musketry and artillery from the other side of the river. Several officers and some of their men fell dead or wounded, and after perhaps half an hour it became evident that their attack was making no further progress.

By that time General d'Arvillars, O.C. of the Division, had succeeded in bringing up some fresh companies to reinforce the front line;[21] but before the new attack could be launched, the Jägers suddenly rushed back over the bridge to their own side of the river. Hardly had they reached the other side than two arches blew up with a tremendous report almost under their feet, leaving only the parapet intact.[22] Evidently the brave Tyrolese company had achieved its object.

The remainder of the engagement consisted in an exchange of fire across the Mincio; on the Piedmontese side, the Bersaglieri, the sailors and various line companies and artillery occupied the houses and the river bank; on the opposite side, the Jägers and Oguliners replied, supported by their four guns.[23] In this manner the fight continued for

[21] We have vivid descriptions of this action in the reports of Bava, d'Arvillars (*Rapporti*, 1).
[22] According to Hilleprandt the charge had got wet (p. 66).
[23] D'Arvillars says they had five, so they may have brought one up from Marengo. Fabris says the Italians only had four guns in action, but this seems incredible. Bava speaks of the brigades advancing, "with their batteries", viz. the Sixth and Eighth with eight guns each. The Austrians say that the Piedmontese had sixteen guns in action, but this may be an exaggeration. In the text we have followed the Italian General Montù (III, 298) who is the accepted authority on the history of the Italian artillery.

three hours more; but the Piedmontese artillery was superior in calibre and far superior in numbers, and moreover was served with great skill and daring, so that finally it made the enemy's position entirely untenable. The houses on the Austrian side began to crumble away, and the defenders were necessarily obliged to abandon them. Later on an Austrian gun was dismounted, and then their general retirement began. Wohlgemuth, however, claims that by that time he had fulfilled the purpose of his orders.

Before evening the Piedmontese had repaired the bridge, had sent a company across to occupy the far side, and had reconnoitred the country for five or six hundred yards beyond. Meanwhile General Wohlgemuth withdrew his whole force to Castel Nuovo and Massimbona.

Thus ended the first battle of the war. It was an encouraging success for Charles Albert; his men had fought with great dash, especially when one remembers that they had had nothing to eat either that morning or the night before. It was the first appearance in action of the now celebrated Bersaglieri. On the other side, the Tyrolese had shown their usual courage. The losses on the whole were light. The Piedmontese had lost 8 killed (2 officers) and 40 wounded (5 officers). The Austrians had lost 19 killed (2 officers) and 38 wounded (3 officers) and 61 missing[24] or prisoners. Total 118. Of the Jägers, their brave officer Knesich was killed, and so were the brothers Hofer, nephews of the celebrated Andreas Hofer who had so nobly defended the Tyrol against Napoleon. One

[24] The high total of men missing is due to the fact that some of the Jägers were cut off before they could get across the bridge and some thirty Italian Tyrolese deserted and joined the Piedmontese. According to the *Feldzug*, 1, 65, half the Jäger company headed by Knesich refused to retire, because the *Kampflust* (joy of battle) was upon them, and were eventually made prisoners. Bava says that about thirty of them were Italian Tyrolese who came over voluntarily. Knesich died of his wound. One of the Piedmontese guns was brought forward so as to sweep along the bridge, and was served with extraordinary gallantry by a sergeant named Milanesio until it was dismounted.

was serving as a lieutenant and the other as a cadet. It seems sad to think that the inheritors of so great a tradition of freedom should, through loyalty, have thrown away their lives for the cause of oppression.[25]

It was Charles Albert's First Army Corps which had taken Goito; but meanwhile his Second Army Corps was preparing a similar attack on the bridges at Monzambano and Borghetto. This was to be the work of the Third Division. Just as in the case of Goito it was prepared by occupying positions in a half-moon round the objectives, before advancing to the attack; so on April 8th while the fight was in progress at Goito, various units of the Third Division occupied Solferino, Cavriana and Guidizzolo; and the Fourth Division, now including Bes' Brigade, occupied Castiglione delle Stiviere and Pozzolengo.

As matters turned out, these two bridgeheads were only defended until Radetzky had completed his retirement from the line of the Mincio. A little firing took place; and the Piedmontese had about half a dozen casualties; but by April 10th they were across the river. Hilleprandt says that Radetzky was no longer anxious about Mantua, because he had received a reassuring despatch from the Governor, and had decided to withdraw to positions nearer Verona.[26]

---

[25] The Southern Tyrol was Italian in feeling, but in the Northern Tyrol there existed a fine sentiment of loyalty to the Kaiser. This loyalty had been appealed to by the Austrians in order to get recruits to hold down Lombardo-Venetia. They had even brought from his monastery old Gaspard Haspringer, a companion in arms of Andreas Hofer, to win recruits; at the sight of the old man with his long white beard the mountaineers seemed to behold once more the heroes of the fight for freedom against Napoleon; sixty companies of Jägers were raised.

[26] Hilleprandt, p. 72; *v.* also *Feldzug*, I, 68. "About the safety of Mantua the Field-Marshal could now feel his mind at ease, since he had received a definite statement from the Commandant and the defence authorities that their fortress was already in a position to make head against a serious attack and that it would hold out to the last."

This was the amazing outcome of the situation. Charles Albert had pierced the line of the Mincio with a loss of only about fifty men. Old Marshal Radetzky was unwilling at the moment to fight a big battle involving serious losses, because he did not know when or if ever he would be able to get reinforcements from Austria; whereas the Piedmontese might find some thousands of men to fill the gaps in their ranks, or might even bring in the French against him.[27]

So he decided to withdraw all the rest of his troops behind the Rideau, the line of defences in front of Verona. This meant leaving Mantua and Peschiera to fend for themselves, and in Peschiera the bread supply was only enough for about a month. Nevertheless he decided to leave them to defend themselves.

[27] Hilleprandt dwells continually on this theme, i.e. the rapidly increasing number of the Italians, and the Austrian anxieties about reinforcements.

Chapter VIII

ITALIA FARÀ DA SÈ. THE OTHER ITALIAN STATES. (ROME: TUSCANY: MODENA: PARMA: NAPLES)

I (ROME)

THE SCHEME FOR UNITING ITALY BY MEANS OF A LEAGUE OF STATES.

What help could Charles Albert get from the other Italian states?

At Rome, Pius was in a terrible difficulty. To declare war meant facing a possible schism in the Church;[1] to refuse to declare war meant losing the hearts of his own people. For him, essentially a man of duty and prayer, the mental struggle must have been terrible. He was now at the culminating point of his movement and on the verge of a great downfall—the downfall for ever of the Temporal Power; and this through the movement which he himself had inaugurated when he proclaimed Forgiveness to his people, and again when he spoke the words: *Benedite Gran Dio l' Italia.*

To a certain extent Pius had foreseen the new situation. In this dilemma his best hope of salvation lay in completing the League which had already been so often discussed; or else a Federation. If a Federation could have been brought into existence, the Papal state might have contributed the prearranged quota of men and money to the army, without the Pope himself becoming so directly involved as to necessitate

---

[1] Corboli Bussi says that the danger of this schism was perhaps not so great as Pius was led to believe; but Corboli Bussi probably did not realise that bitterness increases tenfold in time of war, and especially in time of rebellion. Corboli Bussi, Letter of January 8th, 1850, to Girolamo Sommi—a very interesting review of Pius' policy. Manno, *Corrispondenza*, p. 294.

his preaching a holy war and excommunicating his own Austrian spiritual subjects; if the Federation considered itself attacked it could go to war; all such questions of war and peace would have been decided by the Federal Council of Italy, and that would mark their being secular matters as distinct from ecclesiastical. This at all events was a view very generally accepted at the time.[2]

It will be evident, therefore, that the whole of this negotiation concerning the League of Italian states is of considerable interest, because on it depended perhaps the fate of the 1848 campaign, and also eventually the principles and constitution of the new Italian nation. Had a League or Federation of states been created, by joining it Pius would probably have acquired such popularity in Italy, that the Papal State would have been left to the Holy See—at all events during his lifetime—and consequently the fusion of Italy would have been postponed for many years to come. This negotiation, therefore, is an important thread in Italian history.

It will be remembered that the matter was already in train. Originally this scheme of forming an Italian League had been started by Pius, and had actually borne fruit in the "Basis of Customs Union" signed by Piedmont, Tuscany, and the Papal State on November 3rd, 1847. Since that day

[2] "The Holy Father shows himself more and more desirous to bring this project (the congress of all Italy) into effect, for he holds that this is the only means of providing serviceably for the urgent needs of the present moment and also for the future which etc., etc." (Letter of Monsignor Buoninsegni, Special Envoy of Tuscany to the Holy See, Bianchi, v, 466). And Minghetti, a Cabinet Minister, says: "If any way existed of bringing the Pope nearer to the Italian cause and making him share in national independence—it was this one and this alone. The League would have removed all responsibility as to warlike action, which, as father of all Believers, he abhorred; and there would no longer have been any necessity for him to declare war, because the right to war or peace would have remained in the hands of the League" (*Ricordi*, II, 91).

Bianchi, v, 176, says: "The only open door through which the Roman government could enter into the way along which the nation was moving, was the League."

of rejoicing, the negotiations for a real political League had
been continued almost without interruption, always carried
on with great energy by the Tuscan government, but with
some slowness at first in Rome, apparently because Pius,
although fully approving the scheme, feared that any open
attempt to unite Italy would displease Palmerston, and more
especially Louis Philippe.

For this year, 1848, the efforts to achieve a federal scheme
may be summarised under four headings: (1) Those before
Pius IX's allocution of April 29th; they aimed at forming a
defensive League of all the Italian states, including also the
new Provisional governments. (2) Those during Mamiani's
ministry in Rome, May 2nd to August 4th. This League was
to include only the four principal states, Rome, Tuscany,
Piedmont and Naples. Others might join afterwards. (3)
Those of the Abbé Rosmini, August 1st to September 8th.
His scheme was to set up an Italian Confederation at once,
under the presidency of the Pope. (4) Pellegrino Rossi's
efforts, September 15th to the date of his murder. He proposed that three states should send plenipotentiaries to Rome,
to a Congress presided over by the Pope, for the purpose of
forming a League: others could join afterwards.

During this first period, good progress had been made, and
success seemed actually to be close at hand. On March 6th
a special envoy arrived in Rome from the Tuscan government, namely Don Neri Corsini, the Marchese de Laiatico,
an able and distinguished man. With him Pius and Antonelli
had been working throughout that stormy March, the month
of revolutions, and the trend of events had turned in their
favour. From the first, Pius had insisted that the proposed
League must be *purely defensive*—his conscience as Pope
admitted no other arrangement—but to this stipulation
Tuscany was ready to agree.[3]

At the same time Ferdinand II of Naples had approached
them, willing to join. He had no real liking for the scheme,

[3] Corsini's report, March 9th—quoted Bianchi, v, 452.

but the revolution in Sicily, and the troubles in Naples, had brought him to terms; and on March 4th his Council of Ministers had suggested that there should be held in Rome a congress of plenipotentiaries from the four now-constitutional states, to discuss the affairs of the whole peninsula. On March 18th the Neapolitan minister in Rome had made formal overtures to Antonelli with a view to Naples joining the League.

Thus already there were three states in agreement: the Papacy, Tuscany and Naples. There still remained Piedmont to be considered, and even as early as February 26th, before Corsini's arrival, Pius had written to his Papal Nuncio at Turin directing him to make formal overtures to the government there. But nothing had resulted. And throughout the whole of that month from February 26th until the middle of March no answer arrived from Piedmont. In each of his despatches from Rome, Corsini says that he and Pius are still awaiting a reply; and, without the adhesion of Piedmont, there was no use in forming a League.

But then in the middle of March, as we have seen, came the revolution in Vienna and the universal call for war; this brought home to Pius the immediate necessity for completing the League.

On March 19th, 1848, Piedmont at length signified her consent to a settlement whereby a League between Rome, Tuscany, and Piedmont was agreed upon in principle. As Piedmont was the only one of the four states which had hitherto refused agreement, it seemed that at last the Italian League was an accomplished fact, and it was accepted as being so by the governments of Florence, Rome and Naples. At Rome, Cardinal Antonelli, now Secretary for Foreign Affairs, told Monsignor Buoninsegni, the Tuscan envoy to the Holy See, that "the Italian League is now concluded *de facto* and it only remains for us to put it formally into shape"; that for this purpose it was necessary to call a congress at Rome of representatives of all the states, and that the Holy Father had already manifested the necessity of doing so to all the Italian princes.[4]

It seemed as if the League were virtually accomplished, and almost as if Italy might gradually become a Federation on the lines of Switzerland, the United States, or Germany. When Gioberti wrote about the three powers, "France, Austria and the Italian League", it appeared as if the latter might easily become "the Italian Federation" and then the Italian nation. What a triumph this would have been to Pius after his two years of toil, and also for Gioberti, and indeed for everyone concerned!

In reality, however, this result was farther off than ever; henceforward there is a fundamental divergence which re-appears in every negotiation.[5] Rome wants a defensive bond, Turin is on the offensive; on March 25th Charles Albert had crossed the frontier with his army, and what he wanted now was reinforcements, not federal pacts; men, not governments, and if possible trained soldiers rather than volunteers. He was quite aware that the Tuscan and Roman alliances would more often be a source of weakness than of strength, com-pelling him and his already insufficient forces to defend their frontier as well as his own, and also compelling him at the end of the war to share with them any territories that he might succeed in liberating. He is sometimes blamed for not concluding the League, but, from the military point of view, undoubtedly he was right. What he required now was military support, so before starting on his advance he despatched envoys to the other three courts informing them that he regarded as already in existence "a political league for all purposes", between Piedmont and the constitutional states of Central Italy, but that the details could not possibly

[4] Florence Arch. Esteri. Filza 2485: despatch to Martini, March 31st, 1848. Bianchi, v, 475 (Grifeo's despatch of March 25th (Naples)); v, 465. Buoninsegni's despatch of March 26th (Rome).

[5] Florence Arch. Esteri. Filza 2485: despatch to Martini, March 28th and 31st. Bianchi, II, 180, quoting Pareto's despatch of April 10th.

be settled until the end of the war. Meanwhile, he appealed to the government of Naples to hasten the advance of its troops to co-operate with him, and to the Tuscans to concentrate their troops, with those of the Pope, on the lower Po, for action under his own orders.

Charles Albert's feelings were natural. He wanted to get troops without signing a treaty; but unfortunately his policy engendered some distrust in the other states, because they felt that, once established across the north of Italy, he would be a danger to their existence; indeed Farini says that at times they seemed to be more afraid of Piedmont than of the Austrians. And in their justification we must remember that only a few years later their fears were proved to be well grounded. In 1860 the Piedmontese had not been in possession of Lombardy for more than eighteen months before they had swallowed up every other state in Italy.

For the present, however, the other states continued their endeavours to form a League. On April 1st the Tuscan representative signified his agreement to the proposed congress in Rome. But there again they were met by difficulties. "At this Congress or Diet of Italy, according to the views of His Holiness there should be present not only all the Italian princes, but also all the governments which, during the course of the extraordinary military and political developments, have come into being during the last few days with the title of provisional."

It would have been a congress of Rome, Tuscany, Piedmont, Naples, Lombardy, Venetia, Sicily; but the inclusion of Venetia and Lombardy meant offending Charles Albert, and that of Sicily would alienate Naples. Nevertheless, if a congress had come into being then, it might perhaps, at such a moment of national enthusiasm, have achieved some step forward towards Italian unity.

This, as we know, was the dream of Gioberti, and perhaps the only form of unity possible in 1848—and whatever its demerits, it had to be considered before it could be rejected, just as the republic had in turn to be tried and rejected, before Italy realised that a stage of fusion into Piedmont was the only safe preliminary to becoming united into one nation.

At the beginning of April glorious news began to arrive of the first engagements of the war; it was announced that some Austrian Uhlans and Tyrolese had been repulsed by Charles Albert's advanced guard; that on April 8th the Piedmontese had attacked the Austrians and after four hours' fighting had carried the bridge of Goito, taking one gun, and that on the 9th they had fought their way across the river at Monzambano and had driven the Austrians out of Borghetto. These rather exaggerated accounts of the first successes naturally sent a thrill of pride all over the peninsula.

On April 10th Pius sent off Monsignor Corboli Bussi to go via Florence straight to the camp of Charles Albert, and there on the field to settle with him the terms of the League;[6] on the same day the Tuscan government ordered the Cavaliere Martini (its representative at Turin) also to go to the Piedmontese camp to support Corboli Bussi in his mission.[7]

On this same day, Bargagli tells us,[8] there arrived from Piedmont a despatch almost amounting to a refusal. It pointed out that a congress at that moment was ill-timed because it must necessarily include the Provisional govern-

[6] Bianchi, v, 468: Buoninsegni's despatch of April 9th. *Biblioteca*, pp. 290, 291.

[7] Florence Arch. Esteri. Filza 2485: Letter to Martini of April 15th. Bargagli, who besides being Tuscan representative at Rome was a friend of Corboli Bussi, tells us that "the principal and most genuine part of his, Corboli Bussi's, mission is, in substance, to confine within the limits of moderation the ambitious views of the King of Turin [Piedmont] and to call upon the troops in the field the Benediction which the Pontiff entreated on the Quirinal not long ago, for the land of Italy" (Bargagli's report, April 9th). In other words Pius and the Roman ministers wanted Charles Albert and the Turin government to agree to definite terms of a league before they could bless his cause whole-heartedly.

[8] Florence Arch. Esteri. Filza 2446: Bargagli's report of April 11th; Martini's of April 10th.

ments, and it added that if a congress was summoned at all, the right place for it would be the Piedmontese H.Q.; that they hoped Pius would send a representative to H.Q. so as to encourage the army and the people. They addressed the Tuscan government in similar terms.

Both envoys duly arrived at Charles Albert's camp; and the fact that a prelate should be sent to the field by the Pope, to be with the army of liberation, created a great sensation in Italy. But the Piedmontese ministers at Turin were angry at not receiving more military help; Piedmont, they said, had exerted the greatest efforts, had placed "80,000 men under arms and hoped to raise 20,000 more", but, "so far not a single soldier had joined them from the other states".

Count Cesare Balbo went further: "It is only Charles Albert", he said, "who is imprudent. He exposes his person, his sons, his crown, his people and his resources. The Grand Duke, the Pope and the King of Naples are prudent and I commend them. They issue proclamations and hold councils; but in the meantime while our soldiers have done marches of thirty miles a day, some regiments being without food for twenty-four hours on end, and have got from Turin to Mantua, we have not yet been reinforced by a single soldier from the other states."

This was true enough, but in the same despatch they had virtually refused the proposals. If they had signed a League the other states would have felt safer. They were trying to get the soldiers without binding themselves at all. And right or wrong, they ought to have taken great care not to drive Pius into any kind of resentment.

On April 24th the Neapolitan plenipotentiaries, lately arrived in Rome to negotiate the League, were formally introduced to the Pope, and at once began enlarging on the importance of the scheme.[9] With this Pius entirely agreed, but added that hitherto Piedmont had shown no readiness to take part in it; he had hoped that in answer to his urging she

[9] Florence Arch. Esteri. Filza 2485: Martini, April 12th.

would have sent her representatives, but that since she had proved unwilling to do so, nothing more could be done.

Only five days later, on April 29th, there came Pius' celebrated Allocution which altered the whole situation, as will presently be described. Two months later, when the Piedmontese began to realise that they were unlikely to be victorious, they arranged for a genuine resumption of the discussions under the aegis of the Abbé Rosmini, but this is a later phase of the negotiation.

In March 1848, however, the point of immediate importance was to settle what reply Rome could make to the Piedmontese call for armed men. We may answer it at once by saying that as soon as possible the Romans started off two separate contingents, 7000 regular troops under Durando, and 9000 volunteers under Ferrari, a total of nearly 17,000 in all, but as this is quite a considerable force, we must devote a whole chapter to it; it will be dealt with in chapter IX.

II (TUSCANY: MODENA: PARMA)

"The government of King Charles Albert charges me therefore to make known to your Excellency that now or never is the time to devote to the cause of Italy the last man and the last scudo." These were the terms of the despatch sent on April 14th by the Tuscan representative in Turin to his government in Florence.

Tuscany, with about a million and three-quarter inhabitants, was then a peaceful state, with practically no military tradition. Nominally its army was composed of two regiments, each regiment consisting of two battalions of six companies, and of one depot battalion with only four companies. There was also a regiment of Dragoons consisting of two companies —about 4000 men and 136 officers in all.

During 1847, however, the ministers, seriously alarmed at the Austrian advance, had begun to arm. In October the government had bought 15,000 muskets and 15,000 sabres. In November it decreed enlistment for three years. In January 1848 General Arco Ferrari proposed to increase the artillery. Meanwhile in 1847 the government had applied for several Piedmontese officers to direct their military training; they had also arranged for some of their junior officers being sent to Piedmont for instruction; and the smallness of the army can be gauged by the fact that there was actually some hesitation at the proposal of sending away simultaneously so many as six of the best subalterns.[10]

On the whole Tuscany's response to the call to arms was better than might have been expected. The government, it is true, aimed chiefly at making capital out of the situation, but the people had more national feeling than their rulers, and actually forced their peaceful old Grand Duke to issue a war proclamation, and to send an army into Lombardy. The chief events are as follows:

On March 19th news arrived of the revolution in Vienna; on March 21st many of the Florentines, partly incited by anonymous writings, betook themselves to the Gonfaloniere who happened to be Baron Bettino Ricasoli, afterwards the "Baron of iron", to ask for arms with which to defend the frontier. Ricasoli at once went down to the Palazzo Vecchio to convey their wishes to the Grand Duke, who in reply sent them a message that the regulars were marching that afternoon in two columns and, so Ricasoli added, Civic Guards would be accepted to go with them, if necessary, into Lombardy. Those who had arms might bring them!

Thus on the following morning there started by train from Florence to Prato four companies of regular troops, half a battery and 720 volunteers of the Civic Guard all on their way to San Marcello in Garfagnana, under command of Major Belluomini, a Lucchese officer.

On the same day there started from the town of Leghorn

[10] Florence Arch. Esteri, Busta 283: Martini's despatch of January 1st, 1848.

another column under Major Baldini composed of four companies of regulars, with the volunteers from the Civic Guards of Leghorn, and two-thirds of the university battalion. This column reached Pietrasanta on the 23rd and was reinforced by the volunteers from Lucca, Pisa, Viareggio and Camaggiore, and by 700 more volunteers from the energetic and turbulent town of Leghorn.

Manifestly these troops had arrived not merely to defend the frontiers but also to enlarge them. On their front, round Massa and Carrara, lay a strip of territory, including Fivizzano and Pontremoli, lately acquired by the Duke of Modena in order to connect his duchy with the sea. This strip of territory was now derelict, since the Duke had fled from Modena, and it only remained for the Tuscans to occupy it; indeed some portions of it (Fivizzano[11] and Pontremoli) had lately belonged to them. Similarly, too, the inhabitants of Massa and Carrara were willing to be annexed, for they now regarded Modena as merely an outpost of the Austrian Empire.

The Tuscan government at once issued a manifesto in which it spoke of the danger to law and order arising from these derelict dominions, and gave out that it had decided to advance and occupy them *provisionally* as a matter of duty and self-protection. Fortunately their two columns were already well placed for this purpose. From Pietrasanta the left-hand force under Major Baldini started off on March 25th and entered Carrara, and on the following day occupied Massa in spite of a little resistance. This was quick work, and showed a truly imperialistic spirit, but it was in full accordance with the formal instructions of their government which began: "If we follow the ways of Providence with loyalty and wisdom, we shall attain a good issue: but be careful not to let the Piedmontese get there first."[12] In this way by May 12th these states of Massa and Carrara and the territories of Lunigiana and Garfagnana were all annexed to Tuscany.

[11] As to Fivizzano, *v. Italy in the Making*, II, Appendix A.
[12] Bianchi, v, 242, quoted by Fabris, II, 127.

However, to most people it seemed a joyful occasion, for they regarded this annexation as saving them from Austria.

After this successful advance, the Tuscan government settled down to pursue a twofold policy; it wrote to Turin to push on the League, and, instead of sending any more troops to the frontiers, decided to train them at the depots. This policy has caused the government to be accused of trying to avoid taking a share in the war, but we must admit that the Tuscan recruits certainly required training; they were full of enthusiasm but raw beyond belief, so much so that the Piedmontese officers rather preferred to be without them. The people, however, were not to be satisfied with territorial aggrandisement; they wanted war, and on March 26th Baron Ricasoli called a great meeting at Florence to preach a Holy Crusade. The Grand Duke attended the meeting; on March 29th he issued a decree which decided the matter. Hitherto the volunteers had only been called on to defend the frontier. He now ordered a corps of operations to advance between Modena and Reggio in concert with the pontifical and Piedmontese troops. At the same time he urged volunteers who were the fathers of families to return, and left all others free to do so.

On April 5th the Grand Duke issued a stirring war proclamation in which he reminded them that the holy cause of Italian independence would be decided on the fields of Lombardy.

By April 24th the Tuscans had all crossed the River Po and had taken up the positions allotted to them under command of Charles Albert.[13] They were to form part of the troops blockading Mantua. They numbered 3750 regular infantry, 3186 Civic Guards and volunteers, 230 mounted chasseurs, 605 gunners, six field guns (six-pounders) and two howitzers, giving a total of 7771 men in all. Their left was in the village of Curtatone, over 3 kilometres west of Mantua, their right was at the village of Montanara, and the H.Q.

[13] Fabris, II, 136.

about 5 kilometres to the rear at Castellucchio. Before long they established about 2000 men at each of these places with several guns.

These names, Montanara and Curtatone, are now well remembered throughout all Italy. In Florence two of the streets are called after them.

Thus Tuscany had come into the war, and in view of her exposed geographical position it was a brave decision on the part of her people. But, as everywhere else, the enthusiasm did not reach the soul of the peasant class, which is the hardiest for war. Tuscany with a population of a million and a half had sent only 7771 men and eight guns. However, this line was strengthened by the brave 10th Neapolitan Regiment.

The small Duchy of Modena[14] (population 575,000), regarded by the Austrians as a dependency of theirs, had been abandoned by its Duke Francesco V on March 21st, and was thenceforth living under a Provisional government. Little could be expected from a state whose army consisted only of about 2400 men in peace time, especially as most of the trained soldiers were attached to their Duke. Modena, for its size, produced an unusually high proportion of good officers during the Risorgimento—witness the names of Fanti, Cialdini and Charette, who were trained at the excellent military academy there; but in 1848 its people were divided in sentiment, and consequently their quota of men was small. On April 4th they sent to join Charles Albert a contingent consisting of 800 volunteers, two companies of regulars together numbering 225 men, thirty-five dragoons and thirty gunners; a mixed force of 1090 men in all. Evidently there was little popular enthusiasm. This small contingent was under the command of Major Fontana, a young regular officer without experience of war, but brave and efficient,

---

[14] As to the number of volunteers from Modena we have consulted only Fabris, II, 140; and the general histories, Rosi, p. 196, etc.

who, after some initial difficulties, did excellent service. On April 20th he led his men across the River Po and entrenched and barricaded them at Governolo, 18 miles south-east of Mantua. In this position at Governolo he formed a connecting link between the Tuscans at Montanara and Durando's Papal troops at Ferrara; he also formed part of the half-circle of Italian corps watching Mantua; and on April 22nd he advanced some of his men to Castellaro to cut the Austrian communications between Mantua and Legnago. It was here that he and the Mantuan volunteers who joined him exchanged their first shots with the Austrians, and gave a very creditable account of themselves.

The Duchy of Parma[15] (almost five million inhabitants) took only nineteen days to throw in its lot with Piedmont. Like Modena it was regarded by the Austrians as their dependency, but, strategically, it was more important than Modena, because, with the province of Piacenza, it guaranteed the passage across the Po, and extended like a wedge between Piedmont and Tuscany. Metternich had always wanted it, and by the Treaty of December 24th, 1847, the army of Parma had already passed under the orders of Radetzky.

The result was probably beneficial for the army. Already under Marie Louise its rank and file had been largely in the hands of Austrian N.C.O.s and had imbibed some of their military spirit.

On March 20th, 1848, news arrived of the rising in Milan; Parma immediately joined the national movement, formed a National Guard and made the Duke set up a Regency. On March 21st the Austrian garrison at Piacenza also retired. On April 9th the Duke agreed to the formation of a Provisional government and placed his state under the protection of Charles Albert, "who might regard it as one of the other Italian states which were co-operating in the great work of the independence of Italy".

[15] As to the contingent from Parma v. Fabris, II, 145; Rosi, p. 195; and the other general historians.

On April 18th the young Provisional government offered its armed forces to Charles Albert, but the net result was small. The pre-war army had to be purged of Austrians and in the event only one battalion could be raised, 1026 strong, of whom 200 were National Guards and 180 were unarmed; they also sent a section of artillery (two guns) and a little cavalry. This small contingent must have proved a disappointment to Charles Albert. But in one respect the Provisional government set a good example, namely, that it sent the battalion to form an integral part of the Piedmontese army. When it arrived at Volta on April 23rd it was brigaded with the Savona Regiment in a composite brigade, and thus it enabled the Piedmontese to keep their 15th Regiment in Savoy, on guard against the French republicans from Lyons, who had invaded that province.

III (NAPLES. JANUARY 29TH TO THE END OF APRIL)

Meanwhile, what had been happening in Naples? On January 29th Ferdinand II had published his Constitution; on February 10th he swore it; by March 6th with the help of Lord Minto he had succeeded in collecting a cabinet of which the most prominent members were Prince Serracapriola (President); for Internal Affairs, Bozzelli (ex-revolutionist, now Liberal); for Education, Poerio (ex-revolutionist, now Liberal); for Justice, Saliceti (a law professor and a strong Radical). It seemed as if henceforward all might be plain sailing in the Neapolitan constitutional monarchy, which was modelled on that of Louis Philippe.

Unfortunately during the next three months it became abundantly evident that the Naples of that day was not yet fit to undertake self-government. This is the opinion of all the leading historians. Professor Masi, for instance, tells us that "the concessions granted in Naples were so extravagantly large[16] that the country, passing from the most rigid restrictions to the wildest licence, fell headlong into a state of continuous anarchy, with which three Liberal ministries, which succeeded one another within a hundred days or so of the new Constitution, were never able to cope".[17]

To most people it seems plain that as the Liberals had at length got the King to swear to the new regime, it ought to have been their first and fundamental principle not to break it themselves. But, so far from considering it sacrosanct, the Neapolitan politicians never made any attempt to observe it at all. When they accuse Ferdinand of breaking his sworn oath to the Constitution, they omit the fact that, from the first, the Liberals themselves treated it as a complete nonentity.

When France proclaimed herself a republic, the Neapolitan Liberals seem to have thought that the French Revolution had come back, and that they were entitled to start again on an entirely new basis.[18]

The situation before them required a great deal of commonsense and moderation. In the first place there was the problem of Sicily, and it proved to be practically insoluble.

[16] V. Rosi, p. 188. For a full list of authorities consulted on Naples v. the Bibliography.

[17] Cambridge Modern History (1908), XI, 80; v. also London Corr. II, 285. On April 15th, 1848, Napier (British minister in Naples) wrote to Palmerston: "The laws remain unexecuted, the police and municipal authorities are powerless. The old system has been shattered and none has been constructed to take its place." V. also the latest and best writer on the subject, Signor Paladino, who strongly and repeatedly confirms this view (Il Quindici Maggio, pp. 14, 19, 30, 33, 176, etc., etc.). His remarks are more convincing than those of Settembrini. V. also Tivaroni, Ital. Merid.

[18] Even General G. Pepe, perhaps the most unselfish of the Neapolitan patriots, said openly to Ferdinand: "Now that the French Republic is proclaimed, now that nearly all the states of Europe are carried away by the revolutionary movement, neither mere institutions nor the Constitution itself, with its narrow basis, is sufficient. Peoples are like princes—the more they get the more they want." He then proceeded to claim six new regulations of an entirely revolutionary character. V. G. Pepe, Histoire, 1848, p. 67.

Tivaroni,[19] however, seems to think that, better managed, this Serracapriola-Bozzelli government might perhaps have succeeded in surviving the period of crisis. He groups the causes of its failure under six headings: it failed because the concessions to Sicily were passed too late (March 6th);[20] because the Press was reckless and indiscriminate in its attacks on individuals; because there were too many tumults in the cafés; because in the clubs any scheme was applauded, however fantastic; because in the country districts the peasants invaded private property; and because in the towns there was some prospect of pillage. According to Settembrini—himself the arch-revolutionist—the Plebs said: "If people do not work, and we remain hungry, what sort of liberty is this? In old days the King was only one man, and he used to devour one man's allowance, but now there are thousands, and they devour enough for thousands, so we must begin to look after number one."[21]

Meanwhile, instead of setting to work to nail the King down to the Constitution, the Liberals spent their days in wrangling with each other, apparently oblivious of the fact that the absolutists were still a party in being. The following is the opinion of the well-known revolutionist-historian Baron Nisco: "The real men of the revolution had lost their former authority, and the new Liberals, sprung into life since the 29th of January like fungi from the social mire stirred up by our movement, spent their time declaiming against the inadequacy of their newly won liberties, and calling for new and exaggerated rights in order to exhibit themselves in the leading places, and thus cause it to be forgotten that they had either done nothing at all, or else done very badly."[22]

---

[19] Tivaroni, *Ital. Merid.* p. 192.

[20] *V.* also Massari, *Gli ultimi casi di Napoli.*

[21] Settembrini, p. 263 (quoted by Tivaroni, *Ital. Merid.* p. 192, and by Nitti, p. 92). On March 25th the Sicilians opened their Parliament, and this added to the unpopularity of the government in Naples.

[22] Nisco, *Ferdinand II*, p. 195: *v.* also Massari, pp. 85, 107. But even De Cesare (*La Fine d' un regno*, p. 226) takes this view, a writer

On March 13th the lawyer minister Saliceti resigned, and at once began to form an Opposition. He perceived that, although the moderate Constitution granted by Ferdinand had been received with great gratitude on January 29th and February 10th, since then the scene had changed. Everywhere there was revolution; and he hoped that now they might obtain a far wider concession.

He was not a republican, says Signor Paladino, but he meant to force the King's hand.[23] His programme of seven points ran as follows: (1) The Deputies (Commons) were to have full powers to reform the Statuto; and the appointment of Peers which lay with the King was to be suspended. (2) There was to be manhood suffrage. (3) The provincial, district, and communal councils to be dissolved, and fresh nominations made. (4) Neapolitan *chargés d'affaires* to be sent to the Italian League. (5) Reform of the civil, military and judicial personnel. (6) The line battalions were to start promptly for Lombardy. (7) The Neapolitan flag henceforth to be a tricolour.

This programme speaks for itself. Clauses (1) and (2) meant that the Commons, elected on manhood suffrage, would have the power of drawing up afresh the whole Constitution. Thus they would be, not a House of Commons, but a Constituent Assembly. It is suggested that this idea was an imitation of the French Revolutions in 1789 and 1848.

Thus the Opposition wanted to alter the Constitution from top to bottom before Parliament had ever met. It is hard to see how they could genuinely expect to unite Naples for war to the death against Austria, and at the same time carry out a

who belittled Ferdinand II and the Bourbon tradition in Naples, and makes the following admission, as to 1848: "The Liberal Institutions, which degenerated immediately into turbulent anarchy, were not reconcilable with a temperament such as that of Ferdinand II, nor even compatible with it."

[23] Paladino, p. 53; *v.* also Tivaroni, p. 195. *V.* also Petrucelli, p. 80, a friend and colleague of Saliceti: "Aurelio Saliceti was a man of proud, loyal and disinterested character. He had understood the revolution and wanted at any price to incarnate it. He wanted the governmental machine cleaned of every stain of the old regime."

programme of revolutionary changes, every clause of which would be contested.

The only possible plea in their excuse is their claim that they "did not trust the King". They thought that he would evade the war as soon as possible. Signor Paladino (p. 74) points out that as yet they had no reason to distrust him. Still it is true that Ferdinand, and certainly a good many of his subjects, did not like declaring war against Austria. A victorious campaign might make Piedmont a danger to everybody. In fact, in fearing that Ferdinand would prove lukewarm about the war, the extremists were probably right; but the same consideration would have applied to most of his army, and, after three or four months, to almost everybody else. This is proved by results. And it might be asked, in reality what had Naples to gain by war? Meanwhile Ferdinand was being swept temporarily into the national movement.

After the "Five Glorious Days" of Milan he found himself driven by demonstrations into approving of volunteers starting to help the Lombards. On March 26th the Austrian arms were torn off their embassy and Prince Schwarzenberg left Naples.

The fact was, that whether Saliceti himself was a revolutionist or not, there was now a largish crowd in Naples of people who had flocked into the town "on the make", and plenty of young men who were not unwilling to support any kind of upheaval.[24]

There were some people who really wanted the war; but many of their supporters only wanted troubled waters. If there had been many who really wanted war, more of them would have volunteered for it.

---

[24] Petrucelli, p. 75, expresses these sentiments: "The revolution in France came as a ray of light and cleared the minds of everyone. ...Everyone understood then that the Radicals with their *political pantheism* were not asking for utopias, but that the republic was the aim of the new revolution which was reintegrating society into possession of all the attributes of power." Petrucelli must have known that these sentiments would alienate both Charles Albert and the Pope from declaring war against Austria, which he professed to advocate.

Before the end of March the Serracapriola-Bozzelli ministry resigned—brought down by their failure in Sicily. But on March 29th there arrived in Naples the celebrated General Guglielmo Pepe, the hero of the revolution in 1820. Ferdinand received him with open arms, and immediately invited him to form a government.[25]

With a revolutionary patriot such as Pepe to lead them, it seemed plain that the Neapolitans, if they really wanted to take part in the national war, would have their chance of doing so. Pepe, however, refused to work under the existing Constitution. He threw in his lot with the Opposition; he made six stipulations including that concerning the Peers, and that giving constituent powers to the lower house; moreover he asked for eight colleagues of extreme views,[26] including Saliceti.

This was a disappointment. The King replied that he would stand by the Constitution to which he had sworn.[27]

[25] Pepe, *Histoire*, 1848, p. 69. General Guglielmo Pepe had led the Neapolitan army against Austria in 1821. Since then he had been in exile, but he was remembered as a national hero. Ferdinand invited him to inspect the army and took great pride in drilling and manœuvring first an infantry and then a cavalry brigade before him.

[26] Lord Napier (*London Corr.* II, 366: Letter April 1st) says that at first Ferdinand was disposed to consent "even to these terms", but finally told Pepe that he could not agree to so revolutionary a scheme. It also included sweeping changes among the government employés. *V.* also Paladino, *Il Quindici Maggio*, p. 69.

[27] Pepe himself, p. 70, gives Ferdinand's letter: "S.M. ne peut changer la constitution jurée par elle et par tous. Il appartiendra aux pouvoirs légaux, c'est-à-dire au roi et aux chambres, de développer et de féconder la constitution donnée le 29 Janvier, sans en changer l'essence. Le ministère que l'on propose ne peut donc être accepté. Les adresses que S.M. reçoit de toutes parts ne font que la confirmer dans l'idée qu'elle manquerait a ses devoirs envers son pays, en changeant la constitution existante."

Pepe's reply was that the King was like a man who had sworn to pay 100,000 francs: no one would blame him if now he paid 200,000. Yet Pepe had more sense than most of the Liberal leaders!

On all these points *v.* also Paladino, pp. 70 and 80.

He refused Pepe's demand to have Saliceti as a minister; considerable excitement resulted, but the King succeeded in finding ministers elsewhere.

A new ministry under Signor Troya (April 3rd) proposed a programme of ten headings; the most important of these were the 4th and 5th—those about the Peers and the Constitution. These will be described in chapter xv. It also lowered the money qualifications for deputies and electors and admitted professional and commercial men. The elections were fixed for April 15th. It opened a loan of 12,000,000 ducats, and with that loan there came to its zenith the rush for jobs which in most nations seems prone to accompany a change of regime. Here, the mêlée was such that even Poerio and Settembrini resigned their ministerial posts rather than be seen in such company.[28] Indeed Settembrini's letter of resignation is quite as bitter about the new Liberal regime as his *Protesta* had been about the King and the royal ministers in 1847. He describes the scene as follows:

The Ministries were invaded by people of every species; ignorant, ruffianly, spies worthy of the galleys, and many proposed themselves for appointments. They wrote out lists of names which made one shudder, and then printed them. The maddest ambitions burst forth; even a Beadle of the University came to me, Carlo Basili by name, who had printed some of his

[28] The latter speaks of "this crowd of unmannerly beggars who stand there with their mouths open calling 'Jobs, jobs', from morning until night. They climb all the staircases, they invade the houses, they even threaten people with arms in their hands, and the loudest shouters of liberty are the first people to beg. They beg in a barefaced shameless manner, and, once that they've got their morsel, they are ready to deny God and their own conscience." *V.* Settembrini, I, 324, giving his letter of resignation. As to the general anarchy *v.* also Paladino, *Il Quindici*, p. 100 *et seq.*, with original reports. *V.* also Massari, p. 115, where he relates that Count Pietro Ferretti on his way to a Cabinet meeting was shut into his room by the mass of job claimers, who said that he was now their servant, and no longer the servant of the King.

idiocies, and with those documents in hand, he said to me: Introduce me to Prince Pignatelli, propose me to the Minister of Public Education and I'll soon show you how I'll put things right.

Meanwhile, however, some of the volunteers had actually started for the war. These were the men who were really in earnest about liberating the Lombards, and in most cases perhaps also about uniting Italy. They must have numbered about 3000 souls—and all honour to them! But it was not many in a population of 6,000,000. Thus on March 30th a batch of 184, of whom about 40 were Lombards, embarked for Genoa, and reached Milan on April 6th amid enthusiastic rejoicing. A week later another 250 started, but it was on April 5th and the following days that the best of all the Neapolitan contingents went off; the 10th Regiment of the Line volunteered and was allowed to go. On that day the 1st Battalion (Colonel Rodriguez) sailed for Leghorn to join the 7000 Tuscan volunteers, and it was followed on April 13th by the 2nd Battalion (Major Vigna). They only numbered 900[29] men in all, and only eight captains out of twelve, but still the 10th Neapolitan Regiment was a fine corps composed of hardy men from the Abruzzi, and—as far as they had any chance—they did well during the campaign. Corsi, who saw them, says that they were "two battalions of six companies each, very fine troops and well trained to arms. Their commander was an excellent soldier and a thorough gentleman; the soldiers were talkative, noisy, and not very strictly disciplined—perhaps owing to the recent civil unrest in their kingdom and to their long march." But evidently these men were a credit to their state.

Meanwhile political fever was running so high that on April 7th the now constitutional King was compelled to declare war against Austria, and the Liberals made him issue

[29] Fabris gives 900 in the text, but in a note he makes the battalions 660 and 600 strong respectively. *V.* Fabris, II, 69 *et seq.* Corsi, *Venticinque anni*, p. 86.

a proclamation[30] which was about twice as stirring as that of Charles Albert.

The congress which we were the first to propose, is now about to meet in Rome.... Already we have arranged an expedition by sea, and already a division is moving along the coast of the Adriatic to act in concert with the army of Central Italy. The fate of our common Fatherland will be decided on the fields of Lombardy, and it is the duty of every prince and people in the peninsula to hasten to take part in the struggle.... We intend (though restricted by other necessities which keep a large part of our army engaged) to co-operate with all our forces by land and sea, with our arsenals and with the treasure of the nation. Our brothers await us on the field of honour, and we shall not fail to be there where men will fight for the great cause of Italian nationality.

Peoples of the two Sicilies rally round your Prince....

There must have been many people who felt that they could rely on the King not to carry out these noble projects. However, now they had "done their share" for Italy, and the blame would rest on him. And no doubt they could feel that they had answered the call of Pius IX.[31]

It was suggested that the army should march in two divisions—16,000 men in the first, and 24,000 to follow; some to go by sea to Ancona. It was all under the command of the veteran Italian patriot, General Pepe.

But "it is a far cry to Lochawe!" Only about 14,000 of them ever reached the frontier of Lombardy, where they

[30] The Austrian *chargé d'affaires*, M. Raymond, wrote that the Russian and Prussian ambassadors had tried to dissuade the King from issuing this proclamation, but he told them that he had to swim with the current that was carrying him away (Vienna H.H.S.A. Naples, Despatch of April 9th, 1848).

[31] We are encouraged to make these remarks by the verdict of Signor Paladino on the situation. He blames the Neapolitan Cabinet for sending off a whole expeditionary corps without waiting for an answer from the other states of the League; without any definite plan of operations, without any arrangements as to subsequent compensations. Undoubtedly the Troya Cabinet wanted to give proof of Italian sentiment by sending off the troops, but, at the same time, it did not measure what means the state had at its disposal for the aims which it hoped to obtain (Paladino, p. 89).

were to receive further orders. No doubt, Pepe, like Durando, proposed to try and persuade his men to cross the River Po, but in the event he only succeeded in inducing about 2000 of them, a small body of heroes who did good service during the siege of Venice. Judged as a whole his effort was a fiasco.[32]

The regrettable fact about sending this illusory expedition was that it rather misled the other states, by arousing hopes for which there was no justification. With 40,000 Neapolitans marching against the Austrian communications or even 14,000 Charles Albert ought to have been certain of victory. It was he who had to pay the penalty.

The net military result of Charles Albert's policy, *Italia farà da sè*, of trusting to the Italian states for armed support, may be roughly expressed in the following figures:

Rome	17,000	men	
Tuscany	7,771	,,	
Modena	1,090	,,	
Parma	1,026	,,	
Naples	1,200	,,	(omitting those who
About	28,087	,,	went to Venice)

But out of all this number there were hardly any regular units except the Pope's Swiss (4000), the Neapolitans (1200) and perhaps four or five thousand men in the Roman and Tuscan contingents. We must add to these:

Lombard regulars (mere recruits)[33], about	20,000
Lombard volunteers (mere recruits), about	10,000
Venetian volunteers (mere recruits), about	10,000
The Piedmontese regular army: they brought into Lombardy about	60,000

[32] Pepe, pp. 123 and 169; Tivaroni, *Ital. Merid.* pp. 201, 216; Tivaroni, *Ital. Sett.* p. 548; Fabris, II, 80 *et seq.*; Masi, *Risorgimento*, II, 267–8.

[33] The above totals are those usually stated, but they are entirely misleading. The Lombard troops for instance always appear in these lists. But it seems very unfair to the Italian side to include them,

This gives a total of 128,000, but it is hard to suppose that of these there were ever more than about 80,000 men who were fully trained and reliable.

because they never had enough time or training to become of any use. As to the Neapolitan army: it has been suggested that when Pepe was suddenly taken ill Ferdinand seized the opportunity to prevent the troops going by sea to Venice. But Pepe himself gives the following account of the episode:

"Malheureusement, succombant aux fatigues de la vie agitée et sans repos que je menais, je fus pris d'une fièvre violente qui dura six jours. Le roi profita de cet incident pour s'opposer à l'embarquement des troupes, et, redoutant l'opinion publique, il fit réunir chez moi le conseil des ministres, et voulut qu'il fût présidé par mon frère Florestan. Il adjoignit à ce conseil le brigadier Carascosa et le major Cianciulli. Il serait trop long à dire tous les arguments qui furent produits contre l'expédition par mer. Bien que couché, je crois qu'en faisant peur de l'opinion, sinon en inspirant ma conviction, j'aurais pu faire triompher mon avis. Mais mon avis avait changé: en premier lieu, parce que le corps d'armée qui m'aurait suivi par terre n'aurait jamais traversé le Po sans moi, ainsi que le prouva la suite des événements; en second lieu, parce que le contre-amiral Cosa m'avait assuré que les sept bataillons embarqués auraient entravé le feu de l'artillerie des frégates, et qu'ainsi la division de la marine autrichienne aurait pu nous combattre avec un avantage presque certain. Il fut décidé en conséquence, que les troupes sous mon commandement suivraient la voie de terre...." (Pepe, *Histoire*, p. 78.)

Chapter IX

THE PAPAL DIFFICULTIES. CROSSING
THE FRONTIER

I

In Rome it was very difficult for Pius to render much assistance to Charles Albert. It was a curious situation: a ruler
who was a patriot but could not declare war; his ministers
pressing him for a declaration and carrying on the war without
it; the army under a group of Piedmontese officers who meant
to appropriate it; and the populace almost in revolution.

And the financial situation was even more peculiar, and
very ill-adapted for a war budget; but that is too lengthy a
question to be dealt with here.[1]

How many men was Rome going to send to help the
national cause?

On March 23rd Prince Aldobrandini had started recruiting.
It was a day of sunshine and blue sky, and that afternoon an
immense demonstration was held in the Colosseum whose
historic walls naturally inspired memories of the heroic days.
The principal speaker—a tall figure in the habit of a Barnabite
monk—was Father Gavazzi, whose harangue sounded like a
reminiscence of ancient Rome and of Peter the Hermit's
"God wills it". He preached a crusade against Austria. It
was eloquence of the French revolutionary type—melo-
dramatic. But it carried the people with it. Within the next
twenty-four hours, the recruiting list had to be temporarily
closed owing to the number of recruits crowding round the
booths.

There were other speakers, orators of the most different

[1] Spada, I, 158–72. For Monsignor Morichini's report on the
finances of the Papal State, I, 289; also Tivaroni, *Ital. Cent.*
p. 257.

types. Rosi, a shepherd-poet from the Campagna; the Generals Durando and Ferrari, and one or two of the extremist politicians; the young poet Masi,[2] private secretary to Prince Canino; Dr Sterbini,[3] the journalist; Ciceruacchio, the sturdy wine-carter—the last-named, though aged forty-seven, offered to go as a volunteer, but the crowd shouted out that he would be more useful in Rome; so in his stead he sent his young son Luigi Brunetti. It was in this way that Luigi learnt the methods of violence which, eight months later, led to his stabbing Pellegrino Rossi.

To avoid all unnecessary details we may say that from first to last the Papal State sent about 17,000 men to the war. When operations began they were in two columns, one over 7000 strong, mainly regulars under command of General Durando, the other about 9000 strong, nearly all Civici or volunteers, under General Ferrari.[4]

On March 23rd Durando was appointed to supreme command. Pius did not entirely approve of him,[5] but Durando had the support of the Circolo Romano, of his Piedmontese fellow-countrymen in Rome, and a promise from the Minister

[2] For the lives and characters of these politicians, v. *Italy in the Making*, II, 107 *et seq.*

[3] It is curious what bitter hatred the name of Sterbini seems to arouse among even his most moderate acquaintance. Minghetti, who knew him during this period, describes him as follows: "Sterbini—I have known few men more criminal in mind and spirit and more hideous in face. There was no infamy of which he was not accused, and later on he showed that he deserved these accusations as being one of the principal instigators of the murder of Pellegrino Rossi. He was not esteemed or loved, but only feared. Owing to his playing the demagogue, arousing all the worst passions of the Plebs and keeping in touch with all the worst criminals both in Italy and outside it, he was the type of what we call to-day the Maffia-politician."

[4] Tivaroni, *Ital. Cent.* p. 313; Farini, II, 52.

[5] *V.* Count Guido Pasolini's *Carteggio*, I, 15 and note.

of War. He was admittedly a sound officer who had seen plenty of service in the Spanish civil wars, probably the ablest leader available.

The second-in-command was Colonel Andrea Ferrari, by birth a Neapolitan. He was a republican; but a veteran of Napoleonic days with a fine war record; and he was one who possessed the advantage very rare among the Napoleonic veterans of having been only four years on the retired list.[6] Before starting he was promoted to the rank of General, but it is noticeable that, in spite of protests, Durando kept all the regulars for himself and left the volunteers to Ferrari.

The clerical historians say that, before starting, the volunteers sent up a deputation with their colours to Pius to be blessed; and that, before blessing them, he told them formally that they were not to cross the frontier; they were marching to guard the Papal State.

And so the columns started—Durando's on March 24th and Ferrari's on the 25th and 26th. Their march-out was a scene of enthusiasm. In their ranks were young men of every type: dukes, nobles, citizens rich and poor, all of whom were united in singing the verses addressed to Rome by Sterbini:

> Eri seduta; levati
> Madre di tanti eroi!

They were to assemble at Bologna, and they accomplished the 300 miles in about three weeks; but unfortunately such a hurried mobilisation could not fail to arouse difficulties and dissensions. Ferrari's men soon discovered that they were short of almost every article of kit; those who were Civici had had some training, but among the last-joined volunteers there were too many young men who combined complete lack of discipline with noisy republicanism. This naturally

---

[6] Decorated at Montmirail in 1814; afterwards Colonel of the French Foreign Legion; later, served in Spain and was wounded. During the latter part of this year he served in Venice, and, in 1849, he died during Garibaldi's defence of Rome.

irritated the loyal soldiers, and before long there was no love lost between Durando's regulars and the comparatively untrained column of Ferrari. Their feeling was very plainly expressed in a letter of Massimo d' Azeglio written at a moment when he feared that Durando might be superseded. After referring to himself and his friends as "Durandisti", supporters of Durando, he adds:

in that case we should go to our own (Piedmontese) camps and it would be rather pleasant to be with an army where things are regular. To fight in company with this Babilonia (*sic*) and then find oneself in any sort of mess after risking one's skin and spending money to get things going! You cannot imagine what idiots some of the commanding-officers are....[7]

This division of the small Papal force into two camps was, no doubt, difficult to avoid; but it was a very serious misfortune.

The next month leads us straight to the crisis in Pius' life and to what in reality is a very strange working out of the forces round him.

During those weeks there are three main directing centres around which the story develops itself: firstly Durando on his march towards the River Po; secondly Pius' ministers in Rome; and thirdly Pius himself. It is almost impossible to trace the true intentions of each actor on the scene, but the facts themselves will show how Pius was pushed further and further into the dilemma from which he sought to escape.

Firstly, as to Durando: his orders were to march to the frontier, form a camp, defend himself if attacked, and await further orders.[8] But there is no doubt that when he and d' Azeglio and Casanova once found themselves clear away

[7] Minghetti, *Ricordi*, I, 420.
[8] Minghetti, *Ricordi*, I, 362; Farini, II, 52; Ovidi, p. 17; Fabris, II, 108 *et seq.*

from Rome at the head of 7000 regulars, followed by Ferrari with 9000 volunteers, then the three Piedmontese officers had every intention—orders or no orders—of crossing the frontier and leading the Papal army to help their King.[9] And it would have seemed rather absurd for them to remain on the near side of the river where they would never have been attacked, while on the opposite bank the insurgent Venetians were sending out stories of ravaging and torture accompanied by desperate appeals for help.

Secondly, the mental attitude of the ministers is not very clear to us at first, but there seems to be very little doubt that in a general way they sympathised with Durando. It looks as though they had let him march, trusting to their being able to persuade Pius to declare war during the weeks that must elapse before the army could reach the frontier. It is certain, at all events, that about a month later they were making every effort to get a declaration of war from Pius. Whether they had any previous understanding on this subject with Durando we do not know. But it seems probable. We know that in a private letter of April 12th[10] d' Azeglio re-marked to Minghetti that they two and Durando and Aldo-brandini were all of one way of thinking. And it is noticeable that only five days after Durando's departure, on March 28th, Prince Aldobrandini as Minister of War wrote to him to place himself in touch with Charles Albert's H.Q. and to operate in concert with it.[11]

Thirdly we come to Pius himself. Undoubtedly at the

[9] This we know from a letter of d' Azeglio dated April 10th in which he says that they always intended to do so (v. p. 166). Also from a report dated April 12th of Martini, Florentine minister at Turin, in which he says that the Piedmontese war office had already received a letter from Durando to say that he would not be able to cross the Po before April 19th; it follows that he must have decided to do so early in April, if not before (v. Florence Arch. Esteri, Torino, Filza 2485). Martini had thought that Durando would cross on April 12th (ibid. Busta 2485 : Carteggio al Campo, April 10th).

[10] Minghetti, Ricordi, I, 420.

[11] Farini, II, 53; Minghetti, I, 362; Pasolini, I, 118.

start he did not mean to take the responsibility of any aggression; and indeed it seemed at first quite possible that none would be necessary. He told his young men that they were not to cross the frontier. But, before a month was gone, we may suppose that if anyone could have devised a scheme whereby his troops could take part in the campaign without his being compelled, as Pope, actually to declare war, he would probably have adopted it.[12] Perhaps the clearest indication of his views at first is to be obtained from the reports of Monsignor Buoninsegni, the secret envoy sent by Tuscany to stay in Rome during this period. Monsignor Buoninsegni, being an ecclesiastic, was apparently on intimate terms with Cardinal Antonelli and others at the Papal court.

On March 28th Antonelli told Buoninsegni that, according to instructions from Turin, all the pontifical forces, about 30,000 strong, were to remain lined along their frontier to keep out the Austrians if they came southwards.

In his despatch[13] of April 1st, Buoninsegni says that he suggested, apparently to Antonelli, that sooner or later the troops would insist upon crossing the frontiers in spite of orders. It was replied that in that case the pontifical government would protest that it had merely intended to act on the defensive and not to invade the dominions of others; and

[12] Balleydier and other clerical writers say that Pius refused to bless the banners of the volunteers and addressed their deputation in the following terms: "You know that you are starting merely to go and protect the frontiers of our state. Be careful not to cross them, because in so doing, not only would you transgress my orders, but you would assume on the part of the Pontifical troops the responsibility of aggression. Go then my sons, but only to the frontier, I repeat, not beyond the frontier. That is my will." *V.* Balleydier, I, 104; also Spada, II, 152.

This story is accepted by Tivaroni, *Ital. Cent.* II, 313. He thinks that as Pius had so often given in and accepted a *fait accompli* they supposed that in this case he would do so again. We may see, however, that even if Pius acquiesced in their crossing the frontier it was impossible that he should allow Durando's order of April 5th to pass unnoticed.

[13] *V.* Bianchi, v, 467.

that the troops had violated orders when they crossed the pontifical frontier; but that they could not then be restrained nor prevented from joining the others.

Most probably this was the view prevailing in Pius' mind; that as Pope he could not declare war, but that he could not prevent his young men from going to fight for Italian unity—which was certainly true. It was a precarious situation. Indeed Monsignor Corboli Bussi, one of Pius' most trusted advisers, practically states this view in a narrative of this whole period[14] written afterwards to a friend. He says that the Austrians could not complain of such treatment, because they themselves followed a similar course on previous occasions; and certainly we know that tactics of this type have been pursued from time to time by every government all over the world. But Pius' position was becoming more and more irregular, for his men were marching under the Papal colours, and were being partly equipped and supplied by the pontifical government; so that when he refused to declare war but could not prevent its being waged by his own army with the help of his own government, he had virtually lost control of the temporal authority. His government was now constitutional, and it was forcing his hand.

He was hoping of course for the completion of the League, and did not declare his final decision by the Allocution of April 29th, until he perceived that the Piedmontese would not agree to definite terms. And by that time, other influences, such as the fear of a religious schism in Germany, had been brought to bear on him.[15]

But his patriotism, the genuineness of his desire to help in the national struggle for freedom, is proved—apart from his previous life—by the fact that at this critical moment he placed his whole army under Piedmontese officers and at the orders of the Piedmontese king.

Perhaps the shortest way of dealing with this story of how the Papal State was brought into the war is simply to give a

---

[14] *Biblioteca*, III, 295.   [15] *Biblioteca*, III, 294.

list of the chief communications from the day when the Papal troops left Rome.

On March 27th, after hearing that Charles Albert had entered Lombardy, Cardinal Antonelli wrote to Cardinal Amat, Delegate at Bologna, that the Papal troops were to mass at the frontier, according to Charles Albert's desire; and asked him to inform General Durando of this order.

On March 28th there came an order which takes matters a step further.[16] On that day, Aldobrandini, as Minister of War, wrote to Durando ordering him to place himself at once in communication with Charles Albert's H.Q. and to act in concert with it. For this purpose Durando sent D'Azeglio to the Piedmontese camp.

At this point, therefore, we find that Pius' position is being rendered even more equivocal. As Pope he is acting only on the defensive; but as temporal sovereign his war minister has ordered his army to operate in concert with Charles Albert who is attacking the Austrians.

On March 30th Pius issued an Atto in which he spoke of "this wind which is rending the cedars and the oaks".[17] It reveals a troubled mind.

On April 10th he despatched Monsignor Corboli Bussi to the camp of Charles Albert[18] to try and complete the League of Italian states.

Meanwhile Durando's position was also becoming critical. His orders were to march as far as the frontier, and then await further orders. Every day, therefore, was bringing the crisis closer; he was approaching the River Po and had every intention of crossing it;[19] indeed some writers say that in any case he could hardly have prevented some of his young volunteers from going over to help their Italian brothers.[20]

[16] Farini, II, 53.
[17] V. chap. x. It was not commented on or mentioned in the Contemporaneo. Spada gives it; vol. II, p. 156.
[18] V. Farini, II, 53; London Corr. II, 355, Abercromby to Palmerston.
[19] V. pp. 166–7.   [20] Pasolini, I, 119.

Yet at the same time there was a large section of the troops, including some of the regular officers, who did not mean to cross the frontier unless after a formal declaration of war, because they did not wish to be considered bandits by the Austrians. According to the laws of war all those captured could be shot, and, although such fears might be groundless, it was felt that a formal declaration of hostilities was very necessary.

The chances of the campaign depended largely on what Pius would do; he was in a dilemma; if he tried to halt the army, there would be a revolution in Rome; but on the other hand, if he proclaimed war there would probably be a revolution among his spiritual subjects—a schism. So far, however, he had only followed more or less the same course as the rulers of Tuscany and Naples.

II

In temporal affairs, both military and civil, Pius was regarded as being always anxious to acquiesce in his subjects' wishes and to accept a *fait accompli*—as a man easy to push. It was not realised that there was another side to the question, one on which his mind was extremely determined, namely his maintaining complete control of the spiritual weapons of the Papacy—one might put it that, within the altar rails at least, he meant to be supreme. Although as a patriotic Italian he might acquiesce in his soldiers going to fight under Charles Albert, nevertheless as head of the international Church he did not mean to allow his purely spiritual and religious authority to be made use of as a weapon against the Austrians. This authority is entirely distinct from his ordinary influence. When a Pope declares war, he usually excommunicates his enemies; but it would have been profoundly unjust for the head of the Roman Catholic Church to condemn thousands of its most faithful subjects simply for obeying their officers' orders. And this consideration is all-important because there is no doubt that, during this period, the war party was aiming at capturing the spiritual weapon (quite apart from the military arm) for the purpose of the campaign. This aim is openly admitted by Farini, who was then a minister (*sostituto*), and he deplores it in the following words:

> In 1848 we were waging a war of independence and it was desired to have the help of excommunication for our arms; and so the matter went on and we fell into the same vice which is justly laid to the charge of the clericals, namely that they mix religion and politics; a counsel which, when sincere, is not wise, and when insincere is miserable: and in either case is harmful.... Besides which if our spirit could not be inflamed by the fire of patriotism and the noble and holy enterprise of freeing our native land from foreigners, it was vain to hope that hearts frozen by doubt would be susceptible to the fire of religious faith.

Thus Farini[21] tells us that they wanted excommunication. It would have been better to content themselves with things as they were. As matters stood, the moral influence of the Pope was a far greater military asset in 1848 than is generally realised;[22] his name was rather like that of a constitutional king—all parties could unite around him. Take, for instance, the peasants, the hardiest class for war. In many districts they were an uncertain quantity; so much so that Ficquelmont, newly returned to Vienna, told Ponsonby that Austria could easily raise them against the Italian nationalist party and procure its destruction.[23] Yet after the first fortnight of the war, Mr Campbell, Vice-Consul at Milan, wrote to Lord Palmerston: "A religious feeling predominates throughout, particularly among the lower classes who consider the war against the Austrians as holy, it being sanctioned by their beloved Pius IX."[24] And the Florentine envoy, Commendatore

---

[21] Farini, II, 58.
[22] "He alone can save the only Italian unity that is possible" (Dall' Ongaro to Minghetti, March 29th). *V.* Massimo d' Azeglio's letter of April 19th; both these letters are in Minghetti's *Ricordi*, I.
[23] *London Corr.* II, 290, Ponsonby to Palmerston, April 2nd.
[24] *Ibid.* p. 318, April 5th.

Martini, tells us, when speaking of the provinces in rebellion, that "the clergy of Lombardy, of Venetia and of the Italian Tyrol is entirely compromised on the faith of Pius IX".[25] Thus, as the moral influence of the Pope was producing such valuable results, surely the nationalists should have taken every imaginable care not to make the situation impossible for him.

The military difficulties, such as being considered bandits, were by no means insuperable: as was very shortly discovered. The Papal troops could serve as part of the Piedmontese or Venetian armies.

On March 27th, when Durando was not very far distant from Rome, he had issued an order of the day which made some stir; it was designed to inflame the ardour of his troops; and in this first official utterance there was nothing of which Pius could disapprove. It was a fairly spirited piece of writing said to be the composition of Massimo d' Azeglio, rather too "high-falutin'" for modern taste, but, on the whole, legitimate in form. Its ending was as follows:

> Soldiers and Irregulars! the whole world is watching you and saying, "Let us see the Italian troops at work." The glorious spirits of the men of old who fought at Legnano now smile upon you from above; the great Pius bestows upon you the blessing of the Almighty; Italy places her trust in your valour and hopes that each one of you henceforth will fulfil his duty as an Italian citizen and a soldier.
> Long live Pius IX.
> Long live the Independence of Italy.[26]

In normal times such an order from the G.O.C. would excite surprise; but in April 1848 everyone was talking in this strain, and it was not considered beyond the average. On the contrary it was found to be too mild to sway his volunteers, and Durando seems to have thought that he had better go a step further and issue a stronger appeal which would certainly

[25] Florence Arch. Esteri, Busta 2485, May 9th.
[26] This document is given in full by Ravioli, *La Campagna nel Veneto del 1848*, p. 209.

carry them with him. By this time Massimo d' Azeglio had
returned from his visit to Charles Albert, and it was certainly
he[27] who wrote this second proclamation published on April
5th. The recklessness of the wording may have been due to
Massimo's visit to the Piedmontese camp; but, whatever the
thought behind it, the production itself was a profound
mistake. It began as follows:

Order of the day to the Corps of Operations.

Soldiers!

The noble land of Lombardy, which was once the glorious
theatre of a war of independence when Pope Alexander III
blessed the oath of Pontida, is now again trodden by the feet of
brave men and with them we will share the dangers and victories
to come. For they and we are blessed by the right hand of a great
Pontiff just as were our ancestors of the days gone by. He is a
Saint. He is just. He is kindly above all men, and He has recognised that against those who trample upon every right and upon
every law both human and Divine, the *ultima ratio*, the supreme
argument of arms, is the only one that is righteous and possible.

His saint-like heart could not but be saddened at the thought
of the evils that come with war, and could not forget that all those
who meet on the field of battle, whatever their banner, are equally
his sons; he wished to allow them time for repentance and on his
august lips there remained suspended the words which were to
make those lips the instruments of divine vengeance.

But the moment arrived when kindness would have become
mere blameworthy connivance at iniquity....

The document then goes on to describe how Pius "had
seen Radetzky wage war on the Cross of Christ and beat
down the gates of the sanctuary", and "has blessed your
swords which...are to exterminate the enemies of God and
of Italy....Such a war", it adds, "is not merely national, but
highly Christian." The last paragraph ran as follows:

Soldiers! It is only right and I have made it an order that while
marching to this war we should all be adorned with the cross of
Christ. All those who belong to the Corps of Operations will wear

[27] Minghetti, I, 364.

it on their breasts, in form similar to that which they will see on mine. With it and in it we shall be conquerors—as were our Fathers. Let our war-cry be

God wills it![28]

Massimo had an eloquent pen, and his eloquence was the outcome of genuine patriotism. But here it ran away with him. This effusion was avowedly speaking in the name of Pius as spiritual Head of the Church; the first part of the order, referring to "the words which were to make his lips the instrument of Divine vengeance", foreshadowed excommunication, and the last clauses turned the war into a Christian crusade against Radetzky. In fact, Durando, acting from patriotic motives undoubtedly, had usurped the Pope's spiritual authority almost as completely as Jacob stole his father's blessing. This was a very poor return for all Pius' generosity. Expressed in plain bald terms, the situation between Pius and Durando was that the former, as Pope, could not create a European scandal by declaring war, but that as a good patriot he would say as little as possible if Durando led some of his troops across the frontier. But now, by this order, Durando had proclaimed Pius to the whole world as the initiator and inspirer of a crusade, "the invader of the noble land of Lombardy", the very character which should have been avoided as far as possible, if he wished to retain the support of the Great Powers as guarantors of the Treaty of 1815; his army was still officially acting on the defensive.[29]

[28] We have translated this from Ravioli, p. 209, but it is to be found also in Farini, II, 55.

[29] The ministers were quite of this opinion; Farini's view we have already quoted, and Minghetti in his *Memoirs* speaks of the incident as follows: "When this proclamation reached Rome, Pius IX became furious; and really he may be forgiven for being so, for even if the troops were to cross the river Po, it was not necessary to put the Pope forward as the principal author of the war, by declaring it not merely national but Christian, and giving it the whole semblance and character of a crusade." Minghetti, *Ricordi*, II, 366.

Pius was extremely angry. Minghetti tells us that:[30]

> If the position of the ministry had been difficult at first, the reader can imagine what it was like when the Pope began to complain loudly (*gridare*) that Durando wished to act as Pontiff. This case drew forth the very breath of his Catholic soul; he refused to listen to any consideration of expediency and threatened to raise his protest against this disgrace. It was only with great difficulty that we succeeded in appeasing him by inserting the following article in the *Gazzetta Ufficiale* for the 10th:
>
> An order of the day addressed at Bologna to the soldiers and dated April 5th expresses ideas and sentiments as if they were dictated from the mouth of His Holiness; the Pope when He desires to declare His sentiments speaks *ex se* and never through the mouth of any subaltern.

Even this short statement aroused unfavourable comment; but surely it was right. Indeed one feels inclined at this point to blame Pius for not having broken forth and explained his whole situation publicly, in spite of his ministers. It would have been a great blow to the Italian cause but perhaps not quite so great as that which he afterwards felt himself compelled to strike; however, he was still hoping, says Farini, that Piedmont might agree to the League and help him out of his difficulty.

The following was Massimo d' Azeglio's own rather flippant account of the episode in a letter to Minghetti:

> I know that half of all this screed would have been enough for you and that you see these things as I do. However here's another and a better story. Antonelli has written to Ciacchi that no one is

---

[30] *Ibid.* p. 367. Farini, II, 57, gives an equally forcible account of Pius' great anger at Durando's proclamation: "He complained that people were speaking of him and of religion in terms that would offend the tender consciences of Catholics. He complained, and said that as for himself, he could not keep silence; the Catholic world would be scandalised and perturbed by such words from a Papal general; but he [Pius] would address the Catholic world."

Minghetti and Farini were perhaps the ablest of his ministers and knew him well. They both lived to become ministers of United Italy.

to cross the Po even in his dreams. If he had not said this we should have had patience with things. We are dealing with Rome and the priests. But he did say this, and set everyone calling out; and so I came out with the Order-of-the-day about the crosses! Now, my noble priests, now go and say that we are not to cross the Po! Good-bye old boy; remember me to everyone,

Yours affectionately
Massimo.

This meant of course that they had now got Pius' troops, including his magnificent Swiss Brigade, to fight in the service of Piedmont. Pius had disavowed their order to his army, and they had snapped their fingers at it; but they did not realise that there remained the danger of a schism, and that it might easily compel him to disavow their order to the whole of the Roman Catholic world.

From April 5th onwards there are only a few documents which throw new light upon this episode. Perhaps the most important and therefore the most instructive are some of the despatches of foreign ambassadors in Rome; for instance, there is the Florentine representative, Bargagli. Writing on April 11th he speaks of this episode as

the cause of disapproval which has been aroused against the conduct of the Sardinian government by the General Durando's imprudent proclamation which is to be seen in the *Felsineo*, wherein in the clearest tones he preaches a crusade against Austria and proclaims a religious war against her—contrary to the express instructions given to him by the Holy Father, who intended that action should be taken, but that they should leave it to Himself to justify their actions with such words as might be required by circumstances.[31]

The Dutch minister's report to his government is also interesting because, like that of Bargagli, it has never yet been quoted. He says that His Holiness had especially ordered General Durando

---

[31] Florence Arch. Esteri. Busta 2446. Bargagli, April 11th, 1848.

not to cross the frontiers and not to take up arms except in a case of legitimate defence, that is to say if the Austrians crossed the frontier for purposes of aggression.

This order-of-the-day, of which I enclose a translation with this despatch, is nothing but a very eloquent lie; and it will fully prove to Your Excellency how obedience to the formal orders of his Sovereign is understood by Master Durando, whom one may liken to a condottiere of the Middle Ages without doing him an injustice: who decides on his own account that his men are to march against the enemy, marked with the Cross of Christ; in fact transforming the war against the Austrians into a real crusade, and the subjects of His Apostolic Majesty into infidels....I doubt whether this likening them to the Turks will afford much pleasure in Germany: it might even cause serious trouble for the interests of religion....[32]

The remaining documents seem to show that, there being no formal declaration of war, everyone tried to avoid giving a definite order to Durando to cross the frontier; but that on April 18th Aldobrandini empowered him to do "anything necessary for the welfare and tranquillity of the Papal State",[33] which could manifestly include an entry into Lombardy, so that before starting he was well covered by the orders of his war office.

Finally on April 22nd he crossed the bridge and invaded Austrian Italy: but the matter was by no means at an end.

[32] Regio Istituto per la Storia del Risorgimento, I, 35. 20. 30 K. Ministre des Pays-Bas, 1848.
[33] Farini, II, 55.

Chapter X

PIUS IX. THE PARTING OF THE WAYS

Durando crossed the frontier on April 22nd. It was only seven days later that Pius issued his celebrated Allocution of April 29th, 1848, which is usually considered to have been the first serious setback in the war of liberation. In it he stated definitely that he did not intend to declare war, because as Pope he could not do so.

This came as a crushing blow to the millions of people throughout Italy who regarded him as the champion and justification of the war. It has sometimes been made accountable for all the failures of 1848.

The problem which historians since then have tried to solve is: Why did he think it necessary to issue the Allocution which took him out of the war; what was the decisive reason in his mind at the moment?

It is hard to say which feelings had finally welled uppermost in the soul of Pius during those thrilling weeks. Undoubtedly, he was being torn in two; at the news of the early Italian successes he must have felt in his blood the glorious, incomparable pride of any man whose fellowcountrymen are winning their first victories on the road to freedom.

On the other hand he seems to have been deeply impressed and awe-struck by the ruin all around him, and by feeling that it was attributed to the influence of his own Liberalism. There was not an Italian state, and indeed hardly a European nation, that had not been in revolution. And these uprisings were carried out in his name: *Viva Pio Nono* was the battle-cry. For a man of so sensitive a temperament the strain must have been almost beyond bearing.

In the opinion of Professor Masi it was this conscience-stricken[1] feeling which was predominating in Pius' mind. He says:

Picture to yourselves, therefore, all that must have been passing through the mind of Pius IX—the mind of the poor country curate—when from the heights of the Quirinal he contemplated the universal pandemonium whirling before his eyes. When he turned his thoughts inwards he must have said: "It is I, myself, who was the initiator of all this. All these peoples are hurling themselves against each other with my name upon their lips. Mine was the first spark which set it all ablaze."[2]

During these weeks before the Allocution it seems as though his naturally religious soul had sought relief and poured out itself in his Atti and Encyclicals. They speak with the tone of Hebrew fervour which, through the Bible, has become the most characteristic expression of Christianity. Thus on March 30th when the news of the debacle was arriving hourly, and all the thrones of Europe seemed to be falling in ruins, he published an Atto which reveals the conflict in his mind. It is like a signal of distress:

The events which the last two months have seen following and pursuing upon one another in such rapid succession—these events are not the work of man. Woe to him who in this wind which sways, which uproots, which scatters the cedars and the oaks, hears not the voice of the Lord! Woe to human pride if any should attribute these wonderful changes either to the wrongdoing or to the deservings of men, instead of worshipping the hidden designs of Providence in whose hand are all the ends of the earth. And We, to whom the word is granted to interpret the mute eloquence of the works of God, We cannot keep silence amid the desires, the fears, the hopes which are stirring the souls of Our children.

[1] Masi, *Nell' Ottocento*, p. 198. To find out "what Pius really thought" throughout this April has been considered a problem by historians, but this view of Masi can now be tested by some of Pius' own words, spoken in an interview with Bargagli. *V.* Appendix I.

[2] The weak point in this view—if we may say it about so great an historian—is that Pius was never conscience-stricken during this period. Those who came in contact with him were surprised at his not seeming more downcast. Was not this because he was acting in accordance with his conscience—for him a final court of appeal?

In this outburst there is a realisation of the greatness of the hour, and also, surely, a note of patriotic hope, but its main gist is directed against violence and excesses, and his appeal ends as follows:

May our prayers ascend into the presence of the Lord and bring down upon you that spirit of counsel, of power and of wisdom whose beginning is the fear of God. That your eyes may behold peace over all this land of Italy which We may not call our best-beloved, because of our universal solicitude for all the countries of the Catholic world, but which, nevertheless, has been willed by God to be closest to Us.[3]

This ending is obviously intended to remind his subjects that, however deeply in sympathy with them, he cannot, being Pope, regard Italy as anything more than the country "which God has willed to be closest to us".

At Rome, as the days wore on through the month of April, perhaps one of the most important months in the modern history of the Papacy, the situation developed into a contest as to who should gain the supreme influence in Pius' mind. On the one side were his ministers backed by the representative of Piedmont, who wanted him to declare war; on the other were the ecclesiastics who were supported by the ambassadors of Austria, Prussia and Russia, and wanted him to make some statement against the national war. Lastly, there was Tuscany, urging him daily to issue an Encyclical against the republican and revolutionary movements.

On April 5th there appeared Durando's proclamation followed by angry discussion, and correspondence lasting for ten days, or more.

On April 10th Monsignor Corboli Bussi departed from Rome for Charles Albert's camp, and this left Pius without one of his best friends.

On April 22nd Durando crossed the frontier. This step was doubtless expected by Pius but, nevertheless, he must

---

[3] This Atto is quoted in full by Spada, ii, 156, and various other writers.

have felt that now his army was in the hands of Piedmont, which refused to give him any guarantees.[4]

On April 25th he sadly told the Neapolitan plenipotentiaries that Piedmont would not join the League, so that there was no use in proceeding with it.

On this same date, April 25th, his ministers thought it advisable to present a joint remonstrance to Pius; for some time they had been very uneasy as to what he might do.

The ministers afterwards said that for days he had kept his own counsel, and was evidently thinking deeply over the situation; they could find out nothing. They tell us that the Allocution took them completely by surprise; afterwards they were blamed for it, so they washed their hands of it. But, speaking impartially, was the Allocution in reality a very surprising document, in view of all that had passed? Was it not a very natural defensive statement from the Papal, Roman Catholic point of view? And was there in reality much concealment about it?

Apparently the foreign ambassadors were not greatly surprised at it, and—of the Italians—certainly the Cavaliere Bargagli, the Tuscan minister, was not in the least astonished at it. He knew all about it beforehand.

In the old State Archives of Tuscany, in Florence, there exists a report from Bargagli, who was on very friendly terms with Pius. In this report he describes a long interview which he had on April 20th, actually nine days before the publication of the celebrated Allocution; in the course of conversation Pius told him that he intended to issue an expression of his views, and gave him all the main points which he intended to lay down. Bargagli repeats these points, and they are virtually identical with those in the Allocution published nine days later. Undoubtedly Pius had already got the Allocution planned out in his mind, and as to secrecy, it is true that at one moment he asked Bargagli not to repeat what he was saying, but in a general way he made no secret of it. It is

[4] *V.* Petre's despatch of April 24th, *Correspondence*, Pt II.

hard, therefore, to believe that the Roman ministers could find out nothing at all about it, and were as entirely ignorant as they afterwards asserted.[5]

On their side, it is fair to remember that this was to be an Allocution (spiritual address), not an Encyclical, so that it did not actually concern them.

Unfortunately at that moment Pius' only real friends could be of very little use to him; Monsignor Corboli Bussi was away at Charles Albert's camp. Count Pasolini seems to have taken the view that Pius certainly could and ought to declare war. Pellegrino Rossi also advised war, but on rather cynical grounds; when arguing on this theme, he used, says Farini, to express his views by the following figure of speech:

> The national sentiment and the enthusiasm for war are a sword, a weapon, a powerful force; either Pius IX will grasp it firmly in his hand, or the hostile factions will take it and turn it against him and against the Papacy.[6]

This was a shrewd opinion. He saw that if Pius refused to declare war, he would endanger the continuance of the Papal State. It was a terrible responsibility for its ruler.

Pius' disquietude dated undoubtedly from the day when he read Durando's war proclamation of April 5th; up to that point, in all temporal matters, he had been ready to make any possible concessions to his people, and the Piedmontese officers and Roman ministers evidently thought that they could sweep him with them, spiritual authority and all. But here they were entirely wrong; in spiritual matters he was unshakeable.[7]

[5] For the analysis of this document, v. Appendix I. We found the document in the Florence Archives; it seems astonishing that no one else has mentioned it. It is numbered Esteri, Busta 1446, April 19th, 1848.   [6] Farini, II, 85.
[7] "Though a kindly man and a benevolent prince, as a Pontiff Pius IX was strictly uncompromising. His was a soul not merely pious but mystic. He referred everything to God; he believed that he must guard jealously the temporal sovereignty of the Church because he regarded it as indispensable to the custody and apostolate of the faith." Farini, II, 59. Cardinal Wiseman was of similar opinion; v. The Greville Diary, II, 305 (1927 ed.).

And the following we believe was his supreme guiding motive. At this moment he was particularly troubled, almost conscience-stricken about the position of the Church. Those who were in the best position to inform him were telling him —which he knew to be true—that his name had become simply a revolutionary war-cry, that this had aroused the deepest discontent among the German and Austrian Catholics, that they even considered him to have deviated from the Christian faith, and to be the mover of the war against Germany. So deep was this sentiment among the German bishops—so said his informants—that the Church was threatened with a schism.[8]

From what one reads, the reports sent in to him on this subject may have been exaggerated at the time, but undoubtedly it was a real danger. Those who have lived through a period of war have learnt that however bitter may be the animosity at the start, it is nothing at all compared to the mutual hatred that arises before the end. If the German Catholics were speaking of a schism in April 1848, it is more than likely that by April 1849 they would have accomplished it and, in any case, would not for many years have forgotten their loathing of a Pope who had preached the slaughtering of their sons.

Amid all these fears there was always the feeling that Durando's proclamation had made him the aggressor.[9] At the time, he had been persuaded by his ministers to abstain

---

[8] Farini (ii, 82) tells us that both Monsignor Viale Prelà, the Nuncio in Vienna, and Monsignor Sacconi, the Nuncio at Munich, sent "sinister stories" to Rome, to cause apprehension of a schism.

[9] This point struck the Dutch minister. On April 18th he wrote to his government: "Je doute que cette assimilation aux Turcs plaise beaucoup en Allemagne, et elle pourrait bien même y amener, en dehors des intérêts politiques, des conséquences sérieuses pour les intérêts religieux; car les liens spirituels qui attachent cette vaste contrée au Saint-Siège ne sont pas aujourd'hui tellement forts que l'amour-propre national allemand, profondément blessé, ne puisse sans trop d'efforts les briser pour toujours." Rome Reg. Ist. Busta 1, 35. 20. 30 K., Ministre des Pays-Bas.

from anything like a public wrangle with his military commander, but now it was necessary to clear his position, and
therefore, five or six days before the date fixed, he let it
be known that he intended to make a statement at the next
Consistory.[10]

It was this news which brought the anxiety of his ministers
to its culminating point, because they felt that everything—
the war, Pius' future, their own and that of the Church—
might depend on what he should say during the next few
days. At this crisis, they decided to hand in a remonstrance to
Pius, and it was drawn up at once and unanimously signed
by them under the presidency of Cardinal Antonelli.

It was dated April 25th and, briefly,[11] its main gist was
contained in the view that there were only three possible
alternative ways of dealing with the existing situation.

(1) Your Holiness can agree that your subjects should go to
war.

(2) Your Holiness can declare absolutely that your subjects
shall not go to war.

(3) Or finally, Your Holiness can declare that you desire peace,
but cannot prevent the war being made.

They then proceeded to argue in favour of the first
alternative on the grounds that war was undoubtedly an evil,
yet in this case, it was the least of the evils; that without it,
there could be no Italian nationality, and, without that, no
permanent peace.

[10] Monsignor Corboli Bussi knew Pius' mind perhaps better than
anyone; and he says: "General Durando, on his arrival in Bologna,
not only declared war in the name of His Holiness, but declared a
holy war, a religious war, a crusade.... In Tuscany and elsewhere all
the newspapers were filled with statements that this was a war of
religion; and the self-same thing was cried aloud in Rome in the
ears of the Pope. On the other hand, the opposition were representing to the Pope the scandalousness of such an abuse of religion,
and the very great danger that the Germans would not only embark
on the war with great bitterness, but might also start a schism."
Biblioteca, III, 294.
[11] Farini, II, 86.

Of the second, they said that it would very seriously endanger the Temporal Power, by running counter to the popular enthusiasm.

Of the third, they said that it would be practically an admission that the war was being made in an anarchical way contrary to the wishes of the supreme power. This would annul the moral authority of the government. The Italian princes and people would "feel their zeal cooled" in the cause of independence. One portion of the volunteers would come home, and the remainder would remain in camp, uncertain as to what they ought to do. Being no longer under the orders of their government they would, if made prisoners, be liable to be shot as brigands or assassins, even though carrying the Papal banner and wearing the Papal badges and Cross.[12]

Pius must have realised that now he had come to the parting of the ways, the point where his two duties—firstly as Pope and secondly as an Italian—must necessarily diverge, and one or other of them be made a sacrifice. It is said that during these last four days he spent hours in prayer.

At this time he was evidently reviewing his whole work during the previous two years. Unquestionably it had been good for his people, but had it been equally good for the Papacy? There lay the doubt which troubled him. And his Allocution seems to show that he decided to give a full account of his stewardship to all the Catholics of the world; at any risk the unity of the Church must be secured.

[12] Speaking of Durando's proclamation and the consequent fear of schism in Germany, Monsignor Corboli Bussi says: "It may be that the danger was represented as greater than was actually the case, but there is certainly no absurdity in thinking that the Germans, on seeing the Crusade preached against them in the name of the Pope, just as if they were Saracens, Turks or Albigenses, should regard the Pope as an anti-Pope.

"Being thus assailed in the most intimate sanctuary of his conscience, the Pope thought it his duty to make a final declaration to the world that this was not a holy war, because no war, however just, is holy, unless it be in defence of Christianity." *Biblioteca*, III, 294.

Chapter XI

THE ALLOCUTION, APRIL 29TH

I

On April 29th, 1848, Pius addressed his famous Allocution of
that date to the cardinals in Consistory.

The Allocution is a defence of his policy from first to
last, and is addressed to the Church all over the world. We
might perhaps divide it into three main themes.

His first theme is addressed chiefly to foreign Catholics.

It begins by inveighing against "some men who had had the
boldness to say that the Holy See has deviated from the most
sacred order of our Predecessors, and (horrible to relate) even
from the doctrine of the Church. And to-day there are some
who speak of Us as though We had been the principal authors
of the revolutionary commotions, which have occurred
recently, not only in other parts of Europe, but also in
Italy."[1]

It then recites that, in the Austrian parts of Germany,
stories had been spread among the people that the Roman
Pontiff had sent out secret agents, and by the use of this and
other arts had incited the Italian peoples to initiate new
changes in their public affairs; and that the enemies of the
Catholic religion had seized this opportunity to inflame the

---

[1] There were very definite rumours of the probability of a schism.
Lützow, who says that he was quite ignorant of the contents of the
encyclical beforehand, and had had no influence on the writing of
it, attributes the Pope's resolution to "letters addressed to the Pope
by both Italian and German bishops". Vienna Arch., Rap. Rome,
1848, No. 38 A. Cf. also Pareto, who, writing to his government on
April 17th, speaks of papers arriving in Rome which tell of the anger
in Germany, and even speak of a separation from the Church.
Turin Arch., Lettere Ministri, Roma, 1848.

minds of the Germans with a longing for revenge, and a desire to separate from the Holy See.[2]

And because these enemies can find no proof of what they allege, therefore they cast suspicion on Our reforms as being the cause of all the revolutionary unrest.

"Therefore", he continues, "We propose to-day to explain clearly and openly in your Consistory the cause of all these things, from the start."

He then deals with the whole history of the reform movement from its origin. He reminds them that even in the days of Pius VII, the Great Powers of Europe had recommended the Papal government to adopt methods of administration more in accordance with the wishes of the laity; that later, in 1831, the Five Great Powers had jointly presented to the Pope the celebrated Memorandum, calling on him to install a Consulta (consultative assembly) in Rome, and to allow more powers to the municipalities,[3] to set up provincial councils all over the state, and to admit the laity to public appointments. These they regarded as *vital* principles of government.

These reforms had been carried out to some extent by Gregory XVI, but only in part.

Then, on being elected Pope, he, Pius, had carried on the work amid the general and enthusiastic approval of his own subjects and of the peoples around. And all his measures during that period had been in perfect agreement with the desires of the European powers.

But, apart from the policy of reform, he wishes to defend his general attitude towards the revolution; therefore he reminds them that, on October 4th, 1847, only three months before the outbreak, he had delivered an Allocution urging kindliness on the part of the rulers, and faith and obedience on the part of the people: mutual concord, tranquillity and

[2] We have followed Farini's translation (II, 92) rather than that of Spada (II, 248); and have not translated from the original Latin.
[3] V. *Italy in the Making*, I, 103.

love. Thus no man could ascribe to the work of the Holy See the tumultuous events that had since taken place. Up to that point it had only carried out such measures as appeared to be for the good of its people, "not only in its own opinion, but in that of the princes above-named".

So far Pius was simply defending himself against the accusation of being the originator of a revolution, and his defence consisted in a claim that his reforms up to the end of 1847 were nothing more than the Memorandum of 1831 put into action. And, as against the Five Great Powers, this claim was certainly good. Up to the establishment of the Consulta he might be said to have been carrying out, though generously, the principle of the Memorandum of 1831. But it may be noticed that neither the new constitution nor the other measures passed in 1848 entered into the argument, because they had not been passed until the revolutions had begun elsewhere, and, in any case, they had been more or less forced on him from outside.

Up to this point in the Allocution, he had been mainly addressing himself to the German people, and to German Austria especially; now, however, he puts in a passage intended to satisfy his Italian subjects, but one which entirely failed to do so.

This might be termed his second theme. He gives his definite ruling as regards the war, and it is this decision which ruined him. The position which he takes up is, that he cannot prevent his people marching off to fight for Italy—just as has been permitted to the men in all the other Italian states—but that, as Pope, he does not intend to declare war, because, "We, though unworthy, represent on earth Him who is the author of peace and the lover of concord, and, according to the order of Our supreme Apostolate, We seek after and embrace all races, peoples and nations, with an equal devotion of paternal love".

Finally, we come to what may be considered his last main theme. He ends by strongly and publicly repudiating any knowledge or share in the scheme whereby Italy was to be formed into a single republic under his presidency. These suggestions, he says, are the cunning designs which certain people have spread in the newspapers and elsewhere, and he urges, most earnestly, all the peoples of Italy to guard themselves carefully against such astute counsels, and to remain loyal to their own sovereigns.[4]

This strong statement must have aroused the resentment of the fusionist and republican sections.

The celebrated Allocution of April 29th sounds harmless enough to the modern student; it strikes us as an innocent and—as far as it concerns politics—blundering production, designed rather to clear the conscience of Pius than to meet the difficulties of the time. That he should define his position with regard to the war was inevitable—everyone was calling upon him to publish a statement—but on the political side he might have avoided offering so many openings to his enemies.

In his first theme, for instance, when defending reform he made no mention of the newly won constitution, and thereby enabled his enemies to say that he did not intend to put it into practice; for as yet it existed only on paper. Such an idea had evidently never occurred to him. In his second theme he refused to declare war, and forgot to make any

---

[4] "Once again We declare, the Roman Pontiff directs all his thoughts, his cares and his study to the end that the Kingdom of Christ, which is the Church, shall every day increase, but not through enlarging the boundaries of the civil principality, which the Divine Providence has vouchsafed to the Holy See, for its dignity, and to preserve the free exercise of the supreme apostolate. In great error, therefore, do they wrap themselves, when they think that Our mind can be tempted by the illusive greatness of a wider temporal dominion, to throw Ourselves into the tumult of arms. Rather would it be a happiness to Our paternal heart, if, by Our work, by Our care, and by Our thought, it were granted to Us to make any contribution towards extinguishing the causes of discord, towards conciliating the minds of those who are fighting against each other, and towards restoring peace between them."

provision for preventing his volunteers from being shot as bandits if they were taken prisoner. In his third theme he denounced the republican movement; which was honourable on his part, but no doubt added to the number of his enemies. In this anti-extremist protest, however, we should add that he was only acceding to daily entreaties from both Tuscan and Piedmontese patriots, who regarded the republicans as being the worst enemies of the Italian cause, in fact, as men prone at any moment to wreck the campaign by their factious intrigues.

II

Within twenty-four hours we come to the first act of rebellion against Pius since his accession. For nearly two years he had led the people of Italy in the pathway of Liberalism and nationality, but thenceforward it was no longer possible for him to be their leader.

On the evening of April 29th the gist of the Allocution was gradually becoming known throughout Rome, but at first it did not arouse great resentment.[5] The ministry had resigned, but this fact was not given out until the next morning, and the people had not made up their minds as to what the Allocution really meant.

On April 30th, however, they were up early, and with growing knowledge their resentment soon began to increase. The first point which aroused them was the feeling that their sons who had volunteered to fight for Italy were now liable to be shot by the Austrians as brigands if they were made prisoners; and this fear—very genuine in itself—was, according to Farini, skilfully played upon by the agitators, who

---

[5] This is definitely stated by some of the most reliable people in Rome at the time, as for instance Spada (Papal) and Farini (Moderate). Gabussi (Republican) gives one to understand that the people began to rage at once, but I do not think he was in Rome then. Bargagli writing on the 30th speaks of the growing public indignation. Florence Arch. Esteri, Busta 2446, No. 141.

spread a story that a certain young artist, well known and popular in Rome, had already been captured by the Croats, and hung on a tree in his Civic Guard uniform, with the motto pinned to his breast: *This is how we treat the soldiers of Pius IX.* This fear which spread amongst the fathers and mothers of the volunteers, says Spada, who in this respect would be very unlikely to exaggerate, was the most terrible episode of all, because it was genuine.

The weeping and lamentation that arose from maternal sorrow was mingled with the desperate cries and imprecations of the embittered. There were even some, who, in order to increase the bitterness of the sorrow, and to vent their hatred of the Pontiff, went about insinuating that it was an act of treachery on his part, almost asserting that he had deliberately sent their boys to the slaughter in order to rid himself of those whose sentiments were too hot, or whose spirits were too turbulent....Many of the relatives, and even the mothers themselves in the ebullition of grief and anger, and in their passionate love for their sons, hurled furious curses at the sovereign, the pontiff, the Church, and at religion itself.

Here it may be well to remark that this difficulty was very soon overcome. On May 13th, Charles Albert agreed to take the Papal troops under his orders. This ended any question of their being considered bandits.[6] In this connection, let us remember that, on the day of the Allocution, the people were still quivering with excitement over their miraculous chance of driving out the Austrians; at that moment they were full of great hope and triumph. Charles Albert had crossed the frontier, and driven the enemy before him; he had closed his war proclamation with the words: "Let the angelic spirit of Pius descend upon you, and Italy is made"; the Romans were daily expecting to hear that their own men had been in action. Hitherto all had gone well, and this was the first disaster. Pius, the moral condottiere of Italy, had refused to declare war, and, many of them believed, had condemned the

[6] Farini, II, 139.

war; and perhaps the great chance of winning freedom was about to be lost after all.

Gabussi, though himself a republican, describes the people's anger in the following words:

At first it seemed as if the Romans could not believe their own eyes, so impossible did it appear to them that the Pope had suddenly changed; and an act that thus destroyed in one moment the hope of their whole life, seemed to be a dream, a piece of witchcraft, a spell, an impossibility. But when they were compelled to realise only too clearly, that these words were not merely a phantasm, but a real and positive fact, then their wonder and stupefaction were succeeded by excitement, by anger, by fury, such as one cannot describe in words. The squares and streets were packed with crowds, which gathered together in groups to discuss the phrases of the Allocution, and interpret them. Everyone had his own opinion of it; one man deplored it, another cursed it, there were some who tried to make the meaning of the words as little hateful as possible, but without much success. Some there were who exclaimed that "we must have done with the Pope once and for all". Some accused the cardinals and the prelates, some the ministers, as if they could have prevented the act of the Pontiff; everywhere there was agitation, confusion, and unrestrainable indignation.[7]

All this was partly due to the fact that Pius' rather defensive justification to the Great Powers was taken by the agitators as an attempt to evade his promises. They raged, for instance—some no doubt in good faith and others not so —over his not having mentioned the Constitution.

" Was he betraying us, when he granted it, or had he thoughts of taking it back when the right moment should arrive? And the war," shouted a good many people, "the war so lately allowed and inaugurated in his name, was it merely an outrageous deception for the purpose of urging on our brothers to face an enemy who will deny them the rights of belligerents, and will shoot them like brigands if they're taken prisoner?[8] And the league of princes?

[7] Gabussi, II, 233.
[8] Gabussi, II, 236. Pius regularised their position as soon as possible by placing them under the orders of Charles Albert. As a matter of fact the Austrians treated their prisoners well.

And our independence? Are they merely dreams, clouds, illusions, and no more? Yes indeed. We must make an end of it. The Papacy is unchangeable, it is the chief enemy of Italy, and Rome must not suffer it any longer."

In reality the Pope's view was more or less that of every clergyman when his country goes to war; as a minister of Christ, he cannot possibly approve of slaughter, still less initiate it, but once his nation is at war, he is not called upon to disapprove of its actions; at all events, that seems to be the creed of all Christian pastors alike.

On this day,[9] April 30th, there are two centres of interest, the Quirinal palace and the people.

At the Quirinal the hours were spent in long discussions between Pius and his ministers, during which, with calm conviction, he would return again and again to the saving clause in his Allocution:

"Yes," he would repeat, "I have refused (*disdetto*) the war because I am the Pontiff, and as such I must regard all Catholic peoples with equal affection, and as my sons; but did you not notice the clause in which it says: 'If among Our subjects there are some who allow themselves to be carried away by the example of the other Italians, how would it be possible for me to restrain their ardour?' Is not this the same idea that I have always repeated to you? I bow before necessity, but it is not I, a minister of peace, who can brandish the sword." (Minghetti, *Ricordi*, 1, 376.)

The ministers would then proceed to point out to him (Minghetti tells us) the violent agitation which his Allocution would arouse in Rome and elsewhere; to argue respectfully, and

[9] The principal authorities for these days are:
Cabinet ministers: Minghetti, Pasolini, Farini (*sostituto*). Galletti was also there but remained apart.
Living in Rome: Spada, a banker; British representative, Mr Petre: *Correspondence*, Pt II, pp. 431 and 438; Tuscan representative: Bargagli's despatches, *v.* Florence Arch.; Piedmontese ambassador: Pareto's despatches, *v.* Turin Arch.; Austrian ambassador: Lützow's despatches, *v.* Vienna Arch.
Of historians, the most serviceable are: Tivaroni, Masi, Gabussi (Republican), Giovagnoli (Anti-Papal) and Spada (Papal).

finally to impress on him that, although the decision lay with him, yet in a constitutional state a war ministry cannot remain in office unless the policy is war; they would have to resign. They claimed war; Pius claimed the right of not declaring it. Manifestly they were at cross purposes. The ministers feared a spoilt campaign, whereas Pius was striving to preserve the international character of a world religion.

Meanwhile, among the people there was a growing sense of anger; or, one should rather say, among the citizens of Rome, for the movement did not yet extend to the state. Throughout the next three days the town was simmering and finally boiling with rage, and the government only just succeeded in avoiding a revolution. That it should have avoided it at all was due, apparently, to the tact and ability of Mamiani.

Count Terenzio Mamiani della Rovere,[10] in spite of his noble name, was remembered as a fighting revolutionist in 1831; since then he had spent sixteen years in exile, and had returned to Rome only by the kindness of Pius, who allowed him to enjoy the benefit of the Amnesty without taking the oath required. He was a distinguished writer on philosophical and political subjects, and a great believer in constitutional monarchy, so that although he had no practical experience as an administrator, he was perhaps the most suitable man for the moment.

During these three days the central authority of the ministers faded away, and the real dynamic forces existing in the state stood revealed, namely the Circoli (Clubs) and the Civic Guard.[11] The Circoli were the chief directing influence

[10] V. *Italy in the Making*, I and II. Mamiani was born 1799, died 1885. From 1827 to 1829 he had been a professor in Turin; in 1831 he played a brave part as a leader of the revolution in the Papal State, was imprisoned by the Austrians, and exiled during sixteen years, mostly spent in Paris.

[11] A fairly vivid description of these days is given by the British representative in Rome, Mr Petre, in his letters of May 2nd, 3rd and 4th. *V. Correspondence*, Pt II, pp. 431, 432 and 438.

and the Civic Guards were the armed power. By this time many clubs had sprung into existence, both big and small, but the most important were the Circolo Romano, of comparatively moderate views, and the Circolo Popolare, an extremely democratic institution lately founded by Ciceruacchio. Similarly, the Civic Guard included members with divergent views, the Moderates, led by Prince Doria, Prince Corsini (the Senator of Rome) and Count Terenzio Mamiani, and the Extremists, led by Dr Sterbini, Ciceruacchio and a Neapolitan named Fiorentino.

We shall see that the Civic Guard, though at first obedient to its officers, gradually became mutinous, until it represented in reality the wishes of the Circoli rather than those of the government.

Already on this day, the 30th, there were several rather threatening episodes.

At 10 a.m. the Corso was filled with people, all discussing the situation in a state of half-suppressed excitement. The Circoli were full, and fiery speeches were in progress, resurrecting every grievance against the Pope and vowing vengeance against the cardinals.

Meanwhile at the Quirinal the ministers, after a long interview with Pius, had resigned; they complained that during this interview he was entirely unconscious of the violence of the feeling which he had aroused, and remained unable to account for it; that he regarded his settlement as satisfactory, and thought that the people did not understand it.

At the Palazzo Doria, too, there was in progress an important meeting, which eventually appointed a deputation, headed by Princes Doria and Corsini and Count Terenzio Mamiani, to convey their wishes to the Pope.

This deputation was granted an audience, but soon found that Pius did not mean to give way. Farini says that Sterbini was one of the delegates and that, when talking to Cardinal Antonelli, he let himself go, and threatened that "if the people were not satisfied, deeds would follow words", but that Mamiani at once interposed and said that "he had come as a moderator and conciliator, not to utter threats".[12]

The rest of Pius' day was spent in trying to form a new cabinet, but he could find no one who would undertake the task unless he were ready to make concessions.

As a result of these failures the people were beginning to move. The Civic Guard was under arms;[13] at 4.30 p.m. their men had occupied the city gates, and at 7.30, when the deputation returned unsatisfied, they occupied the Castel Sant' Angelo, which is the ancient fortified castle communicating with the Vatican, and also seized the powder magazines and the prisons.

This was the first act of rebellion against Pius, who had been their adored leader for nearly two years; it must have cut him to the heart.

In the course of the afternoon the representatives of the other small Italian states began to realise that a revolution in Rome might lead to revolution elsewhere, so they formed themselves into two small parties to wait upon Pius and protest against his refusal to declare war. When the first of these, consisting of the Marchese Pareto for Piedmont and the Cavaliere Bargagli for Tuscany—Naples having refused to accompany them—arrived at the Quirinal, they found Pius perfectly firm in his decision. He was ready to talk openly to them as fellow-countrymen, and their descriptions of the interview are identical.[14]

He said, Bargagli tells us, "that as an Italian he desired the prosperity of Italy and considered her independence and

[12] Farini, II, 101. We may remember that Sterbini also was an exile pardoned by Pius; the other exiles despised him because they said he had sued for a pardon before the Amnesty was ever granted.

[13] For the doings of this day v. Pasolini, I, 135; Farini, II, 100 and Minghetti, I, 378. Also Bargagli's reports of April 30th, May 1st, Florence Arch. Esteri, Busta 2446.

[14] For Bargagli's report v. Florence Arch. Esteri, Busta 2446, and for Pareto's report v. Turin Arch., Lettere Ministri—Legazione di Roma, 1848.

federal unity as its foundation. But he added that, as Head of
the Church, and as remaining consistent (*coerente*) to the principles of peace, which he had proclaimed ever since the first
day of his reign, he ought not to, and would not, declare war
against a power which had given him no cause for doing so."
That in order to calm the popular ebullitions he would try,
by means of an Atto, to remove the bad impression which had
been exaggerated with such zeal by the Extremists (*Esaltati*).

If that did not suffice, he said he was ready to face anything,
and not afraid of any consequence which might result to his
power, or to his person, or to the cardinals; that his conscience
imposed on him an absolute command to sacrifice everything
rather than be the cause of the schism which was threatening
Germany.[15]

This was his unshakeable determination. When the second
party of Italian diplomatists arrived, consisting of those from
the provisional governments of Milan, Venice and Sicily, he
said: "I am more Italian than you are, but you *will* not make
the distinction in me between the Italian and the Pontiff."[16]

Surely it is strange that there should ever have been any
doubt as to his motives!

That evening Mamiani went down to the Circolo Popolare,

[15] Pareto's account entirely confirms Bargagli's.

[16] If any confirmation is needed of Pius' convictions on this
subject we have his conversation on May 6th, a week later, with the
newly appointed General of the Scolopians, "in the course of which,
while declaring that 'he remained always a well-wisher of the Italian
cause and desirous for its victory', nevertheless he persisted in his
original purpose, up to the point of concluding by saying 'that the
Pontificate has never been so great and so worthy of reverence as
when it has been in chains'. These are his exact words [says
Bargagli in his report]; and a man who shows that he is indifferent
to martyrdom may be considered inflexible." Florence Arch. Esteri,
Busta 2446, May 6th, 1848.

And on May 11th the Pontifical ministers Mamiani and Marchetti
both advised Bargagli to give up trying to persuade Pius to alter his
view. "To try and force his conscience and his inward conviction,
they both agreed, was trying an impossibility." Florence Arch.
Esteri, *ibid.* May 11th.

where an angry meeting was being held. There he addressed the people with fine and genuine eloquence, urging them to abstain from acts of violence. He found that there were already two alternative proposals under discussion, (1) to set up a provisional government, the beginning of revolution, and (2) to send a popular petition to the Pope. He declared himself in favour of the latter; but, as he perceived that in so limited an audience there was a strong chance of his being defeated, he moved that the meeting should be adjourned to the *Casino dei Commercianti*, where there was room for a more representative gathering.[17] This clever motion was carried; a large meeting was held at the *Commercianti*. Several other associations joined in it—the *Casino Costa*, the *Casino dei Nobili* and the *Casino Artistico*—until there were about 1500 people in all. Discussion continued until midnight, but in this larger assemblage Mamiani, who was greatly respected for his revolutionary past and his sixteen years of exile, and who had the support of the Pantaleoni group, succeeded in staving off the proposed provisional government. It was decided that on the following day he should present a petition from the people to the Pope, asking him to carry on the war by every means possible.

On the following morning, May 1st, the Circoli met again at 7 a.m., but Mamiani did not appear. He had been summoned by Pius, who wanted to avoid the presentation of the petition, and invited him to form a ministry.

Meanwhile the Circoli drew up their petition, but it was more moderate than had been expected. It was the work of men who wanted to avoid a revolution, and merely called on Pius to carry on the war against the foreigner by every possible means.

At midday we have another meeting of the Circoli, in a more extreme atmosphere. Sterbini and Fiorentino enquired

---

[17] Gabussi, II, 230; Spada, II, 261; Giovagnoli, *Ciceruacchio*, p. 393. For this day *v*. Spada, II, 261; Farini, II, 103–5; Gabussi, I, 238. We have also relied on the reports of the Tuscan and Piedmontese ministers, and on Mr Petre's reports in *Correspondence*, Pt II.

what was being done; they talked of the rights of the people, and of a government with no Cardinals as ministers. Outside, the people were shouting for Mamiani and for "No more priests".[18]

By this time the armed men of the Civic Guard were beginning to realise their power. They perceived that, being nine or ten thousand strong, their force was quite over-whelming, provided they acted in unison. Some of them had entered the post office (under Ciceruacchio, says Spada) and had seized any letters addressed to the cardinals. These letters were soon restored. Elsewhere, however, matters were not so easily settled. Cardinal Bernetti was living at the Palazzo della Cancelleria, and Pius, fearing for his safety, sent an order for him to come to the Quirinal. But the Civic Guards flatly refused to let him go, even when ordered to do so by Prince Rospigliosi, commanding officer of the whole force. Bernetti is said to have shown good courage, and a cheerful indifference; but this was a definite act of mutiny on the part of the Civic Guard.

The crowd too was becoming threatening; several of the cardinals were insulted, and when Cardinal della Genga tried to drive away from his house, his horses were stopped and he himself was roughly treated by the mob.

Rome was getting nearer and nearer to revolution. At 7.30 that evening, another meeting of all the Circoli was held at the Palazzo Teodoli, and an attempt was made to set up a provisional government. That would have meant deposing the Pope, but the resolution was defeated by Mamiani. At this crisis, the agitators were rather afraid that if they pressed Pius beyond a certain point, they might cause an outbreak among the poor people across the Tiber, the Trasteverini, who were still faithful to him.[19]

---

[18] Spada, II, 262; Farini, II, 104.

[19] Mr Petre (rather Papal in sympathy) tells us that the Traste-verini were faithful to Pius (*Correspondence*, Pt II, p. 438, May 4th), and Gabussi (republican) says that it was feared that any measure

As yet, Pius was not greatly impressed by what had taken place.[20] He set to work to restore order; he called on the ministers to return to office. At the same time he sent Farini to the camp of Charles Albert to arrange for the Papal soldiers being taken into the Piedmontese service, so as to give them the rights of belligerents; on these terms the ministers returned.[21]

May 2nd. As Pius still believed that, if the people really understood his position, they would be reconciled to it, he had composed a second version of the Allocution, explaining it more fully; and, in it, he told them that their soldiers would now be in Charles Albert's service.

This second version is chiefly remarkable for the evident surprise which it shows at not being understood. In his opinion, it should have been plain to everyone that he had gone as far as was possible for a Pope. He cannot declare war, but he has taken every possible step to provide for the safety of those fighting. He speaks with horror of the danger of innocent blood being shed in Rome simply "to satisfy the unbridled wishes of those who will not use their reason", and then breaks out into a naïve reproach: *Popule meus, quid feci tibi?* (My people, what have I done to you?)

This second proclamation, composed on May 1st, was posted up on the morning of May 2nd, but was soon torn down by the agitators, and did not appear in the *Gazzetta* because, though proclaiming the news of Farini's mission to

endangering Pius' throne would cause a reaction in the Trastevere; that at one moment it was even rumoured that Ciceruacchio had been killed. Bargagli regarded Pius as being practically "besieged". He says that all the gates of the Quirinal were closed except one, and that no prelates were allowed to see him. He describes Pius, however, as remaining entirely unmoved. "The danger to the cardinals, the tumults which may cause bloodshed in the city, the refusal of Cardinal Ferretti to resume the office of Secretary of State, even his own imprisonment, leave him unmoved." (Bargagli, May 1st, Esteri, Busta 2446.)

[20] Gabussi, II, 239 *et seq.*
[21] Minghetti, *Ricordi*, I, 381 *et seq.*

Charles Albert, it was by then considered to be likely to enrage the people even more than the Allocution.[22]

During this day, May 2nd, the movement reached its culminating pitch.[23] Sterbini and Ciceruacchio were raising tumults. "We cannot be the only state left out of the war of liberation." And now the Circoli and the Civic Guard were acting more or less in unison. All over the town were to be heard violent revolutionary speeches, but not even one in favour of Pius. In the course of the day the Civic Guard turned itself, or was turned, into a political body. A project had been suggested that its members should send an address to Mamiani expressing approval of his well-known "programme",[24] which was regarded as his declaration of policy. As it was impossible to consult all the Civic Guards, certain deputies were hastily selected to represent the whole body, and the address was drawn up. This meant that Mamiani was regarded as their leader by all the armed men in Rome.

In reality, he was the only existing authority except the Circoli, for during these hours the ministers had resigned once again; they could not keep order. The Civica was siding with the Circoli against them, so they gave up the situation as hopeless.

[22] Count Pier Desiderio Pasolini (*Memorie*, I, 134) publishes a facsimile of a previous version of this second proclamation. He says that this previous version was composed by Mgr Pentini and corrected by Pius; that it was much more warlike in tone than the final version published; that while it was on the printing press, Cardinal Antonelli came in and altered it into the version which appeared. It is hard to test this statement, but in any case it does not seem to prove much.

[23] Spada, II, 269; Farini, II, 109 *et seq.*

[24] An election programme published by Mamiani on April 25th, four days before the Allocution. It was a statement of Mamiani's patriotic hopes and dreams for the new Italy and included everything from municipal reform to abstract questions, such as the inviolability of the domicile—about twenty headings in all. In the foreign sphere it began with the "holy war" and the immediate founding of a national navy, and ended up with no peace with Austria until "the Alps mark our Italian boundaries from the Var to the Brenner and thence to the Quarnero".

Pius may perhaps have heard that the address was in preparation, but, long before it was complete, he had invited Mamiani to form a ministry and had accepted his terms. No other course was possible.

The terms upon which Mamiani insisted were that the policy as to the Italian cause should be continued just as under the previous minister; the directing of foreign affairs should be taken from Antonelli, and given to a layman, and henceforth there should be two foreign ministers, one for lay foreign affairs, as distinct from the minister for ecclesiastical foreign affairs.

Thus, after three anxious days, the matter had ended in a compromise. Pius had saved his right to declare war, while, on their part, the people believed they had saved their war of liberation. To have obtained a minister for lay foreign affairs was a step forward, and they thought he would be able to carry on the war without offending Pius' conscience.

In reality, however, the position remained almost impossible. Henceforth Pius would be only a constitutional sovereign, but, nevertheless, he would still be the head of the government. In fact, Mamiani had taken office as War Minister under a sovereign who did not intend to declare war, and for this he has often been blamed.

Pius had been spared a revolution, but the true authority had passed out of his hands. In fact, the ways had parted; and while Pius had saved the spiritual unity of the Church in Germany, each succeeding day would carry him farther apart from the temporal authority over his own subjects; and in every part of Italy his moral influence had received a crushing blow.

A few last words about the Allocution of April 29th. It has often been said that on this April 29th he was "ill-inspired", but what is the verdict of history? Let us consider the results of his Allocution.

(1) Undoubtedly it was one of the causes which led to the failure of the Italian arms, but this failure was repaired in 1859.

(2) Undoubtedly it led eventually to the loss of the Temporal Power, but surely this was a blessing in disguise.

(3) On the other hand, it put an end to the proposed schisms; undoubtedly they were a danger and one which would have increased as the war went on.

A very large number of Pius' critics do not go beyond these three results; at the time, even Corboli Bussi did not see much farther. He could not foretell the history yet to come.

(4) Surely the great consideration for Pius—if a layman may venture to suggest it—was something quite different. It was by this Allocution that he saved, perhaps for ever, the *international* character of the Papacy. It was that in reality which was at stake, though very few spectators could foresee this at the time. To lose it would have been a disaster to the Church. Suppose, for instance, that Pius IX had declared war against Austria, he would have been immensely popular, and would have retained his state; and then in 1859 he would have been called on again to declare war against Austria, and again in 1866, and in all subsequent Italian wars. The Holy See would have been an adjunct of United Italy, admitted to be such by its own High Priest.

The Roman Catholic religion would have been swamped by nationalism—which was the true religion of the nineteenth century, but will *not* be the religion of the world to come. In order to retain its international character it was necessary for the Holy See to cast off its temporal and earthly ties *completely*. Not until then could it denationalise itself and emerge as one of the greatest spiritual forces of the future.

Chapter XII

PIEDMONT. THE BATTLE OF
PASTRENGO, APRIL 30TH

While the southern states of Italy had been collecting their small contingents, the Piedmontese army had not been idle.

Firstly, it had reorganised its own units as far as possible, a process which was certainly necessary owing to the hurried mobilisation.

Secondly, it had sent the volunteer forces up into the Tyrol to cut Radetzky's northern line of communications with Austria; but in spite of several small successes these volunteer corps had proved a failure.

Thirdly, now that it was within the Quadrilateral, it had been preparing its own movements. Between April 22nd and 27th it had sent out several very strong reconnaissances, exploring the ground up to six or seven miles from Verona. We must remember that the Piedmontese officers knew far less of the country than did the Austrians, who manœuvred over it every year. Even Charles Albert himself was not yet certain how the Austrian forces were now disposed. Their sudden retirement from the line of the Mincio might be a trap, and the peasantry gave little information on either side.[1] Consequently he was leaving nothing to chance. Radetzky, however, did not interfere; he was biding his time. In fact, although the whole district was a danger zone, only one serious collision occurred: on April 26th an Austrian foraging party—a half-company of infantry, and a few hussars—ran into a Piedmontese force only six miles from Verona and were almost annihilated—four dead, eleven wounded and twenty-three prisoners.

[1] Hilleprandt says that Gorchowski, the Commandant of Mantua, had an excellent intelligence service. Hilleprandt, p. 74.

Under cover of these reconnaissances Charles Albert had moved fairly quickly, and before April 26th he had got about half of his army across the Mincio. His own G.H.Q. was still on the western side, but had been advanced to Volta.

He had organised special reconnaissances against the two fortresses on the flanks; against Mantua (April 18th and 19th) and against Peschiera (April 13th). The results had been unsatisfactory; Peschiera refused to surrender; and in Mantua the garrison which had been reinforced lately with Austrian troops was now strong enough to defy attack or insurrection.[2] This was a disappointment.

Undoubtedly Charles Albert's best chance of success lay in severing Radetzky's line of communications. And this had been left to his Papal and Neapolitan allies.

On April 22nd Durando with the advanced detachments of the Papal army arrived at Ostiglia; and the Neapolitans had already been nine days on their march northwards. Between them these two forces ought to have been able to block the bridges over the Piave and the Brenta and prevent the arrival of any reinforcements from Austria. But they showed very few signs of doing so.

On April 24th Charles Albert held a Council of War at Volta, and decided (1) to besiege Peschiera; and (2) to consider an important operation against Verona, with the assistance of the Papal army. For the time being, apparently, Mantua was not to be assailed.

The result of this decision was that on April 27th Charles Albert ordered the second half of his army to cross the Mincio, and began to allot to each unit its position for the siege of Peschiera.

This involved a considerable movement of troops, but within two days their transfer was completed. Peschiera was surrounded and blockaded by the Pinerolo (Pignerol) Brigade, forming an arc close around its fortifications. And outside

[2] Fabris, II, 167.

that semicircle was the much wider arc formed by the whole Piedmontese army, and cutting off Peschiera completely from Verona.

This wider arc was protective, to prevent any attempts from Verona or elsewhere to relieve Peschiera. It ran from Colà and Pastrengo, through Sandrà-Santa Giustina-Sona-Osteria del Bosco-Sommacampagna-Staffalo-Custoza. In short it ran through the villages on the edge of the high-plateau; and there were also troops stationed at Villafranca on the plain.[3]

In reality, however, the chief problem before Charles Albert was not the siege of Peschiera, but how to oust Radetzky from Verona. This undertaking would have to be faced, and the sooner the better: time was running against him.

Radetzky had now withdrawn his men inside the Rideau or curtain of defences. On April 18th, after three weeks of expectation, he still had only about 32,000 men in or near Verona, of whom 9000 were required for garrison;[4] but he was busy fortifying its approaches by every means known to

[3] The northern half of the Piedmontese position was to be occupied by the Second Army Corps (Third and Fourth Divisions) under General de Sonnaz (H.Q. at Sandrà): the southern half by the First Army Corps (First and Second Divisions) under General Bava (H.Q. at Cerlungo).
The positions of the troops were to be as follows:
Blockading Peschiera was the Pignerol Brigade (Fourth Division).
At Colà and Pacengo was the Piemonte Brigade (Fourth Division).
At Sandrà, Santa Giustina and Sona was the Third Division (Savoia and Composite Brigades).
At Osteria del Bosco and Sommacampagna the First Division (Aosta and Regina Brigades).
At Staffalo, Custoza and Villafranca the Second Division (Casale and Acqui Brigades).
The Reserve Division consisted of the Guards Brigade (at Valeggio) and the Cuneo Brigade (at Castelnuovo).
The Cavalry Division: three regiments at Villafranca, three regiments between Castelnuovo and Valeggio.
[4] Hilleprandt, p. 73, and Fabris, II, 175, both accept the figures in the text. April 18th: Radetzky's First Army Corps, 12,000; Second Army Corps, 11,000; Garrison, 9000.

his engineers, and each day the lines were becoming stronger. The place would soon be safe; but there was one weak point in his position, and one that might prove fatal: he was short of provisions.[5]

On his arrival, his rations had been estimated to last only for another six to ten days.[6] He had been obliged to keep on replenishing them from outside. At the same time he had not enough men for a big attack to enlarge his field of supplies. He depended therefore entirely on keeping his communications open, so as to receive reinforcements of men, food and munitions from home.[7]

Radetzky's position on the military map rather resembles that of a large planet with one ray sticking out northwards to its right front. He had, so to speak, stretched out his hand through the Rideau, in order to keep in touch with the Austrian Tyrol, which was being strongly garrisoned. For there, up among the mountains, in the town of Trent was General Welden with two small brigades, totalling 5700 men and about 40 guns, posted at various important points all over the country. Welden's orders[8] were to maintain communications down the valley of the Adige to Verona[9]—the

---

[5] Wolf Schneider von Arno, p. 67, and quoting Schönhals, I, 162.

[6] "Dearest Fritzie, I am still here [in Verona] bothered on all sides and worried and tormented to provide necessaries of every kind for my troops, surrounded by traitors of all sorts, engaged by a very wary enemy and awaiting Nugent's very deliberate advance—that is my position." Radetzky's letter to his daughter, April 23rd, 1848. Radetzky, *Briefe*, p. 79.

[7] Hilleprandt, pp. 73-4. Also Fabris.

[8] *Feldzug*, I, 80; Hilleprandt, pp. 77, 83 *et seq.*; Welden, p. 195 *et seq.*

[9] Alternatively, if Radetzky retired from Verona and occupied a line farther back, Welden was to hold the Vallarsa, that is to say the line from Rovereto to Schio, thus keeping it open; and if Radetzky retired back to the line of the river Brenta, Welden was to hold Trent until his Commander-in-Chief reached Bassano, and then to maintain communications through the Val Sugana. Thus the old Marshal provided in case of his retreat for keeping open each successive valley and remaining in touch with the Trentino, and thence, through Innsbruck, with Austria. *Feldzug, ibid.*

Adige runs through Verona—as long as might be possible. In fact, the Trentino was now the only remaining means of communication between Radetzky and Austria. Consequently Welden's men had orders to destroy every bridge across the Adige right down south as far as Ponton, only about ten miles above Verona, so as to prevent raids, and maintain this line intact along the left bank of the river.[10]

In all that long and beautiful Alpine thoroughfare there was one really vulnerable point—the place where many French soldiers died and made Napoleon famous—the plateau of Rivoli. At the narrow pass, the river and the road run so close to one another that the plateau commands both of them, and they could both have been made impassable for Radetzky's supplies. In fact some military writers have said that if the Piedmontese had realised that possibility in time, they might have changed the fate of the entire campaign; but on the whole this seems improbable.[11]

One bridge, however, Radetzky had constructed for his own benefit, namely a bridge of pontoons; and on April 24th he ordered General Wohlgemuth's brigade[12] (about 4340 men), fresh from its engagement at Goito, to march out from Verona up the left (eastern) bank of the Adige to bridge the river and cross it at Ponton, and occupy the hill-village of Pastrengo, so as to form a connecting link with some of

[10] What Welden wrote in his *Episoden aus meinem Leben*, is very instructive. He says: "If the enemy had succeeded—as he did very soon—in occupying Rivoli, even the bravest army shut up in Verona would be obliged to surrender from hunger." Schönhals said that to hold this line of supplies was "of the highest importance". But Willisen did not approve of this line of attack.

[11] Rivoli was a point of danger; but Willisen does not regard it as vital; and he holds that such an expedition northwards would have been too hazardous for Charles Albert. During his absence Radetzky could have sallied out of Verona and crushed his weakened main body. In fact, Radetzky was thus defending Rivoli indirectly. As matters turned out Charles Albert could hardly have starved out the Austrians before May 14th when their reinforcements arrived. *V.* Welden, p. 13. Schönhals, I, 211.

[12] *Feldzug*, p. 93.

Welden's men near Sega. And Wohlgemuth's orders did not limit him to a passive defence. If the Piedmontese advanced against Verona he was to come down and harass their left flank by demonstrations; or even to interfere with their operations against Peschiera. And if the Austrians should march out from Verona to attack Charles Albert, Wohlgemuth was to join in this movement on their right flank. In case of his finding himself assailed by powerful forces, he was to retire across the "war-bridge" at Ponton, destroy it, and march down the left bank of the Adige back again to Verona.[13] Or, if for any reason the bridge should fail him, he could retire on Caprino (in the north) and place himself under Welden's command.

Thus Radetzky had joined hands with Welden by sending out Wohlgemuth's brigade to Pastrengo; and he had temporarily cut off the Piedmontese from the Rivoli plateau which was the key to the Tyrol. But undoubtedly he had risked the existence of the brigade, and he has been very generally blamed for doing so, even by so fervent an admirer as Willisen.[14] Willisen argues that it meant exposing a weak corps to be crushed by the superior numbers of the Piedmontese; that it meant dividing the Austrians, who were already inferior in numbers, and that the road to the Tyrol should not have been defended directly, but indirectly;[15] by which he means that it should not have been actually blocked, but that the Austrian troops should have been so disposed that no assailant could take the road to the Tyrol without laying himself open to disaster.

[13] *Feldzug*, I, 93.

[14] Willisen, p. 54; Kunz, p. 20. Hilleprandt, on the other hand, considers that Radetzky was justified in taking the risk (p. 104).

[15] Willisen gives the following verdict: The placing of a division there was based on the intention of a direct defence of the road to the Tyrol and therefore of a division of strength, the greatest mistake the defence can make. The result of this was not only a lost battle, but also the decision to restrict the defence to one line only. From the moment that the Austrian army was thus concentrated before Verona with an inner mass of defence in its grip, the preponderance of the enemy attack was broken (p. 54).

Thus several of the best German military writers agree that Wohlgemuth's brigade at Pastrengo could have been surrounded and cut off by an enterprising enemy; but at the time the Piedmontese apparently knew nothing of his where-abouts, for they seem to have run into him chiefly by accident —according to their reports—while posting their troops for the siege of Peschiera.

This occurred on April 28th and led to the battle of Pastrengo.[16]

Two brigades were marching to take up their appointed positions in the arc north-east of Peschiera; the Piemonte Brigade under General Bes was to occupy Pacengo and Colà, only about three and a half miles north of the fortress. And the Composite Brigade under Prince Victor Emmanuel was to occupy Sandrà, about two miles to the east of Colà.

At 8 a.m. on the 28th, Bes—the same who had led the Piedmontese invasion—started for Pacengo and Colà, which were about half-way to Pastrengo, where Wohlgemuth lay among the rough hills with his 4000 Austrians. Bes had with him a few volunteers, notably a Pavian student corps, but fortunately his advance-guard, about 530 strong, consisted mainly[17] of regulars. He passed through Castelnuovo, still pestiferous owing to the slaughter of its unfortunate in-habitants, and then detached the Fourth Regiment to occupy Pacengo on his left, while he himself marched straight on to Colà with the Third Regiment (three battalions), without diminishing his advance-guard, although it was now rather disproportionate to the numbers of the main body. As they entered the village of Madonna della Neve, "Our Lady of the Snow", they were fired on by a few Austrians, who retired rapidly onto Monte Raso, a steep hill which covers the road to Pastrengo.

[16] For these engagements at Colà, Sandrà and Pacengo we have relied on the official reports of the Piedmontese officers engaged. *V. Rapporti*; also Fabris, II, 183 *et seq.*; Montù, Pinelli, etc. On the Austrian side we have the *Feldzug*, I, 95; Schönhals, I, 206 *et seq.*; Hilleprandt, pp. 94–9. Also Willisen, pp. 40–1.

[17] Bes' report. *Rapporti*, II, 111; also Wehrlin's report, *ibid.* p. 139.

Half the Piedmontese advance-guard at once extended, and started up the mountain in pursuit of the enemy; and soon the hills and valleys were resounding with musketry fire. Bes attacked with his three battalions and six guns; and the Austrians, who were an outpost of the force at Pastrengo, were immediately joined by the rest of their battalion, the First Oguliners.[18] Both sides claim the victory; the truth seems to be that the Piedmontese lines were at first checked; then, on being reinforced, they pressed their enemies back along the mountain—they claim to have gained as much as two kilometres, but the Austrians claim to have repulsed them—and after several hours the fight was broken off. Towards evening, however, both sides were reinforced and the engagement reopened. It is hard to say who was entitled to the honours of the day. Monte Raso, the chief bone of contention, was left unoccupied. One point, however, is certain, namely that the two Piedmontese brigades, the Piemonte and the Composite, had advanced as far as the line Colà-Sandrà with outposts overlooking the valley of the brook Tione; and Wohlgemuth had withdrawn his outposts to the immediate neighbourhood of Pastrengo. Consequently the forces were now within about two miles of each other.[19]

The Piedmontese losses were three killed and twenty-three wounded; and according to Italian sources the Austrians had thirty-two casualties.[20]

But perhaps the most important event of that day was one which contained an element of the ludicrous. Soon after the Pavian student volunteers had occupied Colà, there suddenly drove gaily into the little town a carriage on its way to Peschiera containing an Austrian named Major Platzer, a distinguished officer of their corps of Engineers, with an

---

[18] *Feldzug*, I, 95. Alfonso La Marmora's report, *Rapporti*, III, 56.
[19] *Ibid.* and other reports.
[20] Bes says twenty-three wounded. Their colonel says thirty-eight; but he also says that his outpost line covered the ground as far north as Palu, which is impossible.

escort of eight or ten hussars. The Pavian students at once "precipitated themselves" onto the carriage and pair, which galloped for its life, but unfortunately turned over in trying to round a corner. The hussars opened fire and the Pavians replied; but in the confusion the major suddenly emerged from inside the carriage, jumped up behind one of the troopers, and they all departed headlong on the road to Lazise. Lost to sight, but to memory dear! For he left his papers behind him, and they proved to be a mine of valuable information.[21]

We now come to the battle of Pastrengo.[22]

Even if Charles Albert had originally had no intention of attacking Wohlgemuth, he must now have seen that it was impossible for him to continue the siege of Peschiera with the enemy so close. But apparently he did not perceive what a magnificent chance he had of closing with Wohlgemuth, surrounding him, and inflicting really serious loss on the Austrian troops while he could catch them in the open; a result which he would never achieve so long as they remained in Verona.

Perhaps he may have felt that it was unwise to take risks at that moment. Politically, a victory, however small, was very desirable, and any kind of defeat might be fatal.

On the Austrian side, Radetzky does not seem to have realised how serious was the danger for Wohlgemuth,[23] or he

[21] Also, we are told by Gallotti, the captain of the Pavians, a magnificent Turkish sabre and a rich decoration in brilliants of an Ottoman order, both of which were sold for the benefit of the Pavian volunteers and for that of the Piedmontese company which had taken them in charge. V. Rapporti, II, 436 et seq.; and Fabris, II, 180.

[22] The principal authorities consulted for this battle are the following: On the Italian side: Fabris, Pinelli, Montù, Costa de Beauregard, Baldini; all the official reports of the officers engaged; Memorie inedite, attributed to Charles Albert. On the Austrian side: Feldzug, Schönhals, Hilleprandt, Willisen, Welden, Kunz, Meyer Ott (Ellesmere's Swiss officer), Wolf Schneider.

[23] Willisen, as already stated, regards the occupying of Pastrengo as a cardinal error: but even Schönhals, while remarking on its

would probably have ordered his retirement on the 28th. Instead, on the night of the 28th, he sent Archduke Sigismund's brigade[24] to march up the left bank of the Adige, cross the bridge at Ponton and reinforce Wohlgemuth; and he placed the whole force, now about 7000 strong,[25] under command of Marshal Wocher; he also ordered Welden to send down support to Wocher from his force at Rivoli. Moreover—besides these northern troops—he planned a diversion from the main body at Verona. At daybreak on the 29th he ordered Prince Taxis' brigade (about 3500 men) to march out from Verona seven miles, and occupy Bussolengo, so as to attack the Piedmontese right flank if it moved northwards against Wocher at Pastrengo. In fact, Radetzky evidently intended to defend Pastrengo if he could; and with it, the famous position of Rivoli.

Charles Albert's first plan had been drawn up for a battle on the 29th; but he then postponed it until the 30th. According to the first plan there were to be two simultaneous attacks. He meant to drive the Austrians out of Pastrengo and also out of Bussolengo, and would thus sever their communica-

natural strength, adds: "Behind Pastrengo the bank descends almost perpendicularly towards the Adige. A force which is compelled to evacuate the position of Pastrengo and cross to the left bank may therefore find itself in a very dangerous situation if the enemy presses hard upon it. For ourselves, we have always regarded this position, with such a defile behind it, as very hazardous...." Schönhals, I, 204.

It is perhaps the chief interest of this engagement that it is the last occasion on which the Italians had any real chance of disabling the Austrian army, and that this chance was due to a cardinal error on the part of Radetzky himself. On this subject v. also Kunz, p. 20.

[24] Two and two-thirds battalions, a battery and half a rocket battery, say 2600 infantry, 220 gunners. V. Feldzug, I, 95. This brigade reached Piovezzano at 4 p.m. on the 29th. Hilleprandt, p. 94.

[25] The Feldzug, p. 100, gives their strength as 7000; so does Fabris. Schönhals, I, 207, gives them as barely 6000; Kunz as 5600 muskets and 200 sabres, but with rather different data; his estimates are very low. Hilleprandt, p. 96, says 7000.

tions along the right bank of the Adige. But he did not perceive that it was also an opportunity for surrounding and crushing the comparatively small force of either Wocher or Taxis. His aim was to take Pastrengo, to clear his flank, and to secure it against attacks from the Tyrol.[26] Evidently he did not propose to move against the plateau of Rivoli; and perhaps it would have been dangerous at that moment to transfer so large a proportion of troops to his extreme left flank.[27] Rivoli was over eleven miles distant as the crow flies. So Radetzky might easily seize the moment—as he afterwards did on the day of Custoza—to issue out of Verona with his whole force and hurl it on to the line between Sommacampagna and Santa Giustina, only seven miles to his front along a straight highway.[28]

On this same day, the 29th, Marshal Wocher decided to order out a reconnaissance to see what was happening.[29] He sent five companies along the ridge which leads to Sandrà, and he ordered Taxis' brigade, newly arrived at Bussolengo, to make a feint attack against Santa Giustina. These orders led to some skirmishing and, in the afternoon, to one or two bayonet charges; but without any definite results. The Italians admit a loss of three killed and twenty-one wounded. They claim that there were eighteen Austrians killed; and that twenty-seven Italians in Austrian service deserted to the Piedmontese. The Austrians admit to a total of seventy casualties[30] during these two days before the battle of Pastrengo.

[26] Bava, *Relazione*; *Rapporti*, I, 39; Della Rocca, *Autobiografia*, I, 177.
[27] Willisen, p. 41, said that the Austrians hoped that Charles Albert might make a movement against the Tyrol, when Radetzky would have broken out of Verona and taken him in rear. Charles Albert would have been forced either to retreat or fight in a most unfavourable position with his communications cut.
[28] This was what Willisen meant when he said that Radetzky could defend the Rivoli plateau *indirectly*. When on June 10th the Piedmontese occupied Rivoli, Radetzky was away, attacking Vicenza.
[29] *Feldzug*, p. 96; Hilleprandt, p. 95.
[30] The details work out to sixty-nine.

On the morning of April 30th the Piedmontese left wing, now about 18,000 strong,[31] was only two and a half miles distant from the 7000 Austrians around Pastrengo, and not much further from the 3500 at Bussolengo on its right front. Charles Albert's first plan had been to make separate attacks on each of them.[32]

At 5 a.m., while the men were still in bivouacs,[33] General de Sonnaz and the senior officers sketched out their two simultaneous attacks; but at nine o'clock he received a third version of his orders, directing him only to attack Pastrengo, and to leave the Brigade of Guards to stand on the defensive opposite Bussolengo; the march against Pastrengo was not to begin until 11 a.m., because the King was coming to lead it in person.[34]

This change of plan was due to Alfonso La Marmora, who knew all the ground, and pointed out to the King that if he could take Pastrengo, the communication along the right bank[35] of the Adige would be cut, and Bussolengo would have no further value; which advice proves that they were thinking merely of cutting the communications and securing their flank. The new plan made success more certain. But, even while concentrating all his energies on the hill-village of Pastrengo, Charles Albert was evidently content with the idea of driving the Austrians out of it, and did not aim at surrounding the force there and annihilating it, although some of his officers perceived the possibility of doing so.[36]

[31] 18,000 all told; but only about 13,500 moved against Pastrengo. At Pastrengo itself there remained only about 5900 Austrians, after sending a battalion to guard the bridge at Ponton.
[32] V. Fabris, II, 183; De Sonnaz' report, *Rapporti*, I, 151; Prince Ferdinand's report, *ibid.* 297.
[33] De Sonnaz' report, *Rapporti*, I, 150.
[34] This was one of the occasions on which Charles Albert was accused of having postponed the attack because he wanted to have Mass celebrated. This was manifestly absurd. V. Fabris, II, 186 note.
[35] Of course not those along the left bank.
[36] Colonel Calderina, Chief of Staff to the First Army Corps, and Prince Ferdinand of Savoy state in their reports that the Austrians

At Pastrengo the position taken up by Marshal Wocher and his two brigades (those of Wohlgemuth and the Archduke Sigismund) was almost impregnable on his left; but—the strength of a chain being that of its weakest link—it was not in reality very formidable. He occupied a semicircle of rough hills facing south, bent back like a wide horseshoe half round the village of Pastrengo. His left flank rested on the Adige; several hundred yards to the right of the river rose the steep rugged hills of San Martino; and, west of them, Monte Le Bionde. These two formed rough natural obstacles across the roads leading up from the south; but then Wocher's line curled back northwards on the lower hills of Le Brocche until it reached Le Costiere. At Le Costiere the ground is more open and offered little natural protection to his right flank.[37] Moreover, this horseshoe position, nearly four miles from end to end, was rather too long for the men available. His line of retreat was back to Sega, and across the bridge of boats to Ponton, about a mile and a half along the river-side, commanded from the hills. As he had orders not to defend the position to the bitter end, he had left the 8th battalion of Jägers (Italians) and half a rocket battery, in all about 1075 men, at Sega to guard the bridge; this reduced his defence force to only about 5900 men. Of these he placed about 2220 in reserve at Piovezzano, a small hill-village north of Pastrengo, and the remaining 3700 in the firing-line.

His danger lay on his right, where an attacking force could push its way round his flank and cut him off from Sega and the Ponton bridge. In case of a retirement the prospect was bad. He would have had a line of men about a mile and a half long, who would take several hours to get across the bridge of boats, which was defended at Sega by only the Jäger battalion

could have been cut off and compelled to surrender; so do various other generals. But they do not appear to have suggested this before the engagement. *Rapporti,* I, 124, 297; II, 14, etc. As already stated, the Austrian writers, Schönhals, Kunz and others were of this opinion.

[37] *Feldzug,* I, 100.

and the rockets. During this necessarily slow performance, his strung-out troops could be attacked by superior forces and driven into the Adige; and the unfortunate battalion at Sega, being chained to its position, would probably be annihilated where it stood.

Wocher lined out his men as follows:[38] on the extreme left, from the River Adige to San Martino, he put the 8th Oguliner Borderers (Croats), with two guns; on Monte San Martino itself the 4th Kaiser Jägers (a Tyrolese battalion), with two guns; on Monte Le Bionde, the Gradiscaner Borderers (a Slovak battalion), with half a rocket battery; on Monte Brocche, four companies of Banal Borderers (Croats), with two guns. The reserve, consisting of two Styrian German battalions of the Piret Regiment, a six-pounder battery and half a rocket battery with two squadrons of Hussars (Hungarians), were in rear, on the heights of Piovezzano behind Pastrengo.

Obviously he had considered the question of a retirement; he had placed at Piovezzano a strong force to cover his retreat, and another at Sega to cover the bridge; they amounted jointly to over three-sevenths of his whole strength.

Against this position Charles Albert launched his attack in three columns,[39] converging on Pastrengo; 13,700 men and twenty-six guns.

---

[38] As to the nationalities of the regiments we have followed Fabris, I, 203. Those here mentioned are all confirmed by Ott, whose list does not, however, claim absolute correctness. Meyer Ott, p. 28. His English edition ("Ellesmere's officer") omits this list.

[39] Fabris, I, 187 et seq. It was an attack northwards, launched from the left of Charles Albert's line. V. also Pinelli, III, 312.

From Colà and Pacengo he launched the Piemonte Brigade (the left wing of the attack).

From Sandrà, Santa Giustina and Sona he selected the Composite and Cuneo Brigades to be the centre of the attack.

From Santa Giustina he ordered up the Savoia Brigade to be the right wing of the attack.

From Osteria del Bosco and Sommacampagna came the 2nd line troops: the Regina Brigade (First Division) belonging to the First

His right-hand column began the attack. It consisted of the Savoia Brigade, a column of 5069 men, mainly French-speaking mountaineers, and eight guns; and it was to march along the rough hills from Santa Giustina to Osteria Nuova, and then deploy along the Bagnolo-Bussolengo road and attack the Austrian left on the hills of San Martino and Le Bionde. The distance was about two and a half miles.

The central column of 3500 men with ten guns was to start from the Sandrà district, through the Casa dell' Oca, and attack Monti Le Bionde and Le Brocche—the Austrian centre. Its leading unit was the fine Cuneo Brigade under young Prince Victor Emmanuel.

The left-hand column of 5139 men and eight guns was to march along the road to Pastrengo and attack towards Le Costiere. This column consisted of the Piemonte Brigade under General Bes. Bes had already formed the plan of turning the Austrian right flank and cutting him off from the Ponton bridge; but General Federici, the O.C. of the division, insisted on his conforming strictly to orders—namely, a straight march from Colà to Pastrengo. Bes, who was one of the few brigadiers with initiative, afterwards reported on this episode in his most vigorous French.[40]

Besides the above-named, some other units took part in the fighting, notably several companies of Guards, as already stated.

Army Corps (Bava). It was to support the movement, also the Guards Brigade taken from Valeggio. The Guards were to halt at Santa Giustina and occupy the positions vacated by the Savoia Brigade. But some of their companies went on and took part in the battle.

When these brigades moved off to the attack, the Aosta Brigade was brought forward from Sommacampagna to Santa Giustina to replace them.

The Cuneo Brigade was moved to Castelnuovo (28th), to Sandrà (29th) and on the 30th took part in the attack, in the centre.

[40] *V.* Bes' report, *Rapporti*, II, 114. It is agreed by Piedmontese critics that their commanders lacked initiative, especially at first.

In reserve was the Regina Brigade at Sandrà. It was never engaged.

The three columns started at about 11 a.m., but at first their advance can hardly be called successful. In those days the rough hill-roads were so bad in places as to be almost impassable for artillery; the guns stuck fast, and so did the caissons, long before they had arrived opposite Monte San Martino where the attack was to begin. Of the right-hand Piedmontese column, the three leading companies debouched there alone, led by their commanding officer, Colonel di Boyl; the rest of the column had remained blocked on the hills about a mile farther back.[41] But fortunately for him, he was supported by three or four companies of the Guards who had marched up with their young prince to take part in the battle, although in reality they were intended to stay at Santa Giustina and watch the Austrians of Prince Taxis' brigade.[42] Di Boyl also had with him a company of Bersaglieri and the Parma volunteers, in fact over a thousand men in all.

So he lined out his rather heterogeneous collection of soldiers. The Bersaglieri, Parma volunteers, Guardsmen and Savoyards opened fire on the Austrians on the steep hill opposite, and presently began to advance up the slope in open order. Before very long, the main body began to arrive, and by one o'clock his batteries had opened fire against Monte San Martino and Le Bionde.

Meanwhile, next on his left, the central Piedmontese column, headed by the Cuneo Brigade, had been rather slow in making its way to the cross-roads near Casa dell' Oca farm, which was the point where it was to deploy next to

[41] Fabris, II, 190. The roads must have been very bad in 1848; they are fairly rough even now (1938). V. Colonel di Boyl's report. *Rapporti*, II, 183.

[42] The Guards evidently knew that Victor Emmanuel would not disapprove of their action. He himself was leading the Cuneo Brigade (in the centre) and allowed several Guards companies to come up on his right. The rest of the Guards Brigade was ordered back to watch Bussolengo. *Rapporti*, I, 323.

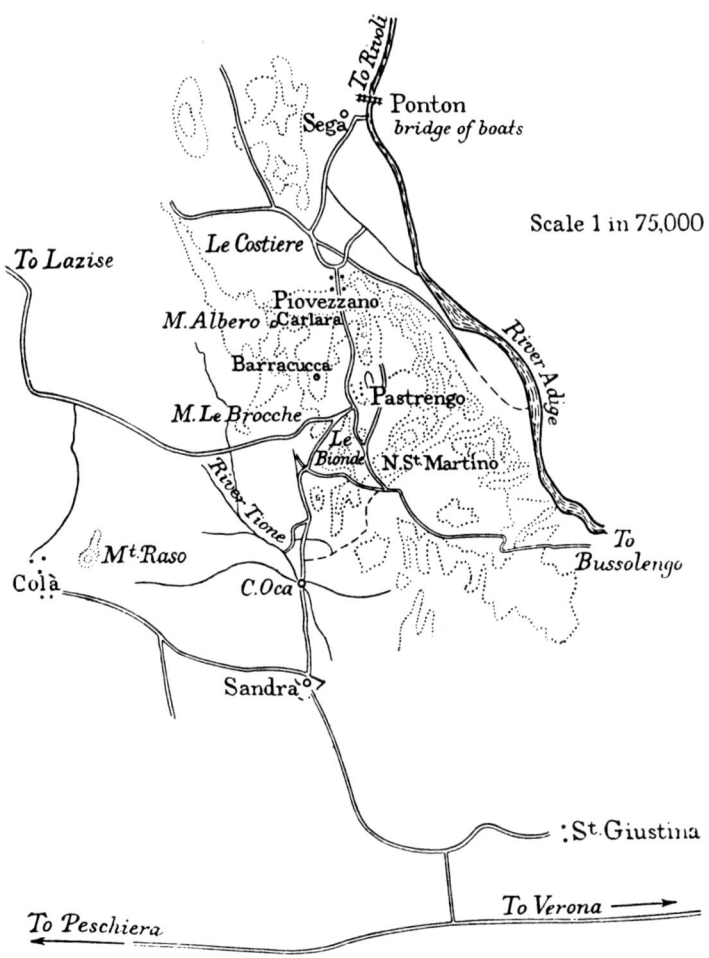

To Rivoli

Ponton
bridge of boats

Sega

Le Costiere

Scale 1 in 75,000

To Lazise

Piovezzano
M. Albero   Carlara

River Adige

Barracucca

M. Le Brocche   Pastrengo

Le
Bionde   N. St Martino

River Tione

Mt. Raso   To
Bussolengo

Colà

C. Oca

Sandra

St. Giustina

To Verona ⟶

To Peschiera ⟵

BATTLE OF PASTRENGO

Colonel di Boyl's line; and even when it arrived the men could only trudge slowly across the marshy ground beside the Tione stream, while Charles Albert sat feverishly on his horse sending them repeated orders to come on; but at last, by about half-past one o'clock, they had reached the foot of Monte Brocche on the left of the line, and their eight guns opened fire.

Between the hours of one and two, these two columns were closely engaged, attacking the hills which formed the strong part of the Austrian position. Opposed to them Wocher had not enough troops to make his defences safe, but still he had over 3000 men and six guns; and, in such congenial positions, their resistance was by no means to be despised. To attack a rough and precipitous slope, which is lined—even thinly—by frontiersmen and Tyrolese Jägers, is to count losses; for they had all learnt how to shoot, though their best shots at a target were not always the best in battle.[43] However, there was also the other element—often neglected in descriptions of attacks—the artillery fire; and in artillery the Piedmontese were probably quite as skilful and far stronger than the Austrians. The report of their commanding officers is simply a record of success.

On the Piedmontese right, opposite Monte San Martino, while the Guards were gradually making their way up the far side, the four heavy guns of the 2nd Battery at length arrived on the scene, and opened fire with such precision against the Austrian pieces opposite, that they drove them off the field in twenty minutes, after firing only sixteen rounds. The Tyrolese then retired, pursued by the attacking line of the Savoy Brigade and the Grenadier Guards.[44] In the Piedmontese centre, opposite Monte Le Bionde, two guns and two howitzers of the 7th Battery opened fire from the Casa dell' Oca and soon caused the retirement of the two Austrian guns at that point. We must remember, however, that Marshal

[43] "Ellesmere's officer," p. 60. He was a Swiss named Wilhelm Meyer Ott.   [44] Major-General Rossi's report, *Rapporti*, III, 9.

Wocher had orders not to resist a serious attack; and for him the attack was becoming very serious indeed. His front was being strongly pressed, and simultaneously his right flank was being surrounded by the left-wing column of the Piedmontese, some 5000 strong. Indeed, most probably he had already given the order to retire, for there was no time to lose if he was to get all his 7000 men over the bridge of boats to Ponton.[45]

On the Piedmontese side it is this left-wing column under General Bes which had the easiest and at the same time the most important work to do.[46] Bes had evidently a firm belief in covering his attack with clouds of skirmishers just as he had done at Colà two days earlier. Before starting, he called for 1000 volunteers from his regular battalions, and added them to the 400 light troops already in hand, so that he had no less than 1400 skirmishers or men in extended order in front of his main body when he moved off to attack at Costiere, Carlona and Barracucca. Four battalions were deployed between Tevoi and Monte Albero; the other two were kept in reserve.

When the attack began, Bes' skirmishing lines were very successfully supported by the eight guns of the 1st Battery, which claims to have entirely dominated those of the enemy, and they gradually carried all the positions before them. Meanwhile, the main body was following in echelon of battalions. The chief resistance took place at the heights of Costiere, from which the Austrians tried to cover their line of retreat; but Bes directed most of his skirmishers against that

---

[45] Willisen blames him for continuing the defence too long; and there is no doubt that if the Piedmontese had pursued him more closely he would have had serious losses. He retired very quickly, but as it was he left over 300 men behind, who were made prisoners, covering his retreat at Piovezzano. According to Hilleprandt he gave the order to retire at two o'clock. Hilleprandt, p. 98.

[46] *V.* Bes' report, *Rapporti*, II, 114 *et seq.* Bes complained bitterly that his French-speaking Savoyards received little if any mention in Salasco's reports.

point, so that the Costiere, like the other positions before him, was taken by men in extended order supported by artillery fire. The enemy's flank was turned, at a cost to the whole brigade of only fifteen men wounded.

By about 1.30 or 2 p.m. the Austrians were retiring—their left wing naturally in some haste—and had very soon passed out of Pastrengo on their way to the bridge at Sega.[47] The Piedmontese made no attempt to cut them off, and their pursuit was not so rapid as it might have been. Nevertheless, with recklessness rather characteristic of their horse artillery, the leading half-battery dashed into Pastrengo ahead of the whole attacking line, came out on the far side and opened fire on the retreating column. Here and at Piovezzano there was serious fighting. The Austrian rear-guard, consisting of one of Piret's German battalions with two squadrons of Hungarian Hussars, probably about 1600 men, made a stubborn resistance; and various wandering detachments of Croats turned to fire on their pursuers. At first the horse battery was in danger, but its cavalry escort charged and relieved it. At Piovezzano, the Austrian infantry stood firm and, where the ground permitted of it, their Hussars charged desperately, but were repulsed by the 1st Savoia battalion. Finally, Piret's men retired; two companies, however, which were defending the Castle ridge, received no orders to retire and were made prisoners. By 4 p.m. all was over.

We may picture Charles Albert's emotion as he sat on his horse gazing down the cliff at the Austrian columns retreating along the river-side below. In the background were the misty outlines of the Alps, which are quite wonderfully beautiful in the opalescent light of an April evening; in the middle distance was the bridge of boats across to Ponton. It must have been a landscape for Turner to paint.

After all the strain and painful sights of the day, there was a reaction of great happiness for him and his officers. His

[47] On this situation v. Alfonso La Marmora's report, *Rapporti*, III, 59.

plans had resulted in a victory, and he had distinguished himself personally by a small "acte de courage" which has always been remembered. It occurred just at the crisis of the day, when the Piedmontese lines were sweeping over the crests of Monte San Martino and Monte Le Bionde, and when Charles Albert himself, though nominally "behind the line", was in reality as far forward as was possible for him and his escort of mounted Carbineers. As he neared the flat top of Le Bionde, he was suddenly fired on by about forty concealed Austrians, and some of the horses in front of him bolted; but the King was quite equal to the occasion. Raising his sword he ordered a charge. It must have seemed like the fulfilment of his dreams, because when the men on the surrounding hills saw their King leading the charge in person, they cheered him enthusiastically, and dashed forward to complete the success of the day.[48]

The battle of Pastrengo was a most satisfactory victory for the Piedmontese, but it was in no sense a disaster for the Austrians, as it might have been. Naturally, writing after the event, we see now that this day of April 30th was the last chance Charles Albert was ever to have of crippling his enemies before they withdrew behind their almost impenetrable Rideau; also that the Piedmontese leaders did not realise the situation before them, namely, that once inside Verona the Austrians were safe; and that Radetzky was only waiting for reinforcements; that he was lying under cover until he could collect enough men there to take the offensive against them on the ground inside the Quadrilateral, where he had an immense advantage because he could make any one of its fortresses his base; whereas they were always liable to be attacked from behind; in fact, that at Pastrengo and Bussolengo they had missed an unrivalled chance of reducing his force while they could catch some of them in the open.

[48] Fabris, II, 198. *V.* also his own account, *Memorie inedite*, pp. 227–8; Della Rocca, *Autobiografia*, I, p. 176; Costa de Beauregard; and many others, including eyewitnesses.

Charles Albert has also been blamed for not pursuing the retiring enemy with greater vigour on the 30th. But, as Fabris shows us, he had to think of the 3500 Austrians at Bussolengo;[49] and apart from them, while fighting was still in progress on the northern side, Radetzky sent out a strong demonstration from Verona against the positions six miles back, vacated by the 3rd Division—namely, those of Santa Giustina, Osteria del Bosco and Sona, now weakly defended. It was a mere demonstration, never designed to be pushed home; but at one point the Piedmontese were so few in number that they were obliged to dismount some of their cavalrymen to meet it.

[49] Fabris, II, 201. *V.* also *Feldzug*, I, 101 and Hilleprandt, p. 98. On this last day at Pastrengo the losses were as follows:

	Killed	Wounded	Prisoners	Total
Piedmontese	9	50	—	59
Austrians	144 killed and wounded		341 (5 officers)	485

The following were the casualties for the whole of the three days' fighting, including the taking of Pastrengo:

	Killed	Wounded	Prisoners	Missing	Total
Piedmontese	15	90	—	—	105
Austrians	25 (1 officer)	147	341	45	558

V. Feldzug, I, 101 and 129. Also Fabris, II, 204. Hilleprandt, p. 99, gives the total of Austrian losses at 855, apparently a misprint.

Chapter XIII

PIEDMONT. THE BATTLE OF SANTA
LUCIA, MAY 6TH

After the battle of Pastrengo the Austrians gave up all hopes of holding the right bank of the Adige or of immediately relieving Peschiera. They saw that they must confine their direct defence to the line in front of Verona; from which, however, they could issue forth at any moment to attack the Piedmontese, and thus indirectly defend the position of Rivoli. But for such aggressive sorties it was necessary to keep their approaches open; and meanwhile they could only pray for the arrival of supplies, either along the left bank of the Adige, or else convoyed by Nugent's column, through Venetia.[1]

On the Piedmontese side, Charles Albert now felt himself secure from interference during the siege of Peschiera, and had restored most of his troops to their normal positions along the line of hills opposite Verona. It was there, at Verona, and not at Peschiera that the real problem before him had to be faced.[2]

There, six or seven miles eastward, at the end of four straight roads, lay the city on the river; and it was too strong for him to take.

[1] "Notre position devenait chaque jour plus critique, et il fallait vraiment beaucoup de force d'âme et d'insouciance pour ne pas être inquiet de l'issue de la guerre." Pimodan, p. 178.

[2] The following is one of the latest opinions on this point (1930): "The difficulty in the military situation lay in this: that for the moment Radetzky was determined not to issue out of his entrenched camp at Verona, and that for the Piedmontese army it was neither desirable nor possible to invest that first-class fortress." Baldini, p. 62.

He decided to fight an action in front of its walls; and it is this engagement, known as the battle of Santa Lucia, which is the saddest to describe of any in the period, for it suddenly reveals to us that the cause of Italy was almost hopeless; it reveals also, most unfortunately, a widespread ineptitude among the senior officers, and therefore a corresponding wastage of man-power among the rank-and-file.

Verona, at that time containing only 52,000 inhabitants, lies in a loop of the broad and swift Adige, so that its walls form a chord across the loop, facing west, with both ends resting on the river. These ramparts and forts bristled with about "three hundred" guns in all. But a mile and a quarter outside the walls there was another strong line of defence, known as the Rideau, which requires some explanation.

To visualise the Rideau let us imagine ourselves to be Piedmontese officers marching to Verona. When we arrive at a distance of about 3000 yards from the city, we shall find ourselves standing, as it were, on the edge of a vast quarry, whose grass-grown sides are about fifty feet deep, with a circumference of about five miles. When we halt upon that semicircle of cliffs we look upon the town of Verona about 3000 yards distant at the lower end of the plain. This plain was dug out by the river Adige, which still flows along the north-western side of it; it is a dry lagoon enclosed by the cliffs which once were the river bank.

Naturally these cliffs face towards Verona. They are a danger to the town. This has often been called a natural line of defence, but in reality it is a natural line of circumvallation for a besieger to occupy.

If an enemy were to establish himself on it, the citizens below would find it very hard to drive him back off the top of that fifty-foot precipice. Consequently Radetzky put up fortifications in front of it. In fact he made it artificially into a Rideau to cover his city of refuge. He meant to keep command of his exits, and would use the last available man before resigning that curve;[3] for it might, just conceivably, be used by an enemy to blockade the town.[4]

The chief villages along the top of the Rideau from north to south are Chievo, Croce Bianca, San Massimo, Santa Lucia and Tombetta;[5] they form an outer arc linked to one another by field fortifications and known as the *Curva*. Each of these places commands one or more roads running into Verona from the west; they had each been strengthened as far as possible in the time available; but, apart from its fortifications, the country between the roadways was very difficult for an attacking force. It was covered with mulberry trees and vineyards, impeding vision; it was a "labyrinth" of walls of loose stones which would check an advance, and often prevent lateral communication from one attacking column to those on either side of it. And here the defenders were at an immense advantage in having behind them an excellent road of circumvallation, along which they could hasten to reinforce any point of danger.[6]

On the Piedmontese side, we must first enquire: What exactly were the aims of Charles Albert in moving against Verona at all? What were the actual objectives in his mind?

In a general way his purpose was political. Peace negotiations were in the air, with England as a mediator. A victory, however small, would be very useful. In Italy he was being accused of inactivity, especially by the republicans in Milan. But according to Bava, Della Rocca[7] and others, his im-

---

[3] Schönhals (*Erinnerungen*, I, 215) says that some of his officers suggested retiring behind the Rideau back into the forts, but Radetzky would not hear of it "and he was right".

[4] "Its loss or surrender would undoubtedly have led to a blockade of the fortress." Wolf Schneider, p. 69. We cannot find, however, that Charles Albert ever had any such project.

[5] The Austrian outposts were at Madonna di Dossobuono, Camponi, Canova, and Feniletto. Fabris, II, 216.   [6] Schönhals, I, 216.

[7] This is definitely stated by Della Rocca (*Autobiografia*, I, 177, 200); also by Minghetti (*Ricordi*, II, 8), who was on the H.Q. Staff. According to one of the Austrian authorities it was they who had conveyed this false information to Charles Albert; but this seems very unlikely.

mediate reason was that the revolutionary committees in Verona were calling for him; they said their citizens were ready to rise, provided that the Piedmontese army appeared before their walls, and drew Radetzky's troops out of the town to defend the Rideau. Charles Albert hoped that if he presented himself before the Rideau, Radetzky would be obliged to come out and fight in the open; this would enable the townsmen to rise; and if the Piedmontese were victorious, perhaps they might enter Verona on its southern side, towards Tombetta.

Unfortunately his orders were likely to generate confusion among his subordinates. Bava in his general plan, which is mentioned in the actual orders of the day for May 6th, spoke of the *Curva* on the Rideau and named the five villages already mentioned (Chievo, etc.) as being occupied by Austrian troops. He then said that the objective was: "to drive back the aforesaid troops beneath the guns of the town, so as to enable us to reconnoitre that part of the fortifications which surround the city on the south-west."

Evidently what Charles Albert wanted his men to do was to attack and take those places above the Rideau, and then await further orders.[8] As there were only about 15,900 Austrians along the *Curva* and he could lead 30,000 men against them, the odds were in his favour. But it would be necessary to undertake a pitched battle, not merely a reconnaissance. His object could only be achieved by driving the Austrians out of all their forward positions. Surely then it was a mistake in his orders to speak so often of reconnoitring, and also of returning in the evening by the same roads on which they had advanced.

Some of the brigadiers afterwards said that they believed that it was only the *Curva* (Rideau) which he intended them to reconnoitre, and pointed out that a mere reconnaissance

[8] "On the heights of Croce Bianca, San Massimo and Santa Lucia—when these are occupied—the forward movement will be at an end, and the troops will receive further orders." Extract from Charles Albert's *Ordine speciale* of May 5th, 1848.

should be carried out by a comparatively small number of men in extended order, so as to gain information as cheaply as possible; whereas to take these Austrian positions would have cost several thousands of casualties. They were evidently unwilling to sacrifice so many lives to win positions, which, according to orders, were to be abandoned an hour or two later.

In any case, however, the plans miscarried from the first.[9] On May 3rd Charles Albert spoke of his proposed movement to Bava, and Bava at once drew up a general scheme for a great reconnaissance in force. It was accepted, and he received orders to come at 3 p.m., on May 5th, to the royal head-quarters to discuss the matter with the King; also with General Franzini as Minister of War; with two divisional generals and with Prince Victor Emmanuel.

On May 5th Bava turned up with all the necessary details carefully worked out; but on arriving at the Council he was met outside by Franzini, who told him that, as there were no operation orders in the plans sent in, he, Franzini, had inserted his own scheme of orders for the advance. Bava replied that he had brought his draft of orders in his pocket. At the Council, however, Franzini read out his own scheme of orders for the advance, interpolated in Bava's general scheme. This irritated Bava, but he agreed to carry it out as it stood. On one point, however, he protested. Franzini now proposed that the reconnaissance should take place on the following day; Bava wanted it to be postponed until a day later, so that all the officers concerned (no doubt including himself) should have time to grasp what was required of them. But unfortunately Charles Albert, supported by all those present, decided in favour of Franzini—partly for political reasons[10]—and thereby made himself the scapegoat for the failure. No doubt they all hoped to surprise the enemy.

---

[9] Bava's report, *Rapporti*, I, 39. Franzini, *Rapporti*, III, 370. For the chief authorities on the battle of Santa Lucia, v. p. 203, note 22.
[10] V. his own statements. *Memorie inedite*, p. 232.

The results are almost inexplicable. The discussion had closed at 5 p.m.[11] and yet—so Bava says—the orders were not fully duplicated until 2 a.m. that night, and his own copy did not reach him until 4 a.m. Whoever was in fault, one thing remains certain, namely, that although the hour of starting was 7.30 a.m. some of the regiments did not receive their orders until 7 a.m. or even later on May 6th, that is to say, only half an hour before they were timed to start. Some of them marched without rations. Such staff-work speaks for itself; the orders are, after all, only about 1700 words long, and could have been dictated by one man to a dozen copyists in about an hour and a quarter; and even the farthest-off units should have had them by 7 p.m.—not 7 a.m. of the day following. But in any case the generals were never told the hour of starting, and do not seem to have warned their subordinates.[12]

Franzini's scheme was as follows: he selected for attack the three central points in the Austrian line, Croce Bianca, San Massimo and Santa Lucia (he omitted the flanks, namely Chievo on the north and Tombetta on the south). The Piedmontese divisions were to move along the four roads leading to the three objectives—there were two roads to Santa Lucia—and attack them full in the face; with a cavalry brigade guarding each flank of the line.

The formation was rather curious; the divisions were to advance in the shape of a wedge. On the central road—that from Sona to San Massimo—was to move the First Division, headed by its forward troops, the Regina Brigade (4300 infantry[13] and eight guns), which was to attack San Massimo

[11] Bava says 6 p.m., *Rapporti*, I, 40. This narrative is taken from Franzini, *Rapporti*, III, 370. It is virtually confirmed by Della Rocca, *Autobiografia*, I, p. 188; Pinelli, III, 325; Fabris, II, 211.

[12] Prince Ferdinand remarks in his Report that such important orders should only be carried round by officers (!). Pimodan said that the Piedmontese defeat was partly due to their starting late: *v.* also Montù.

[13] It included also two regiments of cavalry (but they could not be made use of on account of the ground); the Genova Regiment, 435 men, and the Savoia Regiment, 450 strong. *Rapporti*, II, 505.

(about 3000 Austrians and six guns). On its right, but echeloned back a thousand yards in rear of its right flank, was to march the other brigade in this First Division—the Aosta Brigade—along the road from Sommacampagna to Santa Lucia; but it was not to attack Santa Lucia; it was to incline to the left near Caselle d'Erbe and join the Regina Brigade in the central attack on San Massimo. Thus the central attack was entrusted to the First Division.[14]

The right wing was to consist of the Second Division, which was arranged on the same principle. It was to attack Santa Lucia. The Casale Brigade was to lead the way. It was to start at Gonfardine and advance on the right of the Aosta Brigade, echeloned back a thousand yards as soon as they got sight of each other; on its right again came its sister brigade, the Acqui, which was to advance along the Villafranca-Santa Lucia road, echeloned a thousand yards behind the Casale Brigade. These roads at the start were widely separated from the central highway, but they all converged on Verona.

The left wing consisted of the Third Division; it was to start from Santa Giustina and Sandrà in the north, to attack Croce Bianca; half of the Savoia Brigade echeloned a thousand yards behind the left of the Cuneo Brigade, and the other half of the Savoia marching with the Composite Brigade, both echeloned a thousand yards behind the left of the Savoia.

As the various roads, at the start, are far apart from one another, it was ordered that on reaching the line between Palazzino and Moreschi—a natural ridge[15]—they were all to halt and correct their distances; and the Aosta Brigade was to move up (followed by the Guards) and post itself side by

---

[14] The second-line troops were to consist of the Reserve Division under Prince Victor Emmanuel (the future King); of this reserve, the Cuneo Brigade was to move along the central road, following a thousand yards behind the Regina Brigade, and the Guards Brigade was to follow a thousand yards behind the Aosta. *V.* Fabris, II, 212 *et seq.*

[15] This ridge turned out to be more or less the line occupied by the Austrian outposts.

side with the Regina, so as to unite the whole of the First Division for its main frontal attack on San Massimo.[16] The initial plan of the Piedmontese has been described at great length because this battle was the turning-point in the war. With their eight brigades the Piedmontese must have totalled over 30,000 men and 60 to 70 guns; but their numbers were not of much use as matters turned out, because they could make little headway against an enemy in a strong defensive position, for the most part behind walls. Many of the battalions and most of the artillery hardly fired a single round, and the cavalry was never engaged.

[16] The following is the disposition of the Austrian force at San Massimo and Santa Lucia. I give it for reference in case of anyone's studying the battle; also as a specimen of Radetzky's military methods. (*Feldzug*, I, 104 *et seq.*)

At *San Massimo* was Count Gyulai with outposts from Corte Salvi to Camponi; with the 11th Jägers, two battalions of Archduke Ernst infantry, a six-pounder battery and two squadrons of Reuss Hussars. Their line extended from Sagremoso (right) to Ca Pellegrino (left), where they joined Strassoldo's brigade.

At *Santa Lucia* was Count Strassoldo with only two weak battalions, the 10th Jägers and the 3rd Archduke Sigismund infantry; two squadrons of Radetzky Hussars and a horse-battery (six guns). He held from Ca Pellegrino (some way north of Santa Lucia) to Chioda; and his outposts (10th Jägers) ran from Camponi to Dosso-buono and Trezze.

To north. Four companies of the 10th Jägers and three guns held the line from Santa Lucia to Ca Pellegrino.

Centre. The Villafranca road was swept by two guns.

To south. From Santa Lucia to Chioda was held by three and a half companies of the Archduke Sigismund infantry.

The rest of his two battalions were apparently on outpost duty, but were called in to take part in the defence. They numbered together about 1500 (*Feldzug*, I, 119). He seems to have had about 2000 to 2300 men, and when reinforced by d'Anthon's companies, nearly 3000; of whom, however, about 250 were cavalry.

At this period of the campaign we might perhaps estimate the Austrian battalions (six companies) at about 1090 men; the batteries at 150 men; and the squadrons at perhaps 120 to 140. But the battalions varied in strength. The 10th Jägers, for instance, which had done a great deal of fighting, was probably reduced to about 115 to 120 men per company. (Hilleprandt, p. 108 *et seq.*)

In or around Verona Radetzky had about 31,600 men; but of these about 5100 were at places outside, along the left[17] bank of the Adige, and 10,900 were now allotted to the garrison of the town, and could only be used sparingly, lest its diminution should encourage the would-be rebels. This left him only 15,600 free to strike; but nearly 20,000 of his men and 63 guns took part in the battle.[18] This shows that before the end he had sent out over 3000 of his garrison to reinforce the Rideau.

Its defenders were posted as follows: on his left he had Clam's brigade (about 3700 men) in Tombetta and Tomba; and Strassoldo's weak brigade (perhaps 2300) in Santa Lucia. On his centre and right he had in San Massimo about 3700 men, in Croce Bianca about 2000, and in Chievo about 3700. Each village had been made by the Austrians into a more or less self-contained unit, which could, however, easily be reinforced from other points in the line. But, of those five places, the Piedmontese attacked only the three most central, already named.

Thus Charles Albert was going to push the solid weight of 30,000 men, advancing at first in a wedge of brigades, against the more central portions of the Austrian line. The most probable result of his orders—supposing that they had been carried out to time—would have been that the Piedmontese attacking line would have been checked before the three central villages in its path, but would have gradually forced its way through the thinner defences on either side of them; and would have captured the Rideau or some of it.

But as a matter of fact it was impossible for Charles Albert's orders to be efficiently carried out. Bava says that only one brigade arrived punctually at the ridge where they were all to form up for the attack, namely the Aosta Brigade,

[17] That is to say, about 5600 men of the First Army Corps.
[18] Second Army Corps under Baron d'Aspre. The *Feldzug*, I, 105, says 19,000 men took part in the battle of Santa Lucia. *V.* also Hilleprandt, p. 112; Fabris, II, 215.

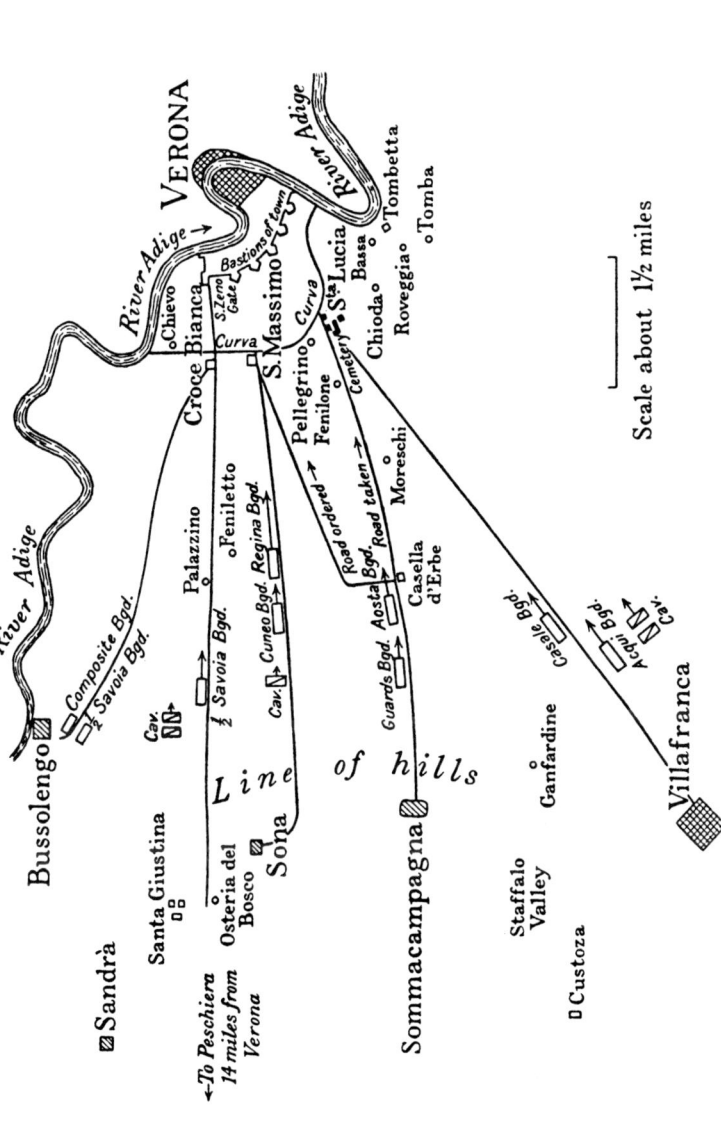

River Adige

Bussolengo

Composite Bgd.
½ Savoia Bgd.

Sandrà

Santa Giustina

Palazzino

Cav.

½ Savoia Bgd.

Osteria del Bosco

Line of hills

Sona

←To Peschiera 14 miles from Verona

Cav.

Cuneo Bgd.

Regina Bgd.

Feniletto

River Adige

River Adige

VERONA

Chievo

Croce Bianca

Curva

S. Zeno Gate

Bastions of town

S. Massimo

Curva

Pellegrino

Fenilone

Cemetery

Sᵗᵃ Lucia

Bassa

Chiodo

Roveggia

Tombetta

Tomba

River Adige

Road ordered →

Road taken →

Aosta Bgd.

Moreschi

Guards Bgd.

Casella d'Erbe

Sommacampagna

Ganfardine

Staffalo Valley

Custoza

Casale Bgd.

Acqui Bgd.

Cav.

Villafranca

Scale about 1½ miles

BATTLE OF SANTA LUCIA

with which he and the King were riding. This is true[19]—but in reality the four central brigades were not long behind the time; it was the wings which, having much further to march, arrived later. On the right wing, the Casale Brigade, starting from Custoza, was evidently unpunctual,[20] though it afterwards did good work; but the Acqui Brigade, starting from the Valle di Staffalo (east of Custoza), was so late that it only reached its post at about one o'clock. And the left wing (Savoia and Composite Brigades), coming down from the north, from Bussolengo and Santa Giustina to attack Croce Bianca, only lined up for the attack at about eleven o'clock and retired at about two.[21]

The battle began in a curious manner. The Aosta Brigade, which was accompanied by Charles Albert and Bava, arrived first on the ridge, and apparently was allowed to march off first, in place of the Regina, the directing unit. But it will be remembered that the Aosta was on a different road and had orders, after about an hour's march, to incline to the left, away from Santa Lucia, and move up side by side with the Regina Brigade to join it in attacking San Massimo in the centre. Owing evidently to a mistake, this long column, strung out among mulberry trees and vines, omitted to incline to the left and kept straight on along the road on which it was marching, which led, not to San Massimo but to Santa Lucia.[22] According to Bava's account, it suddenly found itself fired on from the village of Santa Lucia, so there was no course left except that of pushing forward to the attack. This is rather a strange explanation of the beginning of the battle—

[19] Ferdinand of Savoy, *Rapporti*, I, 298; Victor Emmanuel, *ibid.* p. 324.

[20] Pimodan regarded the lateness of the orders as the principal cause of defeat. *V.* Pimodan, p. 163; Pinelli, III, 326.

[21] Di Ferrere, *Rapporti*, I, 204; *Ibid.* II, 288.

[22] Giustiniani's report, *ibid.* p. 179. The *Feldzug*, I, 111, says that the Austrian outposts opened a lively fire at 8.30 a.m. and fell back slowly and took post in the line of defence; also that the Italians were advancing with clouds of skirmishers.

the wrong brigade attacking the wrong place. However, it opened fire on Santa Lucia at once, although that village had been assigned to the right wing, which as yet was nowhere near.

This was a most unfortunate error. It disorganised both attacks. And at Santa Lucia, where the real fighting took place, the Piedmontese were destined to run up against one of the finest defences of the war. It was a small village with a church and a belfry tower; and within a hundred yards of it there was (and still is) a cemetery on the southern edge of the road. All of these "the Germans had turned into real fortresses"; they had posted snipers in the campanile (steeple), had loopholed the cemetery walls, and had laid an abattis; moreover, the fields around were all intersected with loose stone walls running in every direction. These defences, covering the road from Sommacampagna, were manned by the Jägers of Strassoldo's Austrian brigade. Those to its left, consisting of the village itself with a long garden wall and an abattis, were held by the Archduke Sigismund infantry, to cover the approaches by the road from Villafranca. This brigade of Graf Strassoldo's, though not numerous—only about 2100 men in all, and six guns[23]—was one of the best in the Austrian army. It was composed of German and Italian

[23] Strassoldo's brigade consisted of: 10th Jägers, six companies; 3rd battalion Archduke Sigismund, six companies; "hardly more than 1500 men". One battery Horse Artillery: say 150. In reserve, Radetzky Hussars, two squadrons: 280. Total 1930 or over. Hilleprandt (p. 109) says 2300.

Strassoldo was reinforced by four companies of d'Anthon's Grenadiers from Clam's brigade at Tombetta. These were held at first in reserve over a mile behind. Strength, say 700.

The *Feldzug* (I, 119) states definitely that the two battalions principally engaged—the 10th Jägers and the 3rd Sigismunds—numbered hardly more than 1500 men between them.

According to the best returns available Radetzky considered the full strength of a squaaron to be 150 men and of an infantry battalion 1100 men. General Willisen says that an Austrian battalion numbered 1300 men, but this is surely too high, especially as it consisted of only six companies.

infantry—six companies of each, Colonel Kopal's splendid 10th Field Jägers, and the Lombards or Venetians of the 3rd battalion of Archduke Sigismund infantry. On this day the unfortunate Italian conscripts died heroically for the honour of the Archduke Sigismund's Regiment as opposed to the freedom of their country; and this, even while the Piedmontese were calling to them in their mother-language to come and join them.[24]

Against these defences the Piedmontese leading battalion opened fire, and sent out two companies to distract the enemy's attention while it posted the 8th Battery in "a very advantageous position near Fenilone" to their left rear. The whole brigade then began its advance. To us nowadays it would seem somewhat spectacular. The Aosta Brigade consisted of two regiments. These two regiments were drawn up in "mass of battalions" one on either side of the Sommacampagna road;[25] their general took post on his horse at the regulation distance, fifty yards in front of the brigade, and each colonel placed himself at the correct point exactly twenty-five yards in front of his regiment. Then, to the roll of the drums, the brigade advanced in full ceremonial order, in spite of the fact that it soon began to lose men owing to the Austrian artillery fire. When the leading battalion reached deploying distance, the same ceremonial was observed. Captain Brignone, its adjutant, marked the correct lines of

[24] The *Feldzug* account (1, 113) describes with glee how a Piedmontese *parlementaire*, who came out and called on them to join their fellow-countrymen, was shot dead by them. For their loyalty during these weeks since March 18th (The Five Glorious Days, of Milan) until May 6th (Santa Lucia) they received one gold medal and twelve silver medals for valour, besides thirteen mentions. D'Anthon's Grenadiers received one gold medal, two silver medals and eight mentions.

[25] The other road which runs into Santa Lucia from Sommacampagna was clear; Bava was waiting for the Casale Brigade to arrive on that flank which was the most open. He says that the brigades were too deeply engaged to withdraw any unit and send it round to attack from his right wing.

deployment with the small flags of the guides, and the companies deployed on these with perfect coolness. They then continued their movement with the drums beating and the two tricolours flying, and—so it is claimed with evident pride by Colonel Fabris—in spite of the fact that some of the men were falling, they never hesitated during their advance. "Perhaps for the last time there appeared this spectacle which recalled the days of Frederick II; a very rigid manœuvre which the improved firearms rendered unfavourable if not impossible; but one constituting the supreme proof of a discipline which, though formal, was of iron."[26]

When the companies arrived at effective range they opened fire, no doubt with volleys; but they made little impression on the invisible enemies in front.

On this formation—which they must have regarded as a gift from heaven—the Austrian gunners concentrated their fire; and the Jägers in the cemetery were soon making splendid shooting from behind the loopholed walls, while the Austrian-Italians on the left continued to keep watch down the Villa-franca road. But Strassoldo's whole reserve—to meet the approaching storm—consisted of only two squadrons of Hussars. Presently, therefore, d'Aspre sent him four companies of d'Anthon's Grenadiers, drawn from Clam's brigade at Tombetta. This was the only reinforcement allowed him from any other part of the line.

The Aosta Brigade afterwards proved itself to be one of the best in the Piedmontese army; and this misguided leadership seems all the sadder because evidently the junior officers and men were displaying fine courage, as we know from the testimony of an impartial spectator, young Pimodan, A.D.C. to Radetzky. He said of this engagement that it had been

---

[26] Fabris, II, 222. Major Giustiniani, Chief of Staff of the First Division, says the Aosta Brigade had 350 casualties. *Rapporti*, I, 181. *V.* also some of Alfonso La Marmora's remarks (*Rapporti*, III, 64), and those of Prince Ferdinand (*Rapporti*, I, 301) as to not attacking trenches in close formation.

sanguinary work and that the Piedmontese had fought with great courage.

At every point during the fighting, one saw their officers dash forward, inciting their men to the attack. "Allons! En avant! En avant! Courage! La victoire est à nous", one heard shouted in French. These fearless men were the Savoyards of the Aosta Brigade, as I could tell afterwards by letters found on their dead bodies. Their officers and those of ours who were dead had exposed themselves without reserve. They had been hit full in the chest, and more than once....I was especially astonished, at the beginning of the day, to see the daring shown by the Piedmontese in bringing up their guns even into the line of our skirmishers.[27]

At about 10 a.m. Bava ordered up the Guards' Brigade to strengthen his left: he sent off its Cacciatori battalion to take the Pellegrino farm, which it did without much difficulty, and then returned to attack the cemetery. At the same time Bava sent word to the Regina Brigade, which was by now moving against the central objective at San Massimo, to get in touch with the Aosta Brigade. This message put an end to any attempt against San Massimo; the Regina Brigade moved to the right, gave up its own attack, and placed itself in support of that on Santa Lucia.

At about midday the Casale Brigade at last came in sight on Bava's right advancing along the Villafranca road, and in spite of its being swept by artillery fire, the Casale men succeeded in joining the ring of assailants closing round Santa Lucia. There must have been about 25,000 men concentrating against that small village and its church.

By that time, indeed, the sparsely lined positions of Strassoldo's brigade were gradually becoming untenable. The defenders had held out for three hours; they were behind cover at most points, and as yet their losses had not been heavy, except in the cemetery; but the strain was gradually telling on them. In spite of the advantage of position, the defence could hardly continue.

[27] Pimodan, I, 170.

At about one o'clock the four Austrian guns next the cemetery were at last compelled to retire by the Italian battery at Fenilone and by the musketry fire all around them; and the Jägers were left without artillery. As the guns rolled away out of sight, says the Austrian account, the Piedmontese made a supreme effort, rushing forward "in rapid successive assaults with great force and courage".[28] The Guards and the Savoyards of the Aosta Brigade dashed into the cemetery headlong, with shouts of "Viva l'Italia!", and on the Piedmontese right, General Passalacqua, O.C. of the newly arrived Casale Brigade, took a musket in his hand himself and led about 200 men through the barricade in rear of the village.[29] Most of the Jägers and Sigismunders were already retiring; but they turned among the vines to fire back at their pursuers.

In and around the cemetery it had been a fight of heroes. The walls had been defended by only two[30] companies of Jägers under a captain with a true Germanic name, Hauptmann Brandt. They numbered probably not much more than two hundred men that day, but the casualties of the battalion were returned at ninety-five, nearly all of which must have occurred here.[31] We all realise nowadays that it is a crime to write a stirring battle description—for in reality it is nothing else but the Devil's propaganda—but where so many brave men were killed, their sacrifice can hardly be left unrecorded. And indeed, at this point, the *Feldzug*, which is usually a plain military statement of facts, breaks out into a sort of restrained Teutonic enthusiasm for which an equivalent is perhaps best to be found in Saxon English.

But all the Piedmontese efforts and self-sacrifice were wrecked before the unbendable metal of Hauptmann Brandt and his Jägers. Twice, when the enemy were already thronging in, they

[28] *Feldzug*, I, 112.   [29] Passalacqua's report, *Rapporti*, II, 235.
[30] Schönhals, I, 219. According to Fabris, I, 204, and Meyer Ott, p. 27, this was a German battalion of Jägers, not Tyrolese. Pinelli gives it as Tyrolese.
[31] Including the missing; no doubt surrounded during the retirement, some of them probably wounded.

threw them back with the bayonet. For three full hours there had lasted the unequal struggle, which the 10th Jägers—though deprived of all artillery co-operation after the withdrawal of the guns—had maintained with wonder-worthy daring and self-sacrifice. But as, by that time, this small, fearless band of men had fired away all its ammunition, they were obliged at last to yield before greater strength, and to allow the stormers into the churchyard.[32]

Lieutenants Bognar and Marinovich were dead, and many of the rank and file had been killed or hurt, but the two captains completed their work. Hauptmann Brandt gave the order to retire. He himself did not succeed in getting away, for he was wounded, but he sent word to Hauptmann Jablonsky to cover their retirement. Jablonsky continued to defend a thick wall on the right rear until his turn came to go. In this battalion—Colonel Kopal's 10th Jägers—there were five gold medals given for valour that day; four of silver, and twelve mentions, including the colonel and the doctor.[33] The Austrians—always appreciative of courage—described this defence as a feat which would live in history.

At this point we must leave the Piedmontese troops in their captured village of Santa Lucia to await the coming Austrian

[32] V. *Feldzug*, I, 112. Friedhof = Hostel of peace: the ordinary German name for a churchyard. It is still there, but whereas it was only 28 yards by 63 in 1848, it is now twice that size, and the wall which was then about 6 feet high is now about 8. But the two old monuments to the fallen still remain: one erected by the Archduke Sigismund "to their fellow-soldiers who by their death sealed their fidelity to their sovereign and fatherland". Then follow the names of an Austrian officer, Baron Brakenberg, an Italian corporal and fifteen Italian privates. Near it is a smaller monument erected by Hauptmann Brandt to his brothers in arms (*gefallenen Waffenbrüdern*) of the 10th Jägers who fell in defence of the churchyard.

[33] Gold medals for valour: Oberstjägers Giesmayer and Balthes, Unterjäger Obermayer, Patrol-leader Kranner and Private Bauer. Silver medals: N.C.O.s: Unterjägers Neubacher, Lehr, Bachmann and Private Schmidt. Mentions: Colonel Kopal, Lieutenant Siller, Assistant-Surgeon Winkelhofer, Oberjäger Seiler, Radler, Harrer, Gumpenberger, Fischer, Cadets Klimberg, Payerl, Mattek and Bohm. *Feldzug*, I, 130. Most of these, no doubt, were seriously wounded.

counter-attack about to break on them in an hour or two. It is time to enquire shortly what had occurred at the other two objectives, namely, San Massimo in the centre, and Croce Bianca on the Piedmontese left (north). It is a story of failure.

It will be remembered that to capture the village of San Massimo had been the task originally allotted to the Regina Brigade with the help of the Aosta, supported by Prince Victor Emmanuel and his Cuneo Brigade; about 12 to 15,000 men and 24 guns.

At first, General d'Arvillars, O.C. of the First Division— the same who had been in command at Goito—moved along the road from Sona with great caution, conscious that his Regina Brigade was the guiding unit. His men advanced in battle order "with a vast cordon of skirmishers in front, and flankers of both arms, with the artillery in the centre and the battalions on either side of it forming two lines", carefully examining all the houses round them, the vineyards, the innumerable boundary walls of loose stones which compelled all mounted troops to make wide detours, and were difficult to cross even for infantry.

A few shots from one of their eight-pounder guns drove in the Austrian outposts, and after that the brigade did not come under fire until it was quite close to San Massimo. The Austrians on the road in front of the village then opened fire, but their shots went high; the Piedmontese battery replied and drove them back into the village; the Piedmontese infantry advanced and the Austrian infantry retired behind the houses.[34] "This retirement", says Major Giustiniani, "was perhaps with the idea of drawing us after them"; but General d'Arvillars claims that his attack, which was directed against the left (north) of the village, was on the verge of success, when suddenly a heavy flanking artillery fire was

---

[34] *Feldzug*, I, 112. Further details of the Austrian force at San Massimo and its defences can be found in the footnote to p. 223, where the whole Austrian position is described.

opened on them from an Austrian battery posted in the direction of Croce Bianca. The Italian guns replied to it, but as they were of inferior calibre, and, naturally, not so well placed, they were soon compelled to withdraw.[35]

Thus a fairly successful attack had been begun, and though temporarily checked, could probably have been resumed with good chance of success. But—as already described—at that moment two A.D.C.s arrived in succession, one from General Bava and one from Franzini, stating that the Aosta Brigade was heavily engaged in front of Santa Lucia, and ordering the Regina to march at once to their support.[36]

Whatever may be the rights of the case, the result is certain, namely that the attack on San Massimo was abandoned once for all. The Regina Brigade moved to the right and soon posted itself at Fenilone, in support of the Guards who were attacking Santa Lucia. No doubt these officers felt that they had never been intended to attack San Massimo alone, but to act in conjunction with the Aosta Brigade. The Cuneo Brigade remained behind, and apparently did not come into action at all until the evening.

The third point that was attacked that day in the Austrian line was Croce Bianca on the left wing of the Piedmontese army. This may be very shortly dealt with.

It will be remembered that the troops told off for this attack were those left up in the north after the battle of Pastrengo.[37] They were so far distant that it was impossible for them to arrive in time for the attack.

[35] *Rapporti*, I, 167, 179; reports of General d'Arvillars and Major Giustiniani, Divisional Chief of Staff. Also *Rapporti*, II, 211: report of Colonel Trotti, O.C. Regina Brigade.

[36] This at all events is the order as stated by General d'Arvillars, the O.C. of the Division, by Colonel Trotti, O.C. of the Regina Brigade, and by Major Giustiniani, Divisional Chief of Staff. Bava says that he had merely ordered them to get in touch with his own brigades.

[37] Fabris, II, 227.

At this point Lichtenstein had about 2600 men, fine troops, mainly Hungarians of the Franz Karl Regiment, several companies of Jägers and ten guns all carefully concealed. The ridge near the juncture of roads in front of Croce Bianca and Ca Labbia had been so successfully strengthened that it could not be taken without a systematic bombardment; and such a bombardment was impossible owing to the rough ground and high stone walls, which prevented the attacking batteries from moving off the roads.[38]

The result was a "mix-up"[39] calculated to destroy the morale of any troops in the world. They arrived several hours late, and consequently failed to get in touch with the directing brigade; they made a gallant but futile attempt at a bombardment. At about one o'clock they initiated an infantry attack, but, as the Austrian defences were still intact, it proved abortive. At the end of an hour they were compelled to retire. Their losses were 230 men as against about thirty or forty of the Hungarians and Jägers—figures which speak for themselves.

Thus by about two o'clock the Piedmontese had retired from before Croce Bianca and San Massimo, but on their right, at Santa Lucia, they had been successful. They had penetrated the enemy's line and massed four brigades there— about 17,000 men omitting the cavalry—on his weakest point, with two more brigades in rear. The question remained: What were they to do next?

Charles Albert has been blamed for not proceeding at once to try to roll up the Austrian line by attacking San Massimo in flank and then Croce Bianca, and then bringing all his guns to bear on the Austrians as they filed into the town through the gate of San Zeno.[40] But this was perhaps easier to suggest

[38] Hilleprandt, p. 125; Fabris, II, 228–9.
[39] Pinelli, III, 340.
[40] Kunz, p. 31.

fifty years afterwards than to carry out at the time. He must have had about 25,000 men, guns and munitions treading on each other's heels for several miles back, and he was trying to reorganise his three leading brigades which had become rather intermingled during the course of three hours' fighting, and now included five hundred wounded or injured men.

One action of Charles Albert was noticed; and it is rather pathetic. He gazed long and wistfully at Verona and examined it through his field-glasses, hoping—just as he had hoped before Mantua—that now that he had brought his army so close to the walls there might be some sign of the suggested rising. But the city was absolutely quiet. That morning, at the first sound of the firing, the people had thronged out into the streets, but Radetzky, who was riding by, had told them to go back to their homes, and had sent patrols to see that they did so; in support of his garrison of 10,900 men he had brought in a cavalry brigade. In fact, this town of only 52,000 inhabitants was crammed with soldiers; and Radetzky explained at once in a laconic proclamation that, on the slightest hostile attempt, he would bombard the place from every fort, and turn it into a rubbish heap.[41] As the question was one of life and death to the old Marshal, both sides believed that he was in grim earnest.

So there was no rising, and Charles Albert continued his reorganising of the brigades.[42] He lined them out from the north of Santa Lucia (his left) to the villages of Roveggia and La Bassa (his right) in two or three lines. In front of Santa Lucia remained the brigades that had fought, the Guards and the Aosta; and on their left rear at Fenilone, the Regina, which had taken no active part since it was called off from its attack on San Massimo. To the right of the above-named was the Casale Brigade under General Passalacqua. And on the extreme right, at Chioda, Roveggia and La Bassa, was the

[41] Schönhals (I, 213) evidently admires this attitude.
[42] Fabris, II, 236. As to Charles Albert, v. Pinelli, ibid. 337.

Acqui Brigade, which as yet had not been under fire. In reserve at Santa Lucia was the Cuneo Brigade, which had only been able to arrive there at 2 p.m. after a difficult cross-country march.

Some of the cavalry was sent out to reconnoitre towards Tomba. Thus Charles Albert was offering battle to the Austrians. But there was no sign of any revolutionary movement in the town.

At 3 p.m. he decided to return to his positions of that morning,[43] as he had done all that his orders of the day required. Therefore he sent out the command to retire, and directed the Cuneo Brigade under the Duke of Savoy (his son, Prince Victor Emmanuel) to cover the movement.

But Radetzky was determined not to resign an inch of the Rideau. No sooner had he seen his troops driven back under shelter of the walls than he began to reform them there, at the same time planning a counter-attack by Clam's brigade to retake Santa Lucia.[44]

Thus in one sense Charles Albert might almost be said to have been successful. His capture of Santa Lucia had drawn out every single man whom Radetzky could spare to hold his forward line. The garrison was to be lessened by three or four thousand men. But the citizens saw that a rising would result only in appalling and fruitless slaughter.

Radetzky was extremely unwilling to diminish his garrison. However, he hardened his heart and took one battalion—the Geppert battalion—which he placed on his right to attack Santa Lucia. Next to them the weary battalion of Archduke Sigismund's regiment, four guns, and two Prohaska companies. These formed his right wing. On his left he placed fresh troops, the Reisinger battalion and the (7th) Prohaska battalion to make a wide detour; they were to attack La Bassa, Roveggia and Chioda, to turn the Italian right and to fall on

[43] Fabris, *ibid.*   [44] *Feldzug*, I, 116.

Santa Lucia from the south. In support he placed the rest of Strassoldo's now tired brigade, and two fresh Prohaska companies (also out of the garrison); and one squadron of Uhlans in reserve. In all he launched about five or six thousand men to the counter-attack.

The strange point about this counter-attack is that the Austrian narratives deal with it in some detail, whereas the Piedmontese hardly mention it. Yet it resulted in a Pied-montese success: on the left young Prince Victor Emmanuel brought up his Cuneo Brigade and met the counter-attack with such dash that he stopped the Geppert battalion[45] and drove the Sigismund battalion right back into the zone of the walls, thus making a breach in their line; the 7th Regiment dashed in with the greatest spirit, driving the enemy out of the gardens and hedges before them, while on the Piedmontese right the Acqui Brigade which had only lately arrived, after some unsteadiness at first, gave an excellent account of itself. Its fight is described as follows in the Austrian narrative:

The Prohaska battalion on the flank moved victoriously forward with drums beating, but the enemy redoubled his efforts and was able to hold up the victorious advance of our columns for some time. And the Reisinger battalion met with such a stout resistance, especially at Roveggia, that in spite of its brave attack stimulated by the self-sacrificing example of the officers, it was unable to take the position.[46]

[45] "The enemy received our attack with a feu-de-file which we have never heard equalled. Lieut.-Colonel Lentzendorf in command of the Geppert battalion and Major-Baron Salis, the Archduke Sigismund's chamberlain, present at the battle only as a volunteer, fell as they were leading the Geppert battalion to the charge." Schönhals, I, 221. The losses of the Cuneo Brigade are not stated; but the Acqui seems to have had about eighty casualties.

[46] *Feldzug*, I, 116. He must have been using nearly 4000 of the garrison in this attack, but on the other hand he had brought a cavalry brigade into the town. It is strange that he never sent for Wocher and his nearly 7000 men, who had remained on the right bank of the Adige since their fight at Pastrengo, but not many miles distant.

Thus the Austrian counter-attack was repulsed with the loss of 130 to 140 men. But Radetzky meant to keep Santa Lucia at any cost. If he lost the Rideau he could no longer issue out suddenly, to fall on the Piedmontese if they tried to take Rivoli; nor, later on, could he have struck his crushing blows at Mantua, at Vicenza, and finally at the battle of Custoza. Before four o'clock that afternoon he actually sent out two more battalions and a battery to hearten up another counter-attack; in Schönhals' words he was "playing his last card", that is to say sending out the very last man that could be spared to retake the Rideau. For this second counter-attack the men marched off cheering, and were greatly surprised at not meeting with any resistance. Before five o'clock, without firing a shot, the Austrians had re-occupied Santa Lucia, which was entirely evacuated. The Piedmontese retirement was complete.[47]

Thus the engagement at Santa Lucia had ended in a very unsatisfactory manner for the Piedmontese. It was true that they had retired entirely of their own free will, according to their orders of the previous day. The task set them had been a reconnaissance, not a pitched battle. They had never intended to occupy the positions captured. So they claimed that they had accomplished their object.

But their losses had been heavy: 110 killed, 776 wounded (probably including some of the missing), giving a total of

[47] Charles Albert's own statement is: "This position, within sight of Verona, we held for some time without the Marshal's persuading himself to come out of his fortifications and accept battle; then, as we could not remain like this, without siege-artillery, in front of such formidable fortifications, and as our object had been achieved, the King ordered the troops to return to their positions." *Memorie inedite*, p. 234, which are attributed to Charles Albert. Della Rocca believed that if they had gone on with the attack they would have been victorious; but he does not say how they could take the forts, or prevent Radetzky's bombarding the town.

886 casualties. The Austrian losses were only 72 killed, 190 wounded, 87 missing;[48] 349 in all.

For the men it had been an extremely disheartening and even demoralising experience to be ordered to surrender the village which they had captured at such cost. To most people in fact that day's work had brought the conviction that— owing mainly to the difficulties of the ground—they would not be able to take Verona.

In reality, the Piedmontese plan had been unsatisfactory. It was a mistake to speak of a reconnaissance. Colonel Hilleprandt has pointed out that there were two possible alternatives: (1) a reconnaissance, which would not be worth while; (2) a pitched battle to capture the Rideau. In this latter project, he says—and Willisen and Kunz agree—the Piedmontese might have been successful. They should have launched a mass attack by their right flank, while merely holding the Austrians at all other points. They could have penetrated to Tombetta at the extremity of the *Curva* and from thence cannonaded the defenders in the back.

Franzini's plan had been to attack all three villages simultaneously. This Hilleprandt condemns; but points out that, owing to a mistake in the advance, the central brigades swerved away from San Massimo and joined the right flank in its attack on Santa Lucia. Consequently about 25,000 Piedmontese appeared opposite Santa Lucia and took it.[49]

Having captured this corner-stone of the Rideau he thinks they might, with their 25,000 men, have proceeded to roll up the line and occupy the whole Rideau.

[48] The missing always constituted a large item in the Austrian army; but in this instance they included thirty Jägers who were probably surrounded before they could retire, some of them perhaps wounded. The 10th Jägers lost eighteen killed, fifty wounded and thirty missing. The above figures are those given in Lumbroso, *Memorie inedite*, p. 235 note; and Fabris, II, 245. Pinelli gives the Italian losses at 750, and the missing at 750 more.

[49] *V.* Hilleprandt, pp. 122–6.

It seems doubtful. In front of Croce Bianca the Piedmontese left wing had been completely repulsed. And in any case, apparently Charles Albert and his advisers did not propose to occupy the Rideau for its own sake; but only with a view to supporting movements in the town.

For Charles Albert the repulse at Santa Lucia on May 6th, 1848, was evidently the turning-point of the campaign. He was before a dead wall. The Quadrilateral was too strong for him. The question remained: What was he to do?

Being unable to beat the Austrians single-handed he had two alternatives: either to make peace at once—and the sooner the better—so as to get good terms while Radetzky was still weak; or else to try to starve out the Austrians,[50] with the help of his allies. Everything now depended on his allies—about fifty miles away to eastward—intercepting Nugent's relief column and keeping Radetzky cut off from Austria. But at that moment the failure of the League proposals and the Papal Allocution had gone far to damp their ardour.

Time was short; Nugent with over 18,000 men had almost reached the Piave. Could any confidence be reposed in Durando and the Pontifical troops?

The only military force sufficiently organised to have had any real prospect of stopping Nugent was the Neapolitan army; if Ferdinand had hastened forward his first batch of 14,000 regular soldiers to join Durando's Papal troops, and followed it up vigorously with another 26,000 as proposed by the Liberal leaders, the Italians would have had a really solid wall of about 47,000 regulars and over 9000 volunteers between Nugent and Radetzky. But hastening forward was the very last desire of either King Ferdinand or the majority of his army.

[50] According to Schönhals there still existed a possibility of starving out Radetzky. He says that the Austrian troops in Verona could only be provisioned up to the end of May, but Charles Albert probably did not know this. Peschiera, however, could obviously be starved out; its garrison began to suffer from hunger about a week after Santa Lucia.

Durando, however, would certainly make some kind of attempt to block the way.

It is time therefore that we left Charles Albert to continue the siege of Peschiera, and returned to Durando and the Papal forces, so as to see how they fared in trying to prevent Nugent from joining Radetzky in Verona.

Chapter XIV[1]

THE PAPAL TROOPS DEFEATED
AT CORNUDA, MAY 9TH

I

On April 22nd, 1848, General Giovanni Durando crossed the river Po with his regular division, and committed the Papal troops to the war. He had received orders from Charles Albert to march towards Friuli, as it was all-important that he should reach the Piave in time to cut off Nugent; he moved rapidly, and by May 3rd he was able to establish his headquarters at Treviso.

Ferrari, with the division composed of Civici and volunteers, was some days in rear, and he was receiving entreaties from every quarter to hasten his march. Apparently no one realised that many of his volunteers had only been under arms for four weeks, and as yet could not possibly be fit to face regular troops. Ferrari had applied to Durando to allow him some regulars in exchange for untrained units, and Durando had promised him three battalions, but owing to the insufficiency of numbers at the front he was unable to spare them. Unfortunately, the shortcomings of Ferrari's division were very vividly realised by both its officers and its men.[2]

---

[1] For this chapter there are innumerable contemporary documents in the Roman State Archives. On these we have mainly relied.

[2] On April 22nd Lovatelli wrote to Ferrari that 15,000 Austrians "putting everything to fire and sword" were threatening Venetia, and that Durando had refused to march against them himself and had referred the Venetian government to Ferrari. "I [Lovatelli] had a long talk with Ferrari...and used every possible endeavour to prevent his responding to their summons, so as not to expose his troops to a certain massacre. I say 'a certain massacre' because that is also the opinion of the General himself...and the Austrians are strong in cavalry.

"If Durando refuses and the Venetians insist...Ferrari will cross

On April 30th they refused to cross the frontier until they had received their full kit, and Ferrari was in despair; he sent in an application³ for 5000 haversacks, 5000 pouches, 5000 cloaks, 10,000 shirts, and 10,000 pairs of boots. How many of them ever reached him we do not know, but on May 4th the last of his units had crossed the frontier.

The strength of the two Pontifical divisions was as follows:

Durando's Division. At least 7500 men, nearly all Regulars.

The Italian Brigade (3 regiments).	Grenadiers (2 battalions). Cacciatori (2 battalions). Fucilieri (2 battalions, Nos. 5 and 6).
The Swiss Brigade (2 regiments).	1st Esteri (2 battalions) ⎫ Strength 4257 in- 2nd Esteri (2 battalions) ⎭ cluding battery.⁴
Artillery.	2 Field batteries of 8 guns each (1 Italian, 1 Swiss).
Cavalry.	5½ squadrons (2 mounted Cacciatori: 3½ Dragoons).

Ferrari's Division. Over 9000, nearly all Civici and volunteers.⁵

	3 legions (2 battalions each). 1 legion of 1 battalion. The University battalion. 3 regiments of volunteers (2 battalions each).
Artillery.	1 battery consisting of 1 Roman section (Lieutenant Torre) and 2 sections from Bologna.
Cavalry.	1 small squadron.
Engineers.	1 small company.

the Po, will dash towards Padua and on the first occasion will have half his forces cut in pieces by the Austrians.

In short, these two generals are not in agreement. The one who has taken everything is in a safer position; the one who has only young soldiers, short of all sorts of kit, is called to the more risky engagements." Farini, *Epist.* II, 201.

³ Ovidi, p. 75, quoting the Chief-of-Staff Montecchi. In Roman Arch. Fasc. 149, Busta 25, there is a despairing letter from Ferrari to Durando: "I cannot hide from you, Sir, my bitterness of heart at finding myself unable to satisfy these most just demands several times expressed to you."   ⁴ Ovidi, p. 302.

⁵ 11,746 on May 16th, *ibid.* pp. 304–5 note, but this is the number on paper.

Nugent's[6] adventurous march to relieve Radetzky, and the ensuing duel between him and Durando, may be considered the turning-point of the war and form one of its most interesting episodes.

By April 17th he had already started from Romans near the Isonzo, with his hastily created relief force, then only about 13,000 strong. He himself was suffering from the results of an old head-wound, re-aroused by the hardships of the campaign, and was keenly sensitive to the fact that this would be a hazardous march among mountains swarming with rebels, and that the fate of the Austrian Empire depended mainly upon the success of the orders which he might issue during the next fortnight. Indeed, hardly was he across the Izonzo, when his men ran into a detachment sent out by old General Zucchi, who before the revolution had been a state prisoner in the fortress of Palmanuova, and was now installed there as its commandant. However, after several hours' fighting the Austrians succeeded in pushing their way through at the price of twenty-two casualties, driving back Zucchi's men with the loss of twenty-six killed and wounded and some prisoners.[7] Nugent then left a force to contain Palmanuova, and another to contain Osopo. On April 23rd the town of Udine surrendered to him; but owing to these delays, and to the rebellion all around him, his march was

[6] Count Nugent was an Irish Catholic: b. 1777, d. 1862. In 1793 entered Austrian Service: 1796–1800 served with distinction against Napoleon in the Italian campaigns: 1805 on Staff of the Archduke Charles: 1809 Chief of Staff of the Archduke John: 1813 defeated Eugène Beauharnais: 1814 commanded victoriously against Murat: 1817–20 reorganised the Neapolitan army: 1848 played a leading part in Italy, and later won his Marshal's baton by taking the fortress of Kormorn. In 1859 he volunteered at the age of 82: and, mounted on a pony, was able to accompany the Imperial Staff. V. Fabris, II, 253 and Burke's *Peerage* (1911), p. 2617, *sub* Foreign Titles of Nobility.

[7] The *Feldzug*, IV, 5, claims that the Austrians made eighty-eight prisoners; on the other hand Fabris speaks of twenty-three. Fabris, II, 259.

very slow. He only succeeded in covering about 80 miles during the next ten days, although he was marching against time, to relieve Radetzky.

On May 3rd the bulk of his army reached Conegliano, from whence its cavalry could patrol the eastern bank of the river Piave. His force now totalled about 16,200[8] and thirty-two field pieces. But he had arrived late, for on the far side of the river stood Durando already waiting to receive him.

On April 29th Durando, with the Swiss Brigade and the Italian regulars, by forced marches had succeeded in reaching Treviso. There he found himself in command of over 10,000 men, his own 7500, really good, and about 3000 irregulars (apparently local corps). He was therefore in a position to defend the line of the Piave against Nugent's relief column, but he had only just arrived in time. On the following day (April 30th) Nugent's light troops trotted up to the opposite bank of the Piave, where they found the Priula bridge burnt to the water's edge, and Durando's men strongly posted there to resist them.[9]

Meanwhile Ferrari had not been able to get his volunteers farther than Ferrara, seventy miles distant; the leading column, about 2700 strong, only crossed the frontier on the following day.[10]

At this point the contest of skill becomes interesting. Count Nugent was halted at Conegliano, nearly six miles east of the Piave, with about 16,200 men, and his object was to cross

---

[8] This is the figure given by Fabris and Ovidi, and it agrees fairly well with the Austrian official account, which speaks of 14½ battalions, 9 squadrons and 8 batteries (*Feldzug*, IV, 12).

[9] Ellesmere, p. 100.

[10] Ferrari's troops marched in the following order:

	Left	Arrived	Arrived
	Ferrara	Treviso	Montebelluna
First Column	May 4th	May 6th	May 7th

Various other corps were following him at intervals of from one to three days.

(Ovidi, p. 174 *et seq.*; and Fabris II, p. 284 *et seq.*)

the river and reach Verona; Durando's purpose was to prevent him—in fact to hold that same line of the Piave which was defended twenty-two years ago by the British and Italian divisions under Generals Plumer and Diaz. British officers who were in Italy in 1917 will remember every one of the places mentioned.

Durando's difficulties were, firstly, that he had only a very small allowance indeed of artillery or cavalry; secondly, that the Piave forms an arc on whose circumference he was compelled to operate, whereas Nugent, being on its chord, could reach any given point on the river and attempt a crossing before the main Italian body could get there to stop him. But it remained to be seen what Nugent would do about bringing over his ammunition and supply column. He did not want to arrive in Verona empty-handed.

The problem resolved itself into two alternatives: either operations on the Lower Piave, in the low plain between Treviso and Pederobba, or else operations on the Upper Piave, in the northern mountainous alpine zones between Pederobba and Belluno. Nugent might either decide to force his way straight across the Lower Piave and march through to Verona, or he might take his men to the right, to get across the river by a northern detour.

Durando tried to provide for either alternative.[11] On the Lower Piave he left General Guidotti with the Italian regulars,[12] about 2500 strong, to defend the line of the river from the Montello down to Breda and Barbarana, and especially to prevent the Austrians from repairing the bridge at Ponte Priula. Treviso remained the headquarters, occupied by La Marmora and his 3000 irregulars; but on May 3rd Durando wrote to Ferrari to bring his division up to Treviso, and take over command there. In the Upper Piave zone he practically abandoned any attempt to defend the river

[11] Durando, *Schiarimenti*, p. 15; Montecchi, p. 14.
[12] The Grenadier Regiment and the Cacciatori Regiment of two battalions each: about 2500 men.

between Belluno and Feltre.[13] In case of necessity he would let Nugent across and then hold him up among the Alpine gorges. In that case he decided to make his first stand round Feltre, because it is at the junction of the roads, and blocks both of the northern entrances into Italy, namely the valley of the Piave and the valley of the Brenta.[14] He could hold Feltre itself, and also the smaller places of Arsie and Primolano behind it. Meanwhile he sent officers up northwards to arouse all the local volunteers along the river, even those as far distant as Belluno.

On May 4th he set up his headquarters at Montebelluna, and posted himself there with the Swiss Brigade, his Carbineers, his Dragoons and a Swiss half-battery.[15] From this central position he felt that he could reinforce either Feltre on the upper section, or else La Marmora (and Ferrari when he arrived) on the lower section.[16]

So much for the defence. But across the river was Marshal Nugent, an old officer with an eye for country; he had already planned out a wide encircling movement which completely deceived Durando. Leaving all his impedimenta as a blind at Conegliano under guard of Schaafgotsche's division[17]—6000 men and thirty-six guns—he carried out a fairly hazardous double-back to the north-east with his main body of 11,000. Starting on May 2nd and 3rd, his advanced troops, after meeting with some serious opposition, crossed the Piave at Belluno on the 5th. By occupying that town they got possession of a good

[13] He says that he left the defence of Belluno to the local volunteers who had a few pieces of artillery, and that they were guarding the outlet of the Lago Morte. He can hardly have expected that they would achieve much.   [14] Montecchi, p. 89.

[15] *Succinta Relazione.* D'Azeglio, *Scritti politici*, p. 415. He had 275 Carbineers of whom 75 were mounted.

[16] *Succinta Relazione*, p. 412; Montecchi, p. 18. In case of defeat he had two alternative lines of retreat, either through Treviso to Venice, or else westward through Vicenza to the Piedmontese army beyond Verona.

[17] Hilleprandt, p. 169; *Feldzug*, IV, 20, confirmed by the other authorities.

bridge for future use; and on the 6th Major-General Culoz made a dash forward from Belluno. In order to get into Feltre before Durando could arrive there, he sent a fairly strong force to hasten right along the Piave and occupy that little road-junction.

That same night of May 6th this advanced body entered Feltre unopposed after a march of seventeen miles, along mountain roads which might easily have been made impassable for a week.

Thus at one spring Nugent's advanced troops had occupied Feltre, which was the key to the whole position. From thence he could either push straight on westwards through the Alps and come down twelve miles behind Durando, by the Brenta valley, and then hasten on to Verona, or else he could keep southwards along the Piave, by Quero, to attack the Papal army in flank. And meanwhile—most valuable of all—he could keep Durando in uncertainty as to which course he intended to pursue.[18]

On May 7th Nugent himself started with his rear-guard to Belluno; and simultaneously Culoz in Feltre sent a force eight miles down the valley of the Piave to occupy Quero. This was a very prompt and able move; at Quero he could prevent Durando making any sudden attack on Feltre from the south; and alternatively Quero would cover a debouching movement from the mountains onto the plain.

By their rapid movements the Austrians had forestalled Durando before he could possibly be ready for them.[19] He had been compelled to remain at Montebelluna guarding the

---

[18] The risks of this plan are obvious; he left his baggage and an ammunition column only six miles from the river, and guarded by only 6000 men. Schaafgotsche, the officer in command of these two brigades, had orders to display great activity, and keep the Italians in fear of an attempt to restore the bridge. In planning this march, Nugent disregarded all risks, and treated the local levies as if they did not exist. *Feldzug*, IV, 15 *et seq.*; Ellesmere, p. 101.

[19] *Schiarimenti*, p. 19.

Lower Piave until Ferrari's division should appear on the scene. It was only on this same day, the 7th of May, that he had received news that the first two columns of Ferrari's men had reached Treviso the evening before; he knew, however, that another column was due to arrive on the following day, May 8th,[20] so that he could now feel safe as to the Lower Piave. Throughout the week he had been kept on the alert there by Austrian feint-attempts at crossing,[21] but henceforth he would have nearly 12,000 men in that district, apart from the 4000 Swiss, whom he always kept with him.

On this same day, therefore, May 7th, Durando turned his attention to the northern, alpine zone. He proposed to occupy and defend Feltre, and had received word from the Feltrini that the enemy was approaching, but that they could delay him for twenty-four hours. Consequently he departed from Montebelluna post-haste and marched up along the Piave with about 5000 men so as to place himself near them in case of an attack. He got up that narrow valley as far as Quero, when suddenly the news reached him that the Feltrini had surrendered their town without firing a shot, and that not only was Feltre occupied, but the north end of the Piave valley was closed against his own advance.[22]

It was Culoz' shrewd forward movement which had forestalled him. Feltre was already taken; this was very awkward; in fact, it placed Durando in the dilemma which was soon to prove his ruin. The Austrians might march down alongside the Piave (Feltre-Quero-Pederobba-Montebelluna) to attack the Italian left flank, or else advancing due westward through Feltre, Arsie and Primolano, might hasten down the Brenta to Bassano, slip by all the Italian forces in the plain, and thus reach Verona; or else, after reaching Primolano, they might push on due westward through the Val Sugana until finally they came down to Verona via the Tyrol.

[20] The third column did not arrive until May 9th, according to Montecchi, p. 101.
[21] D'Azeglio, *Opinione.*
[22] Montecchi, Doct. 48; Durando, *Schiarimenti,* p. 19.

Durando's difficulty was: By which valley did the Austrians mean to come?[23] Southward from Feltre to Montebelluna, or westward from Feltre to Primolano? Which route would they select? Because there he must place his main body and block them. It was a dilemma. Nugent, being up at Feltre, could "keep him guessing" between the two.

Durando decided that they evidently intended to come by the north-western route, and that that was why they were closing the top of the Piave valley against him, while they went by.

Undoubtedly there was something to be said for this supposition; for if Nugent intended at all costs, regardless of risking his baggage-train, to join Radetzky, his best course would be to slip along by the northern routes through Primolano. These would bring him out behind the Papal lines, whereas if he came southwards to Montebelluna he might indeed hold the crossing of the Piave, but he would still have the line of the Brenta river between him and Verona. On the other hand, however, if Nugent dashed off by the upper route he would be abandoning for good his valuable pontoon-train and ammunition at Conegliano. (It would be difficult for the two brigades to follow him and probably impossible for a convoy.) Durando must have known this. For six days the Austrians had been bringing up material to build a new bridge, and had set up four battery emplacements. And by Nugent's orders this had been done with a good deal of display to mask his departure.[24]

Durando decided to close both routes; to occupy Primolano in the north, and Onigo and Montebelluna on the southern road, and to post himself with the Swiss Brigade at Bassano, from whence he could reinforce whichever position might be attacked. He turned about at once from Quero, and started back on his way, straining every nerve to arrive at Bassano. At Bassano he would be seventeen and a half miles distant from Primolano (up in the mountains) and fourteen from

[23] *Schiarimenti*, p. 19.   [24] *Feldzug*, IV, 21–2.

Cornuda (on the plain), which was the strong position to be defended in front of Montebelluna.

Late that night (May 7th), during his halt at Pederobba, he was greeted by Ferrari,[25] who most opportunely had marched up that day with his 3800 volunteers to take the C.O.'s place at Montebelluna.[26] Ferrari told him that his Roman volunteers were badly in want of a line battalion or two to stiffen them. And, as on many previous occasions,[27] he urged an entire repartition of the two forces so that the regular trained element should become an object lesson for the irregulars.

[25] Montecchi, p. 101 (Ferrari's A.D.C.).

[26] His first and second columns, which had arrived at Treviso only the day before (May 6th) and had that morning (the 7th) been started on the twelve miles march from Treviso to Montebelluna. On their way up, they had met the company of Bellunese volunteers, 120 strong with two small guns, retiring on Treviso. These unfortunate men, when their town was occupied by the Austrians, had made their way back and reported themselves to Durando, whom they met advancing. He ordered them to join the rest of the volunteers' concentration at Treviso. But Ferrari, meeting them on his way up to Montebelluna, took them forward with him and sent them on again to Onigo to form part of his advanced post there. He kept their two small guns at Montebelluna.

One sees that Ferrari's force was inevitably composed of units which had been hurried in from all sides to unite against the Austrians. The 50 Dragoons and half-battery of regular Papal artillery handed over to him by Durando only arrived at Montebelluna on May 8th at 3 p.m., and had to proceed at once to Cornuda to engage the enemy.

[27] Ferrari had been making this request from the start, and by now it was obviously a very serious question. On April 22nd it had been the subject of a formal application signed by all Ferrari's colonels, in which they said they wanted the two divisions to act in unison, that the Papal army would then be 15,000 strong with a sufficiency of artillery. They added that they had heard rumours that Durando's regulars, with all the accessory services, were to move towards Mantua, while their own division was abandoned to itself without cavalry or artillery and left isolated in Venetia. "We cannot believe this rumour; if it were true, distrust would take the place of confidence, discouragement that of enthusiasm, and there would be a complete disorganisation of all that has been organised hitherto." The whole document is given by Giovagnoli, *Ciceruacchio*, p. 526.

This matter had aroused a great deal of discontent, and Durando, though naturally loth to part with any regulars, assigned him a battalion of Cacciatori—which did not arrive in time for the battle—and also one squadron of cavalry and half an Italian battery, which just succeeded in doing so. Durando says this left him less than 4000 men for the moment. However, with them he continued his march back to his central position at Bassano.

On the following evening, May 8th, Durando arrived there and found everyone in a state of great enthusiasm. Their Bassano volunteers, about 200 strong, had marched up the precipitous valley to defend the mountain roads against the invaders—a glorious adventure. Very soon the news arrived that they had been actually at grips with the Austrians since daybreak[28] near Primolano, and then the whole town went mad, and wanted Durando to lead them out to battle. In reality the engagement was only a most gallant raid carried out by a company of Croats, who had been sent to watch the rebels, and many of whom paid for it with their lives. But the descriptions of the fight were (naturally enough) sufficient to strengthen Durando's belief that Nugent proposed to come by that northern road. He at once sent Colonel Casanova up with a Swiss battalion and 250 Carbineers to defend Primolano, and it arrived there on the following day. This left him only 2700 men[29] under his hand.

That same evening he received a note, written at 9.45 p.m. by Ferrari, to say that he had engaged the Austrians at Cornuda about four and a half miles in front of Montebelluna (over thirteen miles from Durando); that after a brisk fusillade along the whole line, the enemy had retired; he did not know their numbers, but they had artillery.

The fact was that, after all his efforts, Durando had selected the wrong valley. It was natural enough that he

[28] *Schiarimenti*, p. 21.
[29] D'Azeglio. Durando **says only 2400**, but d'Azeglio's figure is more probable.

should do so. But he was now defending the line of the Brenta, whereas the whole Austrian force was coming down the Piave, and he did not yet know that this was so. In all probability Nugent had never thought of moving by the northern valleys unless the southern route were closed against him. His plan was to come down alongside of the Piave, past Quero and Cornuda, and join hands with Schaafgotsche's brigade left behind with the baggage at Conegliano; then restore the bridge and thus establish a direct line of communication from Conegliano in front of Treviso.

But at that moment there occurred another small incident destined to confirm Durando in his wrong idea that Nugent was moving along the Primolano way.[30] When the Austrians had entered Feltre, Culoz had sent a company of Croats, as already related, under a lieutenant called Madgeburg, to watch the rebels towards Primolano. But on the 8th it had been surrounded by the Bassanesi and mountaineers, and had only fought its way back to Arsie with serious losses. Thereupon Schwarzenberg at once ordered out four more companies to its support. These five companies moving along the Primolano road were mistaken for an advance-guard, and this confirmed the idea that the Austrians would march by the northern valleys.

But the true danger was that overhanging the unfortunate Ferrari.

We now come to the small engagement at Cornuda which forms the turning-point in the first part of this campaign; and it has been the subject of furious controversies between the two Papal generals and their respective supporters. The facts seem to be more or less as follows.

Ferrari had done all that was possible in so short a time. On May 7th he had got 3800 volunteers into Montebelluna. On the same day he had formed an advanced post up the valley

[30] *Feldzug*, IV, 28.

at Onigo, six miles farther northward, consisting of Count Mosti's volunteer company (withdrawn from guarding the Montello), the 120 Bellunese volunteers whom he had met on the way, and a regular squadron of mounted Chasseurs (*Cacciatori a cavallo*); about 340 men in all, and all of good quality.

His main body remained in Montebelluna; but about five miles in front of that town, on the road to Onigo, was Cornuda, the last village on the plain before the Alpine slopes begin. In front of it to the north were good mountain positions which he meant to hold.

On the following day, May 8th, at 3 p.m., he received news from the advanced post up at Onigo of the approach of a large Austrian column.

He at once marched out with about two-thirds of his division to Cornuda, to occupy the positions there.

His forces were divided as follows: At Cornuda in the foremost position he had about 1600 men of all arms; back at Montebelluna, in reserve, he had 2400.[31]

At 5 p.m. he passed through Cornuda, and took up positions on the north side of the village, defending the Onigo road, which at this point runs between mountains. On arriving he found the light troops of his advanced post waiting for him, so he ordered their cavalry to send out mounted patrols up the valley. On the hill to the right of it, he posted Mosti's company, and on the height to the left of it, the Belluno volunteers; these were to be thrown well forward on the mountain in extended order to threaten the flanks of an advancing enemy. His centre was farther back. It consisted of a portion of the 2nd Roman Legion. Two of its companies were extended, one on each side of the road, in a small stretch of ground, where they could get good cover among the

---

[31] This is the lowest estimate. He himself said that he had 3800 Civici or volunteers, and he was afterwards joined by the Bellunese volunteers (120 men), the mounted Cacciatori (100) and the Papal half-battery (say 70 men). This would bring his total up to 4090 men of all arms. *V.* Montecchi, p. 22.

ditches and hedges. Other companies of the 2nd Roman Legion were in support. And the remainder of his 1600 men, together with all the artillery, were kept in Cornuda.

"Slightly before Ave Maria", says Montecchi, who was the Chief of Staff with Ferrari, "the company of Bersaglieri del Po which was on the hills to our right, opened fire against the enemy's vanguard, and the fusillade spread at once along the whole line. It lasted for about an hour, and ceased only when the enemy sounded the 'Assembly' (Raccolta). Although there had been slight disorder on our side through the fault of the officer commanding the 2nd battalion of the 2nd Legion which was posted on the road opposite the enemy—he ordered it to retire behind the hedges that flank the road—our men replied to the enemy's musketry, to his guns which kept up an incessant fire, and to his rockets, and did not withdraw from the positions taken up until firing had ceased."[32]

The casualties were insignificant; and, so far, the volunteers had evidently done better than Ferrari had dared to hope. But they were unlucky. After night had fallen, the men of one corps fired on those of another by mistake, and Mosti's company were thrown into disorder by a sudden attack of Austrian raiders. This led to the whole force retiring to Cornuda. That retirement was rather unfortunate. It meant that they had abandoned their strong positions along the hills on each side of the road and withdrawn into Cornuda which is in the plain. However, Ferrari selected a new line of out-posts in front of the little town, and for the moment all was well.

At 9.45 that evening[33] he wrote to Durando telling him of the attack, saying that he did not know how many Austrians there were, but they had artillery. He added that he meant to hold his present positions, but "See, General, what you can do if I am attacked. It is not for me to tell you. I will main-tain the positions which I have taken up." Evidently he felt, as he had explained to Durando the night before, that his

---

[32] Montecchi says "about ten o'clock in the evening".
[33] Montecchi, p. 23.

volunteers required the support of the regular battalions. This note reached Durando at 6 a.m. on the following morning, May 9th.[34]

Ferrari wrote two notes and Durando three during the course of the engagement; and the whole fortune of the campaign depended on those messages.

Durando's *first* note, dated 4 a.m. on May 9th, had already been sent off when he received Ferrari's. In it he said that he was marching to Crespano, and told Ferrari to write to him at Asolo. Crespano is almost half-way, and Asolo is more than half-way, from Bassano to Cornuda.[35] Thus Durando was already starting to come to their support without even being asked; and the news of this message was communicated to the volunteers by way of encouragement.[36]

On receiving that first note from Ferrari, Durando replied to it by a second one despatched at 7 a.m., repeating that he was starting at once for Crespano,[37] but adding that unless unforeseen circumstances arose he meant to return to Bassano that evening to organise the defence of Primolano. He was apparently still guessing as to which valley the Austrians would choose, and still guessing wrong.

On this morning, May 9th, at 5 a.m., a fresh Austrian attack had begun at Cornuda. Fire continued without ceasing until 4.30 that afternoon. In spite of their uneasy night, during all those hours under fire, the volunteers behaved in a way which won the warm approval of their general. They never lost an inch of ground: but luck was against them.

At 8 a.m., after three hours' fighting, Ferrari received the first note from Durando, dated 4 a.m., already referred to.

[34] D'Azeglio, *Relazione*, p. 416.
[35] His marching to Crespano, rather north of the Bassano-Cornuda road, shows that he proposed to make an attack on the Austrian right flank and rear; a plan apparently pre-arranged between him and Ferrari at their previous meetings. Crespano is about seven and a half miles, Asolo about six miles from Cornuda. Montecchi, Docts. 54, 55.
[36] Fabris, II, 309.   [37] Montecchi, Doct. 55.

By that time they had been three hours under fire; but all was going well. As yet there were only about 1500 to 1600 men engaged on either side[38] with three Austrian guns and two Papal; and until about 10 a.m. the volunteers were more than holding their own. Naturally, however, with their inferior arms[39] and complete lack of training, it was inevitable that they would soon begin to feel the strain.

At about eleven o'clock Ferrari received the *second* note from Durando, timed 7 a.m., as already described (*v.* p. 256). He must have felt relieved, for, by that hour the fighting was becoming serious; he replied at once, addressing his second note to Durando's H.Q. at Asolo (according to instructions), informing the G.O.C. that the troops had now been under fire for six hours, and asking him to hasten his march to their support.

By midday the Austrians brought up three more guns and a fresh battalion and "spread themselves out" (*dilatandosi*)[40] apparently with a view to attacking on a wider front. By way of reply, Ferrari brought up a battalion from Monte-belluna.

Shortly after midday (Fabris says 12.30) there arrived Durando's *third* and last note. It was brought by one of Ferrari's messengers. It was short and definite: *Vengo correndo*, which may be translated "I am coming at the double", and was addressed from Crespano, only about seven or eight miles distant. Allowing for the time taken by the messenger and the urgency of the case, they might hope that the Swiss would be with them before 3 p.m.

[38] The Austrians had in the morning fifteen companies, a half-squadron, half a six-pounder battery and half a rocket battery, in all about 2700 men, of whom only half were in action at first. *Feldzug*, IV, 23–4.

[39] There is a story, which is accepted by Baldini in his excellent little work, that one of the volunteer battalions was served out ammunition of wrong bore for their muskets. Baldini, p. 80.

[40] Durando, *Schiar.* p. 24 note. The description of the fight given on May 31st by the *Deputazione* of Cornuda only three weeks after the battle. Also Fabris, II, 310.

The message was decisive.

On the strength of the *Vengo correndo* Ferrari began to form up his Grenadiers and Cacciatori (regulars) with Mosti's volunteers for a counter-attack to keep the Austrians occupied; and this plan produced a tragedy.

In order to gain time for a movement he directed the Papal Dragoons to charge the leading Austrian units and delay their advance.[41] The Dragoons were regulars, probably the best soldiers in the Papal army, but as there were only about fifty of them on the field, it must have been evident that their chances were desperate. Nevertheless, they charged gallantly on either side of the road; some of them were brought down by the Austrian artillery without ever reaching the enemy, others succeeded in using their swords, but in all only about ten men returned. This charge is probably the most gallant episode in the story of the Papal troops during this campaign. In the Austrian narrative it is concisely recorded as follows:[42]

General Culoz noted with real satisfaction the growing intensity of the fire, and that the enemy's dragoons in particular had suffered heavy losses. Many men and horses of these troops were lying on either side of the road.

The counter-attack did not materialise; but after this, for an hour or more, there was a lull in the firing. The Papal troops were expecting Durando to arrive, and the Austrians were waiting for the remainder of Schwarzenberg's brigade.

At 3 p.m. a change certainly took place, but it was not the change for which the Papal troops had been hoping. At that

---

[41] It is very hard to discover for certain when he ordered this charge. We have followed Fabris, Baldini and others, but Ovidi says it was ordered later in the day to cover his retirement. Diamilla-Muller, who was A.D.C. to General Ferrari on the field, describes it as follows: "At about 11 a.m. was announced a sudden forward movement of the enemy's cavalry along the road beyond. The general ordered two troops of Dragoons to charge." Diamilla-Muller, p. 80. But Tosi, a volunteer who was present, says: "Virtually we retired in disorder, and a body of cavalry dashed in to cover our retirement." Tosi, p. 28.   [42] *Feldzug*, IV, 23.

hour, Marshal Nugent himself appeared on the field and warmly congratulated everyone on their successful advance. At the same time Schwarzenberg's last two battalions moved forward, and the Austrians, now numbering some 6000 men in all, attacked along their whole line with their two brigades, Schulzig's on the direct road, and Schwarzenberg's by Levada, so as to turn Ferrari's right flank and cut him off from Montebelluna. Very soon the defence became fairly perilous, but Ferrari kept encouraging his men, promising them "absolutely on his word of honour" that General Durando and the Swiss were coming to help them. So they hardened their hearts and held on to their positions for another hour and a half; but there was no sign whatever of Durando.

It is a pity that he ever despatched that message: *Vengo correndo*, "I am coming at the double", because very soon afterwards he began to change his mind. He sent out a patrol towards Pederobba, and, with his main body, began to march slowly in the same direction but got no farther than Rovo— Rovere he calls it—a village west of Passagno. At that point the patrol returned to report that all was over at Cornuda;[43] that the firing had ceased at 1 p.m. and the Austrians had been only 1600 strong. At the same moment two officers came hurrying after him from Bassano with a message that at Primolano his 1250 men, who had gone up there with Colonel Casanova, were threatened by 3000 Austrians and six guns. "I thought then", he tells us, "that I ought not to abandon a battalion which was about to be engaged by forces four times its own strength", so he turned about and started off at once for Bassano. But, as a matter of fact, this movement at Primolano was merely that of Lieutenant Madgeburg.[44]

[43] Durando, *Schiar.* p. 25, and *Succinta Relazione*. It is believed that the patrol reached the battlefield during the lull.

[44] According to Fabris it was Casanova himself who returned to Bassano to report the appearance of the Austrian advance-guard. The mistake was discovered after his departure from Primolano.

In defence of this decision to reinforce Primolano rather than Ferrari, Durando tells us that he had sent out scouts on all sides and that with one voice they assured him that the Austrians opposite Ferrari's 4000 men were only about 1600 strong; also that the fighting had died down after midday, whereas at Primolano his 1300 men were threatened by 3000. It was therefore his duty to support the unit in greatest danger; and in any case he was still convinced that Nugent would take the Primolano line and slip past him in the north.

But there are several questions which would prove difficult for him to answer. Firstly, as to his misleading Ferrari with the message *Vengo correndo*. He may have had reasons for changing his mind about coming to Ferrari's support; but why did he not let him know? He would thereby have enabled him, when outnumbered, to retire in a normal way. As matters stood, Ferrari believed that he was to hold his position until Durando came up to take the Austrians in flank, and consequently he called up almost his last reserves; and it seems just possible that he might have avoided sacrificing his Dragoons. Durando's defence, that a commanding officer cannot always be bound by his promise, does not cover this point. Moreover, even if all had gone well, Ferrari had the right to know what the rest of the army was doing.

Secondly, Pinelli has asked (Vol. III, p. 378): why was it that Durando tried to stop Nugent by dividing his own force into three, and by occupying Bassano with only 4000 men as against 11,000? "To believe that he did this for military reasons would imply regarding him as destitute of all military knowledge." The true reason, Pinelli says, was that he did not want his Swiss to be contaminated by being with Ferrari's republicans.

As a matter of fact, up in the mountains the Swiss battalion had already retired from Primolano and the Austrian companies from Arsiè; but there had not yet been time for this news to reach Durando.

DEFENCE of the PIAVE in 1848
(Battle of Cornuda - May 8th & 9th)

About 5 miles

Nuger

Alps

Lt. Magdeburg

6th

Feltre

8th

Valleys

Arsie
Primolano

To the
Val Sugana

Valley of the R. Brenta

Mountains

Mt Grappa

7th

Quero

7th

Durando

Pederobba

8th

River

9th

Passagno

Onigo

Levada

8th & 9th

Ferrari

CORNUDA
(battle)

Crespano

8th

9th Durando

Asolo

Montel

4th to 6t
7th Ferra

River Brenta

Bassano

To Verona

Cittadella

Castelfranco

However, whatever the rights of the case, the results were absolutely disastrous. Ferrari's volunteers continued to hold their ground until 4.30, in expectation that the Swiss would arrive. But then their morale broke down. They had been almost twelve hours under musket and artillery fire, and were worn out by the unaccustomed strain and by hunger and thirst. Their own fire began to slacken; Ferrari was compelled to give the order to retire. The volunteers' losses cannot have been very great.[45] The fact was that they were played out; that they felt themselves outnumbered, and were bitterly angry at being left in the lurch. They retreated in good order; but, as Montecchi says, the Austrians numbered about 6000, whereas Ferrari had not got more than 2600 in action out of 4000 available. Ellesmere's anonymous Swiss officer tells us that it was a heavy flank attack which decided the day. Fortunately there was no pursuit.

During the retirement, however, it soon became evident that the day of strain had brought out the dissatisfaction and suspicion of their generals latent among these embryo politicians, more versed in perorations than in soldiering. The ranks began to break up.

No sooner had the young legionaries reached Montebelluna than their discipline gave way altogether. They considered that Durando had broken his promise of coming to their help. They wanted to know which of the two generals was deceiving them. "Chi tradiva?" was the question they shouted. "Which of the two was betraying us?" This train of reasoning, says Montecchi, spread among their ranks and caused a debacle. A large number passed through Montebelluna without halting, and departed for Treviso, twelve miles distant. And

---

[45] Montecchi speaks only of sixty wounded and does not mention the number of killed. The anonymous Swiss officer (Meyer Ott) says the Italians state their casualties at 140. Ferrari's official report says twenty-five to thirty killed and fifty-six wounded, but says that the numbers are not exact. Ovidi (pp. 86–90) gives thirty killed and 150 wounded; that is the number in the Austrian *Feldzug*. The Austrian losses were six killed and twenty-five wounded. *Feldzug*, IV, 24.

at 7 p.m. Ferrari saw himself compelled to give the order for the whole division to follow them.

Before starting, he wrote his third letter of that day to Durando, informing him of his position and retirement. He wrote with perfect dignity about not being reinforced, but ended by saying: "Whatever may be your motives, before military eyes you will not be able to find any excuse, for you received my note at 4 a.m. and you had only fourteen miles to march to my assistance."

That evening he received a fourth letter from Durando, explaining the reasons for his action, and saying that he would arrive at Montebelluna on the following day.

But with the news of the defeat, there was a general fear of being outflanked, and on every side the defence was falling in. That same evening, Ferrari wrote to Guidotti, who was defending the line of the river, directing him if necessary to retire as he thought fit. As a matter of fact, Guidotti's men were already retiring precipitately on Treviso, followed by his various subordinate officers from all the posts along the banks.

Thus there began a sort of natural concentration on Treviso. Guidotti's troops consisted of the Papal regular brigade, namely Grenadiers and Cacciatori, with the second half of the Papal battery and many corps of volunteers. Disorders were rife.[46]

Ferrari saw that it was necessary to end this situation. On May 10th, the day after the fight, he called together the superior officers of the various corps to discuss matters. At this council he proposed that Guidotti's brigade should re-occupy the line of the Piave, as the Austrians had not yet crossed it; while a battalion of Cacciatori (regulars) with the 2nd volunteer regiment, two small guns and twenty-five cavalrymen were to start northwards and occupy Monte-belluna. The officers all agreed, and he wrote to inform Durando; but before long they returned to him and, to his great surprise, said that their men, especially the Papal regulars, refused to march; partly because they were tired

[46] Ovidi, p. 90.

out, and partly because there had been no declaration of war
on the part of their government and they found that they
would be considered rebels. Evidently some of them now
considered that Durando had taken the Pope's name in vain.
This was a far worse blow than the defeat of the day before.[47]
Meanwhile the Austrians were not idle.

The following morning, May 11th, they were beginning to
approach Treviso. Nugent was at Falze, about nine miles
north-west of the town, and Schulzig, after crossing the river,
was at Visnadello, about six miles due north. Ferrari saw
that it was the moment to strike before they joined hands.
He therefore ordered out the Papal regular brigade (two
battalions of Grenadiers and two of Cacciatori), his cavalry
and three guns. At about two miles and a half from the city
they met the Austrian outposts, which they drove back for
about two miles, taking some prisoners. But—it seems evident—they had marched into a trap. The following account
of the engagement is given by "Ellesmere's officer":[48]

The Romans advanced with courage in close column against
the Kinsky Regiment and the Illyrian Croats, who quietly opened
their ranks and received the enemy with a murderous fire of grape.
General Schulzig then took the offensive, captured a gun and many
of the Papal Dragoons who endeavoured to cover the retreat.

According to this account there must have been some very
bad leading.

[47] It must be admitted that by refusing to march they probably
saved themselves from being swallowed in one gulp by the Austrians.
It is hard to see why Ferrari wanted to send off a helpless little force
of about 3000 men with no cavalry and only three guns to march
straight into the arms of Nugent, who had now about 18,000 men,
forty or fifty guns and plenty of cavalry. He had only taken fifteen
hours to bridge the Piave.

[48] Ellesmere, p. 109. This Swiss account is more charitable than
those of Ferrari, Montecchi or d'Azeglio; and in this connection it
must be remembered that d'Azeglio and Durando were absolutely
certain to give the most adverse account possible of the volunteers,
because it was they who had inveigled them over the frontier before
they were fit for a campaign.

The result of this engagement put an end to all discipline in Treviso. Even the officers "shouted treason and dissolution". So Ferrari told off a town-garrison[49] and gave orders that the rest should retire by night to Mestre (a twelve-mile march towards Venice), where he hoped to re-organise them. They arrived there on May 12th.

On the very next day, suddenly there appeared a bright spot in the picture, namely the news from Treviso. The garrison there had made a wonderful recovery. Apparently this was due, at all events partly, to the Neapolitan volunteers.[50] On May 14th General Lante wrote: "By our gunfire and by sorties of skirmishers, we prevented the enemy's advance-guard from approaching the city from Montebelluna, from Visnadello, or from La Carità. Our men behave with daring (*ardire*)." Also "the spirit of the country is for defence, that of the soldiers full of spirit, though not so fully displayed as one would like".

As for General Ferrari, he always upheld that if Durando had come up as arranged on the Austrian right flank, the Italians would have won a victory and have cut Radetzky's communications. It must have been a sad time for a veteran who had begun his career so successfully in the days of Napoleon. Happily we know that before the end he was fully justified by his own officers; in the State Archives in Rome

---

[49] General Guidotti was offered command of the garrison, but he refused it; he was a Bolognese noble, aged fifty-eight, with a very fine military record (including the Iron Cross, won during Napoleon's Russian campaign). At this debacle in Treviso he was in such despair that he went out with a small party, threw himself onto the Austrians and got killed. One of his party was Ugo Bassi, who was wounded.

[50] "An officer of the Neapolitan corps harangued his companions from the steps of the cathedral, calling upon them to swear to defend the city or die. Some of the Romagnol corps who had assembled in order to go to Mestre, began to hesitate; a draft from Sinigaglia joined the Neapolitans; others followed; and a little calm and order was restored among those excited bands." Fabris, II, 326, quoting Santalina, *Treviso nel* 1848.

there is a private letter from Colonel del Grande, O.C. of the 2nd Legion. Del Grande was a Civica colonel, one of those who after the disaster passed on to Durando; he was killed during the defence of Vicenza. This rather touching letter was written to his son, a boy at school. It should be impartial. He says:

Our General Ferrari has been called a traitor; and he made no reply because he did not want to shift the blame onto the men who deserved it. This morning, in the presence of the commanding officers, he had an explanation with General Durando, who has arrived here with his division. Everything was just as Ferrari had promised. The fault was Durando's for not having kept his promise.[51]

This ended Ferrari's division. What happened to all the men is very uncertain. At the end of May Durando issued a new plan in which he claimed that there were 16,400 Papal soldiers left in Venetia; in Treviso there were about 2700 out of a total garrison of 3600; at Vicenza there were 3000; at Padua 1700; and in Durando's mobile force there were to be 9000. His plan was to use his mobile force to march between the three garrisoned towns and attack the Austrian communications; in fact, a plan rather like that of Radetzky in the Quadrilateral. But all these figures are very unreliable.[52]

Certainly—in spite of the accusations of Durando and of d'Azeglio—in many cases the motives for the volunteers' defection were genuinely political; and there is a good deal to be said for them. They had been inveigled over the frontier by Durando's order of April 5th, representing a war appeal from the Pope to which they could hardly turn a deaf ear. Then, after they had crossed the frontier, there came the Allocution, telling them that officially there was no war. Naturally their confidence was shaken; and then, on top of several other incidents, there came the *Vengo correndo*

[51] This letter is in the Archivio politico, B. 25, Fasc. 162, No. 578. (Rome, Archivio di Stato.)
[52] Ovidi, pp. 106, 324 and elsewhere, quoting documents.

episode at Cornuda. After that they could not trust their generals. Del Grande tells us that in his battalion the men most determined of all to do no more service were the same who had stood best at Cornuda. The 2nd Legion was the only one which could never be reconstituted.

II

Nugent had accomplished half his task. He had forced the passage of the Piave; and he had crippled the Papal army sufficiently to prevent its blocking the way. He could get through to Verona. But he had not crippled it sufficiently to prevent it hanging about his line of communication. Durando, though temporarily reduced to a command of less than 4000 men, was still there, able to make Venetia unsafe for the passage of supplies; and the safety of supplies, says the *Feldzug*, was more important than the actual increase of Radetzky's forces in Verona.

Nugent's march along the Piave had been an uncommonly brilliant and adventurous piece of work for a man of seventy-one; but now an old head-wound prevented his going any farther. He had received powerful reinforcements, so he decided to divide his army into two divisions; the largest, 18,500 strong, under Count Thurn, was to proceed directly to Verona to reinforce Radetzky; the second corps, only 16,000 strong, was to remain and secure the territory round Treviso.

In Durando's favour it may be said that in spite of the disaster at Cornuda, he and d'Azeglio could claim one valuable achievement, in the shape of their small but efficient column of nearly 4000 Swiss, soon to be doubled by Italian troops, none of whom, but for the proclamation of April 5th, would ever have crossed the frontier. He was considered a good soldier, and he was on his mettle, for he knew that half the world was calling him *Traditore*. Against the overwhelming numbers of the Austrians it was impossible to block the way; but his first plan was to place himself at points from which he could threaten the bridges over the Brenta; and when that became impossible, he proposed to garrison Vicenza and make it a safe centre of operations.

With these schemes in view he began by occupying Cittadella and then Piazzola, places from which he could threaten the bridges; but the Venetian republic insisted on his coming nearer to their beloved town of Treviso. This left the way open to the Austrians.[53]

On the 19th Thurn passed through Cittadella and crossed the Brenta; on the 20th he arrived at Vicenza and pushed his advanced troops straight into the suburbs. But here he experienced a check. Durando, by a prompt use of the railway, had got the 3rd Roman Legion (Colonel Gallieni) and the University battalion inside its walls just in time to stiffen the defence; and the citizens showed excellent spirit; they raised about 5000 armed men and fired so effectively from their barricades and windows that Thurn withdrew his advanced troops and decided to pass on to Verona. To secure his very long train of waggons, he made a considerable detour; but on the 21st he was caught up by Durando at Sant' Olmo and suffered further casualties. His losses on the first day were 8 dead and 90 wounded; at Sant' Olmo 2 dead and 30 wounded: those of the Italians 12 killed and 70 wounded on May 20th, and about fifty casualties on the 21st.

Thus, on the 22nd the Austrians were free to proceed to Verona. But Radetzky was not satisfied. His communications were not yet safe, and these 18,500 men were too many for him to feed for long. On the 22nd, therefore, he sent Thurn orders to turn back on his tracks and to take Vicenza, so as to clear the whole country behind him, and then to rejoin him by the 25th.

Radetzky evidently believed that Thurn's 18,500 men, with their forty pieces of artillery—howitzers, twelve-pounders and rockets—were quite strong enough to take Vicenza.

[53] *V.* Trevelyan, *Manin*, p. 178, and the authorities whom he quotes.

The problem now before Count Thurn had one obvious solution; the town of Vicenza is in the hand of anyone who can occupy the Berico hills. The long, narrow spur of Monte Berico runs northward for miles until it actually overhangs the city lying in the plain below. Anybody standing on the summit of that final hill could bombard any part of the town; but if attacked from the plain, Vicenza is much harder to take. It is surrounded by beautiful red-brick walls which in parts are guarded by the River Retrone, and evidently are stronger than they seem.

Thurn provided for both alternatives. Advancing along the road from Verona he detached a right-hand column (about 2350 strong with a rocket-battery) to make a detour southwards, to climb the Berico hills, move along the narrow ridge and then attack the town from the southern heights above it.

His central column, under Kleinberg, consisting of about 6500 men and twelve guns, was to advance along the road from Verona and attack the Porta del Castello within the suburb of S. Felice.

His left-hand column, consisting of 3500 men, was to incline to the left and attack the Porta Santa Croce slightly north-west of Vicenza.

His reserve, 5250 men, remained at Sant' Olmo.

To assist this more difficult attack across the plain, he relied on bringing off a surprise-by-night followed by a bombardment during the day, which he hoped would terrorise the citizens into submission. The citizens, however, were much more spirited than he supposed.

The garrison now consisted of about 11,000 men in all; and so far from being taken by surprise they had spent two days in fortifying the approaches with barricades and abattis, and, very much more important, they had cut the river bank of the Retrone and thereby flooded the low ground between the road from Verona and the steep sides of Monte Berico. This was a most fortunate inspiration; it resulted in crippling Thurn's main attack.

The night of the 23rd-24th was dark and rainy. The Austrian troops moved off in the small hours. It was not long before the first column found its advance impeded by the flooded land on the right, but eventually it commenced its attack on the Porta del Castello, while the left-hand column simultaneously attacked the Porta Santa Croce. The most serious fighting was done by Kleinberg's battalions. At first they found themselves shelled by seven Italian guns from Santa Felice. In reply they brought up a battery of six-pounders, and the Italian guns were compelled to retire, but remained in positions from whence they could take the assailants in flank. The Austrian infantry then attacked with great vigour and drove back a Swiss company which was occupying the front line. The Swiss returned and retook the position; and after that the Austrians again took it. (Ovidi, pp. 111-12.)

By now it was 5 a.m., and, profiting by this success, they brought up some forty guns and opened a bombardment.

Simultaneously on their left, Schulzig's brigade had attacked a large warehouse near the Porta Santa Croce, but the defenders, who were supported by the 2nd battalion of the 2nd Swiss Regiment, clung tenaciously to their positions.

Then began the systematic bombardment of the town. It lasted three hours. According to d'Azeglio some 3000 projectiles of all sorts were thrown into Vicenza, but they were of small calibre and no civilian was actually killed by them, and no house completely wrecked. Meanwhile the population showed no signs of alarm; women were looking out of the windows and many people were in the cafés.

As already stated, the only real chance for the Austrians was that the column on their right flank should succeed in climbing up Monte Berico and capturing the extreme point of Madonna del Monte overlooking the town. This endeavour, however, proved to be a complete failure; the flooded ground had compelled that column to make so wide a detour that the men were tired out and never came seriously into action. At

9 a.m. therefore, when the crisis of the battle arrived, Thurn perceived that his left flank was held up at Santa Croce, his centre *embourbé* at Porta del Castello, and that his right flank was not available. Consequently he gave the order to retire. He was followed by a sortie from Santa Croce, headed by the Swiss and some Trevisans, but by noon all firing had ceased. This was a very cheering success for the Italians. According to Ovidi they had only lost about 20 killed and 66 wounded, whereas the Austrians admit to 170 men, of whom one-third were prisoners.[54]

At this point Durando complains, not without justice, that he was "let down" by the Neapolitan army. It had reached the right bank of the Po and he was expecting it to come to his assistance; he was then to become the right wing of the Piedmontese army. But, as we shall now see, the Neapolitans did not arrive.

Nevertheless, to some extent Durando had retrieved his defeat. Although the Austrians had got past him, with his 11,000 men in Vicenza he could still harass Radetzky's communications and make it very difficult for him to get supplies; and he started at once to fortify the city.

It remained to be seen how soon the old Marshal would deal with the military situation; but first it behoves us to see whether the political situation was irretrievably lost in Naples.

---

[54] *Austrian authorities: Feldzug*, IV, 29–31; Hilleprandt, pp. 185–89; Schönhals, II, 14–17; Kunz, p. 39; Willisen, p. 93; Wolf Schneider, p. 74.

Italian authorities: Fabris, II, 340; Ovidi, pp. 111–12. The State Archives in Rome contain hundreds of interesting letters and documents including reports from Durando, d'Azeglio, Ferrari and various other officers. They have been summarised, to some extent, in a valuable book by Ovidi. *V.* also the works of Durando, d'Azeglio, Montecchi already quoted. As to Durando's doings *v.* also his own letters of May 13th, 15th, 20th, 26th (written by d'Azeglio), 30th. Rome, Archivio di Stato (Archivio politico, B. 25, 26; 33, etc.); and, of course, his *Succinta Relazione*.

Chapter XV

NAPLES. "THE 15TH OF MAY"

May 15th, 1848, is the historic date on which matters in Naples came to a crisis.

In a general way Neapolitan history does not often enter into the Risorgimento progress, but—to simplify this two months of tangle—we must quote five principal dates:

January 12th.	The Sicilian rebellion.
January 29th.	Ferdinand grants a Constitution.
February 10th.	Ferdinand publicly swears to the Constitution.
April 3rd.	Troya's ministry of Moderate Liberals appointed.
May 15th.	Parliament is to meet.

The Constitution granted by Ferdinand was more or less a replica of that of Louis Philippe.

Since we last spoke of Naples (April 7th) the political arena had been growing more and more dangerous. The Liberal ministry was unable to keep order, taxes were hard to collect and crimes hard to punish; in some districts the landowners' properties were invaded, but Conforti—Minister of Police, one of Saliceti's extremists now turned Moderate—was unwilling to employ any force except the National Guard. Already there was an agitation[1] in full progress to change the newly granted Constitution before it had ever been set up. With Paris in revolution, the Opposition leaders thought

---

[1] Were the Neapolitans at that time sufficiently trained to undertake self-government? The Deputy Petrucelli (p. 29) was a leading member of the Opposition, an enthusiastic champion of *Il Popolo*, and he tells us that three-quarters of the voters could neither read nor write. As matters turned out very few went to the polls. Tivaroni (p. 200) says 150,000 out of a population of over 6,000,000: Barberisi, who was one of the chiefs of police, says 125,000. *Atti*, p. 145. *V*. also Nitti, p. 78.

they could "squeeze" Ferdinand. In this connection we may perhaps be allowed to repeat a previous opinion, namely, that the wisest policy in Liberal interests just then was to nail the King down to the existing Constitution, while such a course still remained possible.[2] For the moment they had him beneath their hammer, but in some districts the tide was beginning to turn. The Plebs had begun to say that it preferred one absolute King to several thousand amateur statesmen, and that Pope Pius' Allocution of April 29th proved that, after all, he did not consider it such a bounden duty to go to the war.

As to the above consideration, opinions may differ, but there is one point at all events which now seems beyond a doubt, that Liberal historians cannot justly accuse Ferdinand of perjury on the grounds that a year later he dissolved Parliament once and for all, for the Liberals themselves had treated the Constitution as non-existent from the start.

What had happened was as follows:

On February 10th Ferdinand had sworn the Constitution before all the grandees of the Kingdom, in the Church of San Francesco, with great solemnity, and amid heartfelt public rejoicings.[3] All were confident that now, at all events, the King could never revoke his promise of January 29th.

---

[2] This was afterwards the opinion of Massari and several other Liberals. He was one of the United Italy party. V. Massari, p. 89. On p. 10 he divided the Neapolitan public into four parties: (1) Absolutists, strong at Court and in a large part of the army. (2) Muratists and Liberals, numerous but with no aims outside Naples. (3) United Italy, his own party, excellent but not very numerous. (4) Republicans, hardly a party in being. V. also Nitti, p. 98.

[3] Leopardi, *Narrazioni storiche*, p. 81, has two pages of rejoicings over it; v. also p. 101 as to Saliceti's programme and its being influenced by the revolution in Paris and Vienna. Nitti, p. 78: "Enthusiasm reached delirium. Demonstrations succeeded demonstrations and shouts succeeded shouts. For whole weeks the city was beflagged." The Piedmontese ambassador also spends two pages over the "cheers and Te Deum and illuminations". V. Turin Arch., Lettere Ministri Napoli, Feb. 12th, 1848.

But then news arrived of revolution in Paris and Vienna, and Saliceti's Opposition began to think they could claim a more democratic measure. In Saliceti's seven-point programme, there were two main proposals: (1) To prevent a House of Peers coming into existence; (2) To win authority for the Lower House to reform the whole Statute, and thus become virtually a Constituent Assembly.

These two aims ran through the whole crisis, which soon became very bitter. On April 3rd, therefore, when Ferdinand arranged for Troya's ministers to take office, he decided to make a slight popular concession as to the peers. For this first grant of peerages only, he agreed that during the coming general election each constituency should send up a list of names of men suitable for the Upper House. From these lists of 180 candidates in all, he would select his first fifty peers.[4] It was settled also that when both Houses were at work, the two Houses in agreement with the King should have the privilege of developing the Statuto, "especially as regards the House of Peers".

Thus he had bound himself for the first appointment of peers to select fifty of them from the lists returned by the constituencies; and he admitted that, once established, the Constitution (the King, Lords and Commons) might develop its own institutions, especially those relating to the Upper House. Throughout all this period of interminable wrangling, he clung to his word *develop*, whereas the Extremists aimed at forcing him to grant powers to the Commons to "reform" all the rest.

The Opposition at once proceeded to agitate on these lines. In a general way it had little success, but in the constituencies it did succeed in raising opposition against the peers.

On April 18th the General Election took place. Moderate men were returned, but most of the constituencies declined

---

[4] There were some minor points, chiefly a widening of the franchise and of the qualifications for deputies. For the programme *v. Atti*, p. 33.

to give any names for peers; they either refused to vote or they wrecked the returns. About nine out of fourteen provinces were hostile,[5] and apparently the Extremists thought that, in view of its unpopularity, the King would drop the Upper House out of his sworn Constitution.

On May 13th, however, they realised their mistake. Within two days of the opening of the new Parliament the King published his list of fifty peers all drawn from the returns of the constituencies. He has been blamed for not publishing it sooner, but surely that would have been inviting trouble. For every peer chosen he must have made two or three enemies;[6] and it was very important for him and for the propertied classes to make sure of establishing a House of Lords. Once in being, the extent of its powers would become a constitutional question.

No doubt partisans of the Opposition were in a state of irritation, for on that same evening, the 13th, they broke out into resistance over another matter. The elected deputies had been holding a preliminary sitting in the Municipal Hall at Monte Oliveto, and, at its close, the President gave out formally that the oath of allegiance to the new Constitution would be sworn at the opening of Parliament on the 15th. Thereupon a Radical deputy, called Petrucelli, and some of his followers refused point-blank to swear it. They said the Constitution of February 10th could not be sworn by itself without the promises of April 3rd. If the King proceeded to swear it, they would walk out of the church; they drew up a formal protest.

In fact they wanted to make the promises as to the first

---

[5] La Cecilia, pp. 43, 59, says that nine out of fifteen provinces sent up names and that Ferdinand selected his fifty peers from these.

[6] We have not seen this reason for the delay given by any Italian writer, and it is possible that Ferdinand had not much time to spare. He could hardly have received all the election returns required before the end of April, and then it was necessary to decide on his list and make sure that each one would accept. There may have been refusals.

batch of peers, the development of the Constitution and the lowered franchise, part of the Statuto. Obviously these were temporary and controversial issues which could not be interpolated off-hand into a permanent written Constitution, already sworn by the King.

Troya and the great majority of the deputies were in favour of swearing the Statuto as it stood, as that did not preclude their altering it; but some of the recalcitrants did not conceal the fact that they had been elected, not to swear the Constitution, but to draw up another instead[7] of it. Undoubtedly their aim was that the Lower House should become a constituent assembly according to the original plan of Saliceti. The majority perceived this, but they seem to have been alarmed by hints of violence, so they decided to suppress the inaugural ceremony altogether, and with it the oath; and Troya and the ministers actually agreed to this.

Meanwhile, however, the King had published the programme of the inaugural ceremony for the 15th. It began with a solemn swearing of the Constitution in the Church of S. Lorenzo, by the King, Lords and Commons. On the following morning, the 14th, the oath still appeared in the ceremonial. This infuriated the Opposition, who now said that they had been promised that there should be no oath.[8]

On May 14th began a twenty hours' struggle between the two opposing interests, namely the elected deputies at Monte Oliveto, and the King in his palace. This interminable wrangle can only be shortly summarised. It was an effort by Extremist deputies to win power for the Lower House to initiate "reforms" of the rest of the Constitution. The King, on his part, meant to stand by the sworn Constitution of February 10th, but he was ready to undertake that it should be developed by the King, Lords and Commons.

Between these two opposing sides were Troya and his ministers. Certainly during this calamitous day they played the most contemptible part, supporting whichever side

[7] *V.* Paladino, pp. 194-7.   [8] La Farina.

seemed strongest. It looks as if their main purpose had been to retain their posts as ministers, and were not yet certain whether their master would be the King or the Commons.

None of the three contending authorities realised that they were arousing a fourth element, irresponsible, reckless, predatory—the element which in every large city loves a revolution for the sake of excitement, plunder or unpaid scores—and that this element would carry the poor would-be-heroic Extremists into one of the most causeless scenes of bloodshed in all history.

The controversy was fought over the actual wording of the oath of allegiance.[9] Each side wanted it worded so as to protect its own interests. To whom were they to swear allegiance? During the day there were four chief crises.

Firstly, Pica's formula. After a good deal of discussion the deputies accepted a form of oath drawn up by a member called Pica; everyone was to swear allegiance to the Constitution, "together with all reforms passed by the National Representation, especially those concerning the peerage".

This was manifestly an attempt to claim powers for the representative Commons to change anything they disliked, and especially to reform the peerage. Once that they had this power, they might leave the King very little authority except his Veto. Yet it was passed by the Moderate majority, and signed by Troya and his ministry. It must have been an unpleasant surprise to Ferdinand to find his ministers siding against him, in spite of their promises of April 3rd. However, he refused to accept the formula; they resigned, but he did

---

[9] Paladino, p. 206. For use as a general text-book we are largely indebted to the interesting and exhaustive book of Signor Paladino. He is the latest authority on the subject, and by far the most thorough. Moreover, he has had access to the volumes of evidence collected by the Commission of Public Safety (p. 474). But our accounts of the principal episodes are nearly all taken from the memoirs of the revolutionist leader who played the chief part in each case. Our sources are either revolutionary writings or foreign diplomatic reports.

not formally accept their resignation. The net result was that they had successfully made their peace with the deputies without having to retire.

In reply he sent a message by his Radical minister Conforti. Conforti explained the King's point of view to the deputies at some length, and urged them to remember that there was war in Lombardy. But Dr Lanza, the President, received his speech with resentment, told him that the Chamber would discuss all matters, including the war, as it thought fit. "The King is only one man, but we represent a whole people."[10]

This exchange had no great importance, except for the fact that it gave rise to popular rumours that the King had refused to agree to the terms of the deputies, and here and there the first angry mutterings were to be heard.

May 14th was a Sunday, and in one of the squares, it is said, some fifty armed strangers were standing about, on the ground where, later on, arose the first barricade.

At Monte Oliveto some outsiders arrived, and actually walked into the house of meeting; before long they were heard encouraging the deputies. "Il re tradisce la nazione... ma non temete. Coraggio, Coraggio."[11] During the afternoon these people were ejected by a captain in the National Guard, but it turned out later on that he was La Cecilia, a Carbonaro of 1820 and one of the best known Extremists in Naples.

Next we have Dupont's attempt at a compromise. By about 8 p.m. the deputies had received the formal refusal from the King, but it was accompanied by a formula of his own. They might swear allegiance to the Statuto "and such laws developing it as the constituted authorities may adopt". This of course was his original position, that he would agree to the King, Lords and Commons *developing* the original constitution. Obviously, it was the very reverse of Pica's formula, but Troya and his ministers had signed it "because

[10] Paladino, pp. 211–14.
[11] Petrucelli, p. 100. "The King is betraying the nation, but have no fear. Courage!"

the King will have nothing else". In this way they had made their peace also with the King.

The deputies were furious; but for the next two hours there were no further developments.

Meanwhile, however, the ministers had sent to the King a French resident named Dupont, who was well known and respected in Naples. This conversation resulted in Ferdinand's offering another formula to the deputies. In it he clung to his word "development", but it was a little more explicit than the previous wording. The ministers signed it and withdrew their resignations, although the terms were directly opposed to those of Pica's formula, over the refusal of which they had resigned!

When Dupont arrived in the assembly of deputies, the chairman, Dr Lanza, greeted him much as he had previously greeted Conforti, with a shout of "The King is only one, but we, though fewer than a hundred, are 7,000,000, because we represent the whole nation".[12]

Lanza would have refused the new formula, but the deputies had begun to realise that matters in the town were becoming dangerous, and most of them were in favour of considering it. In fact, they seemed about to accept it, when suddenly a captain in the National Guard ran into the assembly rooms, sprang on to one of the seats and shouted out: "Treason! The King's troops have issued from the barracks, their cavalry has occupied the Piazza before the palace, and both horse and foot are about to attack Monte Oliveto!"

Immense sensation! As far as we can tell this was only a

---

[12] This was an extremist statement, for they represented only 150,000 voters in the whole state. It might be retorted by their enemies that they were only a Liberal clique which had temporarily come to the surface owing to the Sicilian rebellion, the revolution in Paris, Pius IX's Liberalism, and the fall of Metternich. Still, among the Moderates there did exist quite a fair proportion of genuine men, though not very practical.

On this chapter, v. Nisco, *Reame di Napoli*, II, 209; *Atti*, p. 88; Paladino, p. 232; also Tivaroni, *Ital. Merid.* 206 et seq.

dramatic coup on the part of La Cecilia. All that the troops had done was to reinforce a guard in the palace, but instantly the room was filled with shouts of "Tradimento!" and with a hurricane of voices, ejaculations, and howls of every kind: "Make the drums beat to quarters to collect the National Guard, and let us construct barricades for our defence." Fortunately, however, Dr Lanza remained cool, and the King's envoys at once told everyone that no movement of troops was contemplated. La Cecilia was still attitudinising ("Time presses...we will defend the assembly with barricades") when Lanza ordered him out. After this the deputies proceeded to vote on the King's latest formula, and threw it out by 58 votes to 22.

At that moment, however, fresh cries arose from the strangers in the corridors. "To arms, we are betrayed!" So Lanza asked Colonel Gabriele Pepe, as O.C. of the National Guard, to go out to the Royal Palace, and enquire whether there was really any movement of troops, and if so, to ask the King to countermand it.

Old Colonel Pepe went out into the town, accompanied by La Cecilia and several other officers. Their walk that night was the most extraordinary experience. They could hardly make their way through the crowds of citizens shouting for barricades, gesticulating wildly, and calling on Pepe to order the drums to beat the "Assembly" in every military quarter—an order which he continually refused to issue. When he reached the Piazza Carità he asked them to let him through to the royal palace, but at that moment four armed citizens, one of whom was wearing the bonnet of a National Guard, crowded round the old man and pointed their bayonets at his throat to compel him to order the "Assembly", while a fifth, who was unarmed, stood by, tearing his hair, thumping his forehead with his fist, biting his fingers, with a thousand other gestures of despair, and shouting, "We are betrayed! Barricades! Barricades!"[13]

[13] Paladino, p. 241, quoting the deposition of Pepe and others. *V*. also descriptions by La Cecilia.

A few minutes later, however, the drums of one of the National Guard battalions beat the "Assembly", and then the crowd precipitated themselves into barricade-building with all the whole-hearted abandon of workers who are using other people's furniture for their raw material. It was every man for himself. Under the administration of Conforti and the Neapolitan Liberal party there was no police except the National Guard, so, that evening, a good many citizens must have begun to regret the regime of Del Carretto.

Meanwhile the King had sent out another formula to Monte Oliveto, but as it differed very little from his previous suggestion, it was refused.

He had only just been told of the disastrous turn that matters were taking. His A.D.C., the Prince of Ischitella, who perceived that the town could defy all authority, and make its own terms once they had barricades, kept urging him to stop their erection. But Ferdinand would not hear of bloodshed. "Why are they erecting barricades?" he asked of Colonel Piccolellis. "Your Majesty, because they have heard that your troops are moving out of their barracks to attack the National Guard." "It is not true," said the King, "no such orders have been given, and if by some mistake any of them issue out of their barracks they will be ordered back at once."[14]

Until midnight there was no movement of troops. After that an order was issued to occupy certain posts in the town, and some detachments moved out. Before they reached the posts, however, they were ordered back to barracks by the King.[15]

Time was now running short, and Ferdinand decided to make a concession which would prevent an outbreak. He sent Colonel Piccolellis to the Monte Oliveto with a message that he would not insist on their taking any oath at all, until after the *Verificazione dei poteri*.[16] This postponed the oath for

[14] Paladino, pp. 248–9, quoting the depositions of Piccolellis and of d' Ischitella.
[15] Maag, p. 66, gives a detailed description by Captain Sturler.
[16] This ceremony does not exist in the British Parliament.

three days, but, in return, the barricades were to be taken down. Colonel Piccolellis dashed off at full speed; it was a message of peace. Parliament would meet without taking any oath at all. This was an immense concession[17] and was received with "scenes of joy". The members embraced one another; here was the end of their all-night sitting. At 5 a.m. they drew up and issued a formal invitation to the young men to dismantle their barricades. After that they retired to bed, leaving a commission of a few deputies to make sure that the demolition was carried out.

The deputies' order[18] was duly posted up for all to see. It was perfectly understood; even La Cecilia went home satisfied that the barricades would be demolished, and all concerned could proceed with the opening of Parliament.[19] But they were about to learn that those who arouse revolution cannot then countermand it merely by posting up a proclamation on the wall—or even a hundred proclamations. It was there to take its toll.

[17] Paladino, p. 253, quoting Piccolellis' deposition, and Troya. The deputies seemed to have assumed that it was even greater than it was. The King did not intend to give in to their wording of the oath. Indeed it is hard to see how he could do so without sacrificing his sworn constitution and letting them reduce his own prerogatives most probably to a mere right of veto.

This final concession is omitted by La Farina; being a Sicilian his whole account is biassed against Ferdinand. *V.* La Farina, *Storia*, III, 515. *V.* Pepe, *Histoire*, 1847-9, p. 114. For standard histories there are Tivaroni, *Ital. Merid.* III, 208. Also Masi, *Il Risorgimento*, II, 285.

[18] The salient words of this proclamation were: "As the purpose at which we were aiming, namely the great welfare of this nation, has been fully obtained, the National Representatives feel it their duty to invite the National Guards to efface from the city every appearance of hostility by demolishing the barricades, so that we may be able to inaugurate the most solemn ceremony of opening Parliament without any reminder of events, which though glorious, were unfortunate." *Atti*, p. 45.

[19] *V.* La Cecilia, II, 63 *et seq.*; Massari, p. 154. Settembrini, I, 286. He says that La Cecilia was there wearing a Turkish sword and proclaiming that this was a revolution.

The Liberal party had mismanaged the change of regime to an incredible degree. They had got rid of Del Carretto without substituting any strong police system for his, which ought to have been their first precaution. Naturally in any city such as Naples there is always an element in the population which wants nothing better than a smashing of authority;[20] and the deputies, in their desire to turn the Chamber conceded to them into a Constituent Assembly, had closed their eyes to the raising of the barricades against the King.[21]

Thus there began one of the most causeless instances of slaughter and bloodshed ever recorded in history. The young men, when approached even by their own side, swore that anyone who touched their defences was "a traitor" and "sold to the government". They forgot that the barricades had no longer any purpose, says Petrucelli (p. 107), who was there. Settembrini, too, was there, but afterwards he carefully disassociated himself from having had any previous knowledge of what was to happen.

According to Paladino and others, there were about a thousand of these heterogeneous firebrands. Many were southerners, Calabrians, a few perhaps Sicilians and a few republicans. Apparently most of the National Guard went home; the ministers retired to the Palazzo della Foresteria, and the deputies sat in Monte Oliveto passing resolutions.[22]

[20] "A body of perennial unsatisfiables, seized by a delirious desire for rebellion at any price, and determined to provoke civil war, imposed itself upon a great city; dragging with it a few national guards, it overturned carriages, wrenched the wooden signs off shops, tore up pavements and smashed up door posts and gates in order to build barricades." Nisco, *Reame di Napoli*, 1824–60, II, 209. Nisco was a revolutionist.

[21] Paladino, p. 175, arrives at almost similar conclusions as to the cause. *V.* Paladino, p. 449, quoting the Royal Circular of May 18th.

[22] "The example of Papirius in his curule chair waiting for the Gauls to kill him decided the deputies not to move from their temporary hall at Monte Oliveto." La Cecilia, p. 75. And Petrucelli, who was in the Assembly, tells us: "The assembly, distracted, tumultuous, on its feet, without any definite aim, torn by a thousand

Even at the last moment the King made another effort to get the barricades peaceably demolished and thus avoid bloodshed. He sent fifty unarmed men to carry out the work, but the defenders would not let them do it.[23] The temper of the extreme "Barricadisti" is exemplified by the claim of a Calabrian named Mileto, supported by a deputy named Ricciardi; they wanted to tell the King that they would not pull down the barricades until he had let them garrison the forts and sent his army forty miles outside Naples—half of it to go to the war.[24]

The garrison was about 12,000 strong, of whom 3784 were Swiss.[25] It included one battery and twelve squadrons.

For several hours the two sides stood watching one another. Then, at about 11.30 a.m., a single shot was fired—one of the National Guards had let off his musket by accident—and the revolutionists followed this up by two aimed shots which killed a sentry in front of the palace and brought down a Guards' officer wounded. Then the fighting began, and it lasted for about six hours. During these six hours the Swiss and the Guards systematically took position after position. First they would shatter a barricade with one or two rounds of artillery, and then they would rush it, but the revolutionists fired on them from the windows on either side, and many houses had to be stormed, and this led to the killing of many innocent people and to pillage by the mob. For the time being the "Lazzaroni" were free to work their will, and the results must have been appalling.

Undoubtedly those were six terrible hours for many families who had had no part or share in erecting the barricades.

doubts, heated by varied passions, understood nothing, took in nothing, would do nothing, and voted nothing." He says, however, that later on it settled down peacefully.

[23] V. Paladino, p. 266, quoting d' Epiro and the depositions of Pepe and other officers.

[24] V. Paladino, p. 270, quoting Ferdinando, Pepe and other officers. Also Ricciardi, p. 1481; Vials, *Atti*, pp. 19, 20, and Tivaroni, p. 208.   [25] Maag, p. 73; Paladino, p. 291.

It is impossible to estimate the losses with any certainty; the wildest figures have been given, but we offer the following: Paladino (p. 257) says that the Swiss had 46 killed and 187 wounded, total 233. Maag (a Swiss) says 36 killed, 169 wounded, total 205. Tivaroni says that the Swiss had 28 killed and 194 wounded.

As to the "Barricadisti" Paladino says 99 killed and 84 wounded taken to hospital, but that naturally there were far more wounded who went to their own homes to escape from the police. Tivaroni believes there were 104 killed and over 400 wounded.

The chief historical importance, however, of this episode of May 15th is that it became the first great lever in the hands of the nationalist party against Ferdinand. It was taken up with extraordinary bitterness all over Italy. The King's defection at this crisis of the war was at once made a damning accusation against him. Henceforth he became "one of the rulers who has betrayed us". At first the outcry was a genuine explosion of fury, but before very long "the 15th of May" became part of a campaign of propaganda by men who saw that there could be no united Italy as long as the Bourbons were in Naples.

Mazzini's paper, for instance, *L'Italia del Popolo*, immediately seized this opportunity to revile Ferdinand. "Raging (*delirante*) with the spirit of his grandfather and of Carolina he masks himself and forms plots; and so the history of his cruel perjuries is the story of his life."

Even in Turin the *Opinione* wrote: "Between the Bourbons and Italy there can be no further agreement. The blood-stained winding sheet in which Ferdinand has wrapped his people must become the winding sheet of his dynasty."[26] And yet the Piedmontese ambassador in Naples had sent to

---

[26] There were innumerable articles of this type and Signor Giovanni Storza has collected scores of abstracts from newspapers all over Italy, most of them more violent than that in the Turin *Opinione. V.* p. 67 of his work, *La Costituzione napoletana del* 1848, Turin, 1921.

Turin a report entirely in favour of the King, and felt so strongly on the subject that on June 8th he wrote: "There is a universal howl of execration all over Italy against Ferdinand, and he is suffering undeserved abuse."[27]

And Napier's opinion ran as follows: "On the whole the crisis has passed over with less harm than might have been predicted, the designs of the ill-disposed have been frustrated, and the apprehensions of those who were solicitous for the preservation of the Constitution have been allayed by the temperate course pursued by the King, and by the convocation of the electoral colleges on the 15th of next month, and of the new Parliament on the 1st of July."[28]

It is a pity that much of the Italian propaganda about "May 15th" 1848, should have found its way permanently into English histories. It has never been accepted by the serious historians[29] not even by the most devoted champions of the Risorgimento, and is less so than ever, now that the Bourbon name is no longer a political influence in Southern Italy.

Before we leave Naples, however, it is best to make clear that our work does not enter upon any of the questions as to prisons and other matters raised by Mr Gladstone in 1851 and 1852. This volume does not go beyond the year 1848— into the eighteenth year of the reign of King Ferdinand II.[30]

We must now return to the main narrative. Three days after the fighting, Ferdinand sent out a definite order recalling the army from the frontier. He required it at home to keep order;[31] and eventually he used it to reconquer Sicily.

[27] Turin Arch. *Ibid*.
[28] Napier to Palmerston, May 28th, 1848. *London Corr*. Part II, p. 541.
[29] Tivaroni, Masi, Rosi, etc.   [30] *V*. Appendix II.
[31] Speaking of the Swiss, Maag, pp. 57–8, says there would have been little order in Naples without them. They were constantly on duty. On p. 60, he says that after the outbreak there were 10,000 firearms found in Naples, but he gives no authority for this.

We can hardly doubt that he was thankful to escape from having to fight Austria, or that the same feeling prevailed throughout most of his people. The soldiers themselves could not possibly be anxious to offer their lives in a struggle which would produce no tangible benefit for Naples.

They had their chance of volunteering. General Pepe, who had arrived at Ferrara, refused to turn back, and made heroic efforts to persuade them to cross the frontier with him. Finally about 1200 or 1400 officers and men followed him over the River Po, and served during the siege of Venice. Those who fought did well.[32]

[32] Pepe himself said openly that without his presence the army would never cross the Po, "as was proved by subsequent events". That was one reason why he accompanied it instead of insisting on going by sea. *V. supra*, p. 152, note. None of the shrewdest judges of the situation believed that the Neapolitan nation or army was enthusiastic. Without going further than Farini's *Epist.* vol. II, we can find the opinions of Cosimo Ridolfi, Cardinal Amat at Bologna, Massimo d'Azeglio, Farini, etc. *V.* Farini, *Epist.* II, 239. Professor Montanelli (*Memorie*, p. 336) says that the soldiers openly shouted out "We want to return to Naples."

Chapter XVI

RADETZKY'S SWOOP. CURTATONE AND MONTANARA. GOITO. VICENZA MAY 29TH TO JUNE 10TH

I. CURTATONE AND MONTANARA

Having disposed of Naples and its King, we can now return to the main thread of the story, the duel between Charles Albert[1] and Radetzky.

For Radetzky the situation had been immensely improved by Durando's failure, and by the defection, now certain, of the Neapolitans.

On May 25th he had been joined by Nugent's reinforcements, 18,000 strong. But his communications were not yet safe. Vicenza, on the road to Austria, was garrisoned by Durando's 11,000 men, and consequently the Austrians in Verona might soon find themselves short of food supplies. Moreover—also an important consideration—the fortress of Peschiera was on the verge of starvation unless he could relieve it. But now he was in a position to retaliate. He had at least 51,000[2] men in Verona, of whom only 11,000 were required for garrison. That left him 40,000 men free to strike in any direction. He must break out from behind his Rideau:

---

[1] There was always some anxiety for Charles Albert's health. On May 14th Minghetti wrote to his friend Pasolini: "The King is always to the fore where there is danger. To see him—tall in person, fleshless, the colour of lead, with all the appearance of a man seriously ill, but with his eyes all alive and bright, though sad and never smiling—moving about fearless and calm under grape-shot from the enemy's guns, makes a very great impression on the army. One might imagine that he had a magnetic influence on the troops, if one can believe in magnetism...." Pasolini, *Carteggio*, I, 20.

[2] Hilleprandt, pp. 205–8.

how wise he had been in keeping open exits! There were two possible ways of doing this.

Firstly, he could march back thirty miles and capture Vicenza; it would be in reality a defensive action, for he would be securing his communications.

Secondly, he could break out in front, and, if possible, compel Charles Albert to retire. He would thus gain new territory, and at the same time perhaps relieve Peschiera.

Theoretically, Vicenza should have been the first objective —security before offence[3]—but Radetzky felt that to march back those thirty miles would mean leaving Verona without much defence. While he was away, Charles Albert, from his forward lines, might assail the Rideau again, or perhaps might even push on and take the Austrian columns in rear while they were still outside the walls of Vicenza. It seemed very advisable to shift Charles Albert from his nearer positions before starting back to clear Venetia.

To begin by an attack on the Piedmontese meant leaving his own communications unsecured while he took the offensive; but on the other hand, if successful, it might decide the fate of the whole war, and consequently that of Vicenza and of Peschiera as well.

The next question for Radetzky and Hess was: Where best to attack Charles Albert. There were two possible plans; they might, of course, try to drive a blow straight through to Peschiera, but this would mean assailing the Piedmontese positions at their strongest points; whereas, in preparing an attack they naturally aimed at striking with their whole force at the weakest point of the enemy, namely, his communications. If they could threaten his communications, they might compel the whole of the Piedmontese army to retire right back across the Mincio, and perhaps even to abandon Peschiera. They decided, therefore, on a bold plan. From Verona they were to march right across the front of the Piedmontese army to Mantua (diagonally from right to left),

---

[3] *V.* Willisen, p. 116 *et seq.*

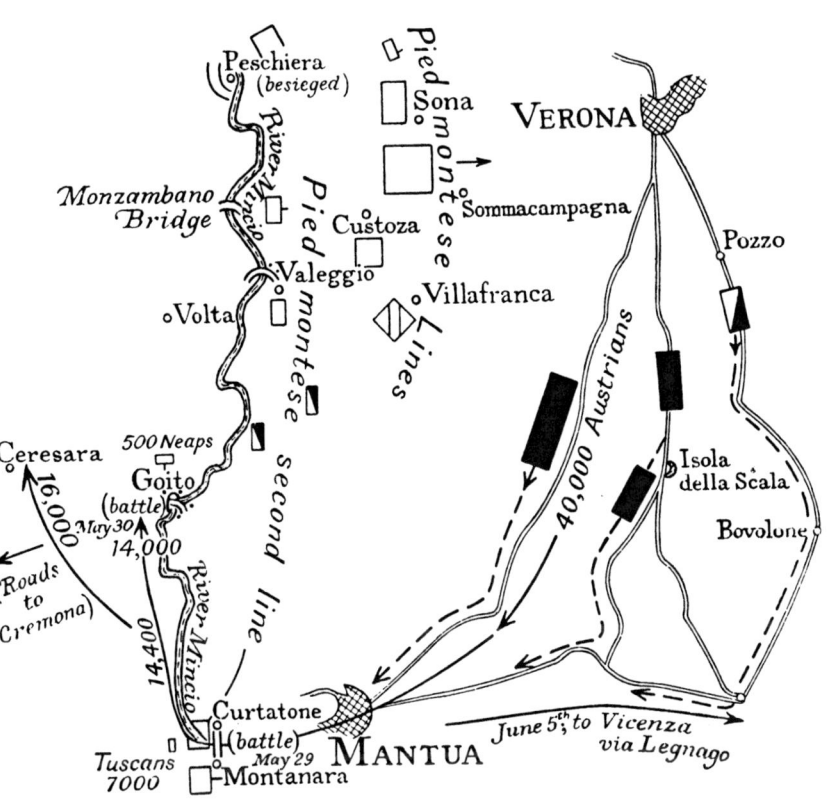

Peschiera
(besieged)

Pied

Sona

VERONA

montese

River Mincio

Monzambano
Bridge

Piedmontese

Custoza

Sommacampagna

Pozzo

Valeggio

Villafranca

40,000 Austrians

Volta

Lines

Isola
della Scala

Ceresara

500 Neaps

second line

Bovolone

16,000

Goito
(battle)
May 30

14,000

(Roads
to
Cremona)

14,400

River Mincio

Curtatone
(battle)
May 29

MANTUA

June 5th, to Vicenza
via Legnago

Tuscans
7000

Montanara

Austrian troops
Piedmontese

Scale about 6½ miles to 1 inch

RADETZKY'S SWOOP

leaving in Verona only enough troops to keep it safe for the time being. Once in Mantua they could make a fresh start. It was a strong fortress just outside the Piedmontese right flank, to which in reality it had always been a danger. Radetzky proposed to put his 40,000 men into the town; to add 5000 more from the Mantuan garrison, and, from that base, to start instantly on an overwhelming flank attack which would roll up Charles Albert's line probably as far as Goito; and thus, by threatening the communications of the Piedmontese, compel them to retire right back from behind the Mincio and abandon Peschiera.

The danger in this plan lay in getting so large a force unperceived from Verona to Mantua. But, once in that town, Radetzky could feel safe, because from there he had a fresh line of retreat. He could retire from Mantua along the southern roads straight to the fortress of Legnago. In that case he would leave Verona to fend for itself.

This was the old Marshal's way of getting himself out of an awkward corner, and it certainly showed that he knew how to use the Quadrilateral.

No sooner planned than done; he only allowed himself two nights' sleep after the arrival of reinforcements. On May 27th, when darkness fell, two columns left Verona for Mantua.[4] The First Army Corps (10,000)[5] marched through Trevenzuolo and Castelbelforte, and reached its destination at 2.30 p.m. on the 28th, after covering twenty-five miles. The Second Army Corps, 16,000 strong and three infantry brigades from the Reserve, marched simultaneously along the road to Isola della Scala, keeping about five kilometres eastward, and arrived at Mantua at 7 p.m. on the 28th, a distance of twenty-seven miles. The Third Corps, 14,400

---

[4] *Austrian authorities:* Willisen, p. 94; *Feldzug*, II, 8; Hilleprandt; Schönhals; Kunz; Wolf Schneider, p. 74; Pimodan; Ellesmere. For other authorities *v.* our Bibliography.

[5] The First Army Corps was 15,000 strong, but Benedek's brigade was already in Mantua. It was this brigade, 5000 strong, which Radetzky proposed to add on to his 40,000.

strong (Reserve and Cavalry Division), started later, in case of mishaps, and it did not arrive until the early morning of the 29th.

This daring night march was carried out with the greatest celerity and secrecy. No halts were allowed. At one time the Austrians must have been passing within a kilometre of the Italian outposts, but they were not overheard. Radetzky himself rode with the First Corps.

At the same time, thirty miles northwards, a diversion was being carried out by his orders.[6] On the 28th, Zobel's brigade, 2600 strong, which was occupying the Rivoli Plateau, marched down from the Alps and took the little town of Bandolino on Lake Garda. On the 29th, however, it was repulsed by Bes at Calmasino and at Cisano with ninety-three casualties, as compared with only thirty-six on the Piedmontese side. This attack was meant to convey the idea that Radetzky was trying to relieve Peschiera from the north. It failed to make any great impression on General de Sonnaz, but he asked Charles Albert not to deprive him of any troops.

We must now turn to the Italian side of the situation.[7]

The position on the extreme right of the Italian line was held by the Tuscan contingent, nearly 7000 strong, more than half of them regulars, among whom we include a battalion of the Neapolitan 10th Regiment.[8] The general in command was Count de Laugier, an old Napoleonic officer with a fine record. They were occupying a line about five miles west of Mantua, to prevent sorties against Charles Albert's flank; nominally they were part of a force "in observation of Mantua", but this phrase almost raises a smile when we remember that 40,000 men and about 150 guns had got into the town entirely unobserved.[9]

[6] *V.* Fabris, III, 41; Willisen, pp. 94, 98; Hilleprandt, pp. 210, 217; also the official reports.

[7] *Italian authorities:* Fabris, II and III; Pinelli, III; Baldini, p. 85; *Rapporti* (3 vols of officers' reports); *Memorie ed osservazioni*; De Laugier; Montanelli, cap. XL; for others *v.* Bibliography.

[8] The second Neapolitan battalion was in Goito.

[9] *Memorie inedite*, p. 245.

Nevertheless this Tuscan contingent, though partly amateur, was good; it contained the pick of the Tuscan youth; it included the Pisa University battalion in which was serving, to his eternal credit, Professor Montanelli,[10] and also his stepson. All these boys were enthusiastic about their Napoleonic general; evidently De Laugier was an officer capable of arousing enthusiasm. Since his arrival in April he had been training them, not only in drill and discipline, but actually under fire, by arranging for raids for forage in the Austrian zone; and the Austrian garrison had retaliated by small attacks (perhaps reconnaissances), which on May 13th culminated in quite a serious engagement, costing each side about thirty-five casualties.[11] De Laugier tells us that on every one of these occasions—five in number—he had been more than satisfied with the behaviour of his men.

Here we must stop to enquire what steps were taken by Bava to meet this entirely altered situation, namely, the sudden appearance of the Austrian army across his right flank, and threatening his communications.

Certainly the most wonderful thing about this operation of Radetzky and Hess was the success of its concealment. Bava suspected nothing of these Austrian movements until within sixteen hours of the first shot being fired; and by then he had barely time to cover the distances necessary for re-grouping his right flank.

His first warning came at about noon on May 28th, when he received a message from General Passalacqua at Villafranca to say that the doctor at Trevenzuolo had seen an Austrian column with sixteen to twenty guns pass through that village at midnight, and had heard that another column had passed through Isola della Scala. This information was rather vague; but in the course of the afternoon, Franzini, who was at the King's G.H.Q. at Sommacampagna, wrote to Bava that

[10] Professor Montanelli was an enthusiastic patriot; a small, bearded man-of-letters, delicate and far from fit for war service: nevertheless he volunteered so as to be with his young men.

[11] Including "several amputations". *V.* De Laugier, p. 14 and onwards.

10,000 Austrians had passed through Trevenzuolo, and asked him to warn the Tuscans.[12]

Bava was not much disturbed; he wrote to De Laugier a letter which we had better note down as No. 1 of the five letters which Bava sent De Laugier before the engagement. These notes are important because, after the disaster to the Tuscans, each general accused the other of having been its cause. In this No. 1 letter, Bava said that although he gave little credence to the rumours, yet if an attack took place and turned out to be serious, De Laugier would find in him, Bava, a zealous and reliable support.[13]

De Laugier received this letter at 6 p.m. He at once warned his people; if attacked they were to hold their positions until Bava's support arrived.

Towards evening of this day (the 28th), however, Bava received from Passalacqua a second letter which made him more anxious. He sent out a young cavalry subaltern to reconnoitre towards Mantua, and wrote No. 2 letter to De Laugier. In it, he now considered it "certain that a large body of troops had been moved from Verona to Mantua", and ended up: "in case of a heavy attack, and if you express such a desire, I will hasten to support you with sufficient forces", but "I urge you to stand firm as long as you can, as I am sure you will": and then he directed De Laugier in last resort, to retire on Goito (nine miles),[14] and to make an energetic defence of the village, "in which defence I will come to your help". De Laugier received this No. 2 letter at 11.30 p.m. that night (the 28th). He took it to mean that he was not to retire except in the last resort (*in estremo*).

Just before dawn on the 29th[15] De Laugier received No. 3

[12] "And tell them, after a good defence, to retire up the Mincio towards Goito" where, Franzini hoped, troops would arrive in time to repulse the enemy. Franzini offered Bava three brigades.

[13] De Laugier, p. 16.

[14] "Per ripiegare poi in estremo verso Goito, onde difendere energicamente il paese ch' io mi porterò a sussidiare." In Goito was a Neapolitan battalion five hundred strong.

[15] De Laugier, p. 104.

letter (the "pontoon" letter). On the morning of the 28th Bava had been informed that the Austrian columns carried pontoons, and he wrote to warn De Laugier that probably they would throw a bridge over the Mincio between Rivalta and Goito, in order to cut off the Tuscans from the rest of the army. He advised him to keep on the watch, and to resist the setting up of any such bridge. But if in spite of all defence, this bridge were thrown over the river, then he directed De Laugier to retire—but not on Goito as hitherto suggested; he was to retreat[16] by Gazzoldo on Volta, where he would find the Piedmontese army in order of battle. About this third letter there are two noticeable points; firstly, that there is no longer any question of his being supported at Curtatone, or of his holding the lines desperately until reinforcements could arrive. Secondly, he was to retire on Volta, not on Goito (fourteen miles as the crow flies instead of nine). De Laugier says in his *Mémoires* that such a retirement was entirely impossible for his inexperienced troops.

On the evening of the 28th, when he wrote that third letter, Bava had at length realised that he was suddenly faced with a giant attack. He hurried from Custoza to Charles Albert's H.Q. at Sommacampagna. There he discussed the whole situation with the King and Franzini and found that their information confirmed his own. Their talk lasted up to midnight, and by the end of that anxious exchange of ideas they had arrived at a definite plan of action. They decided that it was too late to attack Radetzky in flank, but that they would collect as many troops as was possible and form a front to their right flank at some place astride of the river; if time permitted, at Goito; but failing that, at Volta, five miles nearer to them. This midnight decision saved the situation; but unfortunately it could not save the Tuscans.

For the next twenty-four hours Bava was rushing about

[16] *Ibid.* p. 105. "If this bridge in spite of all defence is thrown over the river then it will be best for you to retire, when opportunity occurs, not on Goito as suggested in my last" but by Gazzoldo on Volta.

collecting troops; he did fine work. But for the moment we must return to the tragedy at Curtatone and Montanara.

By 1 a.m. of the fateful 29th of May, Bava was back at Custoza and was writing his No. 4 letter to De Laugier.[17] In this he said: "The whole of the Austrian force is concentrated in Mantua"; that they would probably not make a pontoon attack, and that "you will begin at once to echelon your troops back in order to be in a position—if you are absolutely unable any longer to maintain your defence against the enemy—to retire in good and military order upon Volta, to which place I am on my way with the troops under my command". De Laugier received this letter at 10 a.m. on the 29th, just as the first shot was being fired. It had been written at one o'clock at night, but it had taken nine hours to cover twenty-one miles.

He must have realised that, once in the Austrian grip, it would be very difficult for him to retire to Volta—fourteen miles—or probably even to Goito—only nine. Thus with extraordinary suddenness a disaster had fallen upon him.

How far Bava was to blame for the disaster is a matter of dispute, but it seems to be agreed that after receiving these four letters De Laugier could not withdraw without fighting. In each of them Bava distinctly intimates that he was not to retire until after giving battle. Evidently what Bava wanted him to do was to delay the Austrians as long as possible, so as to enable the Piedmontese army to form to a fresh front. But undoubtedly this order involved endangering, if not sacrificing, the Tuscan corps. To break off contact and retire about fourteen miles, fighting all the way, as Bava had directed, would simply have been courting disaster for these half-trained troops, who were virtually without cavalry or artillery.

As matters turned out, the resistance which they maintained for six hours, until finally surrounded and overwhelmed, was undoubtedly an important factor in saving the Piedmontese army.

[17] De Laugier gives each of the five letters in full. *V.* also Bava's *Relazione*: *Rapporti*, I, 48 *et seq.*, and Fabris, III, 19.

The front of the Tuscan position was about a mile and a half wide, a line of canal between two villages.[18] Its left rested on the lake or lagoon at Curtatone, but its right flank was rather in the air, though protected by the village of Montanara. Each of the extremities had been considerably strengthened, but the line between them was too wide for De Laugier's numbers. He had 2200 men in Curtatone (including Le Grazie) under Colonel Campìa, and about 2400 in Montanara under Colonel Giovanetti, with three six-pounders in each place.[19]

The Osone canal itself was not entirely satisfactory, as it had a high bank on its front side; an infantryman defending it would have to scramble over the canal to get either forward or back, a feat impossible for horses or guns. The only bridge was at Curtatone, on the highway to Mantua.

No other course remained possible for De Laugier but to stand his ground at all costs. He tells us that he remembered Napoleon's maxim about always marching on the sound of the guns, and thought that the sound of his little six-pounders would bring the Piedmontese to his side.

Radetzky, however, allowed them very little time even to think. In the early hours of May 29th, before the last of his details had arrived from Verona, he had already launched his attack.

The Austrians advanced from Mantua in three columns; firstly, Prince Felix Schwarzenberg with two brigades[20]

[18] *V.* Fabris, III, 28.

[19] The following list is from De Laugier, p. 22:

	Men	Horses	Guns	Howitzers
Curtatone (and Le Grazie for reserves, 1¼ miles in rear)	2222	76	3	1
Montanara	2463	24	3	1
Castellucchio (to cover retirement)	163	—	—	—
Rivalta and Sacca	402	4	—	—
The junction of roads from Gaz-zoldo and Goito	80	—	1	—
(Goito)	940	14	2	—
	6270	118	9	2

[20] Benedek's brigade in first line, Wohlgemuth's in support (First Army Corps, Wratislaw). *V. Feldzug*, p. 10, quoted in Willisen, p. 95.

through Castelnuovo on the straight road to Curtatone (8600 men and twelve guns).

Secondly, under Prince Karl Schwarzenberg, two brigades,[21] through Belfiore by the straight road to Montanara (6200 men and twelve guns).

Thirdly, Prince Lichtenstein's brigade, which made a wide enveloping movement on the Austrian left, a detour towards Buscoldo, almost three miles south of Montanara (4300 men and six guns).[22]

The victory of the Austrians was certain; their artillery alone would have ensured that; and they seem to have been feeling confident, for their action began by a frontal attack against the Tuscan left wing at Curtatone. Manifestly this left wing was the hardest to capture, because of its entrenchments, and because, resting on the lake, it could not be outflanked, whereas the Tuscan right at Montanara was more or less in the air. But evidently the Austrian H.Q. had calculated that if they could break through at Curtatone, they would cut off the defenders at Montanara.

At 10 a.m., therefore, the attack was begun by four companies of Szluiners[23] in extended order, supported by two battalions of the Paumgarten Regiment (right) and two of Gyulai's (left). The colonel in command dismounted to lead his men in person, and during these two days he did so with splendid gallantry. It was Colonel Benedek, afterwards famous for his leadership at Solferino, and later on for his disaster at Sadowa. On June 1st, he was able to write to his wife, "I have won the reward which is most coveted by the Austrian soldier, the cross of Maria Theresia".[24]

Here at Curtatone, he led his tall white-coated Szluiners to attack the unfortunate Tuscans, who were very genuinely

[21] Those of Clam and Strassoldo (First Army Corps).
[22] Lichtenstein's brigade was part of the Second Army Corps (d'Aspre); the rest of that corps, about 11,900 men, was not engaged. Nor was the reserve, 14,400 strong. Each of the brigades engaged had two squadrons of cavalry, except that of Lichtenstein, which had four. For these figures, v. Hilleprandt, p. 205.
[23] Croats from the district round Szluin.   [24] Benedek, p. 79.

ready to offer their lives for the national cause. The Croats came on well, but the ground was soft, the ditches deep, and it was hard to bring any guns into action.[25]

Soon after the first shots had been heard, De Laugier arrived at the trenches on a round of final inspection. In order to inspire confidence he walked along the front of the trench inspecting the men from the exposed side. This feat proved a great success. As he passed along the line the young men raised their caps on their bayonets with enthusiastic shouts of "Viva l' Italia!" He says that although he realised the hopelessness of the position, in that moment of sunshine it seemed to him certain that his boys would be victorious, and that in spite of all Bava's letters the Piedmontese would come to their relief.[26]

At about noon the Austrians brought up two twelve-pounders along the road, and opened fire at less than 1000 yards; and soon they succeeded in lining up several other guns on each side of them. The Italian artillerymen tried to reply; but both howitzers became unserviceable after the very first round, and owing to mismanagement one of the guns never came into action at all. So that at Curtatone they never had more than two guns in action. In this predicament De Laugier tried to harass Benedek's movements by organising a small counter-attack with about 200 of his men—150 Neapolitan and Lucchese from the trenches, and fifty drivers, under an officer called Contri. These few men succeeded in creating a diversion on Benedek's left flank, but naturally such an effort could not last long.

For the first three hours, however, the Italians made a good and successful resistance. All that the Austrians could claim was that they had occupied one or two houses within range, and that they had got their artillery in position. By one o'clock their first attack had been repulsed.

[25] Hilleprandt, p. 220, tells us: "In taking Curtatone 19,000 Austrians fought against 6000 Tuscans and Neapolitans", and adds that De Laugier could have been ousted without many casualties if the attack had been begun by the left wing instead of the right.

[26] De Laugier, p. 21 *et seq.*; Montanelli, p. 337.

De Laugier then galloped across to Montanara to see how matters were going there. On his arrival he was received with ringing cheers. So far, the defence was successful; but, naturally, he knew that disaster was only a question of hours. At Montanara there were only 2400 men and three guns, attacked on their front by about 4000 men with twelve guns and a rocket battery; and—which made the position hopeless —the Tuscan right flank was being gradually surrounded by the wide enveloping movement of the Austrian left, namely by Lichtenstein's brigade advancing from near Buscoldo.

When selecting his positions De Laugier had tried to break the face of a frontal attack by occupying various forward points,[27] and similarly, in order to prepare for a possible retirement he had posted men at certain places in the rear, such as La Rocca, La Cascina and La Santa. Moreover, that morning Giovanetti had sent out five companies of Neapolitan and Tuscan Civic Guards under Captain Beraudi to take up positions almost a mile in front of the lines; indeed Beraudi had been surprisingly successful in delaying the assailants, but against such superiority of numbers his effort could only be short-lived. When De Laugier arrived on the scene, he directed him to return to the main body, and he ordered four companies to go back to La Santa in order to protect the line of retreat. He named Castelluchio, to Giovanetti, as being his correct line of retirement. There was nothing more to be done, so he rode back to Curtatone.

At Curtatone also, the second Austrian attack was beginning to overwhelm the defenders. The two unfortunate Tuscan guns were being annihilated by a converging fire from the fourteen Austrian pieces, and presently, by a singular stroke of ill-fortune, a shell exploded on a caisson and spread destruction all around it. Colonel Campìa had used up nearly all his reserves; the University boys had gone into the line singing and were doing well, but this left only the two Grenadier companies at Le Grazie. De Laugier describes his return to Curtatone in the following words:

[27] La Rizzarda, La Palazzina and others.

I hastened to the centre, where the battery was a frightful sight to see; twice the gunpowder had been set on fire by Austrian rockets, and had made tragic havoc of all who stood near it. Various gunners and soldiers, burnt, blackened, scorched, were rushing away crying out and tearing their clothes off as if they were mad. A good many men and horses lay dead and wounded around the shattered gun-carriages and the broken wheels. The guns, overturned on the ground, could no longer be used.[28]

In some of these cases, where the uniforms were on fire, they had to plunge into the canal to save themselves; several of these men are mentioned in the list of decorations.

At this moment De Laugier received his fifth and last note from Bava. Bava wrote from Goito, and told him that he had there a regiment of cavalry and two others within reach, and a battery of horse artillery; at Volta a whole division. He added: "If you can no longer hold the good positions which you are occupying, it will be best to retire gradually on Goito where you will find the necessary reinforcements."

This letter inspired De Laugier to a last effort. There was a Piedmontese force only nine miles distant. He sent off a galloper at once to Goito to ask for help, and meanwhile urged his men to hold out until the arrival of the Piedmontese relief which he fully expected.

The final stand lasted about an hour and a half, and was a very fine effort both at Montanara and at Curtatone, but it did not alter Bava's decision.

At Montanara Giovanetti remained firing until he saw that he was being surrounded; then he sent to inform De Laugier that he was compelled to retire for about half a mile. His retirement was orderly, but when he approached La Zocca, a hamlet half a kilometre back, he found his way barred by three battalions and one squadron of Lichtenstein's enveloping force. He charged headlong, but failed to get through. After that, his force split into several units. One portion of it took to the fields. A second set of detachments occupied La Cascina, Rocca and Villani, and took their guns with

28 De Laugier, p. 28; Montanelli, p. 340.

them; and in these places they made a defence which the Austrian reports describe as "extraordinarily vigorous, even heroic". A third portion, under Giovanetti in person, found itself cut off by Austrian cavalry, which, by then, had passed through Curtatone, but eventually most of this column got away by Castellucchio. The Neapolitan battalion, consisting of about 500 regular soldiers, remained under its officers' orders and eventually was made prisoner; but the volunteers scattered right and left; about 1160 of them reached Bozzolo, and others got through elsewhere.[29]

At Curtatone De Laugier continued his desperate efforts until the dusk was falling. Then he was obliged to give the word to retire. Unfortunately this led to a rush towards the only bridge across the canal, and for a time it became completely blocked. Undoubtedly when the long drawn tension of the defence was brought to an end, simultaneously the threads of discipline were severed. There resulted among some—by no means all—of the men a rush to avoid being surrounded, but only until they got clear of the Austrians.

The three vital points at Curtatone were defended to the end, namely the Casa del Lago, the Mill and the Bridge. In this scene of hesitation and disaster Professor Montanelli lived the moment of his life. De Laugier tells us that the little professor, whose political enthusiasm had so often aroused smiles in the lecture room, on this occasion "raised his voice in generous encouragement which so inflamed his hearers that they were induced to turn back with him to the Mill". In fact, he and some of his young men defended a room in the mill until his stepson had been killed beside him, and they could no longer keep out the enemy. The professor

---

[29] *Feldzug*, p. 14. Pimodan, p. 209. *Re* Neapolitans, Professor Montanelli (*Memorie inedite*, pp. 247, 339) says: "The Austrians had occupied a house and cemetery on our right, from which they were firing into Montanara. Our men tried to drive them out; and in that very bloody fight, the Neapolitan soldiers of the 10th Regiment, now in Tuscan pay, did wonders." He is naturally enthusiastic about his own side: however, the launching of any counter-attack just then was manifestly a fine effort.

himself was shot through the left shoulder and overwhelmed by the inrushing Croats who then greeted him derisively with "Viva Pio Nono!" but did him no harm.

De Laugier was thrown from his horse and trampled on, but that evening he was able to reach Goito with about 2000 men now, once more, in good order. The Tuscan killed and wounded were perhaps fewer than might have been expected, because they had been so completely surrounded: at many points they had no choice but to surrender. Losses:

Tuscan, Neapolitan, etc.:

	Curtatone	Montanara
	79 dead	87 dead
	249 wounded	269 wounded
	328 and 99 prisoners	356 and 1087 prisoners

The Austrians:

8 officers and	87 men killed		
28 ,, ,,	488 ,, wounded		
36	575 and 179 missing[30]		

But the losses do not represent the full extent of the disaster. The real tragedy lay in the fact that this day's work witnessed the end of all enthusiasm in the Tuscan contingent. It could hardly be expected that the men would again have any confidence in the general who had urged them to hold out, but—they complained—had stood inactive only a few miles off while they were being annihilated, without even attempting a diversion. Their feeling was natural; but it must be admitted that Bava had had a very difficult hand to play.[31]

II. THE SECOND BATTLE OF GOITO

Radetzky had won a striking success; his overwhelming masses had forced their way through the defensive line almost up to Goito. But the question remained to be answered:

[30] V. Fabris, III, 40; Feldzug, II, 50; and Montanelli, p. 342.
[31] Bava was promoted G.O.C. of the army for his victory on the following day.

Would he be able to achieve his main object, that of causing Charles Albert's retirement, and thereby relieving Peschiera?

It is very interesting to read how Bava and his King, after evolving their plan of action at midnight on May 28th, spent the next thirty-six harassing hours in collecting forces to form a line-of-battle against the 45,000 Austrians who had suddenly appeared across their right flank. They were only just in time; and undoubtedly it was owing to the hours gained for them by the self-sacrifice of the Tuscans and Neapolitans that they were able to save the Piedmontese army.[32]

It will be remembered how, at 1 a.m. on the night of the 28th, Bava (at Custoza) sent off his fourth note to De Laugier, and then started out to direct as many battalions as he could find to his new line of defence at Volta. He decided first to mass them at Valeggio, close by him. For this purpose he ordered thither various units of the Second Division in his immediate vicinity. By 3 a.m. that night he was able to leave Custoza; he had succeeded in collecting at Valeggio eleven battalions, eight squadrons and sixteen guns;[33] and, as he neared that village, he met the Nizza (Nicois) Cavalry Regiment, two companies of Bersaglieri and the 2nd Horse Battery. In this way he was able to create a unit entirely composed of light infantry and cavalry.

That morning he ordered all the troops at Valeggio to hasten across the Mincio to their place of concentration, Volta (five miles distant), but the Nicois cavalry and the rest of the troops he took with him another five miles towards the enemy, to Goito. They were to reinforce the Neapolitan regular battalion—600 men of the 10th Regiment—which formed its garrison.

He arrived there at noon on the 29th, only nine miles from Curtatone. The battle was raging, but he made no attempt to

[32] For all Bava's doings, v. his own *Relazione: Rapporti*, I, 51 *et seq.* and *Memorie inedite*, p. 246; also Fabris, III, 47.
[33] Also a battery at Molino.

rescue the unfortunate Tuscans. Whether he could have done anything by way of a diversion to help them during their retirement is a matter for military opinion, but it must be remembered that he did not yet know whether his concentration at Volta would prove successful or not; and on that depended the safety of the whole Piedmontese army.

After surveying the Goito position, he sped back to Volta, which he reached at 3 p.m. There he found Charles Albert; and together they watched the distant dust-cloud of battalion after battalion coming in sight. They saw that they would have time to leave Volta to their reserves and march the five miles down to Goito to defend a front-line there. It must have seemed rather like advancing into the lion's den.

Very soon another officer arrived at Volta at a hand-gallop; it was Lieutenant Manelli, De Laugier's adjutant, to beg for help: but they could only repeat the order to retire on Goito. They were waiting anxiously for the troops to join them. Presently the leading units began to arrive; by 3.30 p.m. five battalions were there; by five o'clock two more; and two more by nightfall; also a heavy battery and a horse battery.

By the night of May 29th Bava could feel that he had between 19,000 and 20,000 troops under his hand, in three different groups between Valeggio and Goito (ten miles apart). He had done splendid work since the previous midnight. But he and Charles Albert must have known that it was a very small force to set against that of the enemy.

At 8.30 a.m. on the 30th Bava started off the troops in three columns to occupy Goito.[34] By midday the brigades arrived and began to take up their positions. Some of the battalions were tired—having only completed their previous march at midnight—and did not reach their allotted posts

[34] Costa de Beauregard says most positively that this forward movement was insisted on by Charles Albert in opposition to Bava and the other generals; that they thought that Radetzky had merely tried to draw them away to their right, in order to break through at Sommacampagna and relieve Peschiera: Costa, p. 247. We cannot find any confirmation of this. The advance to Goito was of course covered by a cavalry screen.

until two o'clock. Charles Albert had been there since eight that morning.

His line of battle ran from Goito on the left—resting on the river—through the cross-roads to the Gobbi farm-buildings and thence to the Caldone ditch; a line of less than two miles, with Longhino house on its right front. The Mincio is a river which flows between flat fertile fields with willows on either bank; at Goito it is perhaps thirty yards wide.

The left of the line, in the village itself, was held by the Neapolitan battalion and four others; the centre, at the cross-roads, was occupied by two batteries in line, rather recklessly advanced; in the fields on the right was the Cuneo Brigade under Prince Victor Emmanuel, and some cavalry. It was to be a fight on flat, heavy ploughed land, with here and there a farmhouse to be taken or defended; amid growing crops of corn and lucerne which retarded movements; and amid closely dotted vines and mulberry-trees which rather impeded vision.

Along the Piedmontese front there was a thin line of Bersaglieri (riflemen) and cavalry scouts.[35]

At 2 p.m. the look-out on Goito steeple signalled "enemy in sight". Fortunately for them Radetzky had not been quite so prompt as usual.

[35] The Piedmontese order of battle before they were attacked (Fabris, III, 56):

Right Wing (facing south)	Left Wing (facing south)
Third Line	
The Guards Brigade (six battalions)	Genoa and Savoia Cavalry (twelve squadrons)
A horse-battery	Three horse-batteries
Second Line	
The Aosta Brigade (six battalions)	Nizza Cavalry (six squadrons)
8th Battery	Half-battery (5th)
Front Line	
The Cuneo Brigade	Four battalions (11th and 17th
2nd Horse Battery	Regulars), 10th Neapolitans in
3rd Siege Battery	Goito (one battalion)

In front, three companies of Bersaglieri and some cavalry.

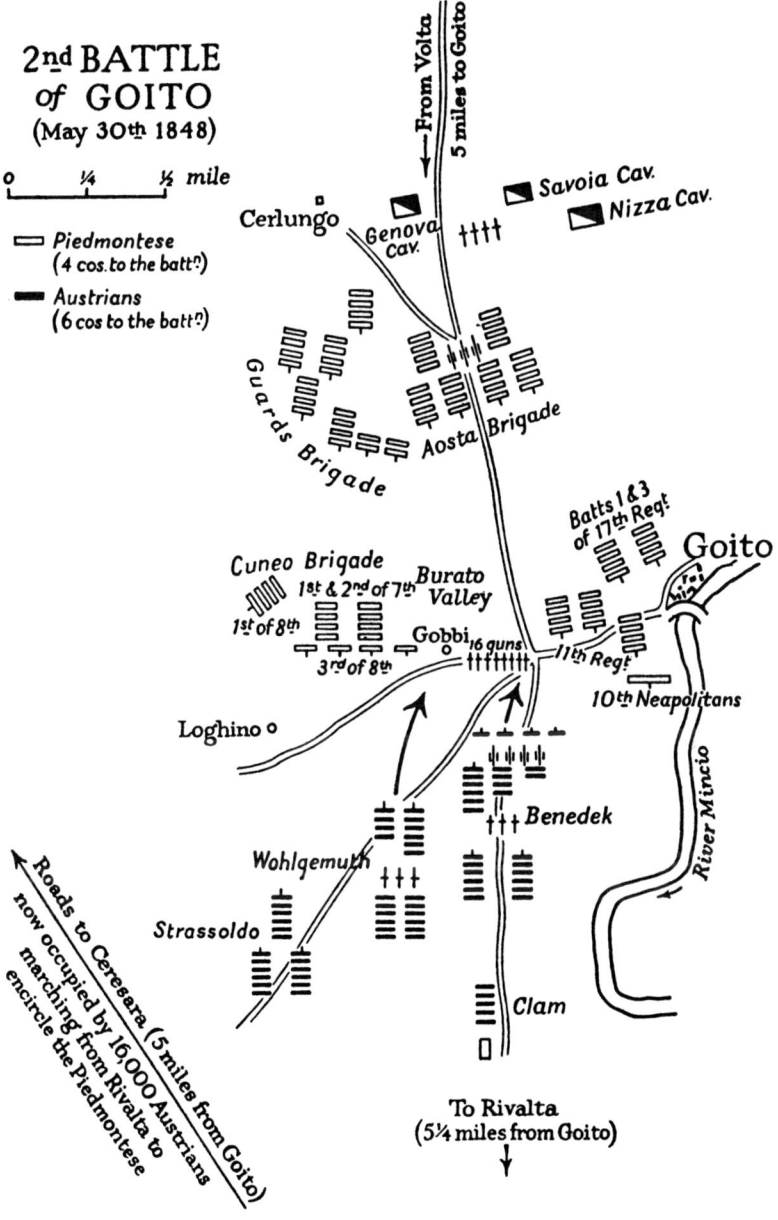

2nd BATTLE
of GOITO
(May 30th 1848)

0   ¼   ½ mile

▭ Piedmontese
(4 cos. to the battⁿ)
▬ Austrians
(6 cos. to the battⁿ)

From Volta

5 miles to Goito

Cerlungo

Genova Cav.

Savoia Cav.

Nizza Cav.

Guards Brigade

Aosta Brigade

Batts 1 & 3 of 17th Regt

Goito

Cuneo Brigade

1st & 2nd of 7th

Burato Valley

1st of 8th

3rd of 8th

Gobbi 16 guns

11th Regt

Loghino

10th Neapolitans

River Mincio

Wohlgemuth

Benedek

Strassoldo

Clam

Roads to Ceresara (5 miles from Goito)
now occupied by 16,000 Austrians
marching from Rivalta to
encircle the Piedmontese

To Rivalta
(5¼ miles from Goito)

His great masses were on the move again. On his right he had the First Army Corps, still over 14,000 strong, of whom 12,884 were actually engaged this day.[36] It was to march on Goito. On his left he had the Second Army Corps, about 16,000 strong, which he sent off on a wide encircling movement to Ceresara, five miles to westward. His Reserve Corps (14,400 men) was to halt about four miles in rear of the fighting, at Rivalta, and be ready to support either corps. He must have had over 44,000 men under his hand, whereas Charles Albert and Bava had barely 20,000.

On the previous day, Radetzky had won a brilliant strategic success. But to turn it into a knock-out blow, he must now follow it up with a tactical victory.[37]

The result might have seemed to be a foregone conclusion. But Radetzky and Hess—we are quoting Schönhals, Kunz and Willisen—were not at their best that day. Their natural plan would have been to advance their right against Goito and thus nail the Piedmontese to their positions; and then bring round their encircling column, which alone was almost as numerous as Bava's two divisions. But they acted on a mistaken assumption.

According to Schönhals, they had assumed that Charles Albert's true line of defence would be at Volta—where he had been that morning—and that at Goito he would only have left some advanced troops. Consequently the arrival of the Piedmontese infantry at two o'clock to defend a line five miles in front of Volta had not been expected. The Austrian officers had thought that their right wing could push its way northwards through Goito; and that then, when they got opposite Volta, their left wing would serve to cut the Piedmontese off from Brescia, and compel them to retire all along the line from Peschiera.

In reality, as General Willisen explains,[38] the march to

[36] *Feldzug*, I, 19.
[37] *Feldzug*, I, 19; Willisen, p. 121; Schönhals, II, 28; Kunz, p. 52; Hilleprandt, p. 230.   [38] Willisen, p. 121.

Ceresara had been planned as a big encircling movement intended to cut off Charles Albert from Lombardy.[39] Therefore it was too wide to encircle the immediate position at Goito. In fact d'Aspre's 16,000 men were lost to them during the battle.

At about 3.30 p.m. the first shots were fired. The cavalry scouts on either side had met. Already the two lines were less than a thousand yards apart and the leading brigade on the Austrian right, that of Benedek, acting as an advance-guard, was pushing forward confidently, straight in the direction of Goito. It was followed by the brigades of Wohlgemuth and Strassoldo. While most of these troops were still in column formation, suddenly they came under heavy artillery fire; during the skirmishes, the Piedmontese had brought up two batteries to the cross-roads just in front of the town, and in all sixteen guns opened a hot fire on the Szluiners and the troops behind them. In reply Benedek brought up twelve guns, and half a rocket battery, but the Piedmontese artillery had the best of the contest. They had ventured into a dangerous position, but they had inflicted considerable losses on their assailants.

It was evidently a good piece of work by Major de Priero and his gunners; and they were efficiently supported by the Neapolitan battalion,[40] which seems to have done well that day. Presently the artillery officers sent four other guns across the river, and soon began to shell the Austrian right flank from the opposite bank.

---

[39] The *Feldzug* states that Radetzky never intended his right-hand attack to be more than a reconnaissance, and thought that his left-hand enveloping movement by itself might perhaps cause the Piedmontese to retire from Goito and abandon Peschiera. It says that the battle went further than he intended. This is confirmed by Pimodan and others.

[40] In the report of Major de Priero, O.C. of the Second Horse Battery, he says: "two Austrian guns were countered by the fire of our two guns; and—attacked by the Neapolitans who fought bravely that day—they were obliged to retire...the 11th infantry were sent out to support the Neapolitans." *Rapporti*, III, 192. *V.* also *ibid.* p. 160.

Benedek's men stood their ground well, but they abandoned any idea of pushing through into Goito. Henceforth the attack was to come from their flank, and Wohlgemuth's brigade was ordered to come up and take post on their left, with the intention that, as soon as possible, Strassoldo's brigade should continue the line and try to encircle the Piedmontese right. In fact the battle developed, as it were, into a contest to see which side could get round the outer flank first.

Wohlgemuth's brigade could only move slowly owing to the heavy ground and deep ditches, but it advanced with great resolution and very well supported by its artillery. On the Italian right, their battery was not yet in position; and it is interesting to see how sensitive to artillery fire was the infantry soldier in the mass-formations of 1848. The Cuneo battalions, which were advancing to the firing line in quarter column, and fighting in close order, were very much a prey to the Austrian guns. The officers afterwards complained that their men were being pounded from the front and flank without being able to make any sort of reply. The result was that after standing their ground for some time, they gave way and fell back into the third line. This was a very serious failure because it compelled the artillery in the centre to retire with them. Consequently Wohlgemuth's Jägers and Oguliners were able to dash forward into the Gobbi farmhouse, where they established themselves firmly, to await the arrival of Strassoldo on their left.[41]

This was the crucial moment of the engagement. There was now a stretch of unoccupied ground in the centre and right of the Piedmontese line. The situation was more than critical, for it compelled Bava to order up both his remaining

[41] According to Schönhals it was Strassoldo's men who entered some of the buildings at Gobbi. He says that Wohlgemuth's men actually took "the rideau" at Goito and some of the houses. If by the "rideau" he means the old river bank, they must have come very near to taking the village. *V.* Victor Emmanuel's report, *Rapporti*, I, 327. Also Biscaretti's, *Ibid.* II, 16; Scozia's, *Ibid.* II, 43.

infantry brigades. To fill the gap in the centre, he sent in the Aosta Brigade out of his second line, and to take the place of the Cuneo on his right he ordered up the Guards Brigade out of the third line. He had no more infantry at all. "Behind us there was not a single soldier left", said General Biscaretti of the Guards. It was now between four-thirty and five o'clock.

Fortunately these were two of the finest brigades in the Piedmontese army. As they advanced, they left intervals for the retiring Cuneo battalions, three of which soon afterwards returned to the fray. When the two leading battalions of Guards came under the Austrian cross-fire they too hesitated, but Prince Victor Emmanuel promptly led them forward at the charge. The Gobbi farmhouses were retaken; and then retaken again by the Austrians; the Prince had to retire wounded. But the Aosta battalions came up on their left, and then, at long last, the artillery arrived on their right and opened fire. That settled the matter. The infantry officers themselves admit it. Wohlgemuth's men were weary and Strassoldo's in difficulties, and their retirement was covered by Clam's brigade.

Bava at once ordered a counter-attack. The Nizza cavalry advanced on the right, and at the same time the Neapolitan battalion sallied out from Goito, supported by three others.

By this time Radetzky had realised that he had more of the Piedmontese army in front of him than he had supposed possible, and that with his Second Army Corps so far away he could not hope for any success that evening; so he ordered a general retirement to their original positions. He could renew the attack next day with the full weight of his 44,000 men. This, says the *Feldzug*, had only been a reconnaissance; but if so, it had been very expensive: it had cost 600 casualties.[42] And the Austrian staff admit that the failure was due, as we have said, to a mistaken assumption.[43]

[42] The *Feldzug* gives 585; namely, 67 killed, 330 wounded, 2 prisoners and 186 missing. Fabris says 622; he gives 4 prisoners and 219 missing.

[43] Schönhals, *Erinnerungen*, II, 28, 29; Benedek, pp. 75–6; *Studie*, p. 15; Hilleprandt, p. 230 *et seq*.

Bava and Charles Albert must have felt themselves well out of it. Their 20,000 men had checked the torrent, at all events, for a day or two to come. Whoever was to blame for the lack of vigilance which had resulted in the loss of the Tuscan division, at Goito most people had done well, especially the artillery. The Piedmontese losses were light— only 43 killed and 253 wounded[44]—and the men were triumphant.

It was a gloriously happy evening, for, at the very moment of victory,[45] a messenger had galloped onto the field with a despatch from Franzini. As Charles Albert opened it, his whole face lit up with joy, and he called out to the soldiers nearest to him the splendid news that Peschiera had fallen. They answered with ringing cheers: "Viva Carlo Alberto, re d' Italia!"

It was the supreme moment of his life. And he realised it. Only a few days later he wrote to a friend that he thought it highly honourable for so small a country as Piedmont to win such successes against a great empire, and that he would welcome peace. But his Parliament thought otherwise.

One permanent benefit for Italy resulted from the fall of Peschiera and the victory of Goito. Coming as they did, just at the moment when the national war had been abandoned by the Pope, by the King of Naples, and—inevitably—by Tuscany, these victories singled out Piedmont as the only champion of Italy. This was the beginning of wisdom; and it was the work for which Charles Albert was giving his life.

III. THE FALL OF VICENZA

Some critics indeed have enquired why Radetzky and Hess with such superiority of numbers did not renew the attack and crush the Piedmontese once and for all. For this inaction, their brother-officer Schönhals supplies us with three reasons: firstly, because of the weather; it rained in torrents

[44] Fabris, III, 63.
[45] *Memorie inedite*, p. 249; *Rapporti*, I, 55 and 126.

for three days until the horses were up to their hocks in mud: secondly, because they received from Vienna news of a fresh revolution so serious that some of them wondered whether Radetzky would have to lead his two corps back to defend the Kaiser in Austria; thirdly—no doubt the truest reason of all—because they saw that Bava and Charles Albert had assembled most of the Piedmontese army more rapidly than had seemed possible. To attack it again meant embarking on a widespread action west of the Mincio while their own communications were still intercepted by Durando with 11,000 or 12,000 men in Vicenza; and the hope of relieving Peschiera was now at an end.[46]

But there still remained the alternative project, that of restoring communications with Austria by an attack on Vicenza.

On June 3rd Radetzky retired his troops secretly and silently from the Curtatone front-positions into Mantua, leaving one brigade behind him to mislead the Piedmontese. On June 4th his army was allowed a complete rest. It meant that he had abandoned his enterprise; but at the same time it meant that this old hero of eighty-one had already embarked on another.

The reappearance of the Revolution was calling forth all his powers, and was to result in one of the most perfectly planned military undertakings of his life. At that moment it must have seemed to him that he was standing alone in defence of the whole world that he had known. Italy was in revolt; and now Vienna was in chaos and the great Austrian Empire itself seemed to be disintegrating. But under his command there still remained the one unshakeable basis of the regime,

[46] Schönhals, II, 33 *et seq.* Exactly how many men Durando had collected by now is very uncertain. Hilleprandt, p. 240; *Feldzug*, etc. For Austrian authorities, *v.* p. 305, note 37. Also Wolf Schneider; *Studie*; Radetzky, *Leben*; Ellesmere; Pimodan. For Italian authorities: Fabris; Pinelli; Ovidi; *Memorie inedite*; Durando; d'Azeglio, *Corr.*; Ravioli; but the most fruitful source is that of the documents in the State Archives in Rome.

the army which he had perfected. It was during this month of June 1848 that the Austrian poet addressed to him the famous line: "In deinem Lager liegt Österreich."[47]

With characteristic promptitude he initiated the new enterprise. Having barely broken off his action with Charles Albert, he started to carry out a rapid and sudden descent on Vicenza. What a sound and irresistible piece of work this was, may be judged by the following opinions of General Willisen:

> Everything belonging to this feat from its beginning to its end: and then the swift return march to Verona, and the immediately resumed offensive against the enemy, forms a masterpiece of contrivance, comprehension and leadership.

Durando, with his 12,000 men and about thirty guns in Vicenza,[48] was sixty miles distant from Mantua. It was difficult to march on him unobserved. The following is a skeleton description of the movement.

On June 5th Radetzky began his march, leaving Benedek and his tired-out brigade in Mantua. His plan was that by June 9th his various corps should have gathered unperceived at five different points around Vicenza, but not very near to the town. They were to close in, and attack on all sides simultaneously on June 10th.

By June 7th, after two days' march along the Mantua-Legnago road, his first corps was at Bevilacqua and his second corps at Montagnana (on the far side of Legnago) thirty-three and thirty-six miles respectively from Mantua, and within one day's march of their objective. At the same time, in order to mislead the Piedmontese, he had ordered two columns of his Reserve, about 11,900 men, to double back from Sanguinetto and Nogara and march into Verona, thus conveying the

---

[47] Radetzky, *Leben*, p. 368: "Since the Kaiser-throne was rocking on its foundations and a further supply of war-materials from within the empire was hardly to be counted on, in these conditions we could not take chances with the safety of the army in which was concentrated the final deliverance of our Fatherland."

[48] Ovidi, p. 116, quoting Ravioli.

impression to the Piedmontese staff that the whole army
was returning to its original quarters behind the Rideau.

Verona was now safe. In fact the arrival of these columns
(June 7th) enabled General Culoz with a brigade of 5400
men to start independently for Vicenza, and take his place
in the ring of assailants. Culoz marched via Montebello
and Brendola, and on the evening of the 9th he arrived at
Arcugnano, on the Berico hills, to form the main spear-head
of the attacking force.

Of all these movements Durando had heard very little. He
had received news that there were 24,000 Austrians at
Montagnana, but as Montagnana is twenty-seven miles
distant from Vicenza, it seemed most unlikely that they
meant to attack him, especially as his positions were considered very strong.

All Radetzky's movements were carried out without a
hitch. By the evening of June 9th, overwhelming forces of
Austrians—over 30,000 men and 124 guns—had gathered
round Durando on all sides. Five miles to the south was Culoz
near Arcugnano (5400 men), prepared to attack along the
line of the Berico hills. On Culoz' right was the First Army
Corps, namely Strassoldo's and Clam's brigades (5500 men),
at Longara, four miles off, which was to advance against
the Rotonda;[49] and on Clam's right lay Wohlgemuth's brigade
(3500 men) at Secula (about six miles off), which was to
advance and take the Rotonda in flank.

On the right of all these First Corps troops was the Second
Army Corps advancing along three separate roads which
lead, from the eastern side, to the gates[50] of the town. Thus

---

[49] The celebrated Palladian villa, about half a mile south-east of
Vicenza; beautiful to look at, but singularly unsuited for defence.

[50] The gates attacked were as follows: Porta Monte, behind the
Rotonda; virtually a back-entrance to the Berico hill; north-east of
that, the Porta Padova; and north again Porta Santa Lucia. Lichtenstein's column attacked up a road between the two gates. Baron
Kavanagh, of the Franz Karl Infantry, was one of Lichtenstein's
colonels and it was while leading a charge against an entrenched

Vicenza was cut off from all Venetia—from Padua where there were 4000 men, and from Treviso where there still remained 3100 of Ferrari's force. But, as stated in chapter XIV, by far the easiest way to take Vicenza was to move along the steep, narrow spur of the Berico hills, the end of which juts out right on top of the town. Radetzky fully realised that if he could reach that farthest point, the town would have to surrender at once, and he would be spared street fighting.

In this connection it seems only right to call attention to the splendid patriotism of the citizens of Vicenza. According to all accounts, they were enthusiastic helpers of Durando, perfectly prepared to expose themselves, and their families, and the town, to the risk of bombardment, or to the horrors of street fighting; and this, although they had twice seen the war at close quarters.

During the last ten or eleven days, Durando had exerted every effort towards fortifying his positions[51] and organising his rather motley forces. He had with him two splendid regiments (four battalions) of Papal Swiss and a battery of their artillery, excellent troops (about 3345 men). After that, about 2700 Italian linesmen; perhaps 6000 regulars in all. But then his army tailed off into Civic battalions (about 4000 men) and volunteers.[52] Some of the volunteers, such as those from Faenza under Pasi, and several of the Venetian corps proved themselves to be good, but naturally they were no match for the Austrians. The commanding officers were Durando, Massimo d'Azeglio, now a colonel, and Casanova— in fact, the same Piedmontese clique which, in Rome, had taken

position that he was killed. *V. Feldzug,* II, 33: "As he galloped up to the trenches, suddenly a wide ditch appeared before him. This checked the stormers for a moment, the enemy seized the opportunity to pour in a murderous fire, and Colonel Kavanagh who was hit by four bullets came to ground together with his horse." His loss was more regretted than perhaps any other except Colonel Kopal.

[51] Durando, *Schiar.* p. 42.

[52] Ravioli, p. 105, quoting return in *Gazzetta di Roma* of June 19th, 1848. Also Ovidi.

such a high-handed line with the Papal army. Apparently they had succeeded in collecting 11,275 men and about thirty-six pieces of artillery.[53] It was not until the evening of the 9th that they realised the hopeless nature of their position. It is remembered that Captain Lentulus, the Swiss Papal officer in command of the artillery, remarked quietly to his superiors: "To-morrow things will be very serious."

On June 10th the action began, some time before dawn, with an attack on the Berico hills.[54] They were defended by the pick of Durando's men, two Swiss battalions (1351 men),[55] the 3rd Roman legion (1000 strong), mostly Romagnols, and 300 men of the Venetian and Paduan volunteers, all under the command of Massimo d'Azeglio and Colonel Cialdini.[56] Culoz' men advanced from Arcugnano, and soon carried the village of Santa Margherita, and after that the Castel Rambaldo.[57] These points were occupied by several companies of Swiss, and *Civici* of the Roman legion, but they were too far from Vicenza to be seriously defended. The men fell back about a quarter of a mile to the Villa Bella Guardia.[58] At that point there was a blockhouse, with a red flag flying above it, and in it were posted several companies of the Vicentine and Paduan volunteers. These defenders made more resistance,

[53] Fabris, III, 89; Ravioli, p. 104.
[54] Culoz ordered his men to start at 3 a.m.: Fabris, III, 99.
[55] The 1st battalion of the 1st Swiss Regiment and the 2nd battalion of the 2nd Swiss Regiment.
[56] The 3rd Roman legion under Gallieno was sent up after the firing began.
[57] One of the present writers lived for several months on Monte Berico, but can write no description so vivid as the following: "The Berici crest, along the top of which a country road winds to Vicenza, is at some places so narrow as to be little broader than the road itself. On both sides the ground falls away steeply into the plain several hundred feet below.... But here and there the crest broadens out into a considerable acreage, and it was the business of the Italians and Swiss to hold these hill platforms, while the Austrians forced their way along the sides of the difficult scarp below, or tried to rush the bottle-neck passages on the crest." Trevelyan, *Manin*, p. 191.
[58] Or Bella Vista.

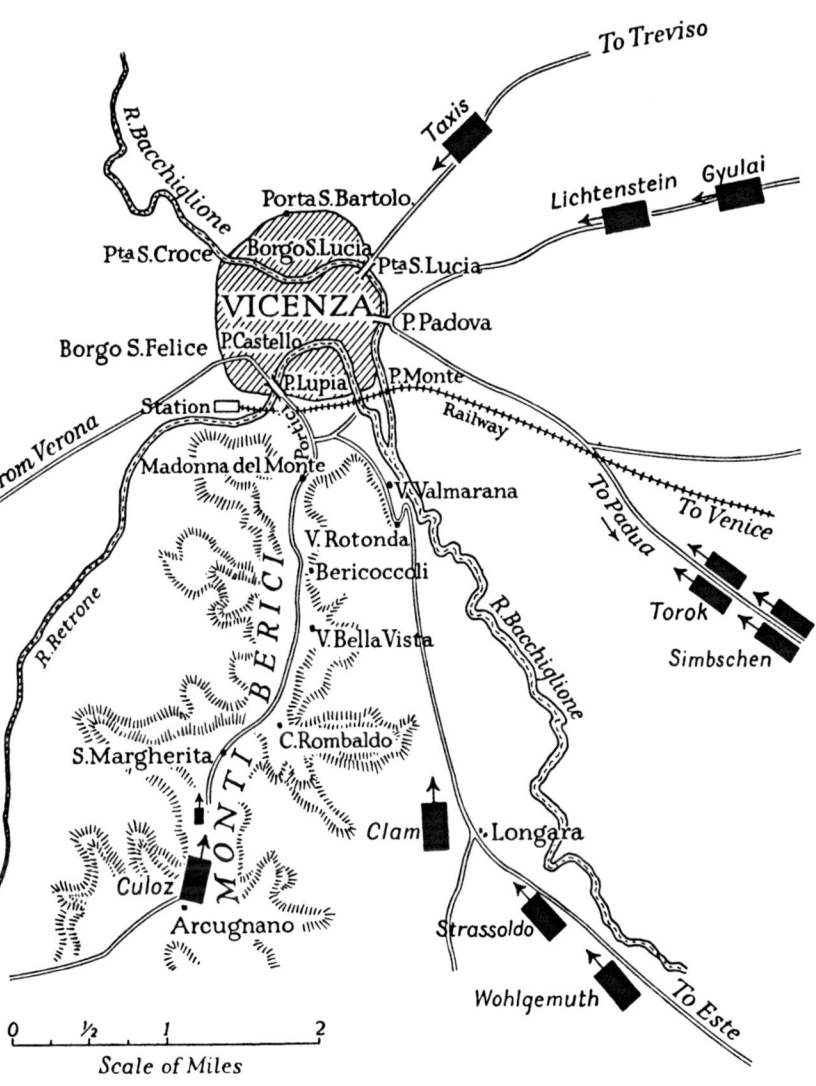

To Treviso

R. Bacchiglione

Taxis

Lichtenstein   Gyulai

Porta S. Bartolo.

Borgo S. Lucia

Pta S. Croce

Pta S. Lucia

VICENZA

P. Padova

P. Castello

Borgo S. Felice

P. Lupia

P. Monte

Station

Railway

From Verona

Madonna del Monte

V. Valmarana

To Padua

To Venice

V. Rotonda

Bericoccoli

R. Retrone

R. Bacchiglione

V. Bella Vista

Torok

Simbschen

M O N T I   B E R I C I

C. Rombaldo

S. Margherita

Clam

Longara

Culoz

Arcugnano

Strassoldo

Wohlgemuth

To Este

0   ½   1   2

Scale of Miles

BATTLE OF VICENZA

and by their joint efforts the first attack of the Oguliners was repulsed; the Oguliners, however, received powerful reinforcements in the shape of seven guns, which they lined out by Castel Rambaldo. With these they proceeded to shower round shot and rockets on to the Bella Guardia position until, at about 6.30, they were able to carry it with a rush. They at once set fire to the blockhouse, while the defenders retired to what was to be the main stronghold of the defence, namely the position at Bericoccoli. At that point stood the Villa Guiccioli, a defensible building, and near it they had placed six guns. It was a good natural position; but it was only about eight hundred yards in front of the Santuario del Monte, the final summit which commands Vicenza.

For the time being, however, the defenders were to have a rest. The Oguliner and Jäger rushes had been carried out under the eye of Radetzky himself, who was sitting on the high ground of the Berico hills watching the progress of the movement. For him, speed was the essence of the contract; but nevertheless, at this stage of the proceedings he decided that Culoz must postpone his main attack until the line of the other units could be formed. He promised him a strong reinforcement of twelve guns and two howitzers, but forbade any further fighting on the hills until the army should be ready for joint action.[59] These guns did not arrive until twelve o'clock.[60]

At 10 a.m. the other Austrian units moved off, but they had some way to march, and apparently they did not begin the actual attacks on the city gates and the outlying points until almost noon.[61] About these attacks upon the gates of the city we need waste no time. The Porta Monte, indeed,

[59] Hilleprandt, p. 250.
[60] Durando in his *Succinta Relazione* speaks of its being general about 11 a.m. *V.* Rome, Archivio di Stato (Archivio Politico). Durando, *Succ. Rel.* Ovidi (p. 119) agrees with this, no doubt relying on Durando.
[61] At the same time he withdrew 600 men and four guns from Culoz and sent them off to close the road from Vicenza to Verona.

which was behind the Rotonda, and a key to Monte Berico, eventually became the scene of close fighting; but the Porta Padova, the Porta Santa Lucia, and the points attacked between them, were never of serious importance. Undoubtedly they provided a certain number of casualties: but the assaults were not pushed home. In each case the Austrians contented themselves with attacks which kept the Italian troops and guns tied to their posts, and also enabled the assailants to throw some hundreds of bombs into the town in hopes of frightening the citizens into surrender—a hope which proved entirely illusory.[62]

Meanwhile Culoz' guns, though their reinforcements were still on the way, had duly opened fire on Bericoccoli. He had 6000 or 7000 men, but he launched no attack, because he was waiting to see what progress was made on his right by Clam, along the lower ground. Out of that plain there arise three successive small hills along the banks of the River Bacchiglione. On the foremost hillock stands the celebrated Rotonda (the masterpiece of Palladio's architecture) which, though undefendable, was being resolutely defended by some 400 young men of the Roman University battalion; and close behind it, the Villa Valmarana, occupied by a battalion of Civic Guards 650 strong from the turbulent town of Faenza, assisted by various volunteer companies of Bersaglieri—about 1420 men in all. These villas were outside the walls, but they were all-important. If Clam could capture them, he could shell the Bericoccoli line from its rear, and probably force the Porta

[62] Behind the Rotonda was the Porta Monte already mentioned:
At Porta Padova were stationed the 1st Roman legion under Colonel Del Grande, a brave officer who was killed.
At Porta Santa Lucia was the Battalion Basso Reno.
At Porta Santa Bartolo and Santa Croce was the 6th Battalion Fusiliers.
At Porta Castello, the Cacciatori.
At most of these were stationed a company or two of Swiss regulars. In reserve on the Piazza, one Swiss battalion, one battalion Carbineers, the Swiss field battery and the native battery. *V.* Durando, *Schiar.* p. 45 *et seq.*

Monte, from which a long steep way and stair lead uphill to the great church of the Santuario. Henceforth it seemed almost certain that the fate of the Berico hill and of the battle would depend on the defence of the Rotonda.

The struggle lasted for about three hours. The defenders were fairly numerous, but weak in artillery, whereas on the other side Clam succeeded in bringing up gradually his whole brigade on the right (west) bank of the Bacchiglione, while, on the opposite side, Wohlgemuth's brigade was also making steady progress. It was impossible for the defenders to hold out permanently against such numbers. By about 2 p.m. they were obliged to retire from the Rotonda to the Villa Valmarana; and after another hour's resistance they were driven from that building as well.

By 3 p.m., therefore, it had become feasible for the Austrians to initiate a decisive attack, both on the lower ground and along the narrow steep ridge of the hill. It was the hill that mattered; and, as far as we can tell, their success was certain; because wherever the ridge became wide enough for a defensive position, they could use their superiority of artillery. By about 4.30 they had made the Bericoccoli position nearly untenable, and on the lower ground they were threatening the Porta Monte. Once inside it, they could seize the steep staircase which connects the Santuario with the town. In fact the end was in sight; but there was destined to be one ghastly episode before Radetzky's victory became complete.

Throughout the day Massimo d'Azeglio had been in command of all the troops up on Monte Berico, and evidently he saw that the position was becoming steadily worse and worse. He determined, as a last supreme effort, to try and counter-attack; so he called upon three of the Swiss companies to retake the old Bella Guardia blockhouse with the bayonet. It was a mistake which amounted to a tragedy. What he was ordering was beyond the power of man. Most probably it had never been possible; but in any case, by this time, Culoz had massed a large number of men in concealed positions, together with his newly arrived guns. When the Swiss had charged forward about fifty yards, these men and guns suddenly opened fire. The brave Swiss tried to press on and were more than half annihilated; and at the same time the leading Austrian battalion rushed out with the bayonet. It seems profoundly sad to read that it was the 10th Jägers, the same men who had made such an heroic defence of the cemetery of Santa Lucia. This was the final blow; the Jägers dashed in among the remaining Swiss, and for some time men of German speech on either side, who had no cause of difference, were shooting and bayoneting one another, in and out of the trenches and even in the Church of the Santuario. Colonel Kopal fell mortally wounded, but his men, headed by Hauptmann Jablonsky, broke up the defence. In this revolting fight the Swiss companies were almost wiped out, and the Jägers lost twenty-eight killed and eighty-nine wounded.[63]

The Austrians had now penetrated the position so far that the Papal officers could no longer organise an efficient defence of the Sanctuary of Madonna del Monte. Cialdini had already been seriously wounded, and during the next hour d'Azeglio, who had shown fine courage, had been hit in the leg. By seven o'clock the enemy were swarming over the hill both from above and from below. From its extreme point they could bombard every portion of the town at their leisure. For Durando, surrender had become inevitable.

Radetzky, as we know, was anxious to get back to Verona as soon as possible, in case of an offensive movement by Charles Albert. So he offered excellent terms of surrender.

[63] Pimodan, p. 246. After the campaign the Austrian army in Italy presented to the 10th Jägers an enamelled hunting-horn with a medallion representing Colonel Kopal leading his men: around it, says Pimodan, are engraved the words: "En avant! Kopal vous appelle." We have seen this trophy in the Heeres Museum, Vienna (1937). The inscription is in German of which unfortunately our copy is lost.

The Pontifical troops were to march out of the town of Vicenza with all military honours, arms and baggage, and to retire beyond the River Po. They were not to serve again against Austria for three months, but after that time, they were at liberty to do so.

Radetzky had finished his task in twenty-one hours. It had cost him 141 dead, 541 wounded and 140 missing, a total of 822 in all.[64] But the work was fully done. His army was no longer in danger of supply failure; reinforcements could come through; and the reconquest of Venetia could be left to Welden. During this last swoop, not a movement had been left uncovered, not an unnecessary risk taken; and by June 12th he was back in Verona, as though nothing had happened.[65]

This feat seemed like a reminiscence of the Napoleonic wars, or rather of the allied crusade against Napoleon. It was directed by a man who had been Chief-of-Staff at Leipzig; but its detail is said to have been largely the work of his own Chief-of-Staff, Hess.[66]

The fall of Vicenza marked the end of the Papal contingent, just as Curtatone marked that of the Tuscans.[67]

[64] The Austrian *Feldzug*, II, 58. The fighting began at about 5 a.m. and lasted until 7 p.m. At that time Durando hoisted the white flag. On p. 35 the *Feldzug* gives the losses as ten less than its total on p. 58.

[65] With the First Army Corps. He left the Second Army Corps behind to reorganise matters and get in touch with Welden; while one brigade (Simbschen) was sent to Schio to open up communications through the Tyrol. Within the next three days he retook Padua whose garrison of 5000 retired to Venice, and Treviso whose garrison of 4000 men surrendered after a slight resistance.

[66] Willisen evidently thought this. *V.* also Pimodan, p. 227.

[67] The Italian losses are very uncertain. Hilleprandt believes they were 1000 to 1400 of which the Swiss accounted for at least 600. There is a pathetic story about the Swiss. After the surrender they brought their standards to Durando and asked him to take them into his quarters so that the Austrians should not be able to insult or drag through the mud the colours for which so many of their comrades had died.

Chapter XVII

THE END OF *ITALIA FARÀ DA SÈ*

I

Charles Albert's chance of victory was now at an end. It seems a tragedy. It was only about two and a half months since March 25th, the day on which he had crossed the Ticino amid scenes of unparalleled enthusiasm. But, after June 10th, although he might succeed in holding his positions, there was never any real chance of driving out the Austrians. They had returned to normal conditions. The Quadrilateral was too strong to be taken by attack; and now there was no possibility of cutting off its supplies. The Papal army no longer existed, and the Neapolitans had been recalled. On the other hand, Radetzky was immensely strong; he could get reinforcements and supplies from Austria; he had at least 45,000 men, always acting between impregnable fortresses. The moment for which Charles Albert had waited for nearly eighteen years had come and gone before harvest-time.[1]

And this new situation was realised by the army even sooner than by Charles Albert himself,[2] as was proved by the events of the next ten days.

---

[1] Fabris' verdict is: "Now, the possibility of an offensive no longer existed for the Piedmontese; it would only have gone and broken itself against the forts of Verona and the walls of Mantua. Consequently the King's army, from being unable to attack, was gradually compelled to defend itself." Fabris, III, 144.

[2] The following was the opinion of Prince Ferdinand, perhaps the boldest of the commanding officers: "We were reduced to the defensive.... In fact with our army of barely 50,000 men, it was temerity to try to attack the Marshal who was protected with fortresses.... For the Marshal, a defeat suffered under the guns of his fortresses was nothing; he could retire into them with the certainty of having time to recoup: for most certainly, with our forty-five guns and army immeasurably inferior to his, we could not reasonably

Charles Albert has often been blamed because he made no attempt on Verona during Radetzky's absence; but in reality he did nearly all that was possible at that moment. Until June 7th, neither he nor any of his staff guessed that Radetzky's objective was Vicenza; and then his information, obtained from one of Durando's officers, was that the place could hold out for five or six days.

On the 8th he wrote to Franzini to get the opinion of the generals as to an attack on Verona, which, he said, could be supported by a rising of the citizens; apparently he did not ·believe in making such an attempt without help from within.

Almost every general had a different suggestion, but it seems evident that they all took the same view as to the unwisdom of attacking Verona. The following account is given by Fabris:

He [Charles Albert] wrote again on the 9th and 10th, according to Farini who was at Headquarters. It seems that Bava wanted to remain at Goito; Franzini wanted to start off for Vicenza; De Sonnaz, Chioda (O.C. Engineers) and Rossi saw the necessity of taking Rivoli before marching against Verona; and only on June 10th did Generals De Sonnaz, Broglia and Olivieri agree to a march by Villafranca to the Adige, to bridge it boldly and follow up Radetzky, in order to separate him from Verona.[3]

Manifestly no one, except Charles Albert, believed in attacking Verona again; and probably they were right. It was a very strong place in 1848.[4] To take it would be a

attempt the siege of Verona." *Rapporti*, I, 305. *V.* also Alfonso La Marmora's report, *Rapporti*, III, 65; and Bava's advice to Charles Albert, *Ibid.* I, 67–8.

[3] Even this was taking a considerable risk. *V.* Fabris, III, 132; Della Rocca, *Autobiografia*, I, 221.

[4] Cf. the following opinions: Baldini (p. 62), speaking about the beginning of the campaign, calls it a "first-class fortress". Salasco (*Rapporti*, I, 13): "These four fortresses made the Austrian position impregnable." Schönhals said that "to free himself from this anxiety the Field-Marshal [Radetzky] sent back most of his reserve" (Schönhals, II, 38). *V. supra*, p. 112. It has been pointed out by Willisen and others that in 1859 Napoleon III never attempted to

question of days, if not of weeks. It was far stronger than Peschiera: Radetzky had left his reserve there to make it quite secure.

Charles Albert decided that the army should set out on the tracks of Radetzky, cross the Adige at Ronco and attack him while he was round Vicenza. Later, however, he received news that the Veronese were prepared to rise, and decided to try a coup. The 12th was spent in preliminary marches to assemble the troops; and at 9 a.m. on the 13th they were at Villafranca ready to start; but they wanted to be reviewed by the King, and consequently spent four hours in getting out of that small town. Meanwhile a deluge came on; by evening they were only four or five miles out in the direction of Verona. Then suddenly Charles Albert received news of the fall of Vicenza and the return of Radetzky with 5000 men. This naturally altered the whole character of the advance; it was necessary to make fresh plans. He called a halt.[5]

Suddenly a Veronese citizen presented himself and said that, in spite of Radetzky's return, the citizens were ready to rise. Charles Albert agreed to attack that night or next morning. It was arranged that the rising should be ordered by sending up a signal at 10 p.m. that night from Villafranca. But he did not say that the signal was to consist of lights; and as the Commandant of Villafranca had not been informed, he vetoed the lights until the time for signalling was past.[6] This was perhaps fortunate, as the soldiers were tired and drenched to the skin.

take the fortresses of the Quadrilateral. *V.* also opinion of Carderina (Chief of Staff, First Army Corps), *Rapporti*, I, 131.

[5] According to Bartolomeis (quoted by Fabris, III, 144), Franzini was very much disappointed at hearing that Radetzky had already returned. He had believed in advancing and cutting him off from Verona. He said (in Italian French): "C'est trop tard, Sire! C'est trop tard!" Bava took the opposite view about this advance.

[6] Fabris, III, 140. Also Bava's *Relazione*: *Rapporti*, I, 64. He calls it a bonfire. Lumbroso, p. 259.

The only result achieved during these days was that the Piedmontese took and occupied the Rivoli plateau. This Alpine post would have been valuable at the beginning of the campaign because it cuts the connection between Verona and the Tyrol. But now it was no longer of any importance. It seems just possible that Charles Albert occupied this celebrated position because he wanted some tangible proof of energy to show to the republicans who were belittling him in their newspapers.

There was one point which should have struck Charles Albert more vividly than it did. The concentration had been very slow and unsatisfactory. One of Bes' regiments coming down from the north had marched all day without food; and others too had suffered. Henceforth there was no question of engaging Radetzky without concentrating very considerable forces. Charles Albert should have perceived that his army was spread out over a twenty-mile front, whereas Radetzky had now got all his troops assembled under his hand to deliver a decisive blow.

II. CREATION OF THE KINGDOM OF UPPER ITALY

When speaking of the Five Glorious Days a Piedmontese writer once remarked that the Milanese were rather like the Creator, because they toiled for five days and, after that, did nothing.

This was partly due to reaction, but chiefly because, after Radetzky's retirement, they remained deeply and bitterly divided against each other. On the one side was the Provisional Government consisting mainly of Albertists headed by Counts Casati, Borromeo and others who had been at the Casa Vidiserti during the fighting. On the other side was the Opposition, headed by Cattaneo, Cernuschi, Terzaghi, Cesare Cantù and others, mostly the active republicans who had fought so well during the Five Days. On April 7th they were joined by Mazzini, newly arrived from England.

The problem which accentuated all their differences was the question of union with Piedmont. The Provisional Government was in favour of uniting the two states by fusion under King Charles Albert, but the Opposition wanted Lombardy to be a republic and to be federated with Piedmont, not fused; and some extremists, headed by Mazzini, claimed that the whole of Italy should be fused into one single republic.[7]

These were vital questions: was it to be Fusion or Federation? Was it to be a monarchy or a republic?

At first, both Charles Albert and Mazzini would have liked to postpone all political wrangling until they had driven out the foreigner;[8] but unfortunately this was found to be impossible. An immediate settlement of the political differences was forced upon them. Before the authorities could raise soldiers to attack Radetzky, they had to decide whether Charles Albert was to be their King, their leader, or merely their ally. And it was this difficulty which became the chief cause of their final disaster.

Consequently, in spite of their good intentions, the Lombards were permanently divided into two parties: the Provisional Government with its paper the 22 *Marzo* and the

---

[7] The clearest account of these weeks on Milan is perhaps that of Tivaroni, *Ital. Sett.* pp. 279 *et seq.* and 455 *et seq.*; also Masi, *Il Risorg.* II, 287; *Rass. stor.* 1927, January–March, a very informative article by Luisa Gasperini; and Antonio Casati, *Milano e i principi di Savoia.* For original authorities Mazzini's *Lettere* at this time: E.N. xxxv. For Hummelauer's mission the Viennese Archives have interesting documents. Also *Correspondence*, II. We have been unable to study the Milanese newspapers.

[8] On March 22nd the Provisional Government had declared: "As long as the struggle continues it is not opportune to bring forward opinions on the future political destinies of our dear country. We are called upon now to win independence; and good citizens should not think of anything except the fight. When our cause is victorious, our destinies will be fixed by the nation." This was quoted against them after the coup of May 15th. *V.* Mazzini, E.N. xxxv, 175 and note.

Opposition which, on April 28th, began to publish *L'Italia del Popolo*. Before long, every newspaper in Milan was either fusionist or anti-fusionist,[9] monarchical or republican, a supporter or an opponent of the Provisional Government.[10]

Meanwhile a reader may ask: What about the war? That exactly expresses the situation. Hardly anyone had the slightest realisation that it was necessary for every able-bodied citizen to be at work all day learning to be a soldier. During this summer campaign the Lombards sent barely 20,000[11] men to join the Piedmontese, and even these men were only semi-trained and almost useless. The fusionists were afraid of raising a separate Lombard army which might oppose Charles Albert, while on the other side many republicans did not want their own soldiers to bring Lombardy under the King of Piedmont. Indeed, throughout these months, the republican party was doing more harm than good to the war of Italian liberation. Yet it was these same men who had fought best in Milan; and some of whom were destined before another year was gone to immortalise themselves in the defence of Rome. And these months produced at all events one great republican success, namely, an independent command for Garibaldi.

On April 7th, when Mazzini arrived in Milan, he published an address[12] in which he spoke only of achieving "national

[9] Gasparini, *op. cit.* p. 45 *et seq.*

[10] One of the most permanent benefits of Charles Albert's movement was the experience gained. Every sort of question was discussed, and the ground cleared for future action. For instance, Milan and Turin were rivals: if fusion were voted, which was to be the capital of the new state? Probably Turin; but if Venetia joined them, then certainly Milan must be the capital. But on either side there were people who did not want fusion if it meant the loss of their capital city, and others who wanted fusion at any price. At length Pareto's formula settled it by postponement; he laid down that Correnti's constituent assembly should settle the *form* of the new government but not its place. Tivaroni, *op. cit.* pp. 279, 464 *et seq.*

[11] *Ibid.* p. 473. Hilleprandt put their number at 17,000 but says they were entirely useless (p. 322).

[12] Tivaroni, *op. cit.* p. 458; Mazzini, E.N. xxxv, 176.

sovereignty" and made no mention of a republic or even of unity; but, before long, he found that there was an Albertist movement already in the field, working for fusion. On April 4th Franzini, Charles Albert's Minister of War, had issued a note calling on all the loyal Provisional Governments in North Italy to return members for an elective assembly to decide the form of government;[13] and on April 8th the Provisional Government of Milan named a commission to arrange for the calling of a constituent assembly which should decide on the composition of the new Piedmont-Lombard state, and also on the form of its government.

Henceforth Mazzini felt absolved from any obligation to abstain from agitating; and he started on a policy of republican propaganda. This undoubtedly did harm to Charles Albert, but it formed a stage in the reorganisation of Mazzini's own following: and a year later, after the failure of Charles Albert and Pius IX, the republican party became the only remaining champion of Italian freedom.

It seems unnecessary to go into all the details of the contest between the Albertists and republicans during the next two months. In the first weeks of April the towns of Bergamo and Brescia, stirred up by Franzini, had voted definitely for fusion. This aroused the Opposition. On April 30th Cattaneo and his followers called on Mazzini and suggested getting rid of Charles Albert and the Provisional Government and setting up a Lombard assembly supported by France. Mazzini, to his credit, replied that so far from stopping the war, they should push it on with greater energy.

On May 12th the Provisional Government succeeded in passing a law that during the next seventeen days a plebiscite should be held all over Lombardy to decide whether to have fusion at once, or postpone the whole question till the end of the war. This was an Albertist success, but Cesare Correnti

---

[13] Tivaroni, *op. cit.* p. 460. *V.* also Antonio Casati, *op. cit.* p. 177. Costa de Beauregard says that Charles Albert insisted on this on account of the trouble Bes had had with the Milanese (p. 156).

succeeded in talking into it a rider that if the union took place, the whole united territory should vote a constituent assembly to decide what form of constitutional government should be established. This suggestion of altering the Piedmontese constitution was very unpopular[14] with the Conservatives at Turin. May 29th was the last day of the poll. And on that day a crowd invaded the Chamber, calling on the government to retire; but the Civic Guards stood by Casati and all was well.

On June 8th Casati published the result of the plebiscite; fusion with Piedmont had been voted by 561,002 against 681. On June 13th the two governments of Turin and Milan signed a Convention whereby Correnti's proposed constituent assembly should be set up before November 1st to decide on the form of constitutional monarchy for the new state.

On June 16th the vote of Parma fusing herself with Piedmont was accepted by the Turin government, and June 21st that of Modena.

On August 2nd the Provisional Government in Milan came to an end. It had achieved fusion, but at the cost of not arming its people.[15] However, there was more to be added to its record.

Meanwhile, on July 4th, Venice had also voted for fusion; with the support of Manin it had been carried in the Assembly by 127 votes to 6.

On July 27th this was accepted by the Turin cabinet; and they sent two commissioners to take over the government. On August 5th the commissioners General the Marchese Colli and Conte Cibrario arrived, and on the 7th they proclaimed Charles Albert King. It was a great moment, but

---

[14] We note, for instance, the indignation of Cibrario who was a type of the best Conservative officialdom: "Cette condition tout à fait neuve dans l'histoire, qui portait en elle une nouvelle et radicale révolution dont les conséquences pouvaient nous amener jusqu'à la dernière forme de la démocratie, et changer de fait le roi en président de république, fut acceptée...." Cibrario, *Charles Albert*, p. 128.

[15] Tivaroni, *op. cit.* p. 468.

alas! too short-lived. On August 9th General Welden, who was clearing up Venetia, notified them that, by Salasco's armistice, Venice was to be evacuated as the price of saving Piedmont from enemy occupation. And on the 11th they were compelled to retire.[16]

The Kingdom of Upper Italy, thus inaugurated, lasted only a month and six days—since July 4th—a short life; but long enough to prove that on some future day, when Italy was again in arms, neither Lombardy nor Venetia would become an obstacle to the unification of Italy.

In fact, although Charles Albert and his army were now inevitably doomed to failure in this campaign, the experience for which they had paid so dearly would prove invaluable to the builders in the next generation.

III. DIPLOMATIC RELATIONS: CHARLES ALBERT'S ONLY CHANCE OF MAKING A SUCCESSFUL PEACE

During these weeks between the middle of April and June 10th (the loss of Vicenza) it would have been quite possible for Charles Albert to make an advantageous peace; and he himself would have been ready to do so;[17] but it was rendered impossible by the political requirements of the various parties, which in both Milan and Turin had become over-confident.

Austria was afraid that the new French republic might intervene,[18] and even as early as April 19th she had offered a scheme of ameliorated government[19] to the Lombards; but

---

[16] Trevelyan, *Manin*, p. 202 *et seq.*

[17] *V. infra* his letter of June 7th quoted by Tivaroni, Costa de Beauregard and others.

[18] Charles Albert, too, was afraid of being stabbed in the back. In the beginning of April two thousand enthusiastic French republicans invaded Chambéry and set up a republic; but the citizens rose, killed four, wounded twenty-nine and took 905 prisoners: Tivaroni, *op. cit.* p. 273. England was also afraid of French intervention which might lead to a general war. *V.* Greer, p. 224 *et seq.*; De Guichen, p. 121.   [19] Tivaroni, *op. cit.* p. 249.

they refused it. Ten days later there came the battle of Pastrengo, and Vienna decided to send Baron Hummelauer to Palmerston, asking the British Government to mediate; they were willing to resign Lombardy altogether and to grant Venetia a very wide measure of Home Rule. Pareto, however, in Turin, refused to accept these or any terms as long as there remained an Austrian soldier in Italy. This was by far the best offer the Piedmontese ministers received or were likely to receive, but unfortunately it only reached Palmerston on May 24th, and by that time Charles Albert was tied hand and foot.[20]

As already described, on May 12th the Lombard Provisional Government had set up the polls for voting on the fusion of Lombardy with Piedmont. After that, it had appointed a deputation to visit Charles Albert at his H.Q. at Sommacampagna and get a promise from him that he would never make peace as long as an Austrian soldier remained in Italy; and they asked him to invite the Venetians to unite with them. To encourage his supporters Charles Albert had bound himself by both promises and had sent out a suitable proclamation to the Venetians.[21] This was unfortunate. The promises were made on May 23rd, the very same day that Hummelauer's offer reached Palmerston, and also on the very day before the Nugent-Thurn reinforcement reached Radetzky; after that success the Austrians were no longer so generous with their offers.

[20] For English translations of these documents *v. Correspondence*, II, which also gives the despatches to Palmerston from May 18th onwards of Campbell in Milan and Abercromby in Turin.

[21] The British official documents confirm in full detail the Italian description of the deputation and its requests. Mr Consul Campbell ends: "His Majesty in reply declared the war at the head of which he had put himself to be Italian, and one which he could not call finished with until every part of the Italian territory was evacuated by the enemy; he confirmed his former pledge not to lay down his arms until the Austrians were driven beyond the Alps...and expressed his conviction that when Verona is conquered Venice would be free." *Correspondence*, II, May 24th.

On June 7th, before the fall of Vicenza, Charles Albert wrote a letter to Franzini which showed that he realised the situation far better than his ministers. He said that if they could obtain through England an offer of the cession of Lombardy up to the Adige, together with the two Duchies, they might consider that

"They had carried out a glorious campaign and made superb acquisitions....To ask more is rashness, in fact, folly. It is risking the loss, the ruin forever of the Italian cause.

You see now, friend Franzini, what my position is like, with a responsible Ministry which has pledged itself in Parliament. As long as the union with Lombardy is not absolutely concluded and there are at Turin as well as Milan such high claims", I can only acquiesce.

"But if they want me to risk everything, I have my military honour to the fore, and I will go forward until a bullet enables me to finish with joy a life of ill-chances, entirely consecrated and sacrificed to my country."[22]

Even the most enterprising of his officers were of the same opinion; Prince Ferdinand, Alfonso La Marmora, all say in their reports that it would have been wisest to negotiate "on the basis of the Adige boundary or even the Mincio".[23]

On July 4th, in reply to Charles Albert's invitation, Venetia gave up being a republic and voted herself into Piedmont.[24] The Venetian deputies came to Charles Albert, who probably regretted the whole situation, for he received them rather coldly;[25] but he sent them on to Turin. On July 7th, just a month after the letter already quoted, he wrote one to Castagnetto in which he said that personally he would gladly accept negotiations on the basis of Piedmont's keeping the Duchies and having the Adige for boundary (i.e. without

[22] This letter is given almost in full by Costa de Beauregard, p. 234, quoting Bianchi, *Scritti e Lettere*; Tivaroni also quotes it, *Ital. Sett.* p. 251.

[23] *V. Rapporti*, I, 306.

[24] *Correspondence*, II: Dawkins to Palmerston, July 5th, 1848: III, 66. *V.* also Tivaroni, *Ital. Sett.* p. 252.

[25] *Correspondence*, II: Dawkins to Palmerston, July 19th.

Venice).²⁶ On July 27th, however, the Venetian offer was accepted, as we have said, by the Turin Chamber.

By that time there was nothing more to get through British mediation.

The British Government had given the most friendly support to the scheme for creating a strong northern kingdom under Charles Albert, but refused to approve of any lesser suggestion because that might arouse French aggression.²⁷ At first the Austrian ambassador had been equally agreeable: but during the months of May and June, when the cession of Venetia was bruited, his replies began gradually to take the tone "after all we're not dead yet". And when the British proposals continued after the Austrian victory of Custoza, he showed some signs of irritation: he insinuated that in principle the case of Ireland was rather like that of Sicily, and the cause of Mr Smith O'Brien rather like that of Charles Albert. On September 1st Austria declined any further Franco-British mediation; and on the same day Palmerston's plain-spoken retort to Baron Koller might be considered the last word on the British side: "Deux arguments militent en faveur de votre profession territoriale en Italie; le traité de Vienne, et la force d'armes. Si l'on me parle du premier, je reponds par *Cracovie—La force d'armes est un fait. Je le reconnais.*"²⁸

When Salasco's armistice was signed, the British minister at Turin was unable to obtain any modification of the provision that all former Austrian territory must be evacuated by the Piedmontese. Radetzky declared that he had calculated the probability of French intervention and was willing to take the risk.²⁹

²⁶ *Correspondence*, II: Abercromby to Palmerston, July 10th. Costa, p. 275, quoting Garnier-Pages.
²⁷ Viennese Archives, Berichte aus London, 1848. Count Dietrichstein's despatch of July 10th. Palmerston swept away the Dukes of Parma and Modena. "Le premier n'a pas une idée dans la tête, et le second est pis (*sic*) que son père."
²⁸ Viennese Archives, *ibid.* despatch No. 48: Baron Koller.
²⁹ *Correspondence*, II: Abercromby to Palmerston, August 4th, 1848.

In this way Charles Albert lost his only chance of success. He had refused, however, to "abandon the Venetians to an Austrian revenge". And some good judges, notably Tivaroni, have thought that it was better for Italy that he should fail, and postpone the settlement to 1860. If he had been victorious in 1848 all that he could have achieved was a Kingdom of Upper Italy, perhaps at the price of ceding Savoy to France.

In this emergency, as in most others, he had been sacrificed; but his sacrifice was to bear fruit. By acceding to the impossible wishes of his ministers and to those of the Lombards and Venetians, he had established the Kingdom of Northern Italy and thereby inaugurated the principle of Fusion (as opposed to Federation) for the whole peninsula. And at the same time he had laid down the true mission of Piedmont—that she was fighting not merely to extend her frontiers to the next river, but to drive the last Austrian out of Italy.

It was these two political influences—Piedmontese hegemony working on the principle of fusion—which brought about the final triumph in 1860.

Chapter XVIII

ROME. MAMIANI'S MINISTRY

At Rome, Count Terenzio Mamiani della Rovere had been minister since the troubled days following on the Allocution (April 29th).

Mamiani was now forty-nine years of age; his face was that of a well-bred man, with a high forehead and straight features, but with long hair and a rather unkempt appearance; evidently he was an "intellectual" of that day; a good speaker, but far more a student of books than of men. At first sight it might have seemed possible for Pius and Mamiani to work in harmony and perhaps to establish a Liberal government in Rome. They were both patriots, and both of the same stock; and Mamiani was indebted to Pius for a very characteristic act of kindness.[1]

Undoubtedly Mamiani was a fine character; his whole life went to prove this. But unfortunately he was just exactly the wrong man to be with Pius at such a critical moment. He had been exiled by the ultra-Conservative Gregory XVI and his writings showed him to be not only politically embittered against the Papal rule, but also philosophically opposed to its spiritual influence during those years. And—although we may often sympathise with his views—naturally Pius dis-

---

[1] In September 1847 Pius had allowed him to re-enter the state, and—to save his face—without signing the oath prescribed in the Amnesty. Mamiani wrote a touching letter to Cardinal Ferretti, Secretary of State, thanking him for permission to see again his family and his friends, and repeated a promise already made to Cardinal Gizzi that he would not raise disturbance in the Papal dominions, adding: "To respect the laws...has become the obligation which is natural, necessary and common to all, since, owing to the miraculous wisdom of Pius IX there now exists true law and order." The oath was absolutely inoffensive, but Mamiani had sworn never to make submission. *V. Italy in the Making*, II, 38 and note.

trusted him in either sphere. It was a pity that they could not agree; for Mamiani, though anxious to limit the authority of the Pope, would never have tried to drive him out.[2]

On May 3rd—the second day of Mamiani's ministry—Pius carried out an idea which has seldom received much notice. He wrote with his own hand a letter to the Emperor of Austria, appealing to him to do a great act of justice. In time of peace this would have seemed a vain conception, but at that moment when Austria was shaken by revolution and defeat, she might perhaps accept him as her mediator; as indeed she had already accepted England.

The letter ran as follows:

Maestà,

It has always been the custom that this Holy See should speak words of peace whenever wars were drenching Christian soil with blood; and in Our Allocution of the 29th of last month, We asserted that to declare war would revolt Our paternal heart; and announced Our ardent desire to contribute towards the restoration of peace. Let it not therefore be displeasing to your Majesty that We should address an appeal to your piety and religion, and exhort you with paternal affection to withdraw your arms from a war which can never reconquer for your empire the minds of the Lombards and Venetians; and can only bring with it the fatal series of calamities that always accompany war, and are certainly both repulsive and detestable to yourself. Let it not be displeasing to the generous German nation that We invite it to lay aside hatred, and to change into the useful and friendly relationship of neighbouring states, a domination which will never be either noble or fortunate so long as it rests only on the sword.

We are confident that the German nation itself, being honestly proud of its own nationality, will not engage its honour in an attempt to shed the blood of this Italian nation; but will rather engage it in nobly recognising her as a sister—for both are Our daughters and very dear to Us; let each of them be content to live within her own borders by honourable agreement and beneath the blessing of the Lord.

Meanwhile We pray to the Giver of all Light and the Author of all Good that He may inspire your Majesty with His holy Counsels; while from Our innermost heart We bestow on yourself

[2] Farini, II, 281.

and Her Imperial Majesty and on the imperial family the Apostolic Benediction.

Datum Romae apud Sanctam Mariam Majorem, die tertia Maii anno MDCCCXLVIII, Pontificatus nostri anno secundo.

Pius P.P.IX.

This letter he despatched at once by the hand of Monsignor Morichini.[3] Its existence was not made public in Rome until twenty-four days afterwards, when it met with general approval. But no answer was returned until later, when all was over.

This was the first event in Mamiani's ministry, and his comment on it is characteristic:

As to the projected intervention of the Pontiff...you may take it for certain that as long as I and my colleagues are at the head of affairs, we do not mean to enter on any treaty with Austria while a single one of her soldiers remains on our territory....Nevertheless, the Pope is perfectly free to go on with his work and in that respect need not consult his ministers. But we shall not cease from carrying on the holy war....I am thinking over another way of getting the Pope to accept the war....

These sentences characterise the whole of Mamiani's ministry.[4]

The chief importance of Mamiani's ministry lies in its having demonstrated that for a Pope to be a constitutional monarch was very difficult, if not impossible.

Pius, under the Statuto, still remained in a position rather analogous to that of an absolute ruler. An act did not become law until he had signed it; and he had the right of referring it to the College of Cardinals. This was his safeguard for the Church and he intended never to resign it. He did not feel necessarily bound to agree to a measure because it had been passed by Parliament. Nevertheless, as it stood, the Statuto might conceivably have been made workable during a period of peace; but, even then, not without a deep sense of mutual forbearance.

[3] Farini, II, 120.
[4] Letter of Mamiani to Farini, May 18th, 1848: Farini, *Epistolario*, II, 320.

Mamiani wanted to alter this state of things. As to the Temporal Power he hoped to turn the Pope into a constitutional sovereign—one who reigns but does not govern.[5] In reality what he and his supporters wanted was an extension of the Statuto. It is said that Pius feared that they might try to abolish the temporal powers of the College of Cardinals. Virtually Mamiani wanted to limit the Pope's authority to ecclesiastical matters.

Thirdly, in the Chamber of Deputies there was the party of the extremists headed by Sterbini and Canino. They wanted to establish a more or less republican form of government, regardless of the interests of the Holy See.

In these changing conditions what most forcibly strikes us is that neither Pius nor his people had any realisation of the workings of a limited monarchy;[6] at the age of fifty-six he was rather old for learning the difficult art of being a constitutional monarch, and the people had not the slightest knowledge of what it meant; its delicate conventions and mutual understandings were unknown to them. The results were almost absurd. Take, for instance, the principle that the King can do no wrong; Pius evidently did not grasp the fact that his ministers' acts and speeches must bind him as a sovereign but did not compromise him personally. At first, he was inclined to state his own views, without much regard for what had appeared in the King's speech, and to justify them to his subjects; and he was quite determined to remain supreme in any matter which affected the Church. The people, on the other hand, far from thinking that the King could do no wrong, were accustomed to blame him for everything; when dissatisfied, their first impulse was to go round to the Quirinal and howl underneath the windows. In fact,

[5] "The farce of the King who reigns, but does not govern, is one that he never understood; to the poet Marchetti he said: 'You are my friend, not my minister'": Cantù, II, 1109. V. also Masi, *Il Risorg.* II, 327.

[6] Farini, II, 141, 142.

the situation seemed to prove that the institutions which elsewhere have taken six or seven centuries to elaborate cannot be appropriated at two months' notice, least of all in a period of popular passion.[7]

"It was necessary to begin by defining the limits of the two authorities", says Farini. But, cutting across everything, was the question of war. Mamiani's aim throughout these months was to annex enough of the secular power to enable him to declare war.

On May 18th there came the first election under the new Constitution, the Statuto. About five-sixths of the deputies elected were ready to support Mamiani; for the time being, the electorate was all in favour of war; but, according to Mr Petre, out of 4000[8] voters in Rome, only 800 took the trouble to go to the poll.

June 5th was the day fixed for the opening of the first Parliament, and early in that month the ministers began to prepare the "King's speech"; but such differences arose with Pius over the subject-matter that at last, instead of reading it himself, he sent down Cardinal Altieri to deliver in his name an entirely colourless speech which offended no one, but satisfied no one. One feature of this ceremony seems almost incredible. This first opening of Parliament naturally was turned into a festival, with "gala" coaches, civic guards in uniform, banners of all the Italian states and of some foreign nations. Yet, so little interest was there among those concerned that only forty-nine deputies had arrived on the scene

[7] Farini, II, 142. Farini felt this very strongly. He often acted as go-between for Mamiani and Pius. V. also the French ambassador, who remarked in a letter to his government, describing the opening of Parliament, that "Tout trahissait leur complète ignorance des pratiques parlementaires": Paris Aff. Etr. Rome, 1848, June 6th. V. also Rosi, p. 203.

[8] London Corr. II, Petre, June 6th, 1848. Tivaroni says, less than one-third, Ital. Cent. p. 328. The French ambassador reported that in Rome, out of 3411 electors, only 1200 voted; in the provinces, out of about 50,000, only 20,000 voted: Paris Aff. Etr. Rome, 1848, May 28th. Spada, II, 302, says one-third to one-fourth.

—not even a quorum—out of a total of a hundred.[9] And on
June 10th there were only fifty-one.[10]

As by that time the ministers were on the verge of resigning,
Pius agreed that they should prepare another speech, and that
Mamiani should read it on the first day of the debate. This
speech therefore was drawn up by the ministers, corrected by
Pius, and read by Mamiani on June 9th. It was known as
Mamiani's Programme, and consisted of nineteen paragraphs
dealing with various subjects, of which the most important
were the following: the restoration of law and order; the
Italian national cause—whose inspiring description they concluded with the words "God wills it", but at the same time
referred to the Pope's true position as being that of mediator;
then, the League of Italian states of which they said: "We
promise never to desist until we have reached the fulfilment of
that noble and splendid undertaking." Then the ministers
mentioned Austria, to whom they offered their friendship
"from that day and that hour when her last soldier shall have
evacuated the last palm-breadth of Italian soil": and they
informed the House that they had urged the Piedmontese
ministers to open friendly negotiations with the brave Hungarian nation; this last clause called forth a strong objection
from Pius, but, as it was a question of fact, Mamiani did not
delete it. As we know, the Hungarians were in rebellion
against Austria.[11]

[9] "We are only 49, not a quorum, therefore we cannot debate.
Many are beginning to think of passing a public resolution in which
they note the shameful negligence of the absent members": Farini
to Cardinal Amat, June 7th, *Epist.* II, 378. The French ambassador
gave their number as forty, and said that there was not actually a
quorum: Paris Aff. Etr. Rome, 1848, June 6th, Forbin-Janson.
Spada more or less confirms this, II, 349.

[10] Florence Arch. Esteri, Busta 2446, June 10th, Bargagli. Spada
says that only fifty-one deputies were present, II, 352.

[11] For the above description of the Programme, *v.* Farini, II, 169
et seq. In reality, the original version of the Programma had been
drawn up by Mamiani and published by him on April 25th: Spada,
II, 244.

Spoken by Mamiani this was an eloquent speech, and was well applauded; and no sooner was it finished than Prince Canino stood up and asked whether it was the expression of the "removable" ministry, or whether it was the programme of the Prince himself, who desired to recognise the sacrosanct and imprescriptible rights of the people; and Mamiani replied that it was "the unanimous expression of the ministry, assented to and approved by His Holiness".

It looks rather as if this had been a pre-arranged scheme for involving Pius in the war: but, from the above speech, was he, as Pope, compelled to declare war? It is rather hard to say: the speech admitted that the true position of the Pope was that of mediator. The question asked was somewhat typical of the part played by Canino; he and Sterbini were very soon to be recognised as the leaders of agitation in the House.[12]

This speech represented the wishes of the ministers; but it also elicited statements of their position from the deputies and from Pius himself.

The Council of Deputies (the Lower House) addressed an "oration" to Pius in answer to those of his delegates and of the ministers. Of the many subjects on which it touches the following are the most significant; the Statuto, they say, may require improvements; the Italian League including Sicily will be completed shortly, with its Diet at Rome; the Papal troops will be under Charles Albert, but at the same time treaties with Tuscany and Piedmont will be necessary; the deputies approve Pius' letter in favour of peace, but consider that "your people ought not to abandon arms": the war is a defensive war. Many reforms are required and "for all of them the Civic Guard is an impregnable bulwark".

These are a few points from the deputies' address read to Pius on July 10th; and it will be seen that in almost every one

[12] For the previous history of these agitators, of Ciceruacchio and others, *v. Italy in the Making*, II.

of them there is a controversial note; for instance, that the Statuto is to be improved, in fact enlarged; the war is to be continued and is defensive; finally the Civic Guard is an impregnable bulwark: each of these might be called a challenge to Pius.

When answering them, Pius assumed that the deputies were merely replying to Altieri's speech and not to the subsequent programme of the ministers. For this Farini censures him, because he was responsible for both utterances; also because he had written his reply without consulting his ministers, which was manifestly wrong. But Pius gives us the impression of having in his head several points which he was quite determined to make public. The following was perhaps the most important of these.[13]

In Mamiani's Programme (clause 3) he had laid down the principle that "*Our Prince lives in the serene peace of the dogmas.* He dispenses to the whole world the Word of God: he prays, he blesses and he pardons." This attempt to limit the Pope's sphere of action to "the serene peace of the dogmas" evidently offended Pius, for even a year later he referred to it with considerable resentment;[14] and now he reminded his people that "the Pontiff prays, blesses and pardons; and that it is also his duty to bind and to loose". He added that, even though as Prince he has summoned the Assemblies to co-operate with him, as Sovereign-Priest he has need of full liberty of action "as to the interests of religion and the state" and that "this liberty remains to him untouched". He reminded them that being Pope he could not declare war, and said that he was greatly surprised at hearing that their consideration was called to this question, "in opposition to our public declarations and at the moment

[13] A translation of this speech is given by Petre, *London Corr.* III, July 11th, 1848, p. 58. For the original *v.* Farini, II, 223.

[14] Masi, *Il Risorg.* II, 328. Already on June 6th the Piedmontese minister had perceived that Mamiani and Pius could not work together. Turin Arch. Lettere Ministri, Rome, 1848, Pareto, June 5th.

when we had undertaken negotiations for peace";[15] that the Statuto must be observed (they had suggested altering it); and in a paragraph apart, he laid down that education is in the province of the Church, henceforth her right and duty.

From the above expressions of opinion, it will be seen that the ruler, the ministers and the Council of Deputies were at cross purposes from the start.

Unfortunately, at that moment there occurred two small episodes which created some controversy in the newspapers. The first was over the vexed question of the lay foreign minister.

On taking office, Mamiani had insisted on having a lay foreign minister for secular affairs, as well as the usual ecclesiastical foreign minister, who at that time was to be Cardinal Soglia. But it was a matter of common knowledge that from the first Pius had hated this double arrangement.[16] No doubt he feared that the lay foreign minister might somehow involve him in war.

Early in July, however, the matter took a rather unfortunate turn. One of the papers discovered that Soglia had written a cipher despatch to the Nuncio in Vienna, Monsignor Viale Prelà, and the newspapers did not hesitate to say that Pius was intriguing with the Austrians. After some delay, Pius told Mamiani that in this cipher-letter, Cardinal Soglia had directed Viale Prelà to take his orders from him (Soglia) and not from Marchetti, the lay foreign

[15] This clause was taken in France as being a restatement of his position that as Pope he still refused to declare war. Farini, II, 178, says that what aroused Pius was the fact that in Paris the *Univers* was inveighing against the Programma and saying that Rome was governed by the enemies of the Church; that the *Epoca* had retorted that the Pope had approved of the speech. Hence a newspaper war round the name of Pius. *V.* also La Farina, *Stor. d' Italia*, p. 490.

[16] Farini, II, 215–16. Spada, II, 387–9, gives rather a different version, but as Farini was in the ministry at the time, we have followed his account. *V.* also Gabussi.

minister.[17] The cabinet was indignant at this, and apparently popular sympathies ran against Pius;[18] but Farini has pointed out that the situation was not entirely what it seemed. In reality the whole of the Pontifical diplomatic service, the Nuncios and all, consisted of cardinals or other churchmen, because nearly all its business was ecclesiastical. The great Catholic powers did not want to be relegated to the lay official of so small a state when they came to deal with the accredited representatives of the Catholic Church all over the world. Indeed Farini considered that Mamiani had been mistaken in trying to establish the lay Foreign Office for secular affairs: there were so many matters which might be considered either secular or religious. The latest historical reference to this episode is that of Count Guido Pasolini, who tells us that Pius had already had a rupture with Marchetti because the latter had sent directions to the Nuncios without reference to the Pope; and that Soglia had directed the Nuncios to send him copies of their despatches to and from Marchetti.[19]

At the same time there occurred another cause of irritation. On June 28th the Alto Consiglio, which was composed of men whom Pius liked and trusted, had decided to keep their voting secret. This decision pleased Pius, but it annoyed Mamiani. Consequently on July 3rd he published an article in the official *Gazzetta*, blaming the Alto Consiglio and remarking that, strictly speaking, an Upper House was not absolutely necessary to parliamentary government, and that some people would rather be without it. This rather tactless

[17] Cf. the opinion of the French ambassador, June 10th, about it: "une nouveauté qui bouleverse toutes les traditions de la Cour Romaine": Paris Aff. Etr. Rome, 1848.

[18] On June 19th, Bargagli, the Tuscan minister, pointed out to his government that a cardinal could not be responsible to Parliament, because of his oath of obedience to the Pope: Florence Arch. Esteri, Busta 2446.

[19] Pasolini, *Carteggio*, I, 45 note 1.   Spada, II, 456, records the fact that when Fabbri became prime minister Pius abolished the lay foreign minister.

article must have alarmed Pius, and naturally aroused some indignation in the Alto Consiglio.[20]

The differences between Pius and Mamiani about the Alto Consiglio soon became public; the papers took sides; the *Costituzionale Romano*, the *Cassandrino* and the *Labaro* attacked Mamiani's view, and the *Contemporaneo* (Sterbini) and the *Speranza* opposed Pius' view. In the course of this controversy Pius, speaking rather frankly to his friends, led them to understand that he would not be sorry if a new minister took the place of Mamiani.[21]

During this period Mamiani made some endeavour to restore law and order and to introduce several beneficent measures. He proposed a minister for education and for public charities. In themselves these projects might have been good; but success was impossible, because at the same time he was trying to force the Pope into war; in fact Tivaroni blames him for having taken office as a war minister.[22] Pius' decision was unalterable, and, in the long run, was destined to bring about the end of his state.

In reality, after the Allocution and after the news of the Piedmontese defeats, the war party very naturally had become less numerous. On July 14th Monsignor Corboli Bussi wrote to his cousin Sclopis that the electorate (the voters) were in favour of war, but that, outside their number, the people were now anxious for peace.[23] But the extremists in the Chamber kept shouting for war at the top of their voices.

It seems impossible that Pius should not have felt that nowadays he was surrounded by men who were showing very little gratitude for past benefits.[24] Not only Mamiani, but also Sterbini, had received special pardons. Galletti had been

---

[20] Spada, II, 380.
[21] Pasolini, I, 150.
[22] Spada, II, 344, puts this very strongly.
[23] Corboli Bussi, p. 234.
[24] As early as June 2nd Pius had spoken of this to the Tuscan minister. Florence Arch. Esteri, Busta 2446. Tivaroni, *Ital. Cent.* p. 329.

serving a life-sentence at the time of the amnesty; and Prince Canino owed his title to Pope Pius VII, who had received his father Lucien in the days when the Bonapartes were political outcasts. Last on the list, Ciceruacchio the wine-carter had been allowed a free hand until he had taken advantage of it to drive behind the Pope's carriage carrying an insolent banner; he was now a danger to the government, because he could raise the Trastevere. In the Trastevere there was a stratum of the better sort of poor people, families long-established there and self-respecting in their own sphere; but beneath them and in the adjoining *Rioni* there were the dregs of the population; and in time of revolution the up-turned dregs of Rome were a fearful revelation; as bad as the dregs of the British seaports or of Paris.

Not only in Rome, however, but throughout the whole state there was a very dangerous failure of authority. In some of the northern towns political murders took place in broad daylight.[25] In these circumstances it seemed a wise inspiration that the idea should have arisen of bolstering up a weak administration by placing it under the leadership of a strong, experienced patriot, and one who had been Pius' friend from the start, namely Pellegrino Rossi. Rossi was now free to accept such an offer, for since the fall of Louis Philippe he was no longer in the service of France. As he was a life-long Italian patriot he had remained in Rome, an interested spectator and adviser during every fresh crisis. He was on friendly terms with the most thoughtful of the reformers, and Farini's description shows their deep attachment and admiration for him.[26]

Fortunately we have excellent evidence of the views in Rossi's mind. During this period he wrote several letters for publication in the papers, but refrained from issuing them,

---

[25] Farini, II, 252. This failure to keep order was a constant source of anxiety. *V.* Farini, II; Pasolini, I; and *Carteggio Minghetti-Pasolini*, I; also reports of the various ambassadors, including Mr Petre.   [26] Farini, II, 253.

when he heard that there was a possibility of his entering politics; but Farini has preserved those portions of them which deal with the political situation, for, he says, "In them Rossi reasoned with profound doctrine. They are a striking expression of thought, and show a degree of romantic patriotism in a dry lawyer which must have come as a surprise to stupid people." They are literary, in fact poetic, supposed to be addressed to a lady. We give them because they reflect the mind of a very remarkable man and also his views on the political situation:

You, Signora, were profoundly stirred by the happenings in Milan.[27]

And who would not have been stirred? Woe to anyone whose soul was not stirred; for not only would he fall short of your *gentilezza* and nobility, but he could have no feeling for the true, the good or the beautiful.

Do you remember the verses which your poet wrote over the lifeless body of Greece? Well, for you, for me and for everyone who has any love for poetry or science or civilisation, Greece and Italy are sisters, differing it is true, in age, but equal in beauty and in glory. Dead they were, both the one and the other; but since the first of the two is well-nigh risen from the dead, it seemed inevitable, when you recited to me those splendid verses, that our thought should linger in sadness over the one that still lies there, fair to see but inanimate and cold. Dio benedetto! We have seen her heart swell anew with health and life, and her veins take colour and her arm be upraised. Her first act of life was a combat, a victory, a miracle. You who are a woman wept over it with joy, and I who am a man (laugh who will) wept too, just as you had.

But your joy and hope are embittered by fear and doubt, and you want me to reassure you and swear to you that the Risorgimento of Italy will be the beginning of a lasting and glorious life.

After some generalities he gives his views:

The conditions in Europe and especially those in Austria are profoundly altered; and to me it is certain that if Italy really wills it, she is now strong enough to drive out the Austrians and oppose an impregnable barrier to any new irruption.

[27] The Five Glorious Days.

He then explains how fully he realises that a victory can only be won at the price of much blood, and continues:

Three movements of a very different character are agitating Italy. The first one is just; the second is holy; but the third is mad and will ruin everything unless it is repressed.

The first is the political movement. Italy will have no more absolute governments whether paternal or not. . . .

This first movement, if Italy shows good sense, is now completed. The constitutions of Naples, Turin, Florence and Rome have reintroduced political liberty into this peninsula. Italy which was but yesterday a slave, is to-day as free as England, and surpasses England in civil equality. What more need we desire?. . .

The second Italian movement is what is known as the National movement; the holy impulse of rearising Italy, which drives her to shake off any foreign yoke and to shatter it by force of arms. . . .

Truly the Lombard insurrection and the corresponding Italian movement could not leave the Pope, and least of all Pius IX, inactive and mute. For the Pope there were. . .two possible lines of action; pacific intervention or war. Great and glorious lines, simple and clear, each of them; the first more suitable to him as Pope, the second more in character for him as being an Italian prince. I am compelled to acknowledge that of these two lines of action which could only be effective if taken wholeheartedly and without delays, neither was boldly adopted. The course taken swayed between the two. War was the stumbling-block. It was neither declared nor prevented. The country made war to a certain extent; the Pope remained at peace. You remember his intervention; a letter, an exhortation which came too late, and was insufficient and perhaps inopportune. . . .[28]

On July 14th, by order of Radetzky, 6000 Austrians under Prince Franz Lichtenstein crossed the Po, drove the Papal garrison back to Ferrara, "and towards noon marched on to the glacis of the citadel from which the town was to have been bombarded; however before that was carried into effect, a

[28] Farini, II, 253 *et seq*. The third possible solution was the Republic, against which Rossi inveighed for several pages. At this moment he refused office, apparently from a fear that as yet Pius could not support his views wholeheartedly. As to Pius' letter being inopportune, no one thought so at the time when he sent it.

deputation of citizens bearing the white flag arrived, and the city of Ferrara surrendered at discretion ".[29]

They compelled the pro-Legate to provision the fortress for two months. But on hearing of their action, Charles Albert detached 6,000 men under General Bava to march on Ferrara; so, on the following day, July 15th, the Austrians hurriedly recrossed the Po, "in the greatest possible confusion" says the Italian story; they had only been there a day, but apparently had achieved their object of revictualling the fortress.

On July 18th Pius issued a formal diplomatic protest to all the European powers;[30] but that did not save Mamiani.

This small incident aroused all parties in Rome to fury. In the Council of Deputies, Canino proposed a threefold programme; that the deputies should declare the state in danger, make their sittings permanent, and call on the Pope to declare war. After a stormy debate the deputies drew up an address to Pius "adjuring him to see that his government lost no time in brandishing arms for defence and offence; and in uniting itself with the princes who are worthy to guide the Italian people because they are fighting for their Italian independence".

This was followed by a less flamboyant address from the Alto Consiglio offering their lives and their property in the cause, and hoping that the League of States would become "a splendid reality".

But the real danger was outside the two Houses; it lay in the Circoli (clubs) and in the revolution. They were not to be satisfied with Papal protests, parliamentary addresses nor even with such military preparations as the government could make. On July 19th the Circoli presented a petition to the Lower House demanding Canino's threefold programme. This petition was received by the President of the Chamber,

[29] *London Corr.* III, 59, Welden's Despatch, July 15th. *V.* also *Ibid.* Doc. 65 (Campbell), and Doc. 60 (Hamilton).
[30] Farini, II, 265. Spada, II, 400, gives it verbatim.

and in due course he announced that it had been handed to a
Commission according to regulation. But Canino wanted the
regulations to be set aside and the question to be discussed
then and there; and while he still spoke, there rang out a
sudden shout in the Piazza below, and, in a moment, the
whole building, the courtyards, the great staircase and the
loggias of the palace were all filled with men shouting
"Armi! Armi!"—calling for arms. It was evidently a pre-
arranged movement;[31] but the president, Sereni, was equal
to the occasion. He put his hat on and the sitting was at
an end.

Sereni seems to have kept his presence of mind very well,
and, consequently, after a short interval calm was restored
and the sitting was resumed. But before long Sterbini arose
and informed the House that grave events were taking place
in the city, and that provision should be made for satisfying
the people. The Duke of Rignano then announced that the
Civic Guard, of which he was the commanding officer, was
in tumult because the men wanted to occupy the city gates
and the Castel Sant' Angelo; whereupon on Montanari's
proposition, the House decided to send for the Minister of
Police; and before long Galletti made his appearance. From
this suave black-bearded lawyer, however, they obtained little
satisfaction. Indeed he was obviously more or less the representative of the revolution, and since then has been warmly
praised by the republican historian Gabussi, because, during
his months as head of the police, he "pleased everyone". On
this occasion he excelled himself; he began by assuring all the
deputies that the Roman people and the Civic Guard could not
be surpassed; that it was true that the Civic Guard wanted

[31] According to Gabussi, both the petition and the movement were
the work of the Circolo Popolare. It looks like an endeavour to
make the Pope responsible for the failure of the war. But now they
were living under representative institutions. As long as they
abstained from declaring war they could invade Austria without the
Austrians being able to retaliate: Gabussi, II, 374. V. also Farini,
II, 270.

to occupy the gates and the Castel Sant' Angelo, but that this was not dangerous because they were the "palladium of our liberties"; that the people had the right to present their petition, and that the noisy interruption of the sitting had been a matter of such small importance that it was not worth discussing. At this point Farini rose to ask for an explanation of this strange opinion on the part of a police officer, but, he tells us, he was interrupted by the audience in the public boxes, and by Canino, Sterbini, Potenziani and Marcosanti, some of them yelling, and others saying that "the people had been sublime", because there had been no violence; and adding that Farini did wrong to complain.[32] For the moment the situation was only absurd, but it was dangerous for the future. The Circolare Popolare and the shouting populace had invaded the Lower House, and the Civic Guard was no longer to be trusted to defend it. What safety was there now for the right of free speech?

Meanwhile Pius had replied to the addresses of both Houses relating to the Ferrara episode, assuring them that he meant to deal formally with the matter as he had dealt with the former Ferrara episode in 1847, and pointing out that the Austrians had already gone.

From this it will be seen that Mamiani's ministry was already weak; it had failed to restore order. And Farini says that Pius was angry because Colonel Galletti had allowed a volunteer legion to quarter itself in the Collegio di Gesù, the Jesuit College; also a young priest called Ximenes had been murdered for writing an unpopular article in a newspaper. Here, too, were dangerous symptoms for the future.

On July 19th Mamiani resigned. He was a well-meaning man, but the disorders and the war made his position impossible.[33]

At this point we may note that his best work had been his undertakings for the Italian national cause. Henceforth the only form that such work could take for the Holy See was that

<hr />

[32] Farini, II, 270-1; Spada, II, 403.   [33] Farini, II, 277.

of trying to unify Italy by means of a League of States—and throughout all this year Pius never abandoned the attempt. It was his most constant political activity. In the Archives there are scores of letters on the subject. But as all these efforts ended in failure, we can only allot them a very short description. Mamiani's negotiations constitute the second of the four main attempts to unite Italy by a league or federal tie.[34] His league was to consist primarily of the four states about whose political existence there was no doubt[35]—Rome, Piedmont, Naples, Tuscany. Of these Naples was still uncertain.

But their inward hopes soared far beyond this. They hoped that the Diet would before long develop into an Italian Congress consisting of representatives from all the Italian states, including Venice and Sicily,[36] and the war against Austria would be considered an offensive war against an invader.[37]

The Piedmontese government, however, was not at all enthusiastic about Mamiani's scheme. It did not want to invite Naples; and claimed that the new capital should be Turin, not Rome.[38] The truth was that as long as Piedmont was victorious, her cabinet had no desire for a league, and would not undertake to defend the unmilitary states; and that, by the time when, owing to reverses, it had become more amenable, the other states had perceived that a Piedmontese victory would mean such a preponderance of power for her, that it would be a danger for them all. What they wanted was a league which would preserve the balance of power inside

[34] *V.* chapter VIII.

[35] He thus avoided naming Sicily whose inclusion had previously offended Naples, and omitted Venetia and Lombardy which were claimed by Piedmont. *V.* Florence Arch. Esteri, Busta 2670: Marchetti's letters June 9th and 17th.

[36] *Ibid.* Marchetti's letter of June 8th; Bargagli's despatch of June 16th.

[37] *Ibid.* Marchetti, *loc. cit.*; Bargagli, June 14th.

[38] *Ibid.* Pareto to Marchetti, June 21st.

Italy. There seems to be no doubt that each of the three governments was right from its own point of view.

During the last week of July, Rome and Florence were absolutely united over the question; but suddenly the whole trend of popular interest was turned in an entirely different direction by the news of a disaster at the front—the battle of Custoza.

Chapter XIX

THE BATTLE OF CUSTOZA[1]
JULY 22ND, 23RD, 24TH AND 25TH

I

Unfortunately it is impossible to acquit Charles Albert and the Piedmontese staff of the fundamental error which began the disaster.

They were in a very difficult position; the real truth was that there was nothing that they could do. Now that Radetzky had received his reinforcements, his defensive position was impregnable, and in a pitched battle he was stronger than they were. The chance of driving him out was gone. It had depended on cutting off his supplies while Vienna was in revolution. In normal circumstances no such chance existed.[2]

As we have seen, Charles Albert wanted to make peace, but his Parliament refused to do so, and in Milan the republican papers were accusing him and his army of being unenterprising, if nothing worse. It was felt that some kind

---

[1] There was a second battle of Custoza in 1866. The principal authorities consulted for this chapter are the following:

Italian. The Italian official account, Stato Maggiore, *Campagna di guerra del* 1848, *Custoza*; *Rapporti*, vols. I, II and III, all the official reports of the officers; *Memorie inedite* (attributed to Charles Albert); various memoirs such as Della Rocca, *Autobiografia*; special histories and biographies such as Fabris, Pinelli and Costa de Beauregard; Montù's history of the Italian artillery; the general histories from Tivaroni downwards; and other works.

Austrian. Feldzug, Schönhals, Hilleprandt, Willisen, Kunz, *Studie* and various lesser works.

[2] Charles Albert's second son, Prince Ferdinand, Duke of Savoy, one of the best fighting officers in the Piedmontese army, put the matter plainly in his report. "In fact, at the point which we had reached, to continue the war was an act of madness. Be it noted that Austria was offering us the most honourable terms": *Rapporti*, I, 306.

of victory was essential to his political welfare in Lombardy and Venetia.

These are the reasons given by Charles Albert and Bava for now undertaking the blockade of Mantua.[3] Before that city he could collect the new Lombard battalions, about 10,000 strong. Already some of them had received him with cheers when he came to inspect them. He proposed if possible to lead them to victory during the siege operations. Therefore, at Bava's suggestion, he decided to invest Mantua —very largely in order to appear to be doing something.[4]

Military critics agree—and obviously—that it was a most unfortunate operation[5] to undertake in the very face of Radetzky and 74,000 men. Charles Albert had now 70,200 men in all, and by this scheme he was obliged to keep 42,150 of his best units at the far right-hand corner of his line, and leave only 28,050 (including 9000 ineffectives) dotted about opposite Verona.

As to these latter contingents he was rather like a chess player who offers his pawns unguarded to a powerful opponent.[6]

The Piedmontese army laid out on the maps before Radetzky, was divided between these two sectors, which were rather too far distant from each other for joint action. This was a cause of the disaster. The two groups consisted[7] of the troops in front of Verona, 28,000; those blockading Mantua, 42,000.

---

[3] Bava's *Relazione*: *Rapporti*, I, 68.

[4] Baldini says the decision was taken on the 8th (p. 109). Bava says that the blockade began on the 13th.

[5] Schönhals blames the Piedmontese for being "rash enough" to try and besiege a fortress such as Mantua in the face of a strong and victorious army: Schönhals, II, 69.

[6] For opinions on the Piedmontese position, *v.* Della Rocca, I, 224.

[7] General de Sonnaz must have been annoyed at having his Second Army Corps reduced by the transference of the fine Piemonte Brigade to the First Army Corps under Bava, and also at seeing his division strung out over so wide a space.

A. *The troops in front of Verona*

	*M.	G.	S.
The Second Army Corps under General de Sonnaz, without the Piemonte Brigade[8]			
1. *From Rivoli.* Left wing up towards the Tyrol $= 3,500$	—	—	—
At Sandrà (H.Q. of General de Sonnaz) $= 1,700$			
	5,200	10	—
2. *Pastrengo to Sommacampagna. Centre.* Includes the strongest fortified belt of the line. St Giustina—Sona—Sommacampagna	8,200	20	2
3. *At Villafranca.* The right wing; with 16 guns and 4 squadrons	2,900	16	4
4. *Second line of Defence.* Garrisons in the places occupied on the Mincio, up to Lake Garda: Sandrà, Oliosi, Goito, Valeggio, Monzambano, Pozzolengo, Peschiera	9,000	—	—
This 2nd reserve, 12 battalions under General Visconti, mainly Piedmontese and Lombard recruits, was found to be useless			
5. *Cavalry Division.* 17 squadrons. General Olivieri. At Roverbella—Belvedere—Marengo	2,750	24	17
	28,050	70	23

B. *The troops around Mantua* (not engaged until July 24th)

	M.	G.	S.
These were the First Army Corps commanded by General Bava			
On the left bank of the Mincio $= 26,950$			
On the right bank of the Mincio $= 15,200$			
	42,150	88	13
	70,200	158	36

* M. = Men; G. = Guns; S. = Squadrons.

[8] The above figures are taken from the Italian official history of this battle. *V.* Stato Maggiore, *Custoza,* p. 145.

Hardly were the troops in position around Mantua when news arrived of a raid southwards by Lichtenstein's brigade to revictual the Austrian garrison in Ferrara. Charles Albert ordered 6000[9] men under Bava to go in pursuit. Before this force could start, news arrived of Lichtenstein's return, but Bava moved at once against Governolo, a place on the Po, south-east of Mantua, and on July 19th captured it and two-thirds of its Austrian garrison of 600 men. This was an encouraging success, but it meant that the Regina Brigade remained at Governolo instead of Roverbella, and became one of the units round Mantua, and that Bava was absent from his H.Q. at Goito.

Roverbella, which was a connecting link between the two halves of the Piedmontese army, was occupied by the Cavalry Division.

On July 22nd, 1848, Field-Marshal Radetzky was aware that he possessed a superiority of strength over Charles Albert:

Troops (1st line attack and support)	52,000
In the Tyrol	7,000
Garrisons (counting Verona and Mantua, but not Legnago for this battle)	15,200
	74,200

From the front-line troops we must deduct the two units which had not yet arrived, namely

Simbschen's brigade, now at Sanguinetto (it did not arrive until the afternoon of the 24th)	6,000
Perin's brigade (Viennese volunteers for garrison work in Verona)	2,900
	8,900[10]

[9] The Regina Brigade, the 6th Battery (eight guns), the Genoa Cavalry and a Bersaglieri Company, some of the best troops that he had.

[10] All these figures are taken from the Italian official account, as being the latest authority; the Austrian figures show no important differences. *V.* Stato Maggiore, *Custoza*, p. 151 *et seq.*

It will be seen that the Piedmontese troops in the line before Verona amounted to only about 19,500 men, including cavalry; with 9000 more (provisional battalions) behind them in the second line. These positions extended up to Rivoli.

To their right, farther south, were the 42,000 men round Mantua, including about 8000 Lombards.

Radetzky must have perceived that Charles Albert and his advisers had given him a fine opening. They had withdrawn more than half their men, and had left the remainder strung out before him on a line far too wide to be safe. In the front line which he proposed to attack, there were only 19,500 men from Rivoli to Villafranca, whereas he had with him in Verona over 43,000 men, with 154 guns, available to hurl against them at two or three hours' notice.[11]

His plan was simple; to break through the centre of the Piedmontese front opposite Verona. He would then march right onwards towards Peschiera. Having split their army into two, he could roll it up either way. For this frontal attack on their lines from the Adige to Sommacampagna he could reserve all of his 43,000 men,[12] and at the same time he could attack the Piedmontese left flank defending Rivoli with his 7000 men, up in the Tyrol.[13]

As far as numbers were concerned he could feel safe, but he believed the Piedmontese trenches to be stronger than was actually the case.

On July 22nd, the first day of the great battle, he began with the attack on Rivoli; it was not merely a diversion, for it was intended to be pushed home, but it was designed

[11] *V. Feldzug*, III, 5; Hilleprandt, p. 339; Willisen, p. 148; Schönhals, II, 74; Kunz, 67; Stato Maggiore, *Custoza*, p. 17; Fabris; Pinelli; *Rapporti*, 3 vols; Baldini, p. 112. These are the principal authorities consulted when writing this chapter. For others *v.* Bibliography.

[12] The First Corps (Wratislaw), the Second Corps (d'Aspre), the First Reserve Corps (Wocher).   [13] The Third Corps (Thurn).

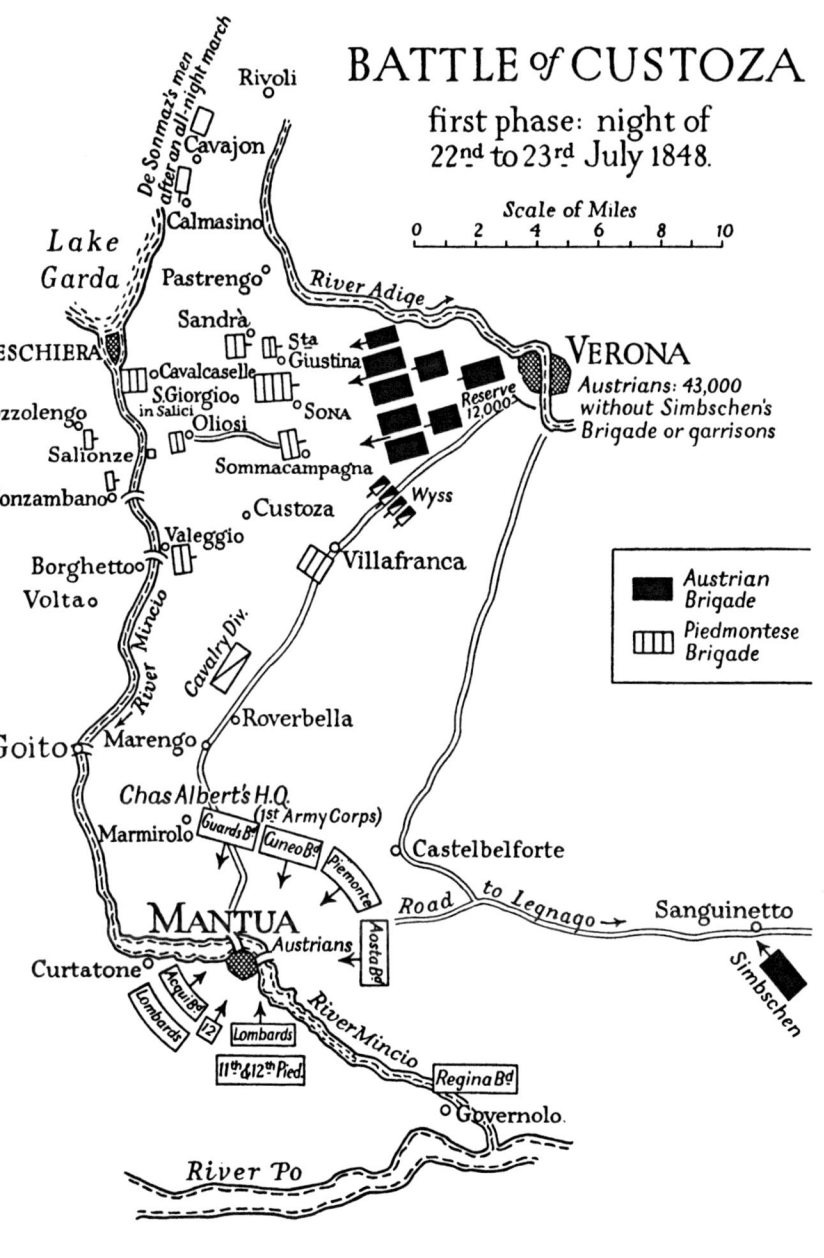

BATTLE of CUSTOZA

first phase: night of 22ⁿᵈ to 23ʳᵈ July 1848.

Scale of Miles

0   2   4   6   8   10

Lake
Garda

Rivoli

De Sonmaz's men after an all-night march

Cavajon

Calmasino

Pastrengo

River Adige

Sandrà

ESCHIERA

Sta Giustina

Cavalcaselle

S.Giorgio in Salici

Oliosi

SONA

Reserve 12,000

VERONA

Austrians: 43,000
without Simbschen's
Brigade or garrisons

ozzolengo

Salionze

Sommacampagna

Wyss

Monzambano

Custoza

Valeggio

Villafranca

Borghetto

Volta

River Mincio

Cavalry Div.

Roverbella

Goito

Marengo

Chas.Albert's H.Q.

(1st Army Corps)

Marmirolo

Guards Bᵈ

Cuneo Bᵈ

Piemonte

Castelbelforte

Road to Legnago →

Sanguinetto

Simbschen

MANTUA

Austrians

Aosta Bᵈ

Curtatone

Acqui Bᵈ

(2)

Lombards

11ᵗʰ & 12ᵗʰ Pied.

River Mincio

Regina Bᵈ

Governolo.

River Po

| | Austrian Brigade |
| | Piedmontese Brigade |

primarily to prevent de Sonnaz from reinforcing his centre. It resulted in a day of hill-fighting.

The Austrians under Thurn, about 5200 strong, pushed back the Piedmontese, who were only about 3900 strong, right down to Rivoli. But then General de Sonnaz arrived from Sandrà bringing up about 800 men and four guns, and the Austrians retired defeated. The Piedmontese were triumphant. All day the Savoyard regulars and the two or three student volunteer companies had shown excellent fighting capacity, both in defence and in counter-attack.[14] De Sonnaz, however, wisely suspected in this move an Austrian trap to draw him away from the main body, so instead of pursuing his success he withdrew his brigade from Rivoli to Calmasino. Unfortunately this long day left his men very tired, and he himself had not quite got back to Sandrà before the battle began next morning.

July 23rd. On this second day Radetzky began his frontal break-through. He selected the strongest section in the Piedmontese line, namely the convex arc of hills between the villages of Santa Giustina, Sona and Sommacampagna; these villages each stood on the summit of one of the hills; and the whole position, with a front of eight kilometres, ought to have been very strong; but between every two hills there is a cleft with a road running through it—between Santa Giustina and Sona it is the main road from Verona to Peschiera; between Sona and Sommacampagna it is a road from Verona to S. Giorgio in Salice.

In these three villages there were only 8200 Piedmontese and twenty guns. General Broglia's H.Q. was at Sona.

To take Santa Giustina (about 2000 Piedmontese and four guns) Radetzky had allotted about 4000 men, and six guns.

---

[14] Austrian losses, according to Hilleprandt, p. 332: killed, 3 officers (including a general) and 20 men; wounded, 5 officers and 148 men; missing, 33; total loss, 209. Fabris says 226.

Piedmontese losses: 3 officers and 31 men killed; 6 officers and 86 wounded; total 126.

To take Sona and its surrounding defences (about 4500 and fifteen guns) Radetzky had allotted three brigades or 10,000 men and eighteen guns.

To take Sommacampagna (1500 men and two guns) he had allotted three brigades, say 11,000 men[15] and eighteen guns.

At one or two other points (notably Osteria del Bosco) there were other units of defenders, making up the total given of 8200; whereas Radetzky, including the reserve of 9000, was sending out at least 33,000 men: at each point in the defence he could deliver a smashing blow, and all the blows simultaneously.

In case of difficulties, what chances of help had these unfortunate little Piedmontese garrisons? On the right at Villafranca there were 2900 regulars and sixteen guns, but they were about three and a half miles distant, and were being observed by Wyss with four squadrons; on their left was Sandrà, the H.Q. of De Sonnaz' brigades, but he and his men were weary after the success of the previous day, and they were being watched by Schaafgotsche's cavalry brigade. In the rear there was no second line except the village garrisons dotted along the Mincio about six or seven miles distant.

The three separate attacks were timed to begin at 6.30 a.m. and the defensive positions were so unsatisfactory that at the end of about four hours a general retirement was found necessary:[16] but there was some sharp fighting. We will describe them in order from south to north.

Sommacampagna is a hill village consisting of strong stone houses and loopholed garden walls. It was garrisoned by a good regular Piedmontese battalion, but on their left was the less strong village of S. Piero (now unknown) defended by a Tuscan battalion. When Major de Bonafoux saw the advancing

---

[15] *V.* Stato Maggiore, *Custoza.* Also the *Feldzug* and Hilleprandt.

[16] *Feldzug,* III, 19, 23 *et seq.* The Austrian soldiers were fine material for war. They had started at 1 a.m. and had marched in a deluge of rain, but they attacked with an enthusiasm which astonished even their officers. At Sommacampagna the attack did not begin until seven o'clock owing to darkness.

Austrian units dotted about all over the plain—two brigades in an attacking line and one in support—he prepared to give them a warm reception; and at first he was successful. But the Austrians always worked by means of enveloping movements. By 8 a.m. they had opened out right and left, and one brigade was attacking S. Piero. Here the Tuscan battalion did better than might have been expected after their demoralising experiences at Curtatone.[17] They fired steadily from their loopholed walls and repulsed the Borderers with serious loss; in fact they remained there until they were driven out with the bayonet. But they were only six companies fighting against fourteen; inevitably they were outflanked before long and forced inwards, on to the centre. Meanwhile a precisely similar episode had taken place on the right. Thus de Bonafoux with two battalions found himself hemmed in on all sides by three brigades. The Borderers were dashing forward on both flanks, and swarming up the hill, and at least twelve of their guns or howitzers were in action.[18]

At about 10 a.m. he gave the word to retire on S. Giorgio in Salice. During those three and a half miles he was furiously pursued by the Radetzky Hussars, and must have thought himself lucky to get through.[19]

Sona. Meanwhile a simultaneous attack had been carried out at Sona, and the result had been almost identical; but at this point the Piedmontese were relatively stronger. In the village of Sona and its cemetery, together with Monte Corno and Osteria del Bosco, they had three battalions of good

[17] *Feldzug*, III, 23. The Austrian account fully clears the character of the Tuscans, which has been very unfairly impugned in the Piedmontese report of the Duke of Genoa: *Rapporti*, I, 268.

[18] These were the brigades of Wohlgemuth, Supplikatz and Strassoldo. They had only six guns each, so they must have got some more from the First Army Corps Reserve of Artillery. *V. Feldzug*, III, 18, 23 *et seq.*

[19] Prince Ferdinand says they killed his wounded men, but naturally that statement requires confirmation. This cavalry regiment had been known as the Carlo Alberto Hussars until the outbreak of war.

Savoyard regulars; also the Parma battalion and the Modena battalion, and fourteen or fifteen guns; moreover, the positions were strongly entrenched across the Verona-Peschiera road. Consequently in and around the village their defence was safe enough, but, between Sona and Sommacampagna, there was a long stretch of line which could only be very weakly held.

The Austrians advanced in their usual formation. The three brigades[20] made a frontal attack which was checked; in fact at 9.30 it was definitely at a standstill. But Radetzky's blows were always overwhelmingly strong. Already General Lichtenstein had launched an enveloping movement. At the hill of Madonna della Salute, half-way to Sommacampagna, the Jägers broke through a point defended by only two companies of Tuscans. Then, followed by various other units, they wheeled northwards and swept into the lower ground behind the main position. There was a close struggle at the village. The *Feldzug* tells us that in places their Jägers came to seizing hold of the ends of the muskets protruding through the loopholes, so obstinate was the resistance. But the Piedmontese were greatly outnumbered. By 10.15 they were obliged to retire to Osteria del Bosco and half an hour later General Broglia, O.C. of the whole line,[21] gave the order for a general retirement. He had received news that his line of defence was irretrievably cut at Sommacampagna and perceived that he was in danger of being surrounded.

Santa Giustina. This village had only been threatened, not attacked by the Austrian brigade, but naturally the battalion there was compelled to retire with the other Piedmontese forces.[22]

---

[20] Brigades of Gyulai, Lichtenstein and Kerpan: *Feldzug*, III, 20.

[21] *V.* Broglia's report: *Rapporti*, I, 218.

[22] Austrian losses for the whole of the second day were: killed, 6 officers and 65 men; wounded, 22 officers and 290 men; missing, 213 (mostly deserters); total 596. Hilleprandt, p. 347.

Piedmontese losses: killed, 4 officers and 22 men; wounded, 7 officers and 72 men; prisoners and missing, 9 officers (1 general) and 182 men; total, 20 officers and 276 men; in all, 296. Fabris, III, 282.

By the evening of the 23rd Radetzky had broken right through the Piedmontese centre. His front line was now established from Castelnuovo to Oliosi, about four or five miles west of the positions attacked;[23] and—rather important—his leading battalions had reached the left bank of the Mincio at Salionze. All the defenders on his right-hand side had been pushed northwards towards Peschiera: at Cavalcaselle there must have been nearly 13,000 men massed together under the command of General de Sonnaz. But on Radetzky's left hand there remained the 3000 men in Villafranca, and all the other units down to Mantua,[24] 42,000 men.

His mind was quickly made up; to push forward across the Mincio bridges and prevent the two Piedmontese halves from reuniting; and to keep pushing them off their line of communication.

Before him on the far side of the river was General Visconti with 9000 men[25], placed to defend the bridges and crossings against him at Salionze, Monzambano and Borghetti-Valeggio. But these were half-trained Piedmontese and Lombard recruits and proved almost useless.

July 24th. Thus the Piedmontese centre had been cut through, but its flanks were still in being. It remained to be seen what Charles Albert would do to retrieve the situation. In such a case there were two possible alternatives: he might retire behind the Mincio and reunite the two severed halves of his army in front of Radetzky; or, alternatively, he might take advantage of the exposed Austrian left flank and throw himself on to it. He chose the latter course.

[23] With the reserve at S. Giorgio in Salice.
[24] Mantua is about 20–22 miles from the Villafranca-Vallegio line. Cavalcaselle, about a mile in front of Peschiera, had become the place of assembly for all De Sonnaz' division. The broken troops from the Sona-Sommacampagna line had found their way thither; and they had been joined there by the general himself with his victorious troops from Rivoli and Sandrà. It was evening by that time.
[25] Apparently there were four regiments of three battalions each; but one regiment was in the fortress of Peschiera.

Thus on the 24th there were two fronts: one was Radetzky's front, where he was forcing the passage of the Mincio; the other was Charles Albert's front, attacking the Austrian left flank. Naturally Radetzky had realised that he must provide for this counter-attack, so he had formed a defensive line from Sommacampagna to S. Zeno (near Valeggio) across his left rear. He had brought up Clam's brigade from Gonfardine to hold the line from S. Zeno to Custoza, and he sent for Simbschen's brigade, on the march from Buttapietra, to hold the line from Custoza to Sommacampagna.

We will begin with Radetzky's push across the river. By the afternoon of the 24th it was successful. At Cavalcaselle, near Peschiera, De Sonnaz had nearly 13,000 men besides Visconti's 9000 Lombards, but many of the units were temporarily demoralised.[26] The men of the Savoia Brigade, which had been driven from the Sona-Sommacampagna position, were perhaps shaken by the ten-mile retirement under constant pursuit; and De Sonnaz' Pignerol and mixed brigades which had fought so well at Rivoli were weary. Apart from the strain of the action, some of them had been compelled to march about twenty-five miles. Consequently old General de Sonnaz[27] entirely failed to defend the crossings at Salionze or Monzambano; and Radetzky was able to get four brigades across before nightfall.

During the morning, however, De Sonnaz had started to lead as many as possible of his men down along the river bank to Volta, in order to get into touch with Bava's H.Q. at Goito, and with Charles Albert at Marmirolo. A certain proportion of his men turned back to halt at Peschiera, but the others came on with him. In this way—at the price of abandoning

---

[26] Generál de Sonnaz attributed their failure to political anger. It is said by others that the French-speaking Savoyards thought themselves unfairly treated by the Piedmontese newspapers. But the poor old general himself appears to have been completely disgusted and discouraged by the sudden disaster to his corps after its first success.

[27] *V.* Prince Ferdinand's report: *Rapporti*, I, 313.

his best line of communications—he had reunited the two main sections of the Piedmontese army. When he reached Volta he had only about 7600 men with him, but there were various other units to follow.[28]

Meanwhile, throughout the whole of this disastrous day Charles Albert had been moving heaven and earth to retrieve the situation. His first warning of danger had been the moment when, early on the 23rd, he had heard the booming of the distant guns to north of him, and rumours had come in of a defeat. Then, before long, an officer freshly arrived from Peschiera had reported that he had seen many fugitives, but naturally for several hours there were no definite details.

It is rather a significant fact for any student of the part played by Charles Albert in the Risorgimento, that at this crisis of his fate he showed excellent calmness and self-reliance.[29]

He had no one with him (except of course Salasco) at his H.Q. at Marmirolo, yet this commander, who has so often been called the undecided King, arrived at an immediate and daring plan of action.

He decided to mass as many men as possible at Villafranca, and throw himself on Radetzky's left flank.

Forthwith he ordered the four nearest brigades, the Guards, the Cuneo, the Piemonte and the Aosta to march to Villa-franca, where already there were nearly 2900 men of all arms with sixteen guns. By midday he himself started,[30] and by

[28] He says (Rapporti, I, 155) that at Volta he had 7000 infantry of the Savoy and Mixed Brigades, fifteen guns and two squadrons. Apparently he had left over 2000 of his Field Force in Peschiera; but by the 27th he had over 10,000 with him. At Volta there were also about 5000 of Visconti's Reserve Division, but they were not sufficiently trained to be of any use. V. also Rapporti, I, 148. Also di Priero's report: Ibid. III, 33.

[29] Cf. modern Austrian military opinion: "The attack was intelligent, bold and carried out with clear purpose": Wolf-Schneider, p. 79. V. also Studie, pp. 26, 28.

[30] Bava also ordered the Regina Brigade and the 1st Regiment of the Acqui Brigade to Roverbella to guard their base of operations. V. his Relazione: Rapporti, I, 78. He saw the Aosta Brigade at Mozzecane.

evening he had collected 19,000, as well as the Cavalry Division, 2750 strong. He left behind the 15,200 men who were on the south side of Mantua, to continue its blockade. They were mainly Lombards.

At the same time he sent for Bava from Goito. The order arrived at 10 p.m., but simultaneously Bava received a report from Valeggio that the Lombard battalions there were unequal to facing an attack, and that their general was proposing to destroy the bridge. As this Borghetto-Valeggio bridge was the principal connection with De Sonnaz' army corps, Bava hastened to Valeggio, had the bridge repaired, gave orders to hold it, and had the passage covered by some heavy guns. He also sent out officers to inform De Sonnaz of the dangerous march that the King had undertaken to relieve the situation, and to induce him to throw himself upon the Austrians at Salionze and Valeggio, in order to hold the line of the Mincio. Owing to all these delays, it was 7.30 a.m. on the 24th before Bava reached the King's H.Q. at Villafranca.[31]

Charles Albert spoke to him at once about his plan, and Bava approved it; they.both considered it possible for De Sonnaz to defend the Mincio; meanwhile they would attack Radetzky's left flank while his troops were still rather dislocated by yesterday's battle. This would ease matters for de Sonnaz; and while thus operating on both banks of the Mincio, they could preserve connection by the bridges at Borghetto-Valeggio, and, farther south, at Goito.[32]

There seemed to be a good chance of restoring the battle;

[31] Willisen, p. 157. According to the Italian official account (Stato Maggiore, *Custoza*, p. 26), by 12 noon Charles Albert had started for Villafranca to direct the attack in person. To assemble at Villafranca he had ordered the Cavalry Division from Roverbella, the Piemonte Brigade from Conedole, the 1st Reserve Division (Guards and Cuneo Brigades) from Marmirolo and the Aosta Brigade from Castellaro. He also ordered the Regina Brigade from Governolo to occupy Goito. The Aosta Brigade started at 11 p.m. on the 23rd and arrived at Mozzecane at 8 a.m. on the 24th after an all-night march of 12–14 miles; thus they did not take part in the attack until the 25th.

[32] For adverse military opinion as to Charles Albert's attack, v. Stato Maggiore, *Custoza*, p. 51 *et seq*.

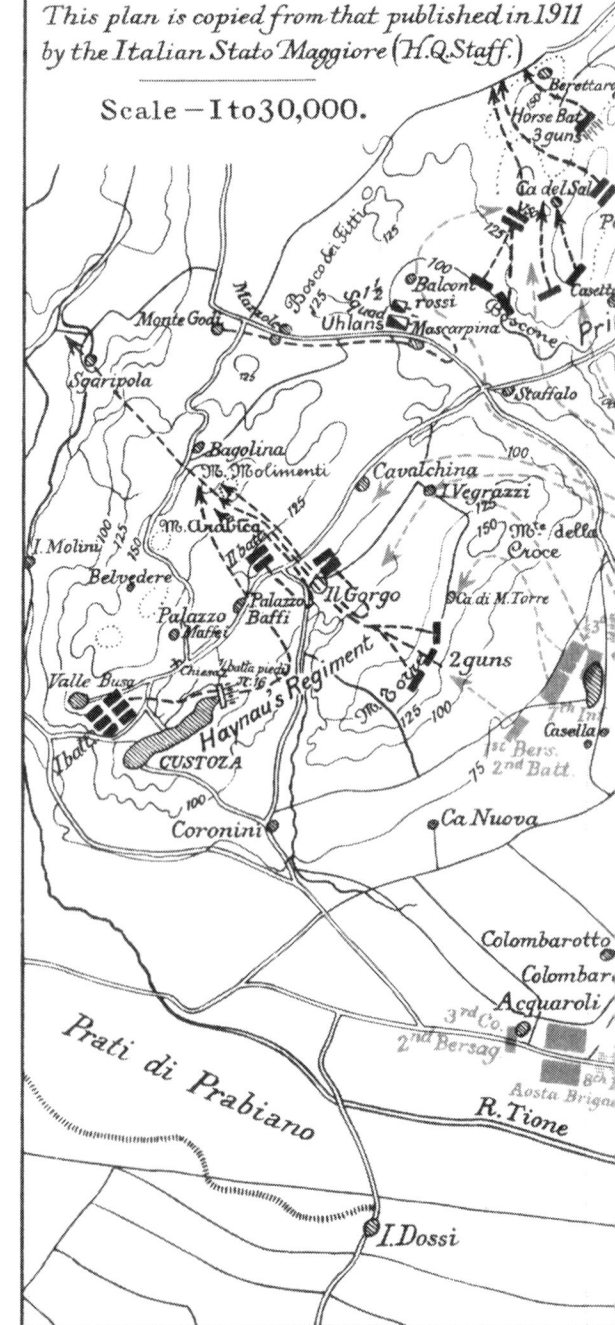

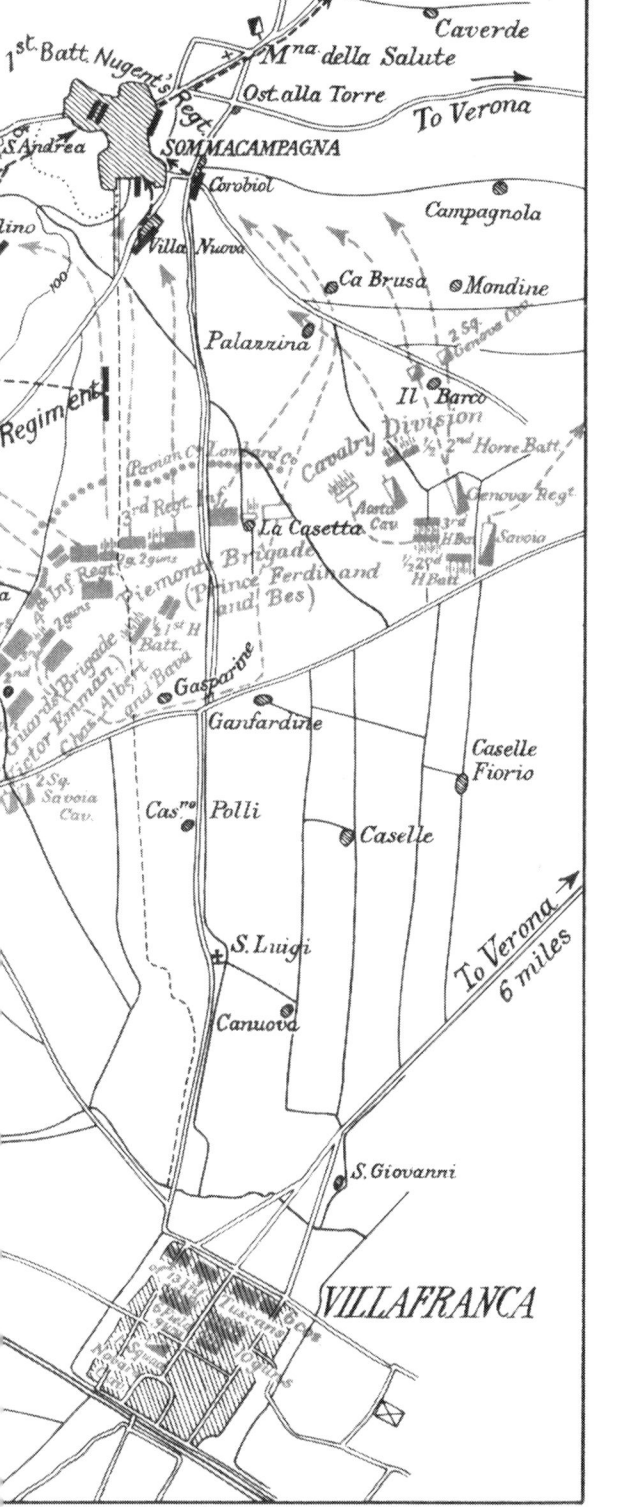

1st Batt. Nugent's Regt.

Caverde

M.na della Salute

Ost. alla Torre

To Verona

S. Andrea

SOMMACAMPAGNA

Corobiol

lino

Villa Nuova

Campagnola

Ca Brusa

Mondine

Palazzina

Il Barco

Regiment

Cavalry Division

½ 2nd Horse Batt.

Roman Co.

Lombard Co.

3rd Regt.

Aosta Cav.

Genova Reg.t

La Casetta

3rd H. Ba.t

Savoia

4th Inf. Regt.

2 guns

2 guns

Piemont Brigade (Prince Ferdinand and Bes)

½ 2nd H. Batt.

2 guns

½ 1st H. Batt.

Guards Brigade (Victor Emman.)

Chev. Albert and Bava

Gaspardine

Ganfardine

Caselle Fiorio

2 Sq. Savoia Cav.

Cas.re Polli

Caselle

S. Luigi

To Verona 6 miles

Canuova

S. Giovanni

VILLAFRANCA

indeed, had they known, this was to be Charles Albert's last glimpse of victory.

From Villafranca on the plain, he could see, about a mile distant, the Austrian positions on the slopes which lead up to Sommacampagna and the other villages captured from him about twenty-four hours earlier. Before him lay the three long low hills to be taken, but his men were full of courage. "Everyone felt that we should win" was Bava's description.

Unfortunately he was obliged to wait until the battalions had had their rations,[33] and also until the Aosta Brigade arrived within reach. By 3 p.m. however he was able to start, and by 4.30 p.m. the first shot was fired.

He had formed up three of the best brigades in the army. On his left were the Cuneo and Guards Brigades, under his eldest son Victor Emmanuel, accompanied by Bava. On his right was the Piemonte Brigade under his younger son Prince Ferdinand, only twenty-six years old but a born soldier.[34]

No doubt these princes always had good officers to advise them, but nevertheless the fact remains that never did the men fight so well as when led by the King in person and his two sons, with Bava in the centre to guide them. It was like the medieval days when the Savoyard mountaineers used to follow their feudal lords, the Dukes of Savoy.

The hope of catching the Austrians off their balance was completely fulfilled.

Their front from Custoza to Sommacampagna (the sector to be attacked) was defended as yet mainly by one brigade, that of Baron Simbschen. It was the biggest in the Austrian army;

[33] Most of them had received none the evening before. *V.* the reports of Generals Lovera (*Rapporti*, II, 30) and Biscaretti (*Ibid.* II, 19). As to the Aosta Brigade, *v.* Giustiniani's report (*Ibid.* I, 187).

[34] The frontage of the brigades was as follows (Italian official account):

The Cuneo Brigade from Casella to Capello.
The Guards Brigade from Capella to La Fredda.
The Piemonte Brigade from La Fredda to the far side of the Fossa, a sort of dyke running along their right flank.
The Aosta Brigade in reserve.
The attack was protected by cavalry on either flank.

it contained six battalions and was about 6000 strong, but the men had been on the march during part of the previous night, and several exhausted companies had gone astray and were late in reaching their posts.[35] This enabled the Cuneo Brigade to dash into the gap near Monte della Croce and cut off two Austrian battalions, making many prisoners. In the centre— so Prince Victor Emmanuel tells us—he ordered the drums to beat the charge, and his men carried the summit of Monte Torre with a rush; "and here", he wrote afterwards, "His Majesty rode up a hill opposite Staffalo from which he could overlook the whole battlefield. In the valley below, our cavalry were pursuing the fugitives, and on the heights in front, the Bersaglieri were still at grips with the enemy."

"Before evening", says Della Rocca, "the tricolour flags were waving on the summit of every hill."[36]

But the greatest success was that of young Prince Ferdinand on the right with his Piemonte Brigade and its enterprising Brigadier Bes. By 7 p.m. he had driven the Austrians off the Berettara and Ca Zenolino hills and out of the Fossa. Then he perceived that many of them had taken cover in the village of Sommacampagna, and although the hour was late, he decided to take that village itself. It was a most creditable piece of work; by about 7.45 in the evening he had retaken Somma-campagna, the first village lost on the previous morning;[37] and in it he made over 200 prisoners.[38]

[35] The temperature was 86° Fahrenheit and everyone agrees that during the two hours' rest at Sommacampagna the thirsty men broke into some cellars and "took more than was prudent in the heat" (Schönhals, II, 94); after which, he adds, the Prince Emil Regiment started three hours late and took the road to Villafranca in mistake for that to Staffalo.

[36] Della Rocca, I, *Autobiografia*, p. 227. He was Chief of Staff to Victor Emmanuel and took part in this attack.

[37] *V.* the reports of Bava, Prince Victor Emmanuel, Prince Ferdinand Duke of Genoa, Bes and others.

[38] The Austrian losses. *Feldzug*, III, 129, gives them as follows: killed, 52; wounded, 105; prisoners, 104; missing, 1056 (many of these dead, wounded or prisoners); total, 1317.

Both the *Feldzug* and Hilleprandt admit that Simbschen's un-fortunate brigade was scattered into three separate blocks, one of

This exploit of Prince Ferdinand marks the close of a very well-timed counter-attack. It was perhaps the greatest Piedmontese success during the campaign. Simbschen's brigade was scattered far and wide. The Austrians admitted to losses of about 1300 men, and—temporarily at all events—Charles Albert had established his attacking line across Radetzky's left flank and rear.

July 25th. Having got their right wing across Radetzky's flank and rear, Charles Albert and Bava evidently proposed that each brigade should wheel inwards half left, and try to roll up the Austrian line.[39]

Prince Ferdinand's brigade (5000 men and twelve guns) was to wheel from Sommacampagna in the direction of Oliosi, and fight its way to the Mincio on his left.

Prince Victor Emmanuel's two brigades were to advance from Staffalo and Custoza towards Salionze.

Next, on their left, Bava and Charles Albert had brought up the Aosta Brigade and one Guards battalion (6800 men with fourteen guns),[40] and would try to roll up Clam and surround Valeggio; in fact, the whole Piedmontese line was to swing round to the left, pivoting on Valeggio.

About a mile or more northwards of Villafranca begin the slopes of a fertile undulating higher plateau, which, here and there, rises into hills; on these cultivated fields the battle was fought.

which retired into Verona. Kunz (p. 83) and Schönhals (II, 96) point out that the officers must have been sacrificing themselves to restore the situation. There were 20 officers killed or wounded as compared with 137 men. Colonel Sunstenau, for instance, was wounded at first but returned to the fight and was killed. Fabris claims that the Italian losses were only 70 which sounds incredibly small; especially as the 3rd Regiment alone had 5 dead and 34 wounded. *V.* Colonel Wehrlin's report, *Rapporti*, II, 154.

[39] With de Robilant's cavalry brigade. On the extreme right Prince Ferdinand was to detail Olivieri's cavalry brigade to watch Verona. *V. Rapporti*, I, 81 (Bava).

[40] The movements during this day are rather difficult to follow and can best be judged from the summit of the monument which commemorates the battlefield at Custoza.

Their reserve was at Villafranca, on the plain. During the battle it supplied 950 men and two guns to the firing line, which brought the total of Piedmontese engaged that day to 21,350 men and 42 guns.[41]

But in reality they had very little chance of victory. They were attacking an enemy much stronger than themselves, and unfortunately on the Piedmontese side there was a complete breakdown. This does not exclude great gallantry on the part of the majority. But there was a general disorganisation which rendered such efforts useless; rations and orders arrived hours late, and there were various unaccountable incidents. There must have been about 35,000 men available—if we include De Sonnaz' troops—and yet only 21,000 took part in the battle.

On the other hand, this day's fighting exhibits the splendid organisation of Radetzky's Austrian army. Whatever were the political sentiments of the rank and file, it must surely have been one of the best organised military machines in Europe at that time.[42] Its commanders displayed a most exemplary promptness and courage in carrying out unexpected and difficult orders, even those for night operations with their tired men; and at the same time there seems to have been plenty of initiative on the part of the subordinate officers.

On the evening of the 24th, Radetzky had realised that his advance across the Mincio, undertaken to keep the enemy divided, was now useless; they had let his four brigades go through, and were now threatening his left flank and rear. But his dispositions had been calculated on the basis that within six hours he could meet any new attack on either side of the river.[43] So during the night, from about 2 a.m. on-

[41] Principal authorities: *Italian*. Stato Maggiore, *Custoza*, which has excellent maps, *Rapporti*, 3 vols., Fabris, Pinelli, Costa de Beauregard and others. *Austrian*. *Feldzug*, Hilleprandt, Schönhals, Willisen and lesser authorities.

[42] Special stress is laid on these points by the anonymous author of the *Studie über der Feldzug...1848*, a shrewd military study published in 1907, for use of officers.   [43] *Feldzug*, III, 41.

RADETZKY'S ORDERS FOR JULY 25

EXPLANATION OF PLAN facing page 369, which illustrates the orders on either side, on July 25th, the last day of the battle of Custoza. See also the map in the pocket at end of book.

On July 24th the Piedmontese had got across Radetsky's left flank; but on the 25th, by masterly counter-attacks, he drove them right off the high plateau (coloured brown on map). So ably combined were his movements that at every decisive juncture he brought superior force to bear.

Radetsky's Orders for July 25th, the decisive day

(Firstly) To form a strong central reserve at *Point A* (on plan p. 369) in the neighbourhood of Salionze. Four brigades at Rocca di Palazzuolo and Oliosi: the brigades of Maurer, Haradauer, Archduke Sigismund and Archduke Ernst.

(Secondly) To attack the Piedmontese.

Against Prince Ferdinand at Sommacampagna, Radetsky ordered out:

(On plan):

At Point 1: Perin's brigade from Verona.

At Point 2: the cavalry.

At Point 3: parts of the Third Army Corps, from Sandrà and Colà.

At Point 4: two brigades from the Second Army Corps to advance from San Giorgio in Salice, Castelnuovo and Cavalcaselle (the brigades of Gyulai and Lichtenstein).

Against Prince Victor Emmanuel at Staffalo and Monte Torre, he ordered:

At Point 5: two brigades (the last two of the Second Army Corps; those of Kerpan and Schwarzenberg, later supported by Maurer).

(Thirdly) *To defend his right,* the line from Custoza to Valeggio:

At Point 6: he sent Clam to San Zeno and Monte Mamaor.

At Point 7: at Valeggio, his stronghold, he kept Wohlgemuth and Strassoldo.

Piedmontese Orders

Having got their right wing across Radetsky's left flank and rear, they proposed that each brigade should wheel inwards half-left, and try to roll up the Austrian line.

The following were the orders given by the Piedmontese generals but it became impossible to carry them out:

At Point 8: Prince Ferdinand was to advance from Sommacampagna towards Salionze.

At Point 9: Prince Victor Emmanuel's Guards brigade was to advance from Staffalo towards Monte Vento.

At Point 10: his Cuneo brigade was to attack Monte Mamaor.

At Point 11: the Aosta brigade was to attack Valeggio.

At Point 12: a cavalry division was to accompany it.

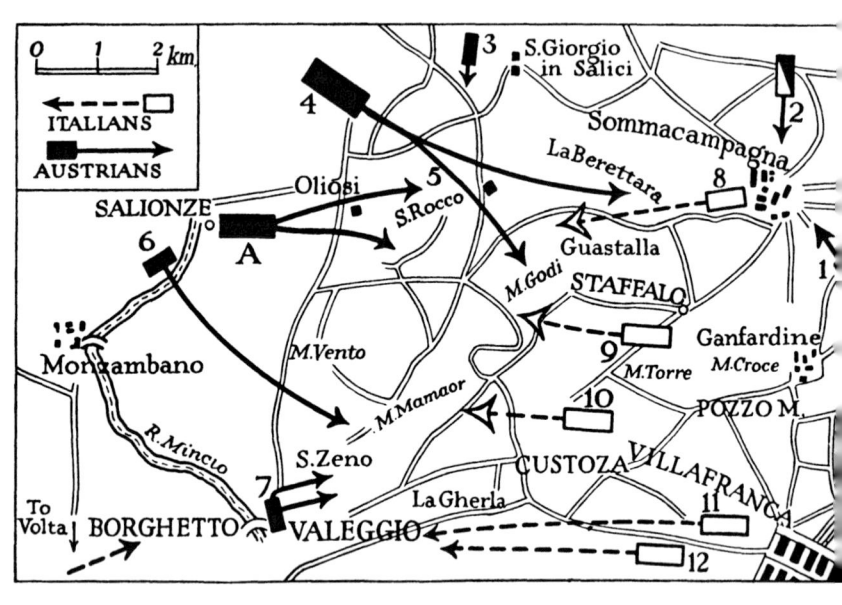

RADETZKY'S ORDERS FOR JULY 25

wards, he sent out messages which formed the whole Austrian army to a new front on its left flank, with orders to attack the Piedmontese that morning and drive them off the high plateau.

He had two main zones of action. On his right Valeggio, which he occupied with the whole of the First Army Corps, about 16,000 men. This was his defensive zone. Evidently he meant to hold Valeggio at all costs.[44] It was the "Stützpunkt" of his army (point of support).

Secondly, the zone on his left rear in which he was the attacking force. He had planned an advance against the two young Dukes between Custoza and Sommacampagna.

For this attack, he formed up his Second Army Corps, of which perhaps 27,000 men were engaged that day; he selected two brigades to act against Prince Ferdinand in Sommacampagna,[45] and he even brought an extra brigade (Perrin's) out of Verona to operate against Ferdinand's extreme right flank. This strong combination was intended to roll up the whole Piedmontese line.

Against Prince Victor Emmanuel's two brigades he opposed two, and eventually parts of two more.

At the central point of the army, near Oliosi and Rocca di Palazzolo, he had a reserve, intended to reinforce any point of weakness. It consisted of three brigades, mostly units withdrawn from across the river.

Thus, there were 42,000 men at his disposal, of whom probably about 27,000 actually came under fire on the 25th, without counting the two brigades garrisoning Valeggio. The two latter were not engaged, but their presence there made victory certain. Radetzky had been able to arrange that, of

[44] Wohlgemuth and Strassoldo at Valeggio itself; Clam and Supplikatz holding the line towards Monte Mamaor about 3200 yards to westwards. Kunz (p. 96) considers that Radetzky's dispositions might "fairly be compared with the best performances of Napoleon": v. also the *Feldzug*, III, 48; Hilleprandt, p. 366; Stato Maggiore, *Custoza*, p. 70.

[45] Gyulai's and Lichtenstein's brigades: Hilleprandt, p. 361 et seq.

all the Austrian units in his attack, there was not a single one which had had to fight on the previous day, and several were now firing their first round during this battle; whereas for Charles Albert no such arrangement had been possible. His only fresh brigade was the Aosta; the others had been fighting up to ten o'clock on the previous evening.

We will begin our description from left to right of the Piedmontese line. Charles Albert and Bava moved off at 8 a.m. to attack Valeggio. The other brigades were to support them.

Valeggio ought never to have been in Austrian hands. It was a natural stronghold, the key of the position, entrusted to two Lombard battalions; and only twenty-four hours earlier Bava himself had adjured them to hold it. Yet before evening the Lombard battalions had abandoned it,[46] and marched down to join De Sonnaz' force near Volta. As the distance from Valeggio is hardly five miles, it seems strange that De Sonnaz sent no one to take their place. Naturally the Austrians got into it before midnight, and the occupation of Valeggio was equivalent to a battle lost.

The whole of Charles Albert's counter-attack had been planned on the basis that Valeggio was in his hands; it covered the bridge at Borghetto, connecting the two halves of his army.[47]

[46] Apparently none of the Lombard battalions were expected to achieve anything. They were undisciplined and only half-trained, and had only two packets of ammunition each. Many of them refused to swear allegiance or fight, because they feared that the Austrians would shoot them as rebels. *V.* Bava's *Relazione: Rapporti,* I, 66; also Carderina's and other reports. But if they were not in a condition to do anything themselves, they ought surely to have got someone to relieve them before departing. The supreme importance of holding Valeggio is agreed to by everyone. *V. Rapporti,* II, 195; also *Custoza,* p. 54; and many other Italian opinions. Also Austrian opinion: Hilleprandt, p. 378; Willisen, p. 161, and others.

[47] Della Rocca (p. 228) says that he and Prince Victor Emmanuel started at daybreak and occupied Custoza; but the prince himself says 10 a.m. Bava (*Rapporti,* I, 82–5) says that both princes failed to start until 11 a.m. because their rations had not arrived. Ferdinand admits that he could not start until 11 a.m. owing to lack of rations.

His attack proved a complete failure. The original plan had been that he should assail Radetzky's positions from the east; that De Sonnaz should join in from the south-west; and that the advance of Prince Victor Emmanuel should envelop them and cause an Austrian retirement. But De Sonnaz said that his orders did not arrive until late, and consequently he never moved from Volta all day. Both princes were late in starting owing to failure of rations, and when they did finally move off, Victor Emmanuel's advance made little progress; so Charles Albert, after a brief effort, withdrew on to the plain to await all day the reinforcements of De Sonnaz, which never arrived.

On his right was Prince Victor Emmanuel, with orders to start an offensive movement towards Salionze; but, similarly, his chances were wrecked, mainly owing to the block at Valeggio. At 11 a.m. he had begun his proposed advance[48] by occupying Monte Godi, about a mile distant on his right front, with one of his battalions of Guards. But the two guns despatched with it had to be recalled. Bava wanted them on the left, and also claimed the three remaining Guards battalions to help his Aosta Brigade in rolling up Clam's line down to Valeggio. Thus Victor Emmanuel's fine regiment of Grenadiers was split in two and fared badly. After some preliminary success the three battalions found themselves blocked on Monte Mamaor by the joint brigades of Clam and Supplikatz, and also by the remnants of Simbschen's brigade, some companies of which were returning to the fight in spite of their unfortunate experiences on the previous afternoon.[49]

These Austrian movements resulted eventually in their launching a combined attack of seven battalions and fifteen guns, before which the Guards and the Aosta Brigade were

[48] *V. Rapporti*, 1, 78 (Bava) and many other Italian opinions: also Austrian *Studie*.
[49] *V.* the reports of Prince Victor Emmanuel, Della Rocca, Biscaretti and others in *Rapporti*, 1 and 11. Also *Custoza*, and its excellent maps.

compelled to retire. This was the beginning of the end. Already at 4 p.m. Charles Albert had received word from De Sonnaz that he would not attack before 6 p.m., and simultaneously he was informed that the Cuneo Brigade on his right was in difficulties.

At 4.30, therefore, he and Bava withdrew the Aosta Brigade into Villafranca; at about five o'clock the Guards followed them.

On his right flank Prince Victor Emmanuel had done rather better. True, his battalion of Guards had been driven off Monte Godi by Kerpan's brigade. But when, at 2 p.m., Kerpan attacked the main central position, he was definitely repulsed by the Cuneo battalions. By 5 p.m. the assailants were back again on top of Monte Godi.[50]

On the extreme right of the Piedmontese line, the brave and able Prince Ferdinand was allowed no chance of success. This was due to an excellent act of initiative on the part of Field-Marshal Haynau, the Governor of Verona.[51] On the previous evening, this officer, from one of the Veronese towers, had seen Simbschen's men in full rout, and in consequence he took it upon himself to alter the destination of a whole brigade. He had received orders to send out Perin's brigade to Castelnuovo, but he now ordered it to march at once to Sommacampagna to relieve the situation. By 10 a.m. Perin was actually attacking the village itself, and threatening the Piedmontese line of retreat. At first he was repulsed, whereupon he attacked again; he was again repulsed, apparently with some loss. But he had checked any advance on the part of Prince Ferdinand; and presently Gyulai's brigade arrived from Sona to support him. Against these two assailants the Prince held out strongly until about one o'clock. Then, however, he saw a third brigade (Lichtenstein's) pushing in between him and his brother. Bes promptly moved to

[50] Hilleprandt, p. 364, gives a clear account of all this. *V.* also *Custoza*, p. 84.
[51] Schönhals, II, 100.

the left, on to Monte Berettara, and engaged these newcomers; but their arrival compelled the Prince to evacuate Somma-campagna and follow Bes. From that time onwards the defence was unsteady; the temperature was 90° in the shade and the men had no water, and finally a battalion and a half retired—in good order—all the way back to Villafranca. Prince Ferdinand remained on the positions with the last ten companies that he could get to stay with him, and then he followed the others; his defence had lasted until six o'clock, and Bes' 3rd Regiment had lost another 103 casualties. Their retirement was covered by his brother Victor Emmanuel, whose Cuneo battalions held out obstinately on the hill in front of Custoza.[52]

At 5 p.m. there suddenly arrived near the centre of the field another Austrian force, Karl Schwarzenberg's brigade. It had marched from Cavalcaselle, near Peschiera. A third of the men had fallen out by the way and sixteen were dead of heat-stroke,[53] but it was able to give the *coup de grâce*. At about 7.30, Prince Victor Emmanuel was at last compelled to retire. That evening, the bulk of the Piedmontese army was assembled round Villafranca.

This general retirement is often considered to be the end of the battle, but in reality it was the end of the counter-attack. The losses had not been enormous:[54] and although there was great exhaustion and some discouragement among the troops, Charles Albert believed that De Sonnaz and his four brigades, now rested and restored, might hold the Volta-Cavriana line, until he could join them with the rest of the army. But fate had another crushing blow in store for him. The story is short but exasperating.[55]

[52] *Rapporti*, I, 263 (Ferdinand) and p. 330 (Victor Emmanuel).
[53] *Feldzug*, III, 49; Hilleprandt, p. 365; *Custoza*, p. 90.
[54] *V.* Table of Losses at the end of this chapter.
[55] It is taken from the Italian official account, *Custoza*, p. 126 *et seq.*

At 5 a.m. on the following morning, the 26th, De Sonnaz unexpectedly arrived at Goito with his two brigades from Volta. He had evacuated the Volta position, and he was within his orders in doing so, for he had received an order on the 25th from G.H.Q. authorising him to retire if he thought fit.

On arriving at Goito he was met by a later order directing him to stand fast at Volta. Being a little uncertain as to whether this second order was to override the first, he decided to await the arrival of Charles Albert. But within less than an hour he was informed that the King proposed to line up his army on the Volta-Cavriana front and offer battle.

At that moment it cannot have been later than 6 a.m., but De Sonnaz postponed his start until 4 p.m. He said there were no signs of activity on the part of the enemy and that his own men were tired out and required rest and food. But during the afternoon[56] Charles Albert arrived and upbraided him bitterly for not having carried out the order. At 4 p.m. therefore he started off, and arrived at Volta just in time to see the Austrians entering the village.

The whole distance was only about four miles, but he had let them get in half an hour before him.

He now proceeded to turn a mistake into a disaster. Although it was late, he sent his men at the defences, battalion after battalion, and brigade after brigade. The Savoyards fought splendidly. They showed what they might have done on the previous day. They stormed the hill and attacked the Jägers with the bayonet; they carried on the struggle into the night and renewed the contest on the next morning, but without the slightest chance of success. Schönhals has since explained that Radetzky meant to hold Volta at all costs, and that he had a whole army corps available for doing so.

[56] Bava says at 2 p.m.: he calls it three miles from Goito to Volta (*Rapporti*, I, 91). De Sonnaz' version is that at 4 p.m. on the 25th he received an order to leave Volta and march to Goito: that he arrived there at 4 a.m. on the 26th: that in the afternoon he was ordered back to retake Volta: and that he began his attack at once (*Rapporti*, I, 155).

Finally they were compelled to retire. The Austrian losses were 79 killed, 200 wounded, 177 prisoners and missing; total 456. The Piedmontese losses totalled: dead 67, wounded 263, prisoners 352, total 682.[57] Schönhals says that this repulse seemed to break the spirit of the Piedmontese troops more than their defeat at Custoza.

II. THE RETREAT

It was a Via Crucis on which Charles Albert was compelled to lead his army.

On the 27th his Council of War agreed unanimously that he must apply for a truce, but Radetzky's terms were such that the Piedmontese decided to refuse them, and resumed their march westward. Bava urged that the army should cross the River Po and retire via Piacenza and Pavia, but Charles Albert insisted on going through Milan. To retire via Milan was courting disaster, but he refused to abandon the Milanese. To Bava's arguments, he replied: "We will fight side by side against the enemy. I have been assured that the city is well provisioned with food and war munitions; they have erected defensive works. We will complete them, and victory will turn to our side." This undaunted spirit aroused Bava's admiration. "I was reduced to silence by this chivalrous outburst so characteristic of our august Sovereign."[58]

Consequently the King and his weary soldiers directed their footsteps straight on Milan, closely pursued by the Austrian army only one day's march in rear. He arrived at the gates on August 3rd.

Here another disappointment awaited him. He found himself coldly received. The Milanese were still divided against each other. When news of the defeat had first arrived, they had formed a Committee of Public Safety, composed entirely

[57] Hilleprandt, p. 386.
[58] Bava, *Relazione*, p. 100.

of republicans; it had decreed a *levée en masse* and had constructed some fortifications. But the spirit of the Five Days was now asleep. No great results had been obtained. Consequently the Committee of Public Safety had been superseded by the Royal Commissioners; and then most of the enthusiasm had disappeared.

The next three days, August 4th to the 6th, in Milan were destined to become famous. On August 4th the Piedmontese were halted outside the Porta Romana, when at about 1 p.m. their Austrian pursuers dashed on to them under cover of artillery fire, drove back the exhausted defenders and succeeded in cutting off five of their guns. In this sudden emergency, it is on record that, once again, Charles Albert set a splendid example to his troops. "His Majesty", says Bava, "went with his escort on to the road, and became at once the target for all the enemy's fire, which killed three horses of those with him. I entreated him to retire about 200 paces...to which he agreed rather unwillingly, and thus put himself a little under cover."

He and Bava ordered up four guns. Charles Albert then placed himself between two of them, and from three o'clock to nightfall the action continued, so Bava says, "in the presence of the King, near whom other horses and men were killed by cannon balls". That evening a further retirement became necessary, and Charles Albert moved his H.Q. into the town, to Count Greppi's palace, where he called a Council of War.[59]

At this council it became evident that any attempt to defend the city would only involve the Milanese in the horrors

---

[59] Bava, *Relazione*, pp. 105–7. He was with Charles Albert and his account is more or less official. Cantù (*Cronistoria*, II, 943) speaks of "seeing the bombs raining" on the King, but perhaps was not with him at that moment. Costa de Beauregard quotes De Robilant (*Les dernières années*, p. 314). Della Rocca, *Autobiografia*, I, 240, says: "Our men fought under the eye of the King who, at the first shots, came to place himself where the fighting was closest, like a man who is desperate and determined to die."

of unsuccessful street fighting. The Piedmontese artillery ammunition column had gone astray; of musket cartridges there remained only what had already been issued to the battalions, and of food there was only enough for three days. Consequently it was decided to send two officers at once to Radetzky to discuss the terms of a convention.

The officers started off in the darkness, and soon found themselves threading their way through hundreds of barricades. The fact was that, with the sound of the guns, the spirit of the citizens had risen. They were throwing up defences for a fight to the death. Indeed, that night of the 4th and 5th August has remained a terrible memory for both Milanese and Piedmontese. A furious storm had raged during the evening; in the suburbs there were some houses blazing, and the two armies stood face to face with their outposts firing at each other, while inside the town the crowds were becoming rather dangerous.

Radetzky, however, did not keep the officers waiting long. He agreed to a convention whereby the Milanese were to receive fairly humane terms; his own troops were to occupy the Porta Romana at 8 a.m. on the following morning.[60]

By 6 a.m. on August 5th the Convention had been signed. But it had not yet been communicated to the municipal authorities and committees. As yet the citizens had no idea that they were to be handed back to Austria. It was felt that the man to inform them would have a terrible task; Charles Albert entrusted it to Bava.

That morning Bava summoned the deputations to the Greppi palace, and set to work to explain the whole situation to them; and at first all went well. The deputation seemed to understand him; but suddenly two of the younger men sprang

[60] Our account of these days is taken from Bava's *Relazione*: *Rapporti*, I; from Cantù, who was also an eyewitness (*Cronistoria*, II, 943 *et seq.*); Della Rocca, *Autobiografia*, p. 239, also an eyewitness; Costa de Beauregard, *Les dernières années*, p. 322; Tivaroni, *Ital. Sett.* p. 262.

up and began protesting in the most violent terms against any convention. Before long they had got to shouting "Tradimento".

In a very short time the harm was done, because they were appealing from the committees to the streets, and the streets were filled with people already half insane[61] at the idea of a surrender. Bava saw the danger for Charles Albert; here was the King in the middle of the town, cut off by a thousand barricades from his army which was over a mile distant. He was defended only by a squad of about twenty National Guards, who would probably side with the mob. Bava said afterwards that he himself had never yet felt his life in such danger.

He warned Charles Albert and urged him to rejoin the army as soon as possible. His advice was received with a kindly smile: "We will mount presently", said the King, and he proceeded to hold an interview with General Zucchi and two other visitors.

Half an hour later the drums beat the "Generale" all over the town, and the crowds rushed down to the Greppi palace to secure Charles Albert for the defence of Milan. His carriages were smashed up; the National Guards vanished, and soon a howling mob filled the streets around the building.

Bava went out on the balcony and attempted, but in vain, to make his voice heard; meanwhile some of the citizens were in the courtyard, and one of them, "a man with a big apoplectic head and eyes starting out of it", went upstairs and penetrated the King's room. Cantù was there and describes it in the following words:

"Some of the mob," he says, "people whose names I prefer not to remember, penetrated upstairs to the King, and told him that his life was in danger. He received them with the impassiveness of

---

[61] The word is not too strong. Cantù tells us that early in the day a man was shot as a spy simply because he had a musket and cartridges; that later on he saw a man galloping his horse headlong all through the street without saddle or bridle shouting "Tradimento!" at the top of his voice.

a statue, without a movement of his body or a quiver of his brow. And with that quiet slow speech of his, and the gestures of his long and fleshless hands, he intimated to them to remain calm; and to go; that in a few minutes he would send them an answer."[62]

The next episode[63] in this eventful day was when Anelli and Litta, the last two remaining members of the Provisional Government, called on Charles Albert, and told him solemnly that "he must either fight or die".

This request hardly came well from the Provisional Government, but as the Milanese populace seemed so anxious to fight, Charles Albert told them he would cancel the agreement with Radetzky and resume hostilities. He issued a proclamation: "Citizens, I and my sons will remain with you...we will all unite in welcoming the dawn of our liberation..." and, by this means, one all-important point was achieved. Bava succeeded in persuading the crowd to let him pass through to the Piedmontese army, on the plea of making preparations for the renewal of hostilities. He found his soldiers longing to dash into the town and rescue their King. But—heart-breaking as it must have seemed— he was obliged to restrain them. Such an attempt would have meant storming a thousand barricades, and an internecine struggle between the Piedmontese and Lombards under the very eyes of Radetzky. So the rescue had to wait until Bava could get through the barricades without a conflict.

Yet, in reality, there was no probability of any further resistance to the Austrians. The more sensible citizens had always seen that it was impossible, and at four o'clock their Podestà waited on Radetzky and obtained from him the renewal of the armistice.

Meanwhile Charles Albert was still at the mercy of the crowd.

[62] Cantù, *Cronistoria*, II, 948.
[63] We can only select the episodes essential to the day. Costa de Beauregard spent some twenty-five pages over this day, and Cantù twenty-one. We have followed chiefly Bava's eleven pages; none of the accounts entirely agree.

The final scene of that ghastly day must be related, because it is the last occasion on which Charles Albert appears in this book. It is best described by the historian Cantù, who was serving as a volunteer.[64]

I returned quickly to the Greppi palace to see whether there was anything more for me to do. . . .
The scene there was worthy of a Greek tragedy, and will never leave my memory. The people were shouting that they wanted "The king! The king!" so that I was obliged to urge the chamberlain on duty to call him. Charles Albert had been suffering from fever, and these scenes were not calculated to allay it. He had thrown himself on the bed: but we were obliged to interrupt his period of rest.
A sigh, more than any other mark of impatience, revealed his state of suffering. He put on his military tunic and buckled his belt, and then stumbled out and grasped hold of the balcony: I was on his right. He began to address the people, but his voice gave out; so I asked him to tell me what he wanted to say. But the howling of the populace prevented my understanding what he said, even at the trifling distance which separated his very tall figure from my short one. At that moment a bullet whistled just between us, and, raising his hand with a gesture of compassion, he stumbled back into his room. I followed him there.

For a short time Charles Albert spoke to Cantù and began to explain some of the reasons for his actions, but then:

He wanted to continue, but a great weakness overcame him, and he threw himself back again on the bed. Then it was plain that even the eyes of a King may fill with tears and his heart with despair. I was overcome with pity and went out regretful that I could find no better phrase of comfort than "the testimony of his own conscience".

That first shot was the forerunner of many others; and an hour later the crowd set the gate of the palace on fire; but fortunately Alfonso La Marmora had been able to get through them to his division, and he returned quickly with some of his Bersaglieri, followed by a battalion and two guns. After that the King was able to start.

[64] Cantù, *Cronistoria*, II, 956.

Radetzky's terms were a suspension of arms for three days: the Piedmontese to retire behind the Ticino within 48 hours: the Milanese to receive generous treatment: and all citizens wishing to expatriate were to do so within twenty-four hours. It is said that about 60,000 of them availed themselves of this permission, and Radetzky's triumphant return to Milan was the scene of a national exodus.

On August 9th it was agreed that the armistice should last for six weeks; the Piedmontese to evacuate Venice and the Duchies, and to surrender Peschiera. Since then this has always been called Salasco's armistice, after the Chief of Staff who signed it.

It must have been a time of desolation for Charles Albert: after taking his chance of mutilation or death so generously and so often, he found himself now regarded merely as the incompetent commander; the man who was to bear the onus of the disaster throughout all time.

Some friends he has always had, among writers of history. Only in recent years, however, do they seem to have agreed that they can visualise him as he really was—a heroic "trier" in matters of duty, but unfortunately a commander without enough professional experience to initiate victorious campaigns, or to drive his subordinates into efficiency; he was no match for Radetzky and Hess within their Quadrilateral; but certainly he was a patriot of incomparable devotion—one to whom the war had always meant the supreme sacrifice.

And above all, a gallant heart. At that moment of disaster he alone remained undiscourageable. The day after the armistice he issued a proclamation to his whole people, and it is a fine instance of undiminished resolution. After summarising briefly the course of the campaign he says:

I am not unaware of the accusations with which some people wish to stain my name; but God and my conscience are witness to the integrity of my intentions. I leave it to impartial history to be their judge.

For the present a truce of six weeks has been arranged with the enemy: during that interval we shall either obtain honourable conditions of peace, or we shall resume the war....

Peoples of the Regno![65]

Prove yourselves strong during the first days of adversity.

Consider the free institutions which are newly springing up among you. Just as I was prompt to grant them on learning the people's needs, so henceforth, at all times, I shall be unswerving in maintaining them.

I still remember the cheers with which you then greeted my name: they have rung in my ears even through the din of battle. Have confidence in your King. The cause of Italian independence is not lost.

[65] The Kingdom. That is to say the new Kingdom of Northern Italy which Piedmont claimed henceforward now that Lombardy and Venetia had voted for fusion.

The battle of Custoza, 1848. Losses

AUSTRIANS

		Killed	Wounded	Prisoners and Missing	Total
July 22		23	153	33	209
„	23	71	302	213	586
„	24	50	104	1160	1314
„	25	175	723	423	1321
At Volta „	26 ⎫				
„	27 ⎭	79	200	177	456
					3886

PIEDMONTESE

		Killed	Wounded	Prisoners and Missing	Total
July 22		34	92		126
„	23	26	79	193	298
„	24	16	54		70
„	25	212	657	270	1139
At Volta „	26 ⎫				
„	27 ⎭	67	263	352	682
					2315

Authorities: Hilleprandt, pp. 332, 347, 357, 371.
Fabris, III, pp. 253, 282, 317, 358.

On the 24th Fabris gives the Italian losses at "about 70" and Hilleprandt states them at 16 killed and 51 wounded. But this seems a very low figure, especially as the 3rd Regiment alone returned more than half that number. Colonel Wehrlin states their losses at 5 killed and 34 wounded: he names four officers of whom two died of their wounds; *v.* Colonel Wehrlin's report, *Rapporti*, II, 154. This regiment was one of Bes' Piemonte Brigade and on July 25th it had 23 more dead and 92 wounded.

Chapter XX

AFTER CUSTOZA

A terrible disaster had fallen upon Italy, but it was perhaps a blessing in disguise. Like a great storm it stirred the elements below the surface. It starts a new phase in the story, the phase which ended a year later with Garibaldi's glorious defence of Rome.

Its first reactions were democratic, revolutionary and republican. As yet there could be only a town-movement; but in each principal town it aroused the Plebs to anger against Austria and to fury against its own government. That was why, for a year to come, the national movement was democratic and republican. At first it was limited to the insurgent towns and their outskirts, but in October we begin the period of the "Costituente", of the various proposals that a Constituent Assembly should be set up, to erect a supreme national government for the whole of Italy. This seems to prove that national feeling had become more uniform than ever before.

Many good patriots argued more or less as follows: Italian freedom can never be won through the Princes; Pius' Federalism is useless; Charles Albert's *Italia farà da sè* is a failure; Leopold does not count; Ferdinand is a minus quantity. To fight for unity and freedom there remain only the democrats. Let the democrats have a trial.

"The monarchical principle is condemned. Let God and the People triumph. They do not fail."[1]

---

[1] In Rome, Spada (strong Conservative Papal) described the press-campaign as follows: "*Disloyal and a tyrant* was the King of Naples: Charles Albert was a *traitor*; the Grand Duke of Tuscany was an *imbecile*; and the Pope was *too weak*. And what other consequence could there be of this outcry, except a more pronounced advance towards the pre-arranged republic?" Spada, p. 449.

The chief centres of happenings now are Venice, Turin, Rome, Bologna, Leghorn, Florence and Milan. They will be described in this order. It will be seen that each of these towns except Turin is working up, through democratic advance, towards republicanism or revolution.

In the north, the territories of Piedmont, Lombardy and Venetia had only just completed their unification as the Kingdom of Northern Italy. We may recall the dates: on June 13th Lombardy had voted itself into Piedmont; on July 4th Venetia had joined them; on July 27th this fusion had been proclaimed at Turin; and on August 6th the Piedmontese Commissioners, Conte Cibrario and General Marchese Colli, had entered Venice to represent the royal government. But unfortunately they were too late; on this same day Radetzky was entering Milan; the news of Charles Albert's disasters had already arrived, and next morning the people were shouting: "A republic! Away with the Commissioners of the Re traditore! We want help from the French republic!" These were merely their first reactions to the news; but on the 11th the Commissioners were formally notified by Welden of the terms of Salasco's armistice, and they realised that their authority was already at an end. They were lucky to get away alive; for an angry crowd dashed up their stairs, and there was some danger of the Commissioners being lynched. It was then that there occurred the celebrated scene when Manin appeared on the balcony and called out: "For the next forty-eight hours it is I who govern"; and thereupon the people returned to their homes calm and pacified, because they knew that the state was in the hands of Manin.

The defence would continue as before. Henceforth there was no·hope of a Piedmontese relief force; but nevertheless the defence would continue.

Venice was now again a republic and in this way the Kingdom of Northern Italy had ceased to exist. At the longest computation it had lasted only fifteen days. It had been merely a fleeting vision for Charles Albert of the time to come; but here, as everywhere else, the experience for which he had to pay so dear proved invaluable in 1859; in that year there was no delay nor hesitation when the Lombards joined themselves to Piedmont; nor do we hear of any in 1866 when Venetia was united to the rest of Italy. The Regno was an idea in being.

With the events in Piedmont or its new Parliament at Turin, we shall only deal quite briefly because there was very little attempted of a constructive nature until Charles Albert began preparations for the campaign of 1849; and that is a subject which does not enter into this volume.

At the time of the disasters, Gabrio Casati, Podestà of Milan during the Five Days, was President of the ministry; but after the armistice, he retired and was succeeded by Alfieri (15th August to 11th October). Alfieri was then replaced by his War Minister, General Perrone, who remained in office until December 16th, when he in turn was succeeded by Gioberti.

Now that Piedmont was in difficulties and without allies, her thoughts turned more readily to the idea of a league of states; and on this occasion there seemed to be more chance of a successful negotiation because at first she was willing to work on the basis of a genuinely defensive agreement. The envoy selected by Casati—on the proposal of Gioberti—for this mission, was the Abbé Rosmini, who was beloved as a kindly old priest and well known as a distinguished philosophical writer. We may note that before starting he stipulated definitely that there should be no question of his trying to persuade Pius to declare war. He would begin by a Concordat with the Holy See, and then would proceed to suggest a confederation of states.

The old Abbé left Turin on August 4th; went to Charles Albert's camp (10th) and reached Rome on the 15th. He was back in Turin early in October. During this short stay he seems to have charmed everyone. Pius held long con-

versations with him and let it be known that a successful
mission might be rewarded with a cardinal's hat; meanwhile,
Monsignor Corboli Bussi was chosen to discuss the whole
subject with him at informal conferences, which were joined
by Pareto the Piedmontese ambassador and the Cavaliere
Bargagli for Tuscany.

Bargagli, well pleased at finding himself in this distinguished company, has left some interesting despatches on the
subject; but, as the whole scheme seems rather Utopian, we
need only deal with it very briefly.[2]

Rosmini's project differed from all others, as it was not
merely a League—namely an alliance between separate states
—but it provided for setting up at once a *permanent confederation* with a Diet at Rome. It would in fact have given
form to the new nation: it would have initiated for the Italian
states a single individuality such as that possessed by the
United States.

At first he would only have the three "reforming states":
the Papal State, Tuscany and Piedmont. But forthwith they
were to proclaim themselves a nation, with the Pope as
President. Within a month, three representatives, elected by
each legislature, were to meet in Rome and draw up a constitution under a permanent Diet.

This Diet was to have such wide powers that we may
wonder how Rosmini and Pareto ever supposed that Turin
would agree to such self-effacement. Its powers were to be:

(*a*) War and peace: allotting the contingents to be sent by
each state.

(*b*) Regulating the customs system for the Confederation.

(*c*) Dealing with foreign treaties.

There were also many other very wide innovations, such

---

[2] Rosmini has left an interesting account of these weeks. *V.
Missione a Roma* by Antonio Rosmini Serbati. And in the Florence
Archives (*Carteggio Martini*, Busta 2670 and elsewhere) there are
interesting despatches from Bargagli, especially that of September
4th. *V.* also Bianchi, vi, 8; Farini, ii, 335.

as providing uniformity of the monetary system; and as far as possible of military discipline, and of civil and criminal legislation and procedure.

Surely this would have made Piedmont very like an out-lying province of Rome! It would have turned most of Italy into a confederation, and Italy was not yet prepared for so sudden a change.

Rosmini and his friends had the greatest hope that they had achieved unity for their country; but meanwhile in Turin, Casati's ministry had fallen (August 7th). The new ministry was reverting to the traditional Piedmontese policy: their new instructions were, to obtain the energetic co-operation of the Pope in the war against Austria, in case of its being resumed; also to form a political league, and fix the military contingents from each state.

On receipt of these warlike instructions the Abbé Rosmini saw that his mission was at an end. Pius would never agree to a league of princes for war.

At Rome the new ministry did not come in until August 6th. At first,[3] Pius would have liked to appoint his friend Pellegrino Rossi to the ministry; but Rossi did not yet feel himself in a position to accept office, and the political clubs raised such violent objection that Pius named old Conte Eduardo Fabbri, until a better moment should occur for Rossi.

Fabbri's ministry only lasted six weeks. Perhaps it can best be described in a paragraph devoted to it by Masi:

Pius turned to Count Eduardo Fabbri, a poet and conspirator from Cesena, who had paid for his patriotism by prison and exile; a man of kindly spirit and moderate ideas...."I am here against my will", wrote Fabbri from Rome to Vincenzo Fattiboni, "and I do not know what good it will do. The Chamber, the philo-sophers, the extremists, the obscurantists, the job-hunters and the high-command-hunters are the heroes of Italian liberty....Every-

[3] Pasolini, 1, 162; Farini, 11, 262; Spada, 11, 420; Ledermann, p. 165: he quotes a letter of Rossi to Salvagnoli, p. 347.

thing ends up in vain, ridiculous disputes and mad pretensions. The Pope wants one thing; the philosophers, the Chamber, the canaille want another....I am here to be a useless part of an entirely useless ministry, which is still in process of formation and according to all appearances will never be got together."[4]

Only two days after its formation, this stop-gap ministry was faced with a sudden invasion from the north. General Welden, who had been detached by Radetzky to guard the southern border and prevent volunteers from the Papal State from reaching Venice, decided to block the stream at its source by occupying Bologna. On August 8th his advanced brigades were already at the gates of the town, and two companies had stormed several of the houses. But during these years of the Risorgimento the Bolognese were always among the best fighting populations in Italy. On this occasion, although many of their regular soldiers and volunteers were serving elsewhere, when they saw the Austrian uniforms the people suddenly took fire: not only the poor people —the "Santa Canaglia" which so often does the fighting— but students, shopkeepers and citizens of all classes. Regardless of the bombardment by howitzers, they threw themselves on the Austrians, and with such good effect, that after two or three hours the troops outside the walls were in full retreat, and one of the companies in the town had been captured. Welden then recalled them, apparently because he was unwilling to stir up a political hornets' nest.

This episode is very significant: after their triumph the Bolognese remained in rebellion. The Italian spirit of resistance was not dead, but it was changing leaders.

It was in Tuscany, however, that the new democratic phase found its most violent exposition, headed as usual by the city of Leghorn. Thither came Father Gavazzi, the Barnabite monk whom we last saw preaching a holy war to

---

[4] The chief point of importance about Count Fabbri is that in him Pius continued his custom of selecting laymen and ex-revolutionists to be his prime ministers under the Statuto.

thousands of young Roman volunteers in Romagna, and who was now equally busy proclaiming the republic of Mazzini.

On August 24th he landed at Leghorn in the very teeth of the Tuscan government, although he was a Bolognese by birth and a Roman subject, and was soon at work arousing the mob. His arrest was followed by a revolution. Leghorn became virtually separated from the rest of Tuscany, and refused to accept the governors sent to her from Florence.

In this new dilemma the Tuscan ministers decided to send Professor Montanelli to govern Leghorn. It was a bold choice; but Montanelli was a well-meaning man and, at that moment, immensely popular owing to his wound and his gallant conduct at Curtatone. As matters turned out, the results were extraordinary. No sooner did he arrive in Leghorn (October 8th) than he addressed the mob in the market-place and suddenly proclaimed the *Costituente*, a constituent assembly for the whole of Italy. His proposal was to form a democratically elected assembly over the heads of the eight or nine existing governments; a democratic assembly directly elected by the whole Italian people.

The immediate result of this simple scheme was that on October 12th the Tuscan ministry fell, and the Marchese Capponi, who in spite of his blindness had been so long the mainstay of Liberalism, was succeeded by Montanelli and Guerrazzi, the confirmed revolutionists.

From that date onwards Tuscany, the third of the "reforming states", had definitely become ultra-democratic; in fact, four months later on February 9th, 1849 her Grand Duke was compelled to seek safety in Gaeta, where the Pope had already preceded him.

In Milan hitherto the Republicans had been of little use to the national cause. Their presence had been a source of embarrassment; but at this moment there suddenly appeared on the scene a leader who knew how to turn them to account.

On June 22nd Garibaldi had landed at Nice,[5] a returning exile who had now abandoned his great position and the results of all his toil in Montevideo, in order to help in the unifying of his native land. Already his name was one to conjure with among the people, but legally he was still a condemned rebel. When he presented himself before Charles Albert at Roverbella, the King referred him to Turin; and at Turin the Minister of War suggested his going to Venice. Evidently they did not like his politics, nor perhaps his methods of soldiering.

Garibaldi was a republican, but he was ready to serve the King or any authority that would help the national cause. He offered himself to the Provisional Government of Milan and was accepted. Between Milan and Bergamo they had nearly 3000 volunteers of one type or another: men of Antonini's Legion, a small Pavian battalion, a hundred Milanese, a corps from Nice and the Ligurian coast, all of them stiffened by the war-veterans of Garibaldi's own Montevideo Legion. When he heard that the Piedmontese army was retiring hard-pressed by the enemy, he started in pursuit, intending to hang on to the Austrian flank and rear.

Then came the armistice; Garibaldi decided not to observe it until he had got in a blow at the enemy. He was at Monza, which is on the plain, so he retired into the steep hill-country near Como. There he proposed to start guerilla warfare among the mountains, but the adventure seemed to be so desperate and impossible that many of his men deserted him. For the moment he withdrew over the Piedmontese boundary to Castelletto; but there, he promptly received an order to disband his volunteers and leave the Kingdom.

As he regarded this order—to disband his republicans without fighting—as an insult, he marched straight back into

[5] Baldini, p. 142; Fabris, III, 521–32; Garibaldi, *Autobiography* (Eng. edit.), I, 276–86, III, 81–2. For authorities on Garibaldi v. Trevelyan, *Garibaldi's Defence of the Roman Republic*, p. 49, and Bibliography.

Lombardy. In a single night he reached Arona, on Lake Maggiore; seized the two small steamers that plied on the lake; filled them with Red-shirts, and sped over to Luino, followed by an excited flotilla of smaller craft. On the following day, August 15th, he and his eight hundred[6] stalwarts with their two small guns were attacked by three Szluiner companies from Varese, but the Garibaldians drove them back with the bayonet, after a fight which cost the Austrians over forty casualties.[7]

Garibaldi then advanced to Varese, where he was received in triumph. Already his picturesque republican Red-shirts were a centre of great enthusiasm all over the district. We know this from the Austrian side. "Garibaldi", says Hilleprandt, "had divided his volunteers into several small bands, in order to deceive the Imperial commanders. By making rapid appearances and disappearances at various points in the district between Lake Lugano, Varese and Lake Maggiore, he succeeded in producing a feeling of insecurity." Evidently Radetzky decided to make an end of the matter. On August 20th d'Aspre appeared with most of the Second Army Corps. Garibaldi was still at Varese. He cannot have had more than six or seven hundred followers left, because his men naturally perceived that the game was up; and d'Aspre was advancing with no less than six brigades, from six different points in the south and west. He meant to cut off Garibaldi from the Swiss frontier on the east, and from Lake Maggiore on the west.

On August 23rd four Austrian brigades made a combined rush and seized Varese; but Garibaldi had already slipped away northward. On the 24th d'Aspre determined to cut him off from Lake Maggiore; he ordered Maurer northward to seize Luino and the two steamers there, and sent his other

[6] He says he only had 800 on this day. The Austrians believed that he had 2000. V. Hilleprandt, p. 442; Garibaldi (Eng. edit.), I, 277.

[7] Hilleprandt, p. 442, admits 4 dead, 14 wounded and 24 missing.

brigades westward to various points on or near the Lake. But Maurer was first met by Medici, who, with only 110 men of the rear-guard, succeeded in delaying him for four hours, and then slipped over the Swiss frontier. Garibaldi then exchanged a few shots with him, but let him go on to Luino, as the steamers were no longer there.

For the next two days Garibaldi himself did a wonderful march through that mountainous country; on the first day he wheeled to the left towards Lake Maggiore, but when the Austrians occupied places in front of him, he wheeled again to the left and passed by, along the hills, with only two or three miles to spare. By seven o'clock on the evening of the 26th he had got down south to Morazzone, actually behind the Austrian H.Q. at Varese, and in touch with the Swiss frontier.[8]

Here his fortune deserted him. Simbschen was close on his track, with a Kinsky battalion (Germans), a squadron of Polish Kaiser Uhlans and two guns.[8] After dusk, they suddenly rushed through the tired Garibaldian outposts, and some of them entered the village. Garibaldi and his officers were just sitting down to a meal, but they rose, sword in hand, rallied their men and drove out the assailants. For a time, fighting continued outside the barricades; but at 9.30, when d'Aspre himself arrived with Edmund Schwarzenberg's brigade, he ordered a retirement to Bizzozzero; he thought that he would do better by daylight. The Austrians admit twenty-one casualties.

After this last piece of heroic bravado, Garibaldi perceived that the end was at hand. At eleven o'clock that night he led out his last seventy men, disbanded them and ordered them to cross the Swiss frontier. After the fight at Morazzone there were only two points left in all Italy where resistance could possibly be continued by the republican party—namely Venice and Rome.

[8] Fabris, III, 525 et seq.; Garibaldi, Autobiography (Eng. edit.), I, 280, III, 81 note.

Undoubtedly it had been a marvellous piece of guerilla work, by water, as well as by land. Its successful defiance of all impossibilities had come like a ray of sunlight to the dispirited Italian patriots. It gave them fresh belief in their people. And it had revealed a born leader. After the experiences of the previous campaign, his daring seemed amazing; indeed throughout all Italy there were people—even Moderates to the core—who felt that he might be an ex-rebel and he might be an avowed republican, but, before Heaven, he was the type of man whom they required.[9]

[9] As the name of Garibaldi is celebrated in England, it may be of interest to read the official Austrian account of this fight at Morazzone:
"When our troops were in position we raised the signal for the attack; the skirmishers fired, and they, together with the supporting columns—each consisting of one company—pressed forward with the bayonet, raising loud shouts of 'Hurrah!' and rushed with such impetuosity against the weakening enemy that he threw himself back in most disorderly flight into the village. It was there the defence began.
"Meanwhile night had fallen; and several times our detachments —led by brave officers and inspired with their courage—thronged into the entrance of the village. They laid low many of the insurgents, and then they withdrew back into the open country, only because of the fear that they might fall into some ambush and be cut off. The guns now came forward, and at first opened fire on the entrance at very short range. But as a great number of the insurgents had gathered together in the nearest houses and those beside the exit and had opened a very lively fire on our troops as if preparing to charge out on us, our guns were brought up almost to a distance of thirty paces of the nearest houses, and poured out grape-shot so that the enemy abandoned his idea. An hour after the beginning of the fight there appeared two battalions of Kaiser infantry, and a horse battery, to support the attack, under Major-General Fürst Edmund Schwarzenberg. These also now took part in the battle and contributed towards dislodging the enemy. The pitch darkness and the ignorance of locality decided their leaders against any further attempts to surround or pursue the enemy." *Feldzug*, III, 92.
Hilleprandt, p. 445, says that Garibaldi had only fifty men left to disband; and that the Austrians found seven dead and three wounded in the village.

Chapter XXI

PELLEGRINO ROSSI

I

The tragedy of Pellegrino Rossi is a subject that Italian writers naturally approach with regret; it is an episode that they would gladly omit from their history. In reality, however, they are fortunate in having so few of these tragedies to record at the end of 1848. Italy was then passing through a stage when they were inevitable. The Italians had been defeated in war, and in every town the populace was angry. We know now that when the Plebs is angry, it usually raises the cry of "The Republic"; and unfortunately, when the cry is "The Republic", murders are sure to occur. There have been many of them in most of the European capitals since 1918. In Italy in 1848, very fortunately, the leaders were idealists—Mazzini and Garibaldi—men to whom their cause was a religion. And so Rome was spared anything in the nature of a Terror.

Of all the Italian patriots living in foreign lands, there was perhaps none whose career so genuinely proved him to be one of the distinguished men of Europe as Pellegrino Rossi. Exiled for supporting Murat in 1815, he had sought refuge in Switzerland, and—although he had to begin by learning the French language—before many years were gone he had become known as one of her ablest citizens. In 1832, when he suddenly found himself a ruined man, at the age of forty-five he had made a fresh start in Paris. In his new career he had moved from success to success; he had become a friend of Guizot; was created a Chevalier, then an Officer of the Légion d'honneur, a member of the Institut de France, and had eventually returned to Italy as French ambassador and a peer of France. Yet amid all his honours he had not forgotten the land of his birth. For two years he had been the Pope's ablest friend and adviser; and it was in answer to an appeal from Pius that he now undertook the immense task of trying to save the Papal State from revolution and disaster.[1]

Although Rossi was a lifelong Italian patriot, there were now fundamental differences between him and the new school of revolutionists. He stood for the existing Constitution, the Statuto; he believed in using the Papal State as a haven of refuge within which to develop Italian nationality on a federal basis; and above all he intended to restore law and order, and to prevent Rome from being overrun by refugees from other states.

Throughout the whole country there was bitter discontent and much unrest. The extremist leaders were tired of a ruler who could not declare war. In that respect we cannot help feeling that they were right. Pius had refused ever to attack the Austrians. On his side it might be retorted that in 1849 the Republicans, who had succeeded him, never attacked the Austrians,[2] so that after all their talk of war, they did no more than he had done. But that was because events moved too fast for them. And in any case they had an absolute right to claim a ruler who was not debarred from ever declaring a war of aggression; it meant that their nation would never be unified. From the religious point of view, Pius had been right: but—as we see now—this meant that it was time that

---

[1] "He was tall for a southerner and rather thin and pale; and clean-shaven as befits a barrister; the Roman Law had left its stamp on him; in fact, with his wealth of now-whitening hair, his grey eyes deep-set but very bright, his cravat and his low-breasted frock-coat he must have looked more like a distinguished Scottish advocate of that period than an Italian exile. His face (on his monument in S. Lorenzo in Damaso) is fairly broad but sunken, as if from too much brain work; the forehead wide, cheek bones a shade high, the nose and chin slightly hooked, and the expression rather sad. His long lips are closely compressed and, normally, would break into a grave smile, probably tinged with irony." *Italy in the Making*, II, 21.

[2] They voted 15,000 men to march with Charles Albert, but they could not possibly be ready in time.

the Papal State came to an end; on that point we think that nowadays almost everyone is agreed.

Consequently we hold that at that moment there was justification for a rebellion; but it is impossible to agree with those who say that the murder of Pellegrino Rossi was justifiable. They spoke of "the dagger of Brutus". But even for the most fanatical republican there was no need of Brutus. Rossi was only a prime minister, not a dictator. The Roman people could defeat him in the Chamber;[3] as we know, they had had four different prime ministers in the previous six months.[4]

From the first, he was faced by a hatred both bitter and brutal, and the cause of its being so has not always been realised. In reality it was because he was in opposition to the new wave of the national advance. The republican revolutionists had been gaining ground every day—owing to the discouragement of all other parties—when suddenly Rossi, a man from outside, had appeared and thrown himself across their path. Their reasoning ran more or less as follows: "Venice is still resisting; Charles Albert is still armed; Tuscany is with us; the only absentee is our Papal State.[5] And now that Vienna is again in revolution and Garibaldi is coming south the struggle is not yet hopeless." Their cry was, "either war or else a republic in Rome"; they called for a League, a *Costituente*, and if possible for French intervention.

On all these issues Rossi poured a douche of cold common sense: war was now hopeless;[6] a republic would never be

---

[3] The *Contemporaneo* observed that the death of Rossi made no difference politically, because every single deputy was opposed to him. Pantaleoni and others, however, afterwards said that Rossi would probably have carried his proposals in the assembly.

[4] Recchi, Mamiani, Fabbri and Rossi.

[5] *Contemporaneo*, September 26th and 28th.

[6] In this opinion he was right; the Papal State could not raise men for war in Lombardy: *v. London Corr.* III, 141 (Abercromby); p. 101 (Hamilton). *V.* also Pareto's opinion on July 12th, Turin Arch., Lettere Ministri, Roma, 1848. And that of the French Ambassador, Paris Aff. Etr. Rome, 1848, August 8th and 11th.

allowed by the Great Powers, and would only lead to the re-establishment of foreign domination all over Italy; a League was right, but it must be approached quietly if they wanted to bring in Piedmont; a *Costituente* was useless. As to the idea of French intervention, most probably he foresaw the line which it actually took only two months later.

In this manner Rossi settled down to defend the life of the Liberal Papal State. He alone, if anybody, could ever have made it a possibility. And, although we may see that it was better for the future that he should have failed, it must be admitted that his analysis of the situation was absolutely right. Step after step, the events which he foresaw followed one another as surely as night follows day; first the revolution, then the republic; and with it, the foreign occupation, voted in fact by the French republic only two days after Pius left Rome, and assented to by the other great Powers.

There was one result, however, which he could not foresee; and it is one that is very rarely foreseen by men of his type, namely, that out of all the ruin around him there would rise a glorious legend which would go farther towards the creation of the new nationality than any other influence during the Risorgimento—Garibaldi's defence of Rome. No one in the world could have foreseen such an achievement of the impossible. When all hope of victory had become unthinkable, when Charles Albert was in exile, when the Venetian resistance was weakening and Rome was face to face with three hostile armies, at that moment of disaster Garibaldi boldly raised the tricolour out of the dust and turned this scene of humiliation into a glorious national memory. His defence of Rome proved that there were thousands of Italians who felt it better to throw their lives to the winds than to see their cause fail without honour. And such an example went straight to the heart of the people. More than any other episode in the story it inspired the romantic tradition which has been the strength and the saving of modern Italy.

II. INTERNAL AFFAIRS

Rossi was the strong, able, determined man who knew what he wanted and how to set about it. He intended to save the state from revolution.

His ministry[7] was "a one-man show". The cabinet of seven ministers consisted of one cardinal as President, one other churchman (for education), one learned lawyer, one young professor, one duke, one count and—Pellegrino Rossi. Some wit of that day[8] expressed its specific gravity by the symbol 0000001. But Rossi had made his position even stronger by accepting two of the principal portfolios, those of the Interior, and, temporarily, of the Finances, to which, shortly afterwards, he added a third, by suppressing the Ministry of Police and placing that body under the Interior or Home Office, as is the custom in England and elsewhere. He could thus get rid of Galletti, and of his subordinate Accursi, an ex-carbonaro and extremist, for both of whom he found posts elsewhere. But the extent of his authority aroused a great deal of comment in Rome; even the kindly

---

[7] In his despatch of September 24th the Dutch minister quoted a friend of his who said that Rossi's ministry was described as "Tu solus Peregrinus in urbe" and by the symbol in the text. He added that the other ministers rejoiced in "une réputation de nullité la mieux établie": Rome Reg. Ist. Ministre des Pays-Bas, I, 35. 20. 30 K.

[8] Rossi's ministry:
Cardinal Soglia Geroni. President, and Foreign Affairs.
Count Pellegrino Rossi. Ministry of the Interior; into which the Ministry of Police was soon afterwards absorbed. Finance (ad interim).
Professor Montanari. Commerce; a young professor of moderate Liberal views.
Duke of Rignano. Public Works (ad interim).
Cardinal Vizzardelli. Education.
Avv. E. Ciccognani. Mercy and justice; a learned lawyer, but in politics so moderate as to be considered a reactionary.
Count Pietro Guarini. Minister without Portfolio.
  There were also Cav. Pietro Righetto, Sostituto to the Ministry of Finance, and Monsignor Francesco Pentini, Sostituto to the Ministry of the Interior.

old Abbé Rosmini said: "This is a dictatorship rather than a ministry"; Sterbini pointed out that the fewer the ministers, the more independent of popular control; and Bargagli wrote to his government in Florence that Rossi's occupying three offices of state amounted to a *coup d'état*.[9]

Once established, he started on his task of saving the Papal government; and set about it with extraordinary energy and fine indifference to opposition and danger.

His first care was for the fundamental necessities, the finances and the army. He began by abolishing the vexatious Accursi ordinance forbidding the export of money, and, soon afterwards, several other causes of irritation.[10] For the army, which was now in a disorganised and undisciplined condition, it was necessary to obtain a strong and distinguished commander-in-chief. Rossi sent an invitation to a fellow-revolutionist, General Zucchi, the old Napoleonic officer who had been the hero of the rising of 1831, and had only lately emerged from his long defence of Palmanova against the Austrians. Zucchi accepted the appointment. In connection with his arrival, historians have remarked that during this last effort to save the Liberal Papacy, Pius succeeded in gathering round him, among many able men, three of the most distinguished in Italy: Rossi the administrator, Zucchi the soldier, and the Abbé Rosmini the philosopher—for Rosmini remained in Rome in touch with Pius, and it was expected that he would become Minister of Education.

General Zucchi soon got to work on the army, trying to

[9] Both Rosmini and Bargagli, though charitable men, were enthusiastically hopeful about their scheme for the confederation of the whole of Italy; and they believed and stated at this time that Rossi was secretly influencing Pius against them. Thus they were temporarily biased against him. In reality Rossi was no more than a Home Secretary whose department included the Police; his tenure of the Finances was only temporary. For Sterbini's opinions, *v.* the *Contemporaneo* of September 23rd.

[10] His further financial reforms will be given in the list which we quote from Farini, II, 353.

substitute order for the existing military chaos; but among other things he dealt with the financial side of it, and, whether on that account or because he exacted Napoleonic discipline from the troops, he soon began to lose popularity. The extremist press, which saw in this heroic old patriot merely a bulwark of the Constitution, lost no opportunity of attacking and even slandering him.

On September 22nd Rossi printed in the *Gazzetta* an article announcing these measures, and expressing his own views upon them, especially upon the army: also on the necessity of law and order. Everyone, said Rossi, has rights and duties, and it is for the government to see that they can enjoy them and carry them out in peace.[11]

In this article he boldly declares war against the extremists on either side. He stands for the Statuto, the existing constitution. On that basis he calls for loyalty and popular support. "In a constitutional government such as ours, everything would result in confusion and disorder, if the opinions and actions of the whole people did not, so to speak, breathe a spirit of life into the law."

He was plunging into a mass of complicated reform which involved more work than seemed possible for one man. But this great effort of Pellegrino Rossi does not in reality concern our subject. This was administrative work within the Papal State and consequently had no influence on the development of the Risorgimento. It is touching, however, to see the long and careful record left by Farini, in honour of his friend and colleague; there are three pages of such items as the following:[12]

He provided for a subsidy from the clergy of 80 baiocchi on every 100 scudi assessed on all ecclesiastical property. By this means, with the Pope's assent, he raised 2,000,000 scudi from

[11] *Gazzetta di Roma*, September 22nd, 1848.
[12] These can be verified in Spada, II, chap. XVIII; in Ledermann, pp. 173-4; Giovagnoli, I, 225-6, and in other authorities. They are mentioned in the diplomatic reports, notably in those of Bargagli: *v.* his despatches of September 4th, 27th; October, various dates; November 2nd.

Church property which had already been mortgaged for 2,000,000 scudi....

He sent to Paris in anticipation, the money for interest on the Rothschild loan (*Gazzetta*, October 17th, 1848)....

He named a Commission for putting the finances in order; also another for the military forces, and another for reforming the monetary system....

He simplified the transmission by post of bank-notes and treasury bonuses, reducing the tax to one scudo per thousand....

He effected economies in all the estimates, and aimed at having them all in order, so that when Parliament met on November 15th, it would be able to discuss them at once, and thus start exercising the first and most important right of the free peoples....

He busied himself about concluding a contract with a company for the construction of a railway from Rome towards the Neapolitan frontier, and tried to encourage the citizens and the municipalities to form companies for constructing others elsewhere....

He established a central statistical office at the Ministry of Commerce....

He instituted an inquiry as to improvements in the system of producing and manufacturing salt....

He considered the question of establishing chairs of political economy and commercial law in Rome and Bologna....

He created within the Ministry a Directorate of Police....

The above truncated sentences represent only about half of the subjects mentioned by Farini.[13]

In the *Gazzetta* of October 2nd there appeared another article written by Rossi; in it we find that he mentioned his two ordinances of September 29th, namely, one providing relief for wounded soldiers and the other for the immediate construction of three lines of telegraph: Rome-Ferrara, Bologna-Ancona and Rome-Civita Vecchia. By this means, he said, he would unite the Adriatic and the Mediterranean and extend the influence of Rome throughout the state; not only this, but he would bring nearer to her the whole Italic peninsula. In this article, then, we have Rossi's own statement of his hopes. It runs as follows:

The telegraphs and railways will be the most powerful aids in rendering more serviceable, more effective and more national

[13] Farini, *loc. cit.*

the great vision of our illustrious Pontiff, the idea of an Italian League.

We have hopes that before long we may see it carried into effect, for the honour of Italy, for the guardianship of her rights and of her freedom, and for the salvation of the lately-established representative monarchies which will inaugurate a splendid future in the civil and political life of the Italian people.

May God grant that our hopes may not be deceived by the evil passions and mad impulses and the inexcusable errors whereby our magnificent and just hopes have been only too miserably disappointed.

III. POLICY OUTSIDE THE PAPAL STATE

Rossi's negotiations over the League and over the *Costituente* are the most important part of his work from our point of view. His negotiations with Piedmont constitute the fourth and last attempt at uniting Modern Italy by a league or federation. The idea died with Rossi.

Here we can only give the very briefest skeleton outline, and quote the principal dates.

On August 4th, when the subject was resumed after the battle of Custoza, the scheme under discussion was that of the Abbé Rosmini—a Confederation, as differentiated from a League or Alliance. It was not finally rejected by Piedmont until October 9th.

On October 3rd and 4th, however, two alternative plans had appeared. Both envisaged a league or alliance of separate states as distinct from a confederation.

On October 4th the Turin cabinet, headed by General Perrone, had produced a plan to succeed that of Rosmini. It contemplated war rather than peace. A league was to be formed between the Papal State, Tuscany and Piedmont; its principal aims were to be:[14]

1. To assure the nationality and *autonomy* of Italy; to

[14] Spada, II, 471-7; Giovagnoli, I, 232 *et seq.*; Florence Arch. Esteri, Busta 2670, *Carteggio di lega politica*; Bargagli's despatches of October–November 15th; Farini, II, 342; Bazzoni, I, 117.

guarantee the territory of each state, and the defence of the country by contingents furnished by each Power.

2. A Customs-Union and a uniform system of posts, money, weights and measures.

3. Uniformity of legislation, administration, education.

4. A meeting of plenipotentiaries from each state to be held in Rome as soon as possible, to draw up organic laws.

In reality this proposal amounted to a military league. Its aim was to assure the *autonomy* of Italy; in other words, to attack the Austrians: this attack was to be considered defensive. Manifestly the Pope would not agree to declare such a war.[15]

The league was to guarantee the existing territory of each state. But that was not enough. At that moment Piedmont was claiming, through Gioberti, to include Lombardy, Venetia, Parma and Modena, lately fused with her as the Kingdom of Alta Italia—the North-Italian Kingdom. Were the smaller states to guarantee this? Undoubtedly it would be dangerous for them, as was proved in 1860.

What they wanted guaranteed was not merely the existing territories, but the *balance of power within Italy*.[16]

The rest of the *Progetto Sardo* was indefinite. A meeting of plenipotentiaries "as soon as possible" might mean anything.

On October 3rd, a day before General Perrone, Pellegrino Rossi had already produced a scheme to set opposite the *Progetto*,[17] of which, no doubt, he knew the probable gist.

---

[15] Rosmini claimed that his Confederation would meet this difficulty. By establishing a permanent Diet in Rome for all Italy, the Pope would not have to declare war individually.

[16] It is true that the Piedmontese were doing the fighting and deserved the spoil; but what they were asking now was that the Pope should guarantee them Lombardo-Venetia and all the other states still to be reconquered. In return, they offered to guarantee the Papal State itself which was already protected by the Great Powers of Europe.

[17] Florence Arch. Esteri, Busta 2670, No. 413: Bargagli's despatch of October 3rd. In this letter Bargagli sends the outline of the scheme to his government. *V.* also Farini, II, 342.

His scheme seems to go, as far as is possible for a Pope, towards persuading the Piedmontese to come to a meeting in Rome—also perhaps the Neapolitans. No one is asked to bind himself to anything beforehand; but evidently Rossi hoped that, once round a council table, they would succeed in producing some sort of useful result under his guidance.

His preamble began by reciting that the league was intended to preserve the liberty and independence of the states of Italy, and also to restore public order.

The terms were as follows:

A league was to be formed between the Papal State, Piedmont and Tuscany; Naples was uncertain; but any other sovereign might join it afterwards.

The league was to be guided by a congress of plenipotentiaries in Rome, presided over by the Pope or by one of the Papal plenipotentiaries as his representative.

Each state was to select its plenipotentiaries as it preferred.

There was to be a preliminary congress in Rome, not later than   ,[18] for the high contracting parties to discuss and ratify the organic regulations of the congress.

That was all. Proclaim a league of three states; assemble a preliminary congress; leave the rest to the plenipotentiaries. If we can once get Italians to meet round a table, we shall arrive at some result.[19]

Nothing about nationality; nothing about independence; nevertheless on October 3rd, Bargagli, after a long talk with Rossi, came away satisfied that the ideas of nationality and independence were "enclosed within these expressions", and that Rossi intended that all the attributes of Rosmini's Diet

---

[18] This date was never filled in.
[19] "The Pontifical plan is exceedingly simple; it can be summarised in a few words. *There hereby exists a political league between the constitutional and independent Italian monarchies which agree to the pact; the plenipotentiaries of each independent State are meeting forthwith in Rome in a preliminary congress, to deliberate upon the common interests and to draw up the organic conditions of the League.*" Extract from Rossi's Discorso of November 4th.

should be definitely fixed at the preliminary congress of plenipotentiaries; "in fact", wrote Bargagli (with rather absurd optimism), "he does not now differ substantially from Rosmini".[20]

Rossi felt that to harp on nationality might rouse Piedmont's fears about his wanting a confederation; and to speak of national independence might commit him to war.

His feeling may probably be expressed in the following words: War is a mistake for the present; but that is no reason why we should not move towards one another on federal lines.

Rossi hoped that, as he had cut out the Diet, Piedmont would agree to his plan.[21] And, the league once formed, he would proclaim it as an accomplished fact for the honour of Italy, for the guardianship of her rights and liberties, and for the salvation of the representative monarchies; but he would say nothing that would imply war or fusion, both of which were impossible for the Papacy.

Meanwhile the Piedmontese were pushing their own warlike scheme, and apparently at first they agreed with Tuscany that, at once, they should send envoys to Rome to draw up organic laws of an Italian federation.[22] But in return for coming to Rome they demanded the old terms; and, as before, a formal guarantee to Piedmont of the North-Italian Kingdom (naturally a very big demand). On that basis Rossi could not treat. "History", he said, "will take account of this avidity which is full of danger for Italy; and will blame them for their failure to form an Italian federation."[23]

[20] Florence Arch. Esteri, Busta 2670, No. 413.
[21] "Rossi believes that, in view of his having struck out all questions concerning the powers of the Diet, the Sardinian Cabinet cannot delay its acceptance of the scheme; and if, as is extremely probable, that government agrees to the scheme, he intends to proclaim the league at once." *Ibid. V.* also Florence Arch. Esteri, Busta 2670, *Carteggio Martini*. Letter from the Tuscan Minister of Foreign Affairs to Marchese Ridolfi in Paris, October 5th, 1848.
[22] Clause 4 of their scheme. *V.* p. 403.
[23] Florence Arch. Esteri, Busta 2670, No. 440.

By the middle of October the whole situation was being invaded by the new schemes, and the league was no longer possible. In Tuscany they were ultra-democratic. On October 8th Montanelli had proclaimed his *Costituente*,[24] a Constituent Assembly to be elected by the people of Italy, regardless of the nine existing or would-be existing governments. Apparently he was thinking of the glorious days of the French Revolution. And when on October 27th he and Guerrazzi came into power, Rossi saw that in Tuscany the democratic *Costituente* had supplanted any other project.

At the same time in Piedmont, there was a second *Costituente* on the tapis. Gioberti's congress,[25] which sat from October 10th to the 30th, was proposing a Constituent Assembly composed of government envoys from each state; it was to draw up a scheme of federation for all Italy. But what differentiated it most of all from the others was the fact that Piedmont claimed to include in its own territory all the Kingdom of Alta Italia or Northern Italy, namely, Lombardy, Venetia, Parma and Modena. This alarmed the other states.

The situation was not without humour. In Venice, where the people were republicans, a rival congress had been called to counter that of Gioberti. They raised the cry of: "Not to Turin: to Venice."[26] And at Rome, Padre Ventura tried to call a congress of Moderates. But neither of these two efforts produced important results.

There is this much to be said for Gioberti: his *Costituente* was a step on the right path. The only hope of Italian unity was that Piedmont should swallow up all the other states, "like the leaves of an artichoke"—as was said in 1860. But,

[24] *V.* chap. XXII, p. 416. Also the *Contemporaneo* of October 11th.
[25] On September 17th Gioberti, through his *Società politica federalistica italiana*, had called a congress of representatives from every Italian state. This congress had sat in Turin from October 10th to the 30th and had proposed his federal *Costituente*.
[26] Bargagli forwarded a leaflet which they were distributing in Rome in his despatch of September 30th. Florence Arch. Esteri, Busta 2670, No. 403; and No. 413 (October 3rd).

in 1848 and 1849 this was quite impossible, because Piedmont had no ally against Austria.

None of the existing schemes were likely to succeed. Montanelli's democratic plans could only lead to a Mazzinian republic, which was odious to Piedmont, to the Church, and to the Great Powers. Gioberti's *Costituente* meant war against Austria; and Piedmont, single-handed, was not strong enough to be victorious. She required an ally.

Gioberti's congress did indeed draw up a scheme of confederation consisting of two chambers, one elected by the states, the other by the people. This Central Authority was to override the existing governments and provide military and diplomatic unity. Such a scheme, however, had no chance of being accepted.[27]

For Rossi all these upheavals had brought immense toil, and inevitably a greatly increased number of enemies. The ultra-democrats hated him because he was a bulwark against Montanelli's *Costituente*, and against revolution, fusion, or republicanism. Many federal nationalists hated him because his scheme said nothing about nationality, or union, or the people; they thought it merely a treaty of governments for safety—which was partly true; the people who were calling for war hated him because he stood for peace. As soon as Piedmont began to re-arm she became again the champion of Italy.

Thus, for the Liberal and modernised Papal regime set up by Pius, the end was very near. It had only another seven weeks of life; and once the Liberal institutions were gone, the loss of the Temporal Power would be merely a question of time.

[27] Gioberti, on October 14th, argued that what Italy required was a strong northern state to protect her from invaders. He argued that if Piedmont annexed Modena, for instance, this meant increased safety for everyone: but if Modena were added to the Papal State the rest of the peninsula would be no safer.

Unfortunately for Rossi, during these last weeks there occurred a definite breach with Piedmont which must have done him a great deal of harm. In some of the Piedmontese papers articles had been appearing accusing Pius of having been the true cause of the failure to form a league. On November 4th[28] Rossi wrote an answer in the *Gazzetta*, defending Pius, his friend and sovereign, and retorting with some acerbity:

Why these accusations? The answer is simple; it is because he, the Pontiff, the initiator of the League, did not blindly agree to the Piedmontese proposition.

He discusses the Piedmontese claims to have her territories guaranteed:

It would be well to say clearly which territories Piedmont wishes to have guaranteed by Rome and Tuscany. Are they the old or the new? Those she possesses or those she hopes to possess?
If it is the old there is no objection to be made.
If it is the new, who is there who does not perceive that Tuscany and Rome, by making themselves sole guarantors of such magnificent accretions, would arouse a smile all over Europe.

This retort must have been highly unpalatable to Sterbini, who was on his way back from Turin with two *Costituente* schemes in his pocket.

At the same time, Rossi insinuates that he would not oppose the cession to Piedmont of Lombardy and Piacenza. And this after all was more than Piedmont received in 1859.

Perhaps his own policy is best expressed in the following extract:

But when one is thinking of Italy above all other things, it seems healthier, more sincere and a more patriotic counsel to begin by establishing firmly the bonds of the league and at the same time to allow leisure to the states, intending to become members, to reform their armies on a more solid basis.

---

[28] *Gazzetta di Roma*, November 5th, 1848. *V.* also *Contemporaneo*, six weeks earlier on September 19th, which had an article by Agostini, attacking the view of the Piedmontese papers.

IV

Everyone admits that the hatred against Pellegrino Rossi was due primarily to his political views: but some writers have attributed it partly to his stand-off manner; Spada, for instance, says he was proud and sarcastic.[29] Of this view we find very little confirmation in the letters of the diplomatists who knew him. But in his own despatches he was certainly a little didactic; his tone reminds us sometimes of Mr Woodrow Wilson, who, like him, had been a lecturer. And, as an able barrister, no doubt Rossi would have taken a sarcastic tone when faced by such opponents as Canino.

The real reasons for the hatred were, not his manner, but his work. Rossi's enemies in Rome are summed up by Farini as follows:

The turbulent or those who wanted a new state, the enemies of all order and all discipline; conceited people, impostors, magistrates who were good hands at making their profit out of the abuses; Sanfedists who busied themselves with turning licence to their own account, clerics greedy of gold or honours—all these were greatly displeased at seeing Pellegrino Rossi invested with ministerial authority. To them may be added a number of honest youths who hated anyone reputed to be severe; many others who were inclined to be extremists from sheer incurable distrust of priestly government; and certain journalists accustomed to make their pickings at the expense of others' reputations. Add also the mediocre and the vain and all their following, who saw snatched from them a chance of rising to the summit of power.[30]

[29] The chief hostile opinion about Rossi's manner is that of Spada, which is more or less accepted by Ledermann. "He was hard, proud, taciturn. He had too high an opinion of himself and did not know how to hide it. He was not expansive and did not encourage others to be so with him.... In fact he was generally unpopular and *antipatico*": Spada, II, 470. Spada is on the whole impartial; but he and other Roman citizens were ashamed of this crime in their city and perhaps a little inclined to lay blame on Rossi. Giovagnoli gives lists of writers who liked or disliked Rossi: in reality their views follow their politics.

[30] Farini of course was a Moderate, a supporter of Rossi and a hater of the extremists; so we must allow for some natural bias. Still there is probably a great deal of truth in the list he gives; it too

The revolutionary agitation against Rossi's government may be broadly divided under three headings: firstly, that of the old Gregorian Sanfedists who loathed Rossi's liberalism; secondly, that of the democratic republican politicians whose leaders were Sterbini and Canino and whose principal organs were the *Contemporaneo*, the *Epoca*, the *Pallade* and *Don Pirlone*; and thirdly, the uneducated plottings among the populace. Before long, the second and third rather tended to coalesce.

During Rossi's ministry he was attacked with unparalleled bitterness by all these sections. The Gregorians would never trust him; they recalled his early Carbonarism and his subsequent Protestant wife; and also his recent taxation of Church lands. Already on an earlier occasion the liberal-minded old Cardinal Micara, when introduced to Rossi, had greeted him warmly with the following words: "I have known you extremely well, Sir, ever since you were burnt in effigy"— a piece of wit no doubt directed against his own Sanfedist colleagues.[31]

The chief opposition, however, came from the party headed by Sterbini, Canino and their satellite Ciceruacchio, and in a lesser degree from the constitutional Liberals such as Mamiani; and certainly the three first-named were a more dangerous clique than might have been supposed. Sterbini had the brains, Canino had the money and Ciceruacchio had the mob.

The third section, that of the uneducated plotters against Rossi's government, affords us a melancholy picture of mob-movement seen from the inside. The trial of 1849–52[32] (to discover the murderers of Rossi) afterwards revealed an

is accepted by Rossi's biographer, Ledermann. *V.* also the *Contemporaneo*.

[31] This was the same Cardinal Micara who had supported Pius' election to the Papal throne. *V.* Pelczar, I, 386.

[32] The *procès-verbal* of this trial is preserved in the State Archives in Rome in twenty manuscript volumes. It affords an interesting cross-section of the life of that time. It is our chief source of information for the plots against Rossi.

appalling condition of affairs in the lowest strata of Rome in 1848; and it is sad to think that many of these people must have formed part of the following of Ciceruacchio who, although probably genuine in his motives, was inevitably becoming more unscrupulous in his methods. These would-be revolutionists included men of all types, from officers of the Civic Guard and small shopkeepers down to loafers and informers such as Bernasconi. At the moment, the slum population was more dangerous than usual. No doubt the Roman Plebs, like that of any town, had always contained a percentage of riff-raff, but not for many years had the city included so many violent characters as now. On July 25th the Legions had returned from Vicenza and the town was full of armed men, of whom even the better sort were completely out of hand;[33] they had begun by seizing the monastery of the Gesù and turning it into a barracks; and on the self-same day Rome had been invaded by a number of Neapolitan and other revolutionists from Calabria. Spada gives the names of thirty of their leaders;[34] the most important was Vincenzo Carbonelli, one of the two best orators of the piazza in Naples. Others who afterwards figured in the trial were a fiery young enthusiast called Nicotera, Bianchi an ex-priest, Bomba, Maiolini and finally Colonello, who had been condemned in 1844 at the same time as Galletti, now Minister of Police. Some of these refugees were probably well-intentioned; but they were in a frame of mind to avenge their Neapolitan defeat upon the government of Rome, and especially upon Rossi.

From these conditions there developed the notorious Facciotti plot, which was afterwards made a cause of accusation against the Liberals of every type and section. It began as follows:

In the Salita del Marforio there were living two brothers named Bernardino and Filippo Facciotti, natives of Palestrina, aged twenty-eight and twenty-six respectively; they were

[33] Nino Costa, p. 47.   [34] Spada, II, 415–19.

ordinary small shopkeepers, *ebanisti* or cabinet-makers, hitherto of good life, but the elder Bernardino was a strong and enthusiastic patriot. He was one of those who had been profoundly disappointed by Pius' Allocution and refusal to declare war. Since that date he had become a politician; he raged against the cardinals, hoped to restrict the Pope to matters purely spiritual, and to set up a republic.[35]

During this period he made the acquaintance of the Neapolitan exile Carbonelli and very quickly fell under his influence. Carbonelli,[36] aged twenty-six, was an educated man, a Bachelor of Medicine, a Carbonaro, an enthusiast who had been implicated in every revolutionary plot, and had fought at the barricades in Naples on May 15th. He was now probably at the full tide of his bitterness, and poured forth all the revolutionary fervour of his own soul into that of Bernardino Facciotti; it was not long before the small shop of the two brothers became a meeting-place for Carbonelli and his compatriots Tomba, Maiolini and Colonello; also for any Romans who wanted to talk revolution. Apparently almost anyone was welcome; in fact, it is thought, but not proved, that Canino supplied money for general propaganda.[37] In this manner the Facciotti collected quite a large number of associates, but it was not a very dangerous conspiracy because it included two officers of the Civic Guard and three secret service men, so that all their doings were fairly well known to the police.[38]

Before long there were no less than 120 people concerned —quite a crowd—but no one of any importance unless it be the Assessore of Police, Michele Accursi, whose loyalty is rather a matter of doubt; it was soon after this that Rossi got rid of him.

[35] Giovagnoli, I, 250–51.
[36] *Ibid.* p. 251 note, quoting La Cecilia, *Memorie*, IV, 167. Also *Dizionario del Risorgimento*, II, article *Carbonelli*.
[37] *Processo Rossi*, VII, 3205 *et seq.*, Toncker's evidence. He claims to have seen Canino there and says Rossi was very anxious to find out who was behind the Facciotti.
[38] *Processo Rossi*, evidence of Toncker, Rufini, Salvati, etc.

But the plan was being betrayed every day by at least four of the conspirators, three of whom were in touch with the police and the fourth with Rossi himself. This fourth was an officer in the fourth battalion of the Civic Guard to which the Facciotti also belonged. Thus Rossi was keeping himself well abreast of the conspiracy, but he did not consider it very serious.[39]

On October 24th, however, he received news from the Duke of Rignano, G.O.C. of the Civic Guard, that on that day Carbonelli with true Neapolitan eloquence had harangued about a hundred of the conspirators, urging them to take action and fixing a gathering for the following day, October 25th, at a place between the Foro Boario and the Colosseum. Rossi directed the Duke of Rignano to have the place watched; and consequently Colonel Tittoni of the same 1st battalion of Civic Guards sent a strong detachment to the spot in question, but they found no signs of disturbance although they remained there until midnight. Evidently the proposed action had been abandoned.

It seems unwise on Rignano's part, when trapping conspirators, to have selected the very battalion to which the ringleaders belonged, even though it was their colonel, Tittoni, who had reported the existence of the plot. But the fact remains that now there existed in Rome a definite conspiracy against Pius; its originators had failed in the first attempt, but were busily continuing their propaganda all over the town.[40] The Neapolitans, Carbonelli and Bomba, were

[39] Monsignor Pentini, who was Rossi's Sostituto, or Under-Secretary, at the Home Office, said in his evidence at the trial of 1849 that there had been several plots after the Allocution, but that they had come to nothing as they all differed in their plans of action. Rossi may have taken the view in November that this isolated plotting was not dangerous. *Processo Rossi*, XIV, 6784, Pentini's evidence.

[40] For an account of the propaganda, *v. Processo Rossi*, III, 1445; IV, 1544, Bonomi's evidence; IV, 1682, Menarini's evidence; IV, 172 *et seq.*, Politi, and many others. Also VII, 2994 *et seq.*, Bernasconi. This man had turned King's evidence and some of his statements about individuals were disproved, but his description of the plots and propaganda is probably accurate enough.

preaching openly in the streets against the government to which they had fled for safety.

Moreover, within this mob-movement, side by side with the Facciotti, there was also another and more dangerous element, that of the *Reduci*, "the returned men", which had come into existence as follows: when the 1st Roman Legion arrived back after the surrender of Vicenza, it was found to contain so high a percentage of undisciplined men that on September 4th it was ordered out of Rome to garrison the province of Forlì, where the Colonel dismissed all those whom he considered undesirable, and, we may add, formed a good battalion out of the remainder.[41] But the unfortunate result was that the undesirables, about a hundred and forty in number, drifted back into Rome in their volunteer uniforms, and organised themselves into a so-called battalion, which they christened the Battalion of the *Reduci* or returned volunteers, and chose a man named Grandoni to be their colonel. These men, though in uniform, were dangerous because they were drilled and completely undisciplined, carried *dagas*, and having been at the war, set only a war-value on human life; and they were evidently under the influence of the revolutionists. Their chief meeting-place was the Teatro Capranica.

Nino Costa has described them in the following terms:

The *Cassandrino*, edited by the priest Ximenes, aimed at repressing violence by dealing with it in a joking way. But one evening, when joking in the street, they settled the Editor with a knife through his carotid artery. I was not far off and saw the deed. It was carried out by conspirators whom I knew.

He then proceeds to describe another similar stabbing, this time at night.[42]

[41] There are several letters on the subject of these volunteers in the Roman State Archives. Archivio del Ministero della Guerra, Archivio Politico, 1848.

[42] Nino Costa, p. 49 *et seq*.

Chapter XXII

THE MURDER OF PELLEGRINO ROSSI
NOVEMBER 15TH

I

There is no actual proof that Sterbini planned the murder of Rossi, but his signed articles in the *Contemporaneo* prove that if he did not murder him, it was not for want of hatred. Sterbini was at the turning-point of his career. The old wave of Moderate Federalism had died away, and in its place there was a new advancing tide of nationalism, chiefly represented by Montanelli's *Costituente* in Tuscany, Gioberti's *Costituente* in Turin, and the republican movement in Rome which Sterbini felt himself entitled to lead. When, on October 10th, Gioberti opened his Congress in Turin, Mamiani was sent from Rome to represent the Circolo Romano: and Sterbini also went up to Turin, as a delegate from the Circolo Popolare.[1] While there, he tried to arouse animosity against Pellegrino Rossi; and on his way home, he and Canino were entertained at a public dinner in Florence, where, too, they made another bitter attack on Rossi.

When he returned to Rome, it seemed as if he might have been on the verge of a great advance in his career. He and Mamiani had been two of the eight Commissioners who drew up Gioberti's *Patto* (Pact), and Canino had been a vice-

---

[1] The Dutch minister was a strong Conservative and his opinion of Sterbini may be biased, but not by any personal rivalry. In a letter of October 4th, he says: "Le Sieur Sterbini...est un de nos meneurs les plus exaltés, cachant sous le manteau de son patriotisme une ambition démesurée, et qui à l'occasion, serait, je crois, peu scrupuleux sur la nature des moyens à employer pour la satisfaire." And on November 11th, four days before Rossi's murder, he referred to Sterbini as "l'homme, fougueux et irascible, qui voudrait à travers des ruines se frayer une route au pouvoir": Rome Reg. Ist. Ministre des Pays-Bas, despatches of Oct. 4th and Nov. 11th, 1848.

president. At Turin, Gioberti and Charles Albert wanted to renew the war; at Florence, there was Montanelli with his *Costituente*-by-manhood-suffrage, and he also wanted to renew the war. The programme was war under democratic guidance.[2] These two proposed constituent assemblies were entirely dissimilar, but Sterbini hoped that he might be the man to reconcile them. In Rome, however, he was faced by this newcomer Pellegrino Rossi, who would hear nothing of war or of either form of *Costituente*.

On October 8th news arrived that Vienna was again in revolution and that the Hungarians were victorious. This fresh chance of winning Italian freedom must not be lost! Sterbini and those with him hoped to unite Alta Italia (Piedmont), Tuscany, Sicily and Rome—Naples was also mentioned—to form a national confederation for the purpose of attacking Austria. In reality his scheme was chimerical. On paper there might possibly be something to be said in its favour, but even on paper the hard facts were manifestly all against him. Alta Italia no longer existed, Tuscany and Sicily were of no military weight; and in Rome, Pellegrino Rossi would, probably, carry the Chambers with his peace policy.

Pius' Parliament, however, was not to meet until November 15th; so Sterbini and his friends proposed to turn the full blast of their newspapers against the prime minister, and bring him down.

And there for the moment we must leave Sterbini until the second week in November, when he got back from Turin.

In Rome the revolution was rising higher and higher around Rossi. For the time being, the temporal authority of the Pope still represented the law of the land; but if it failed, anything might happen; hundreds of families all over the state might

---

[2] At Turin, Sterbini had insisted on the proposed federal army being under the proposed federal congress, so that the Kings might not be able to use it to suppress liberty.

suffer.[3] The most likely result would be the erection of a republic; the majority of the population was probably not very republican in feeling, but as all other parties were now discredited, a republic seemed to be the shortest way of ending the Pope's right to veto a declaration of war.

What impresses a student most about Rossi during these last days is his coolness. He stood almost alone, and was venomously attacked on all sides; but he moved on his course with a calm deliberation and a fine contempt for danger, working more or less single-handed at everything, so as to have a clear statement of his policy ready for the opening of the Chamber on November 15th. If he could but state his case, he might very possibly win through and save the Liberal Papacy.[4]

Among his opponents the importance of his coming speech was fully realised. It would carry a majority in the Chamber against Sterbini and Canino and their followers, if it got a fair hearing.[5] The following is Farini's description of these days:

All these events aroused the anger of Rossi's enemies—the journalists, the leaders of the populace, the Circoli of Rome. The advices received by the government from Tuscany informed us that there would be a fresh movement attempted in Rome on the day of the opening of Parliament. The bitter feeling was hardly dissimulated and the intention of raising trouble in the state was barely concealed. There was no form of abuse that was not heaped on Rossi, and no kind of accusation that was not made against the Roman government. If the police sent off one or two Neapolitans to the frontier, an outcry was made against tyranny; if Rossi brought carabinieri into Rome he was accused at once of a *coup d'état*;[6] if the Minister of Public Works made alterations in the

[3] On November 15th, when Pius spoke of leaving Rome, Sturbinetti (then his prime minister) reminded him that if he did so, hundreds of families would suffer. Consequently Pius stayed in Rome until it became impossible to do so.

[4] This was Pantaleoni's view: *Processo Rossi*, XII, 5796. Also Pentini's.

[5] Farini is referring to the *Contemporaneo* of November 14th and 15th. On these dates Sterbini let himself go against Rossi and brought the revolutionary agitation to its crisis. Farini, II, 359.

[6] Mgr Pentini, who was Rossi's Under-Secretary (Sostituto) at the Ministry of the Interior, has left an interesting paper giving as

hall of the Council of Deputies and in its public loggias, a rumour was promptly spread that he was restricting the space for the people (which was not true), and that he wanted to shut them out; that an attempt was being made against publicity, against liberty and against a constitution. True, Rossi had ordered a good many carabinieri into Rome, two or three hundred perhaps, and he did not conceal the fact that he had called them in to defend order; just as the raisers of the outcry made no concealment of their will, their hope and their desire to disturb it.

During these days Rossi continued to receive secret information as to the meetings of the Facciotti plotters and others. He knew that there were conspiracies in progress against his government, though it does not seem that until the very last morning, November 15th, he knew definitely that there were any against his own life. Before the end he received thirteen anonymous threatening letters, but these of course he despised.[7]

Nevertheless, the strain must have told upon him. One evening, when he and Count Pasolini were dining with the Duchess of Rignano, towards the end of dinner the Duchess whispered to Pasolini: "You can't think how it worries me to see a man so silent and so much concentrated in himself. It seems hardly worth while speaking to him, he barely answers." And Pasolini replied: "When a man has very serious preoccupations and thoughts, and finds himself in such terrible conditions as those of Count Rossi, he has the right to be silent and self-centred like that."[8]

It was this kindly Duchess of Rignano who warned Rossi of the conspiracy a few days later; though she seems not to have known that it was directed against his life.[9]

his opinion that what finally decided the murderers to act, was Rossi's complete success in converting to his views the Consiglio or Upper House, many of whose members had previously been hostile. Consequently there seemed little doubt of his success with the Lower House on the 15th. Rome, Reg. Ist. Carte Pentini, Busta 71, No. 7.

[7] Rome Reg. Ist. Carte Pentini, Busta 84, No. 7, gives several specimens of these threatening letters.

[8] Pasolini, I, 183–4.   [9] Giovagnoli, I, 271 note 2.

On November 12th the conspiracy of Carbonelli and the Facciotti again came to a head. They had collected their force, had tried to bribe the Dragoons and Carabinieri, and had formed the following plan of action. Their rising was to start at Trajan's Forum; the date was not named, but we may suppose that it would probably have been November 15th. Their plan was to attack the Quirinal, make the Pope prisoner and take him to St John Lateran, compel him to abdicate the Temporal Power and retain only the spiritual dominion, to make hostages of the cardinals, and to proclaim the republic.[10]

Of this plan Rossi received information, and he took immediate action.

He sent orders to the Carabinieri all over the Comarca to come into Rome; there were between two and three hundred of them. They were more trustworthy than the Civic Guards.

On the evening of November 12th he arrested the Neapolitan revolutionaries Carbonelli and Bomba. Of the other Neapolitans, Galeotti, Maiolini and the ex-priest Bianchi fled from Rome. Orders were given that Carbonelli and Bomba should be repatriated.

By now Sterbini was back in Rome, hard at work on his press-campaign. On the same day, the 12th, he published a furious article, over three thousand abusive words, under the heading "Deceiving and corrupting", in which he tried to pillory Rossi as an unscrupulous adventurer and a hater of the people; his climax was:

"But this same pride which leads them [ministers such as Rossi] to exalt themselves, may, by Divine Justice, afterwards ruin them. That public opinion, which they so greatly despise, finally drives them out. And happy are those princes who can free themselves from them in time."

Louis Philippe for instance; it had only taken "a breath of popular opinion to overthrow him"....Ferdinand of Austria, "where is he now?"[11]

On November 14th Rossi published an article in the

----

[10] *Processo Rossi*, VII, 3217.
[11] *Contemporaneo*, November 12th, 1848.

Gazzetta which showed that he meant to put an end to Rome being governed either by organised mobs or by Sanfedist intrigues. Speaking of the opening of Parliament he says that the extremists on both sides are trying to overthrow the existing form of government and intend to achieve their purpose by means of disorder:

but let them both remember that the government of His Holiness is watching them, and is determined to carry out its duty by offering a vigorous resistance to every attempt made against the integrity of the Statuto.[12]

He then addressed his words to the assemblies themselves. He called on them to restrain the extremists from trying to reproduce an event which occurred elsewhere (namely the revolution in Tuscany) and from carrying out a pact agreed *inter scyphos* over the wine, in a neighbouring city.

This latter reference, "inter scyphos", was directed against Sterbini and Canino who, while in Tuscany, had attended a banquet to Garibaldi, had abused Rossi and had drunk toasts to the fall of his ministry.

Possibly some news of Rossi's article leaked out on November 13th, because in all probability that is the day on which the plan was laid to murder him. In fact, the crisis had already begun. The Facciotti conspiracy had been comparatively innocent; but now, a smaller and far more deadly plot was in progress. The agitation had stirred up the dregs of the Roman populace, and it was bringing to the surface some of the worst specimens that Europe had seen since the yelling crowds which followed the tumbrils in 1792.

The actual facts are not entirely ascertainable. But it seems probable that on the evening of the 13th, at a small inn, some six or seven men were sitting together debating how to carry out the murder of Pellegrino Rossi.[13]

---

[12] *Gazzetta di Roma*, November 14th, 1848.
[13] At the trial (which lasted from 1849 to 1852) Colonel Tittoni, C.O. of the Civic Guards, related the following pathetic story. We have not included it in the text because it is merely hearsay, and

It is certain that such a plot was arranged in detail for the opening of Parliament on the 15th. The plotters were all, or therefore cannot be positively asserted against Sterbini; but it seems to be quite a probable description of what occurred among the plotters at the inn. Colonel Tittoni, among other things, deposed as follows:

"The tenth or eleventh of July 1849, Filippo Trentanove, a stone-cutter, presented himself at my house; he was a sergeant in my battalion, a young man whom I had always known as an excellent Civic Guard of good conduct and fond of me because I had done him a good turn while he was out of work. He threw himself on his knees before me, and begged me with tears in his eyes to lend him a small sum because he was compelled to flee from the state. I told him not to be afraid and encouraged him by assuring him that he could have nothing to fear if he had not committed any crime.

"Trentanove then begged me to take him into another and more out-of-the-way room, and when I had taken him to one, he revealed to me, still weeping, that he was an accomplice to the Rossi murder, and told me what had happened in that affair."

Trentanove then told his colonel that on November 14th, 1848, at a late hour, he had been sitting in an inn in the Ripetta, near the Piazza del Popolo, drinking with five others, of whom one was Luigi Brunetti (Ciceruacchio's eldest son) and another called Neri, when Sterbini came up to them and began to "upbraid them for being cowards and carrion, good only for drinking, while Rossi was preparing ropes and fetters for them and their native land, insulting the people with his carabinieri, and preparing to extinguish liberty, and yet no one had the courage to cut his throat" (it is noticeable that there is no mention of Carbonelli's repatriation which is given by Giovagnoli as one of the chief causes for Rossi's assassination).

Luigi Brunetti, hot-headed and inflamed with wine, retorted angrily that they were not carrion and that Sterbini was insulting them wrongfully; that if no one else would cut the minister's throat, he, Brunetti, would do it. Thereupon Sterbini took him at his word, and called them all to follow him into the Piazza del Popolo, and there made them bind themselves with an oath. After which, he planned the whole assassination with them, and instructed each of them to bring some of their comrades, though apparently without letting the comrade know that murder had been planned.

On the following morning Luigi Brunetti was sorry that he had given his oath, but felt bound to stand by it; especially on hearing fresh incitements from Sterbini.

Trentanove ended his story by recommending his family to the care of his colonel, and after receiving twenty scudi, started for London.

Tittoni added: "I believed and still fully believe Trentanove's narrative, which he told me, trembling and weeping, in that solemn nearly all, *Reduci*, "senselessly brutal", says Nino Costa, who knew them intimately and who afterwards saw the blow struck. That evening they worked out a plan in detail; it was agreed that in the crowd on November 15th, one man should hit Rossi to make him turn his head; a second should stab him through the carotid artery; a third should stand by, daga in hand, in case of errors; and a fourth should hold up a cloak to cover the deed. Each of the plotters was to invite some of his *Reduci* friends to be present in uniform—for a "demonstration".

In spite of their small numbers, apparently they did not succeed in keeping the matter secret. Throughout the 14th there were sinister rumours going about Rome. Owing to the extraordinary stupidity of one of the plotters, named Bezzi, the news leaked out to a lawyer called Zanini, and throughout the whole of that afternoon of November 14th and the following morning, Zanini was trying to convey his knowledge to Rossi without being discovered. Had he been even a tiny degree bolder Rossi's life might have been saved. The events ran as follows:

On the 14th Zanini happened to meet Bezzi, an acquaintance of his; and Bezzi inveighed loudly against Rossi's politics and ended by saying that "to-morrow vengeance will be taken on Rossi...it only remains to be seen whether Rossi will die the same death as Prina or whether he will be killed in some other way". On hearing this news, Zanini says that he expressed his horror, and Bezzi left him brusquely.

The whole of that evening and the following morning, I spent in giving information and working for the life of the threatened Minister. I went to Monsignor Corboli Bussi and informed him: I left a few lines for the Duke of Rignano—as I had not been able to see him—but I made the note anonymous. On the following morning I went again to the Duke of Rignano and the Minister of Arms (*sic*), and not being able to find them, I informed one of the heads of the Civic Guard—I think it was Colonel Cleter.[14]

moment when he was leaving his native land, his family and friends. More than once he cursed Pietro Sterbini as the cause of his ruin." *Processo Rossi*, IX, 4223 *et seq.*
    [14] *Processo Rossi*, VIII, 34, 38 *et seq.*

But his anonymous letters had no influence on the Duke of Rignano; and Colonel Cleter apparently took him for an alarmist; and his efforts ended on the 15th in his being actually one of those who were close to the scene of the murder of which he had given warning.

On the 14th the excitement increased in political circles. For this, there were several reasons; firstly, Carbonelli had been sent off to Civita Vecchia that morning to be repatriated; secondly, Rossi's article had appeared in the *Gazzetta*; and thirdly, he was parading several hundred Carabinieri and making them march through the streets. The handing over of Carbonelli is said (by Giovagnoli, I, 266) to have been one of the chief causes of resentment, because in Naples he had been condemned to death for fighting at the barricades on May 15th. But as far as we can trace, he was never handed over to the Neapolitan government; at all events he returned to Rome as soon as the Roman Republic was proclaimed, and he lived to be one of Garibaldi's Thousand.[15] Further, Rossi's article was interpreted as a threat to the Opposition; an insinuation that, if attacked, he would dissolve Parliament, overthrow the Constitution and return to absolutism.[16] And thirdly, there were loud assertions that his parading of the Carabinieri was an attempt to cow the people.

Whatever the truth may be, on the evening of the 14th

[15] Carbonelli only left Rome on the morning of the 14th; whereas Rossi's death had certainly been thought of before then. It was true that Rossi's reviewing of the Carabinieri was intended to warn people that he was in earnest, and thus forestall trouble. And his article in the *Gazzetta* was written with somewhat similar intentions. What he really expected was a renewal of the former shouting demonstrations outside the Council room; or perhaps one in favour of the *Costituente*, or some offensive move against himself, or a march of armed petitioners to the Pope. No one believes that he ever thought of a *coup d'état*.

[16] The witnesses when interrogated as to what people had against Rossi, invariably answered that it was said that he wished to put an end to the Statuto, or "return to the government of the Middle Ages". *V. supra*, p. 414, note 40.

there was great ferment in the clubs, all of which were crowded with members, and, more especially, in the Circolo Popolare. In the last-named, Sterbini and several friends were declaiming against Rossi's expected *coup d'état*. Rusconi gives us their exact words:

"Rossi, the minister in Rome, had only one project in view," they said, "namely to tame democracy and to destroy, or indefinitely postpone, the conception of nationality. Rossi, as minister in Rome, repudiated the league with Piedmont, but courted the alliance with Naples; sneered at the War of Independence; ridiculed the idea of a *Costituente* which had been acclaimed by all Italy and sanctioned at Turin and Florence, and called it an idea conceived by drunken men;[17] restored to Bomba the political refugees, and made the Carabinieri parade up and down the city with great pomp in order to terrorise the people. He maltreated high and low alike, so that Rome seemed stunned, and imagined herself back under the old despotism."

Finally, during one of these discussions at the Circolo Popolare—one which, says Giovagnoli, was no longer a discussion but a tumult—on the proposal of Ciceruacchio it was decided to issue to each of the Circoli an order that, on the following day, all the Civic Guards and all the *Reduci* from Vicenza should appear in their uniforms; in case of alarm each man was to run for his musket and make for the Piazza di Spagna.

On the morning of November 15th the first matter which aroused interest among the citizens was another article in the *Contemporaneo* headed "Intimidazione" and signed by Sterbini, and two other unsigned articles also attacking Rossi, and calling him a disciple of Metternich. The following are a few extracts from them:

Obedient to the words of their master (Metternich) the great diplomats of all Europe have girded themselves for the work, and the floods of citizen blood outpoured, and the many illustrious

[17] This referred to the "inter scyphos" sentence. It will be noticed that when referring to the *Costituenti*, the speaker did not know the difference between them.

cities bombarded, are evidence of a vast conspiracy against the peoples; a conspiracy not in the interests of the monarchies (against which there is accumulating an immense hatred, the precursor of certain ruin), but in favour of a ministerial clique which has associated to itself the great lords of finance, so that they may render mutual service to each other in order to establish their domination by force and by money....

The work of so many centuries, the marvels of human intelligence, would soon become cinders and ruins if society did not arise like one man and put a chain on the barbarism now summoned to their help by the Metternichs and the Guizots.[18] But before this can come to pass, we must expect to see often renewed the scenes of horror and desolation which were witnessed at Naples, at Messina, at Palermo, at Prague, at Berlin, at Frankfort and at Vienna. And this is because there exists a school which follows the same principles, serves the same arts, and has always before its eyes the principles of Metternich. This school unfortunately has found its way also into Italy, having been initiated with sanguinary auspices at Naples; it is now threatening Rome....

Rossi is entrusted with the duty of making in Rome an experiment of the policy of the Metternichs and the Guizots.

The motive for this attack seems to be personal, for he must have known that Rossi had sent his son to fight against the Austrians in Lombardy. It is very difficult not to believe that Sterbini and Canino were mainly actuated by blind rage, because when they had felt themselves at last approaching the summit of authority, an outsider had suddenly been brought in, of a very different calibre from their own, and put over their heads; similarly, later on, when another outsider had been brought in, Sterbini again objected, though in that case it was Garibaldi.

II

Rossi's movements during these last days are fairly well known. He had no definite information of the plot against his life, but he knew that there would be a demonstration of some

[18] The Guizots, of course, meant Rossi, who had been the friend and minister of Guizot.

sort and had taken steps to meet it. He had ordered police-agents to stand in the Piazza outside the Cancelleria palace where the deputies were to meet, and also in the Piazza Sant' Apollinare where the Alto Consiglio (the Upper House) met, so as to discover the ringleaders in any disturbance. But he had arranged that the main body of the Carabinieri should remain in barracks, and thus avoid any collisions between them on the one side, and the people and the Civic Guards on the other. Some patrols of Carabinieri had been sent out into the town, but he had forbidden them and the police-agents to come into the Cancelleria. This mistaken order was given in deference to the expressed wish of the President that the service of the palace should be carried out by the Civic Guard.

Why the President could not allow the police to carry out their ordinary duties it is hard to see! The Civic Guard proved themselves entirely incapable; they evidently did not realise that in such cases the police responsibility is one of life for life.

To arrive at the Chamber of Deputies it was necessary to drive through the great gateway of the Cancelleria palace into the portico and pull up with the heads of the horses looking into the central courtyard; they would stop on the left side of the entrance, and on alighting from his carriage, Rossi would have to walk about twenty yards along the passage to the foot of the wide stone staircase which leads up to the first floor. During this walk he would be entirely unguarded, although he would be making his way through a crowd.

The streets were quiet; but as the morning wore on, the twenty-seven police-agents dotted about the square in front of the Cancelleria began to notice that groups of people were collecting there, and that they seemed to be excited and spoke in loud tones against Rossi. But what first struck alarm into Rosalbi, the chief detective, was the furious threats which he heard uttered in some groups of *Reduci*, of whom quite a number were gradually arriving in their short grey tunics and blue trousers with their *daga* (long straight knife or dagger) at their sides. They said loudly that it was time to get rid of that scoundrel Rossi once for all, and seemed so much in earnest that Rosalbi departed and by 10.30 had reported the matter to the Cavaliere Rufini, who immediately rushed off to the Quirinal to warn Rossi. He found that Rossi, so he tells us, was "greatly perplexed" owing to his having already received some other warning; on hearing Rufini's news, he simply sighed and said: "What can one do?...I must go." He then told Rufini to send for Colonel Calderari, to inform him of the news, and to direct him to distribute his Carabinieri on the Piazza so as to repress any disorders. It seems, however, that he gave no special orders about the inside of the Cancelleria palace which was in charge of the Civic Guard. Rufini returned to the Palazzo Madama,[19] sent for Calderari, and gave him his orders. Calderari replied, "I will go at once" (Vado subito).

Meanwhile Rossi had returned to work. From twelve o'clock onwards he was talking to Professor Montanari, the Minister for Commerce and Art, and they were joined by the Duke of Rignano, who was Minister of Public Works, and by Count Luigi Mastai, the Pope's nephew. When it was nearly 1 p.m. Rossi looked at the clock and said it was time to go to the Chamber of Deputies. Rignano and Mastai took their departure, and Rossi asked Montanari to drive with him: Montanari refused on the plea that he had to take some papers to the Palazzo Borromeo;[20] whereupon Rossi invited Righetti,

---

[19] *Processo Rossi*, IX, 4040 *et seq.* Why did not Rufini drive off and find Calderari at the Palazzo Borromeo before going on home to the Palazzo Madama? Rosalbi's warning reached him at about 10.30 a.m., yet between them, these two officials had not got the Carabinieri out before one o'clock, though the distances were short. But in any case, Calderari would not have sent many Carabinieri to the Cancelleria, because it was in charge of two battalions of Civic Guards.

[20] Giovagnoli evidently believes this to have been an excuse, but it seems hardly fair to assume this without proof; Montanari turned up just after Rossi's death and remained at the Quirinal throughout the fighting next day. *V.* Carte Pentini. Also the letter of the Spanish ambassador.

the Sostituto to the Minister of Finance, to accompany him "if he was not afraid". Thus Rossi drove off to face his ordeal with only one companion.

At the Cancelleria palace there was certainly no lack of armed men. In the square outside there was a composite battalion of Civic Guards drawn up eight hundred strong; moreover there was the guard of the 6th Civic battalion whose H.Q. was close by; and in the Piazza Farnese, not far distant, there was the 7th battalion. All these Civic Guards were at the disposal of the President of the Assembly; and, by the request of the Questors of the Chamber, ten sentries had already been posted at various entrances and exits, but none inside. With all these hundreds of Civic Guards on the spot, they allowed the prime minister to be murdered in broad daylight and made no attempt to arrest anyone!

In the square was now a large crowd, consisting of men and women of every type: nobles, citizens, Civic Guards off duty, shopkeepers and poor people; and about sixty *Reduci* in uniform. Ten Carabinieri and sixteen police-agents were strolling up and down. In all, there were perhaps three thousand people waiting to receive Rossi.

Within the palace, in the central courtyard, the crowd at some points was fairly thick; and in the entrance portico there was a largish contingent of the *Reduci*, in uniform and wearing *dagas*.

At length a sound of raised voices and of shouts in the Piazza was heard by those inside; and a thrill of expectation swept over the assemblage; it was noticed that the *Reduci* seemed to be talking to one another in rapid and excited tones, turning their eyes to the great gateway; some of them moved rapidly from the portico towards the foot of the stairs; two of them who had been on the look-out at the corner of the Via dei Baulari came back almost at a run towards the gateway, saying "Eccolo! Eccolo!" (Here he is).

A few minutes later the carriage arrived at the gateway, stopped, and out of it stepped a man of medium build, dressed in black clothes, whose features were well-known to most of the people. There was a moment's pause and then a cheer: "Viva Sterbini! Viva Sterbini!"

Dr Pietro Sterbini got out, conscious of his popularity and walked away to the left to the foot of the stairs.

After that, ten minutes went by; some of the *Reduci* were heard to mutter: "Sta a vedere che non viene questa carogna. ...Dovrebbe avere paura" (It looks as though this carrion were not coming. He must be afraid).

But at this moment, another carriage drove into the square, and again everyone was on the alert; this time there was no mistake; it was Rossi and Righetti; and neither of them seemed afraid.

As the carriage clattered in under the portico a profound silence fell upon the crowd; but everyone pressed forward towards it and craned his head to see it; Rossi was to alight on the left-hand side; and the *Reduci* with some civilians among them, some fifty to sixty men in all, formed two long lines one on each side of the way which led from the carriage door to the foot of the stairs.

The carriage door opened and Rossi stepped out, a tall figure in a dark blue overcoat. His thin, intellectual face, which contrasted strongly with that of Sterbini who had just gone in, was pale; but he surveyed the crowd as calmly as usual.

The following description may have some interest because it concerns a crime which has become world-famous and it is pieced together from the evidence of the three principal eyewitnesses, namely, the coachman and the footman on the box, and Righetti who pushed his way along close behind his chief. It squares exactly with the account given later by Nino Costa and other eyewitnesses. The presence of so many as fifty *Reduci* and their concerted action show that the scene had been previously organised.[21]

Rossi and Righetti left the carriage and took their way

[21] *Processo Rossi*, I, 137, Righetti's evidence; I, 10–17, Jean Ponadier's (the footman) evidence; I, 158–72, Deck's evidence. Also Nino Costa, p. 53.

between the two lines of *Reduci*; but after they had taken
four or five steps, the lines closed in before them and blocked
their path. Then they opened again to let Rossi walk forward,
but closed again behind him so as to shut out Righetti. Thus
he was now surrounded by a crowd of some fifty men, whose
faces were distorted with rage and hatred. On every side
there were whistles, cat-calls, yells of fury; "Abbasso Rossi!
Abbasso Rossi!" (Down with Rossi!) and here and there a
shout of "Morte a Rossi! Ammazzalo!"

Nevertheless he moved on, showing no signs of hearing
them, except—so it is said—a quiet contemptuous smile,
until he reached the broad stone staircase. Then, just as he
was placing his foot on the second step, he received a light
blow from a young man on his right. This caused him to turn
his head quickly to that side, and at that moment another
young volunteer, about two paces on Rossi's right front,
crossed like a flash to his left, and drove his hunting knife[22]
right through the left side of Rossi's throat. A great fountain
of blood spurted up, for he had made no mistake and the
carotid artery was severed; Rossi fell to the ground; and
immediately all the *Reduci* raised their daggers high so as to
prevent the striker from being identified; one of them,
Mecocetto, threw a cloak over the murderer's shoulders and
they all trooped out.[23]

Rossi was thus left lying on the ground. His French servant
and Righetti, both of whom showed good courage that day,
and several of the crowd remained with him; they carried
him up to the first floor, broke open the door of Cardinal
Gazzoli's rooms and laid Rossi on a sofa. During the next
twenty-five minutes he groaned often, but was unable to speak.
At the end of that time, Cardinal Gazzoli appeared and tried to
give him Absolution, but found that it was already too late.

Who was the murderer of Pellegrino Rossi?

As to the proposed rebellion, there seem to have been
three different centres: the Facciotti plot, perhaps under the

---

[22] Rosi, p. 218.   [23] *Relazione*, p. 12 *et seq.*

influence of the Neapolitans Carbonelli and Bomba; the
Teatro Capranica, to which the Vicentini went; and the
secret clique in the Circolo Popolare. The government afterwards believed that all three united for action, an evening or
two before the murder.

Who was the head of the rising? Undoubtedly Sterbini,
and probably Canino and Ciceruacchio. But there is no
actual proof that they planned murder.

They may have joined forces, for undoubtedly there was a
formidable plot to overthrow the Papal government; but
most of these conspirators had probably no connection with
the actual murder.

But there was within this rising a small detailed plot to kill
Rossi. His murder was carefully and accurately planned
beforehand and very skilfully carried out. The people most
concerned in carrying it out were the *Reduci*; and the actual
knife-thrust was certainly delivered by Luigi Brunetti, eldest
son of Ciceruacchio.[24]

The guiding spirit of the murder plot was very probably
Sterbini; but, as we have said, there is no actual proof of his
guilt.[25]

But it does not much matter who struck the blow; the blow
was merely the first act of a rebellion; the man who struck it
had nothing to gain by his action, and was probably no more
to blame than many others. The rebellion aimed at destroying
the government in Rome, just as Montanelli had overthrown
that in Florence, in order to produce a union of democracies

---

[24] Giovanni Costa, whose memoirs, dictated to his daughter,
Signora Giorgia Guerrazzi Costa, were published by her in 1927,
puts this beyond doubt. He gives a perfectly straightforward eye-
witness' account: Costa, *Quel che vidi e quel che intesi*, pp. 52–4. He
says that the night before, Grandoni had got wind of the plot at the
Osteria and gave him a list of conspirators practically identical with
that of Trentanove. *V. supra*, p. 422 note 13.

Masi, *Il Risorg.* II, 357, quotes Rusconi as saying in his *Memorie
Aneddotiche* that he was told at the time by Galletti in confidence that
Rossi's murderer was Luigi Brunetti.

[25] Sterbini, some years later, when taxed with it by a friend,
indignantly denied the accusation. Tivaroni, *Ital. Cent.* p. 354.

or a united democracy against Austria. And Rossi was murdered mainly in order to prevent his having a chance of speaking in the Assembly.

As far as we can tell now, Sterbini seems to have been the principal mover; under a government which was, after all, constitutional, he had preached violence. One can only hope that his motives were better than his actions.

But lastly we ask: How was it that a man such as Sterbini was even a possible murderer? The answer is obvious. The root cause of all the suffering in Italy was the Austrian domination in the northern provinces. Such a domination was an injustice to seven million inhabitants, and a danger to the rest of the peninsula. It created a situation in which wrong seemed right, in which outbreaks of mad resentment will inevitably occur, again and again, in any nation in the world. If the Austrians had not been there, there would have been no call for war, and no political murders. It was they who created a situation in which even such crimes as this will always take place, because they are justified in the eyes of many patriotic men. This particular crime was justified even by Garibaldi.[26]

Garibaldi was right in perceiving that the holy work of driving out the Austrians could only be accomplished over the bodies of innocent men; and for the next twelve years, scores of tragedies were enacted whose root-cause was simply the Austrian continuation in the provinces of Italy.

[26] Garibaldi justified it (*Autobiography*, I, 297 and III, 83 note), though he would rather have died than do it himself; because he saw in it a step towards driving out the Austrians. Later on, too, he granted a small pension to the mother of Agesilao Milano who tried to stab the king of Naples. And those who have lived through times of revolution succeeding war, know that the wildest crimes can be received with approval even by the most honourable men and women; and that the perpetrators may possibly have the noblest ideals. As a matter of fact there were plenty of other people, on both sides, who justified Rossi's murder; there were public rejoicings over it in some places, and one ardent Sanfedist went so far as to say that it was the work of the Blessed Virgin. Carte Pentini, Busta 84.

Chapter XXIII

THE REVOLUTION IN ROME

I

Even before Pellegrino Rossi had finished bleeding to death, it was already evident that without him the Moderate party was almost helpless. In the Chamber of Deputies, for instance, although it was known that the prime minister was dying in a room close by, yet no attempt was made to adjourn the House, from fear, apparently, that this mark of respect should be resented by the revolutionists. The President, old Avvocato Sturbinetti, ordered the minutes of the last meeting to be read; and presently when the news went round that Rossi was dead, the members looked grave, but there were no voices raised—except a rather significant comment from Prince Canino: "What is all this fuss about? Is it the King of Rome who is dead?" It has been suggested that the President was afraid that the armed crowd might rush the Chamber, and was gaining time for the ladies in the galleries to get away safely. We read, however, that many of the members had gone out at first to see whether they could assist Rossi or his friends, so Sturbinetti was presently able to order a count, and to adjourn the House in a normal way for want of a quorum. Thus they were able to leave without venturing upon any sign of sympathy for their murdered leader. By that time it was a quarter past two.[1]

Later on, a priest, Padre Vaures, who had been a friend of Rossi, came and took the body and hid it in the vaults of San

[1] The chief authorities for this and the following chapter: *eye-witnesses*, or in Rome at the time: Minghetti, Pasolini, Farini (*History* and *Epistolario*), Spada, Gabussi, Nino Costa, the Ambassadors of France, Spain, Holland, Piedmont, and Tuscany; Lützow's correspondent Gutières; and Monsignor Pentini. *Not eye-witnesses*: Tivaroni, Rosi, Masi, Giovagnoli, La Farina, Pelczar, Balleydier.

Lorenzo in Damaso for fear of outrage. In the town, naturally enough, there was a general fear of the violence to come.

Up at the Quirinal, the news was brought to Pius of the assassination of his friend, and at first he seemed, to use Farini's phrase, like "a man thunder-struck". But he acted at once; indeed even Giovagnoli, who seldom speaks in his favour, says that "on this day he showed more energy than his ministers". When the young minister Montanari arrived[2] shortly afterwards, Pius was in "a state of grief", but he immediately appointed Montanari to take Rossi's place at the Ministero dell' Interno, and to carry on the administration for the time being. He then sent for the two men[3] who were now perhaps his best friends, Minghetti and Pasolini; Minghetti had arrived back from the war that morning to take his seat in the Chamber, and was staying with Pasolini.

Certainly it was one of those days upon which a ruler finds out who are his real friends. Farini thus describes the situation at the Quirinal:

On that day there came no fair-weather courtiers to the Papal Court. It had become a house of sorrow and the storm was raging round it; few of these friends were there and fewer still came there.

Giovagnoli says that Pius was abandoned by all his ministers,[4] and certainly the Duke of Rignano had resigned,

[2] It was probably between 2 and 2.15 p.m., but Pius had already received news of the tragedy. Montanari left the Cancelleria before the House rose. The Spanish ambassador says that he himself, when he heard that Rossi was dead, went straight from the Chamber of Deputies to Cardinal Soglia at the Quirinal: "It was from me that he heard of Rossi's death....At that moment the Pope sent for His Eminence and I begged him to tell the Holy Father...." Madrid, Ministerio de Estado, Roma, Sucesos de 1848, No. 46 ,November 18th.

[3] Farini, Spada and Count Pier Desiderio Pasolini all give one to understand that Pius sent for Minghetti and Pasolini at once, namely at about 2.30. But the two latter speak of being sent for "in the evening" and Minghetti says "a late hour". Farini, II, 370; Spada, II, 511; Pasolini, I, 186; Minghetti, II, 125.

[4] The Spanish ambassador says that he saw none at the Quirinal except Cardinal Soglia and Montanari who remained faithful. Madrid, Ministerio de Estado, Roma, Sucesos de 1848, No. 46.

completely overcome by the death of his friend Rossi; but Montanari stood firm, and, for several hours, his colleagues remained in office. Without Rossi, however, they were not fit to cope with the terrible situation.

At the Quirinal, now that the leader was gone, there was no commanding brain left. What was required was a man who could put life and loyalty into the Civic Guards and spirit into the Carabinieri, and strike right and left. Prompt action was necessary at any cost, to stem the revolution before it gained strength. But by now, even for Rossi, this would have been a very difficult task.

In fact, the reign of law was coming to an end and the reign of physical force and violence had already begun; the revolution was advancing and each hour brought fresh proof to Pius that for his defence he had no reliable officers and very few reliable men. But his first care was to try to reconstitute the ministry in order to keep the machinery of state working.

Evidently it took Montanari about half an hour to install himself in Rossi's office; for one thing, he was obliged, with Pius' leave, to break open the desk before he could collect the papers that he wanted,[5] and start work. He began by making some enquiries as to the armed forces. By about three o'clock he was interviewing Colonel Calderari, O.C. of the Carabinieri, and directed him to keep his men in barracks (so as to avoid fraternising with the revolution). This was a matter of great importance, the more so because, owing to Rignano's resignation, the Civic Guards were without a C.O. and the soldiers of the line were not considered reliable. At Ave Maria (about 4.45) Calderari returned to report that his order had been carried out, but as there was a cabinet council in progress he was directed to come back two hours later.[6]

[5] *Processo Rossi*, XI, 5235–6, Montanari's evidence. He says that Monsignor Pentini went through the papers with him. *V.* also Rome, Reg. Ist. Carte Pentini, Busta 21, fasc. 2.

[6] *Ibid.* Also Calderari, *Il 15 e 16 Novembre* 1848; Carte Pentini, Busta 20, fasc. 24.

When he finally returned, he reported that his men had fraternised with the people, but that it was all over and order was restored:[7] he admitted that this was a very serious piece of insubordination, but thought that perhaps it was preferable to a collision with the people. From this last statement it was evident that neither he nor his Carabinieri were to be trusted; and after a personal interview with him, Pius remained quite convinced of that fact.[8] Captain Lentulus, the Swiss officer wounded at Vicenza and now in command of all the troops, said that he would keep order but that he would not open fire on the crowd.[9]

Meanwhile a cabinet meeting[10] was in full progress in Monsignor Pentini's room; but when the ministers discovered that neither the Carabinieri nor the soldiers were to be relied on, they decided to resign. By midnight there was no longer any cabinet in existence.[11]

Thus matters were going very badly indeed. Minghetti and Pasolini had been sent for, and it is strange to think that out of all Pius' court, these two quite young men should have represented his best hope in this crisis; Pasolini, the sharer of his first plans, and Minghetti fresh back from the war. As soon as they arrived at the Quirinal, Pius sent for Minghetti,[12] who has left us the following account of the interview:

I found him sad and thoughtful, but calm. That mystic sentiment which always dominated him made him even then resigned to the Will of God. He spoke to me in a very general manner about the necessity of forming a ministry, but without specially calling on me to do so; to me it would have seemed an act of cowardice to refuse at that moment to enter the government; but there were two points which I could not conceal from him.

[7] Giovagnoli, II, 315–17.   [8] *Processo Rossi*, XI, 5240, Montanari.
[9] Carte Pentini, Busta 20, fasc. 24.
[10] Pettinaro, Pentini Docs., fasc. 62.
[11] *Processo Rossi*, XI, 5240, Montanari's evidence. Carte Pentini, Busta 20, fasc. 29.
[12] Minghetti, II, 125. It does not seem that Pasolini saw Pius that evening, though his own Memoirs would rather lead one to suppose so.

And thereupon Minghetti told Pius that, in his opinion, any new ministry would have to be frankly liberal and national (which meant that it would be pledged to war), and secondly, that having only arrived in Rome that day, he himself required a night to talk over matters with his friends, and therefore asked leave to be allowed to return at 10 a.m. the following morning. On the way home, Pasolini said to Minghetti that although they two might make some attempt and some sacrifice as a proof of good will to the Pope and to their country, it was impossible to suppose that they would achieve any success. And we may add, after a long night of hard thinking, they decided that they could make no other reply to Pius. But evidently he had rather anticipated this view.

Thus on the evening of the 15th, Rome was "a ship without a rudder" (Spada). There was no authority; the mob was free. But into this vacuum there was rapidly rushing a new power, namely that of the Circolo Popolare, and its President Sterbini.

While the Quirinal had been discovering its weak points, the Circolo Popolare had been acting.[13] Their men had been going all over the town inviting the Civic Guards[14] to fraternise with them. That evening they held a meeting of delegates from other Circoli, and had thousands of bills printed announcing an immense popular demonstration for the following morning, November 16th. The people were to march to the Quirinal and obtain Pius' agreement to four fundamental principles:

1. The promulgation of Italian nationality.

2. Convocation of the *Costituente* and putting into effect of the Federal Act.

---

[13] The Dutch minister was struck by the promptitude of their action. Rome Reg. Ist. Ministre des Pays-Bas. November 24th, 1848.

[14] Their C.O. had resigned. Colonel Gallieno was named as his successor, but at first he refused the appointment; on the following morning he accepted it. Colonel Lentulus, as we have said, was appointed to command the Line. Spada, II, 511; Farini, II, 371.

3. Carrying out of the deliberations of the Council of Deputies as to the war of independence.

4. Entire adoption of Mamiani's programme of June.[15]

And it was claimed by the Circoli in the name of the people that the following ministers should be appointed to carry out the above programme: Count Terenzio Mamiani, Count Pompeo di Campello, Doctor Sterbini, Doctor Fusconi and the two lawyers Lunati and Sereni, all deputies.

These four principles might be justifiable from a twentieth-century point of view, but undoubtedly they meant depriving Pius of all power to protect the temporal interests of the Church; and consequently he would be compelled to resist them.

As to the names suggested for the new ministry, the chief popular aim was to get Sterbini appointed because he was the president of the Circolo Popolare. Of course it was not generally known that most probably he had been the principal organiser of Rossi's assassination, but still it seems a

---

[15] Spada, II, 519; Pentini, Busta 20, fasc. 33, contains one of the original proclamations. The above-quoted were their four fundamental principles for presentation on the following morning. About them we may say that the first was very indefinite; the second was a curious mixture between the two rival schemes, Montanelli's democratic *Costituente* and Gioberti's Federal *Costituente*. Apparently it meant that a *Costituente* (constituent assembly) on Montanelli's model was to draw up a federal scheme on Gioberti's plan—a mixture of contradictory principles. Gabussi, the republican historian, remarks that many people did not understand the difference between the two *Costituente* schemes. But this clause as it stands is a success for the Piedmontese scheme, which had, as we remember, been proposed during Gioberti's congress at Turin by Mamiani himself, and was soon to be proposed by him in Rome. The third fundamental principle meant war with Austria, and the fourth, namely Mamiani's programme of June 7th, meant relegating the Pope to the spiritual sphere; "He lives in the serene peace of the dogmas, dispenses to the world the Word of God, prays, blesses and pardons." Cf. chap. XVIII.

A later and good opinion on the situation is that of Rosi (p. 218); he says that "the plans of the extreme Liberals and the *Costituente* signified that they wanted to destroy the Temporal Power".

strange turn of fate whereby a man who probably organised murder at 1.30, is proposed for a cabinet minister before the day is out.

The next step of the Circolo Popolare was to send some members to the Carabinieri barracks to invite the men there to come out and fraternise with them in the town. For the time being, the C.O. of the Carabinieri took a middle course and merely allowed seven or eight men to go.

Night was now falling and the mob would soon be free. With the darkness a good many loathsome reptiles were coming out into the streets. The men of the Carabinieri quickly joined themselves on to the procession of members of the Circolo Popolare and revolutionists, about a hundred strong, who were now marching up the Corso under a tri-colour banner and cheering wildly. They were rejoicing like men who had won a victory.[16] As they progressed they were joined by others singing feast-day songs and carrying torches and loudly applauding the murderers of Rossi. At their head marched some of the *Reduci*, singing the couplet " Benedetta quella mano, che il Rossi pugnalò " (Blessed be the hand that stabbed Rossi). From time to time they raised the murderer shoulder-high with shouts of " Viva Bruto Secondo! " " Brutus the Second forever! " But here a curious point arises, which seems to show that there was some method in their madness. None of the men whom they raised on their shoulders was the actual striker of the blow—Luigi Brunetti. He was not with them.

At about half-past one that night, they went down to the house of Rossi's widow near the Palazzo Doria.

These hours of darkness are vividly described by Count Pier Desiderio Pasolini:

This clamorous crowd kept increasing as it went, and late that night it went off, torch in hand, until it came beneath the windows of the truly unfortunate widow of Count Rossi, where by way of

---

[16] Madrid, Ministerio de Estado, Roma, Sucesos de 1848, No. 46.

a supreme insult and horrible harrowing of all human feelings it intoned the psalm Miserere. . . .

I remember that more than twenty years afterwards my mother could not recall without trembling and turning pale the horrors of that night, and the terrible indignation and anguish that she had felt.[17]

This scene is one that has several times been described in English and might well be curtailed but for the horrifying effect which it had upon all those in Rome, and the influence which such a remembrance must have exerted on Pius when he abandoned Liberalism.

No doubt these blackguards were carrying out the terrorism of Sterbini and the Roman agitators; and in common fairness to Rome one must remember that they were only an infinitesimal part of the population, about a hundred and fifty men in a town of a hundred and twenty thousand. The dregs of the city had been stirred up, and as usual the worst refuse was rising to the surface. And there is one strong point that should be made, even in their favour; namely, that no pillaging nor assaults took place. Although all authority had vanished, and any imaginable crime might have gone unpunished, nevertheless throughout all that and the following nights there were no acts of plundering and no physical violence. None of the rich palaces were touched. In such circumstances this is really a very remarkable record, and seems to prove that the motives even of these ruffians were genuinely political and not personal.

II

When morning broke on November 16th Pius had already been informed that the crowds proposed to march up to the Quirinal and claim the four popular principles already stated,

[17] Pasolini, 1, 187; Nino Costa, p. 54. Bargagli and M. Gutières de Estrada, a correspondent of Lützow, say that the crowd shouted "Light up the window". Florence Arch. Esteri, Busta 2446, November 16th, and Vienna Arch. Rome, 1848, *Verschiedene Varia*.

and he had decided to forestall their demonstration. He sent out messages to the President and Vice-Presidents of both Houses to be with him at 7.45 a.m. and to bring some of the more influential representatives with them. Minghetti was included in these invitations, but he did not arrive until ten o'clock according to his original arrangement.[18] Pasolini was one of the Vice-Presidents.

Meanwhile Colonel Lentulus, who was acting Minister of War in Zucchi's absence,[19] reported that the leaders of the people were asking his officers to take part in the demonstration "in favour of the people and of the Italian *Costituente*",[20] assuring them that it was to be of a purely peaceful and reverential character. Pius sent for Lentulus to ask for his advice; but Lentulus' advice, Farini says, was merely an expression of doubts; he said that he was new to Rome, and very new to his present post; that he did not yet know the spirit of the Italians, but that he knew the bonds of discipline were weak if not broken. He ended by saying that it would perhaps be as well to let the officers mix with the people in order to prevent worse evils. Farini says that he himself "does not know what order was given, probably none", but that the troops certainly did mingle with the people. He regards this as a fatal lack of decision on the part of the government. But as a matter of fact, outside every barracks the troops had already fraternised with the people that morning.

Thus by about 10 a.m. the Papal Court was brought face to face with the fact that it no longer had any defence against the revolution. The mob would soon be at the gates. At that moment the people were down in the Piazza del Popolo preparing a giant demonstration for the afternoon; as matters

[18] Minghetti, II, 125, 126 for his account.
[19] Zucchi had been sent for the day before on the suggestion of the Abbé Rosmini. Farini, II, 372 and 375–6.
[20] The *Costituente italiana* meant Montanelli's *Costituente*; and this is evidently what the people expected to get, not Gioberti's, which they were afterwards given.

turned out, they did not arrive until about three o'clock. But meanwhile the Quirinal had no defenders except about eight or ten of the Noble Guard on duty, a dozen Carabinieri and the company of Swiss: about 100 armed men in all.[21]

Pius himself did not mean to accept the four demands of the people. Throughout all that day he maintained his refusal with great persistence, and with astonishing indifference to the howls and shots from outside. In fact, it was fortunate for everyone that finally Monsignor Pentini succeeded in finding a formula which Pius could accept without loss of dignity. In his hour of trial, only two of the cardinals had remained with him, namely Soglia and Antonelli; hence, perhaps, the confidence which Pius always retained in the loyalty of Antonelli.

Before long the Presidents and Vice-Presidents arrived; Monsignor Muzzarelli and Count Pasolini for the Alto Consiglio and the Avvocato Sturbinetti and Doctor Fusconi for the Chamber of Deputies; and with them were various other members such as Sterbini, Torre and Guiccioli, who were presently joined by Minghetti. Very soon it was announced that the Pope would receive the four Presidents and Vice-Presidents, and this interview represents the final crisis in the whole history of the Liberal movement of Pius IX. We have three accounts of it; those of our old friend Pasolini, of Fusconi a middle-aged doctor, and an account written by the republican historian Gabussi which perhaps represents the version of the old lawyer Sturbinetti.[22] As far as we

[21] Pentini says 140 men in all but only 86 muskets. He evidently counted clerks and others. The above number is given by Farini, II, 378.

[22] Pasolini's account gives the most reliable summary of the situation. It was written to Minghetti in 1850 (Pasolini, I, 189). Fusconi has left two accounts, one given in evidence at the trial of the murderers of Rossi (*Processo Rossi, Deposizione Fusconi*) which is the best. He wrote another account of it in 1886 to Pasolini (Pasolini, I, 217), but this one speaks only of his own doings, and is evidently meant for posterity. The third account upon which we rely is that of Gabussi because we cannot help thinking that it was

know, Muzzarelli, the literary-political Monsignore with rather extreme views, has left us no record of the scene.

Pius, who was "visibly agitated" according to Fusconi, or in Gabussi's words "disturbed and sad", began at once to speak about Rossi.

I had found a man who not only could discover and point out to me the needs of the state—but could also indicate the remedies —and this man whom I had found, they have assassinated.

Then Monsignor Muzzarelli began to say to the Pope that Rossi was "a man rather badly thought of. . . that in fact his assassination need not occasion such distress to His Holiness. . . ." Full of indignation at this speech, Pius turned towards Muzzarelli. "What!" he exclaimed, "a Monsignore, dressed in that colour, a man whom I have placed at the head of the Superior Council, comes to me and makes an apologia for an assassination like that!"

Sturbinetti had already spoken in the same strain, and had mentioned the fact that he had heard two cab-drivers the day before suggesting that they should carry Rossi's body out to the Porta Leone where the carcasses of animals were buried.[23] These remarks aroused such indignation in Pius that Pasolini was obliged to interrupt the conversation by urging that at the moment the future was of more importance than the past.

inspired by Sturbinetti to whom Gabussi was apparently much attached. It makes Sturbinetti the leading figure and omits his *faux pas* about the cab-drivers. It seems fairly likely that the sayings of Pius recorded by Gabussi are accurate, because they are the very reverse of what a republican historian would have invented for him at a time when a republican crowd was at his gates. And some of his points are confirmed elsewhere. Gabussi, II, 219.

[23] Both Pasolini, and Fusconi whose letter he prints, speak of this very tactless allusion on the part of the ordinarily kindly old lawyer; but Fusconi puts it at the very end of the interview, and says that Pius' face was so much convulsed with anger that he, Fusconi, suggested ending the interview because he feared that the Pope would have an apoplectic fit. He adds that Pius sent him a message of thanks next day for having "saved him from so serious a danger". This all seems to us an exaggeration.

Pius then told them that he was extremely anxious to prevent the demonstration taking place, because he considered it simply an ovation to assassination. To which Muzzarelli replied that there were only two ways of preventing it, either by force, or by appointing a ministry according to the people's wishes; and that force was non-existent—a statement which came as a disappointment to Pius,[24] who had hoped that some of the Civic Guard would have stood by him from personal attachment if from no other motive. This answer of Muzzarelli led to discussion over the appointment of a new ministry, and soon revealed the fact that no one wanted the task of forming it. The two representatives of the Lower House were invited to do so, but Fusconi refused, and then Sturbinetti also refused.[25] It must have become evident to Pius that he would have to face the mob without a ministry even on paper. He turned to them and said, apparently with some scorn:[26]

"Do you know the next thing to be done, gentlemen? I shall give up the whole thing and go away."

Whereupon Muzzarelli replied: "Oh! but Your Holiness will not do a thing which will bring ruin on your people."

And Sturbinetti, adding "some grave and noble words", ended his phrases by saying: "There lies upon the conscience of Your Holiness the peace of so many families which have a right to government and cannot be thrown amid the horror of anarchy."

The face of the Pope lit up, and he answered in a passionate voice: "In that case, We will stay, and await the thunders from Heaven."[27]

[24] This point, recorded by Gabussi, is confirmed by Spada.
[25] The words in the text are all reported by Pasolini and Fusconi.
[26] This exchange is reported only by Gabussi, p. 219.
[27] This was his decision. The words are reported by a republican writer who was certainly not prejudiced in his favour, and they give the reason for his remaining at the Quirinal when others urged him to seek safety elsewhere. It seems strange that this scene has not won more sympathy for his memory.

At this moment, however, Pius received an unexpected proof of support which must have come to him as a great relief and encouragement, because it proved that, although his small Italian state had turned against him in order to be free from international ties, yet, as the guardian of the Holy See, his action was considered right, and was justified in the eyes of the whole Catholic world. During that morning he was waited on by the ambassadors or ministers of all the foreign embassies in Rome.[28]

The first to arrive was Count Martinez de la Rosa, the Spanish Ambassador;[29] after him the Duc d'Harcourt (for France), and then the lesser Catholic powers. These men came, not only to lend him their moral support, but to remain in the Quirinal and risk their lives at his side if need arose.

[28] Carte Pentini, Busta 20, Fasc. 29. *V.* the despatches of the Spanish, French and Dutch Ambassadors; also that of the Tuscan minister, who was very much on the watch, though not himself in the Quirinal until the following morning.

[29] "I had realised for some time that our presence might be a support to the Pope who was surrounded by very weak advisers, and that at any rate it would be extremely useful to him to have such authoritative witnesses of anything that might occur." Madrid, Ministerio de Estado, Roma, Sucesos de 1848. We were fortunate in being in Madrid just before the Civil War and finding a long and interesting despatch, now perhaps destroyed, from the Spanish Ambassador describing minutely the events of this day.

Chapter XXIV

NOVEMBER 16TH. THE END OF THE LIBERAL PAPACY

I

The following is Farini's description of the Papal Court during these long-drawn-out hours of November 16th, 1848. He himself was in the Quirinal and his account is fairly well confirmed by Pentini, by Galletti and others; but the most impartial descriptions are probably those of the foreign ambassadors.[1]

The Court was in a state of anxiety and it had very good reason for being so. There were some courtiers trembling in their pulse and veins; others stood there motionless and dumb; some shuddered; some ran up and down the palace. Bold counsels were met by desperate answers and despairing sighs. There were some who said—and I myself heard them—let the rioters rage as they like; it is all the better, it will be over sooner. Some commended themselves to God, others invoked Providence. Some exhibited many of the Christian virtues, but of the governing virtues none whatsoever; their minds were resigned, but not strong. And there were also some who tried to deserve the help of God by showing that they themselves were helpful and energetic; they proposed to send for the Carabinieri at once and persuade the Pope's brother to take command of them; and said that the palace ought immediately to be put in a state of defence, or else that we ought to move quickly to the Vatican, or outside Rome to Castel Gandolfo, or Civitavecchia; any plan was better than staying there purposeless and awaiting the rebels.

When the Presidents and Vice-Presidents rejoined the other representatives, they began at once to consider the selection of a new prime minister. After some discussion, they all agreed to recommend Galletti to Pius.[2]

[1] Farini, II, 376; Carte Pentini, Busta 20, Fasc. 27; Vienna Arch. Rome, 1848. *Verschiedene Varia*, Gutières to Lützow; Galletti, *Memorie*, p. 21.   [2] Minghetti, II, 126; Pasolini, I, 190.

Galletti, as will be remembered, was a Bolognese lawyer, who at the time of Pius' accession had been undergoing a life-sentence for rebellion and had been pardoned under the Amnesty. After his release, he had obtained an interview with the Pope and had thanked him with expressions of the most profound gratitude. Since then he had returned to politics, and had been very successful. Minghetti has called him a windbag, but he was a captivating talker with a charming smile, very popular, and most deservedly respected for his early sufferings. He was Chief of Police under Mamiani and Fabbri. His opinions were still of the extreme type, but it was believed, especially by Minghetti, that the bond of gratitude would ensure his fidelity to Pius. Galletti had not been one of the five men chosen by the Circolo Popolare, but there was no doubt that they would accept him with joy. In short, he seemed to be the best man available at that moment.

Pius knew of course that Galletti was an extremist, but perhaps he relied on the same hope as Minghetti, for he agreed at once to send for him; and Minghetti and Pasolini dashed off at once in a carriage to get him. They were successful; Galletti came up post-haste to the Quirinal; but, he tells us, on his arrival he was rather surprised to find that the Pope was in no great hurry to see him. Pius, however, received him in a friendly way and invited him to form a ministry; but, as this would take time, invited him to return that evening.[3]

By this time it was nearly two o'clock,[4] and the crowd had actually started on its march from the Piazza del Popolo to the Quirinal. It was gathering strength and enthusiasm as it went. And soon the news was brought to the Papal Court by a dragoon, who arrived scared and breathless, to warn them of the approaching danger.

[3] Galletti, *Memorie*.
[4] Harcourt, Despatch of November 17th, 1848: Paris Aff. Etr. Rome, 1848.

By an odd chance, however, on its way the crowd met Galletti; he was just returning from his interview with Pius, so they greeted him with loud cheers. Here was the very man whom they wanted. They told him at once that he must come with them and lay their demands before the Pope. Galletti, having only just left Pius, felt himself in an awkward position and made various efforts to temporise.[5] He mounted on the terrace of Villa Colonna and addressed the people below; but the people meant to achieve results and to get them then and there. A great roar went up from the crowd. "Subito dal Papa", they shouted, "e risposte a tutto": "Straight to the Pope and get answers to everything", and Galletti saw that he must go.

When he arrived back at the Quirinal, the gates were closed and, as usual, the two Swiss sentries were outside the great entrance armed with their long halberds. The leaders of the crowd precipitated themselves on the two young Switzers and a struggle ensued, in which one of them lost his halberd and the other broke its shaft—no doubt over an assailant—and they both managed to get back into the palace. Inside the building there were a hundred men, but only eighty-six muskets.[6]

At the moment of Galletti's entry Pius was walking up and down in the lofty rooms. He was almost entirely deserted except by the foreign ambassadors and representatives. That is a point which is commented on not only by Farini and Pentini, but by all the diplomatists alike. The Spaniard speaks of Pius being "abandoned by nearly all his subjects for several hours"; D'Harcourt said: "Pas un seul...n'a eu le courage de venir offrir ses services au Pape dans cette triste con-

---

[5] He says that he, with a deputation of the crowd (Canino, Sterbini and Mariani) re-entered the Quirinal, but came out without seeing the Pope; and, to satisfy the crowd, told them that he [Galletti] had been asked to form a ministry, which was true. But the crowd refused to be put off without an answer to their questions. Galletti, p. 20.

[6] Pettinaro, Doc. 68.

joncture": and the Dutch minister, who was always very conservative, reported that: "Jamais un souverain...ne s'est vu si lâchement et aussi complètement abandonné."[7]

Pius must have realised that in Italy there were now very few friends for a Liberal Pope. What the agitators had wanted ever since the Allocution, was a sovereign who would reign but not rule; what the crowd now wanted was virtually a republic with a Pope who would merely pray and bless. In his view, such a status would be equivalent to relegating him to the position of the Patriarch of Constantinople. Evidently he felt that he was defending his very last tenable position as guardian of the Church. The final crisis had arrived. According to Galletti he was very pale and his eyes wandered. From time to time he muttered: "No; martyrdom is better— God has no thunders left."[8]

In spite of Galletti's utmost efforts, Pius, who became extremely indignant,[9] refused to agree to the demands of the demonstrators, and as time went by, the impatient crowd on the piazza could be heard in tumult, howling so as to reach his ears: "A democratic ministry or a republic!" Colonel Calderari arrived in the square with his Carabinieri, and the Ambassadors hoped to hail this police-officer as a defender, but he let it be known at once that he was "on the side of the people". Presently some of the crowd, unable to attack the great gate, made a dash at the side entrance and succeeded in setting fire to a door near the Quattro Fontane. This compelled the Swiss to fire a few shots at them and drive them

[7] Madrid, Ministerio de Estado, Roma, Sucesos de 1848, *loc. cit.*; Paris Aff. Etr. Rome, 1848, *loc. cit.*; Rome Reg. Ist. Ministre des Pays-Bas, *loc. cit.*

[8] Galletti, *Memorie*, quoted by Tivaroni, *Ital. Cent.* p. 351. Galletti's account, like most others, aims at proving himself to have been the only cool man in the place. In this connection, the Ambassadors' reports speak of the "sangfroid et fermeté" of Pius (France); of his "calme et sérénité la plus parfaite" (Gutières to Vienna); "never for a moment lost his accustomed serenity" (Spain); the Piedmontese and Tuscan Ambassadors were not there.

[9] Galletti, *ibid.* p. 22.

back, so that the flames could be extinguished by the firemen. The sound of these shots was greeted with fury in the piazza. In fact the fray was on the verge of beginning, when Galletti suddenly appeared in the little turret on the right of the great gate—the same from which Pius had so often blessed the people—and shouted to the thousands below that nothing would be conceded under pressure of violence. By adopting this wording, he had rather softened the direct refusal sent out by Pius, but nevertheless he was greeted by a "horrible" shout of "All' armi!" (To arms!) from the whole crowd. It was followed by cries for vengeance, as they all dashed off to get their weapons, and the news went throughout Rome that the Swiss guards were firing on the people.

To obtain an impartial account of what next happened, perhaps out of all the historians it is best to select the republican Gabussi, who tells us that he was a spectator; it agrees well with those of Mgr. Pentini, and the foreign ambassadors who were inside the Palace:

Within less than an hour, that broad piazza of the Quirinal was filled with armed men; for, besides the great numbers of the Civic Guards and of the numerous individuals who possessed either a gun, a pistol or a sabre, there were also two Line regiments, Galletti's legion, the University battalion, and the Carabinieri, of whom there were rather less than a hundred. The latter, however, were regarded with suspicion, as was also their commander Calderari, who—though one cannot exactly say why—received a wound in the face from some unknown hand. The armed men numbered at least six thousand. When the Swiss saw the whirlwind approaching, they closed the little side door which had hitherto been left open beside the great gate; some of them went up to the turret from which Galletti had spoken to the people, and some took post in the windows in the front and on the sides of the Palace. And then—either because they hoped to disperse the multitude with a few musket shots, or because they wanted to anticipate rather than await the attack, or because they had hopes of help from outside as soon as the signal for fighting was given, perhaps from a portion of the Roman people or from the Carabinieri, or possibly because there were among them a few rash men who obeyed their own instinct or a reckless order—the fact remains that some shots were fired upon the crowd and a few people were hit.[10]

Gabussi thus gives a goodly list of possible reasons for the action of the Swiss; but he omits the most probable master-motive with both officers and men: namely, that they were tired of being howled at, and that their blood was up.[11] This is very commonly the second act of these dramas; and on this occasion one can scarcely blame the Swiss for firing, as the crowd was some thousands strong, mainly consisting of drilled men supplied with good firearms.

"This", he continued, "was the signal for the fray. Because then the musket-firing began from the Piazza, and off the base of the two colossal statues of Castor and Pollux—those which are said to be by Phidias and Praxiteles and are situated in front of the Palace a little to the left of the great gate. And the Swiss answered back from the inside so that several soldiers and some of the people were wounded, and two of them, apparently, were killed."[12]

Within the palace, says Farini, there was uncertainty and resignation. Some few were advising their sovereign to resist, and many were advising him to give in; the diplomatists offered no advice. But the ambassadors and ministers of nine nations[13] were beside him, and showed a fine indifference to danger throughout the day. Their names were: the Duc d'Harcourt for France, Señor Martinez de la Rosa for Spain,

[10] Gabussi, II, 224 *et seq.* Carte Pentini, and the Ambassadors' reports already cited.

[11] Since writing the above we have found that this is the motive given by the Spanish Ambassador. About Pius he said: "At the first shot the whole Corps Diplomatique went up to the side of the Pope who never for a moment lost his accustomed serenity; only showing himself careful and solicitous for the lives of others."

[12] Gabussi, *Ibid.* Carte Pentini, also the Ambassadors' reports.

[13] Spada, II, 523, says ten, but he included Pareto, the Piedmontese Ambassador. Pareto reported to Turin that he had been at the Quirinal in the morning but left it at 1.30, and afterward could not get back owing to the crowd. Turin Arch. Lettere Ministri, Roma, 1848, despatch of November 17th. Perhaps the same reason accounted for Bargagli's absence.

Count Spaur for Bavaria, Baron Migneis Venda da Cruz for Portugal, Count Buteniew for Russia, Count Liederkerke for Holland, Cavalier de Figueiredo for Brazil, Meester de Ravenstein for Belgium, and Baron Kanitz und Dallwitz for Prussia. Two others were absent from Rome, namely, the ambassadors of Austria and Naples; and Bargagli (Tuscany) was not in the Quirinal that afternoon, but he spent the next morning with Pius. The presence of these diplomats at this moment was extremely important. They spread true versions of the situation all over Europe, and these are still in existence; the Bavarian Ambassador shortly afterwards helped Pius to make his way to Gaeta; and (only three days later) the government of the French Republic voted an expedition to reinstate him.

By this time the firing was becoming more serious; marksmen were posted on the campanile (church tower) of San Carlo and on other points of vantage so as to "snipe" the defenders; three bullets, it is said, penetrated to Pius' anteroom, and at about three o'clock Monsignor Palma, a bishop acting as one of the Pontifical secretaries, fell dead, shot through the head beside his own window.

On this winter evening the dusk was coming upon them. It was quite obvious, of course, that a permanent defence was out of the question, so Pius decided to send again for Galletti, who was now regarded as the leader of the insurgents, and see whether they could arrange for an honourable compromise. Meanwhile at about 6 p.m. the crowd had brought a field-gun up into the square—the gun known as S. Pietro, the gift of Count Carlo Torlonia to the Civic Guard—and placing it under cover of the Colossi began to sight it at the great gate. It was evident that one single shot from this gun would shatter the door, and that a breach would be made; the crowd could break in, overpower the Swiss, knock Antonelli on the head, and work their will on the others.[14]

[14] *V.* Nino Costa, p. 51. Pius never forgot the devotion of Antonelli on this occasion. In a letter of November 26th to Count

THE END OF THE LIBERAL PAPACY

It was at this moment that old Captain Mayer de Schauensee, commanding officer of the Swiss, presented himself before Pius, and offered in his own name and that of his men to defend him to the death.[15] The ambassadors were profoundly touched.

Pius, however, was naturally unwilling to call upon his guards for so useless a sacrifice; moreover, says Farini, most of the courtiers were *convulsi* and "were wearying both God and the Pope with prayers that he would give in".

Before receiving Galletti, the Pope had the Corps Diplomatique summoned, and made his formal protest to all Europe.

"Seated before us at his table", says the Spanish Ambassador, "he spoke to us in a grave and solemn tone the following words: 'They require that I agree to these Ministers', and he read us their names; 'they demand that I accept a programme which is against my conscience. If they carry their violence to such a point that I am obliged to yield, I declare to you that I do so against my will, and I protest before you all against the force which is being used towards me; and I wish to say that do what they will, I do not consent!'"[16]

The ambassadors replied by a few words, formally accepting the Pope's protest, and then retired. This protest to the European powers was destined before many weeks were past to bear its fruit.

Lützow, M. Gutières de Estrada said: "Le Cardinal Antonelli est celui qui s'est montré le plus dévoué au Pape, en restant auprès de lui, et malgré les instances les plus pressantes, jusqu'au dernier moment. Il faisait tout ce qu'il pouvait pour inspirer ou pour soutenir la fermeté du Saint Père." Vienna Arch. Rome, 1848, *Verschiedene Varia*. Gutières de Estrada was apparently a friend of Lützow and wrote him an account of these events.

[15] The Dutch minister wrote as follows about this episode: "Lorsque ce vieux soldat, l'épée nue, et avec une contenance intrépide, est venu offrir au Pape de mourir, lui et les siens, à ses pieds, tous les regards se sont tournés vers lui, et il a pu lire dans leurs expressions, combien cette héroïque proposition le plaçait haut dans l'estime de tous ceux qui l'entendaient faire." Rome Reg. Ist. Ministre des Pays-Bas, despatch of November 17th, 1848. *V.* also Farini, II, 380.　　　　　[16] Madrid Ministerio, *loc. cit.*

At about eight o'clock, Pius received Galletti; and for over half an hour remained in close discussion; but finally a formula was produced by the help of Monsignor Pentini. Pius was to accept the new ministers, but as to the four points demanded by the crowd, he only agreed that those questions should be discussed in the Chambers. By this condition he had succeeded at all events in postponing the matter.

Having thus obtained the terms stated, Galletti was soon addressing the crowd from the very same terrace of the Villa Colonna on which he had made his speech before the fighting began. He was able to tell them that His Holiness had agreed to the following cabinet: Mamiani, Galletti, Sereni, Sterbini, Campello, Lunati, and, as Pius had insisted on retaining one Churchman to be President, the post was to be offered to the Abbé Rosmini.[17] These included all the men whose appointment had been demanded by the crowd, and their names were taken as a guarantee that war would be declared and a constituent assembly called; consequently the insurgents were satisfied. As to the other great question at issue, the *Costituente*, Galletti announced that the organisation of a Constituent Assembly should be left to Parliament. The news was greeted with great enthusiasm by the crowd, who fired a volley into the air and then disappeared, regarding their victory as complete.

II

In one sense their victory certainly was complete, namely that they were now in a position to overthrow the Statuto and compel the Pope to carry out any measures planned by the democratic ministers whom they had selected. They had in fact for the moment destroyed the Temporal Power of the

---

[17] As a matter of fact the Abbé refused the post on the following morning and his place was taken by Monsignor Muzzarelli. Mamiani was in Genoa and he refused at first, but afterwards took office for a short time. *V*. Farini, *Epistolario*, II, 704.

Holy See; and on the following day they were roused to a recrudescence of fury at the sight of the Swiss Guards, and insisted on their being disarmed and sent away. In place of these traditional defenders of the Pope's person, various batches of Civic Guards were installed all over the Quirinal, so that, for good or ill, Pius must have felt that he was now entirely in the hands of the revolution.

But in another sense the republicans had achieved very little success. They had started their movement with the intention of establishing four fundamental principles, and in that respect they could hardly claim to have made much progress. When the new cabinet under Muzzarelli's presidency issued its programme, that document was found to be, in the words of the republican Gabussi, "somewhat weak and irresolute, as if the ministers themselves knew that they must not promise things which they did not believe they would be able to perform".[18]

It will be remembered that the four fundamental principles claimed by the crowd had been the following:

(1) The promulgation of Italian nationality. This the ministers undertook to carry out, adding, however, that Pius had long ago proclaimed it in his letter to the Emperor of Austria.

(2) The Constituent Assembly. The people had claimed the democratic *Costituente* of Montanelli; but what the new cabinet proposed to carry through was the Federal *Costituente* of Gioberti; that is to say, a constituent body called to organise a federation of states (including the enlarged Piedmont), not a democratic diet for all Italy. Gabussi refers to this alteration with resentment, but adds that many people did not understand the real meanings of the terms.[19]

(3) Carrying out Mamiani's programme of June 5th.

(4) Carrying out the decisions of the Chamber concerning the War of Independence.

[18] Gabussi, II, 229. *V.* also Farini, II, 381 *et seq.*
[19] Gabussi, II, 229.

As to sections (3) and (4), the new cabinet expressed its determination to put them into practice, but the war itself was not mentioned by name. Gabussi remarks on this situation with disgust. "Of the war itself, that terrible rock upon which the Pope had run aground, there is no explicit mention."

The fact was, that an immediate war of aggression against Austria was impossible and always remained impossible. After Pius' departure to Gaeta, Sterbini's government increased the armed forces—by only 1390 men! And after six or seven weeks of public chaos, the pro-Piedmontese faction succeeded in getting into power and made a secret treaty with Piedmont whereby they promised to declare war, and send 15,000 men. But at that moment the republican party came to the fore, and when the Piedmontese reopened hostilities on March 20th, 1849, they had to fight single-handed at Novara; no help was sent from Rome or Tuscany, which were both still occupied in consolidating their republics and not yet in a position to do anything else. And the mere fact that they voted only 15,000 men, in a state of three million inhabitants, proves that there was no longer any widespread enthusiasm in the Papal State for the war; if there had been a genuine, national, soul-stirring war-fever, the people would have raised at least 100,000 volunteers, and no power on earth could have prevented them; witness the Venetian risings against Austria, and the first Sicilian rising against Naples.

To return to Pius; he was now living in solitary grandeur at the Quirinal while the city of Rome was under the sway of the Circolo Popolare; during the fighting on November 16th it had elected a committee consisting of Sterbini, Mucchielli and Polidori, and this committee remained the only centre of authority in the town until November 19th, when it was dissolved.

The Chambers had lost all authority and were rapidly becoming useless. On November 17th they did not sit. On the 18th they met, but the Lower House was unable to raise a quorum.[20] On the 21st both Chambers sat, but six members resigned, including Minghetti. One of the chief causes of difference was a point upon which the cabinet showed a regrettable though inevitable weakness, namely, the pursuit of the murderers of Rossi. Many of the members, especially those from Bologna, wanted to pass a resolution strongly condemning the crime, and to institute an enquiry about it, but Galletti succeeded in evading their demand by saying that the government itself would express its indignation about the matter; an indignation, however, to which it carefully refrained from giving utterance. The fact was that quite literally the ministers felt themselves in the same difficulty as the celebrated Texas juries described by Mark Twain, which never found anyone guilty of murder because such a verdict would be "kind of casting a reflection on the judge". In this case, Galletti could hardly condemn the murder of Rossi without casting a very credible reflection upon the conduct of his friend and colleague Sterbini, and upon that of several other prominent members of the Circolo Popolare. And an enquiry into the matter might have produced fatal results, as was proved by the trial in 1852.

But more serious was the fact that members of Parliament could now be terrorised from the galleries, which were often full of partisans who did not hesitate to shout advice to the legislators coupled with threats in case of failure to follow it. So serious did this evil become, that when a loyal address to the Pope was being voted, Doctor Pantaleoni made a formal complaint to the Speaker that some members had voted twice, first on their own initiative for the Ayes, and secondly, after hearing the shouts from above, for the Noes; many others, he added, had not voted at all. Consequently this loyal resolution was defeated, although at the first count it was believed to have been carried.[21]

[20] As to the quorum, v. Gabussi, II, 234; Spada, II, 531. As to Sterbini's guilt, v. Rosi, p. 218: Rosi says "Sterbini undoubtedly contributed to the killing of Rossi".

[21] Minghetti, II, 128–9; Farini, II, 385. The system of voting

Thus Pius had no longer any genuine legal authority on whom he could rely; constitutional government had given way to mob-rule. As yet, however, the mob-rulers were able to keep order.

During the week which followed the disbanding of the Swiss Guards, Pius remained at the Quirinal. During those days he was very sad;[22] he must no doubt have realised, and realised finally, that the end was come; his hope had been the preservation of the pontifical authority by inspiring it with enlightened ideals; by making Rome the beacon-light of a Liberal state within a free Italy. But it seemed that he had been wrong; Italy was not free; the Temporal Power was gone, and he himself was virtually a prisoner. He was watched day and night by the Civic Guards, and knew that he would not be allowed to leave Rome. Meanwhile, at the palace, there were very few supporters to be seen, either official or unofficial, for "it had now become a crime and a peril to go to the Quirinal". His old friend Pasolini offered to come and stay there, but Pius said:

No, no, you must go to your family. I merely asked about you, so that if on any evening the tumult increased beyond measure, I should not find myself alone, face-to-face with the people.

In those days Pasolini wore his pistols when he went to the Quirinal.

When the new ministry published its programme, Pius must have realised that they intended, and indeed would be obliged to proceed with the chief measures to which they were pledged. This meant that he could be called on to ratify the passing of the *Costituente* and the declaration of war, and

seems to have been that when the Speaker called for those in favour of a motion, all those who were in favour stood up and were counted; then he called for those against the motion, and those in favour sat down and all the opposition rose to their feet to be counted. What Pantaleoni said was that many of the Ayes resumed their seats too quickly to be counted.

[22] The events and crimes of November 15th and 16th left Pius IX's spirit in a state of profound discouragement and emotion. Pasolini, I, 194.

anything else placed before him by any faction in power, who certainly would be indifferent to the spiritual, ecclesiastical and international needs of the Church. In these conditions his wisest course was to leave Rome; he had stayed there through the revolution for the sake of the many families which might otherwise have been thrown amid the horrors of anarchy, but it was now evident that he could no longer protect them. Already several nations had offered him their hospitality, and he decided to accept that of Naples, because he did not wish to abandon his friends and supporters; by crossing the frontier and establishing himself at the town of Gaeta, he would be near enough to remain in touch with them.

On the evening of November 24th he left Rome, unrecognised by his guards, in the dress of an ordinary priest. The details of his escape have often been written; here we need only say that its success was due to the fidelity of one of his servants and of Signor Filippani, the Marshal of the Papal Court; also to the help of the Duc d'Harcourt, the French Ambassador, and to that of Count Spaur, the Bavarian minister, assisted by his wife, the Countess Spaur, who was Italian by birth. Owing to the ability of these friends-in-need, Pius was able to make his escape from the Quirinal by passing along a secret passage which led to a secret door into the courtyard where a carriage was waiting for him; and then, after driving for nearly twelve hours during the night, he found himself, at six o'clock next morning, safe on Neapolitan territory.[23]

This then was the conclusion of a great effort to do what was right. Pius had started with the noble ambition of being at once a Liberal Pope and an Italian patriot King. But the

[23] Carte Pentini, fasc. 27. Also Madrid, Ministerio de Estado, Martinez, November 26th, 1848. Spada, III, 13; Rosi, p. 219. Pasolini, I, 194, puts Pius' departure a day later; so does Farini, II, 389 and Masi, II, 362.

Austrian domination had checked normal progress and vitiated the whole situation.

For two and a half years the experiment of being a Liberal Pope had certainly been tried to the very utmost limit. Having begun by appointing commissions largely composed of life-long reactionaries such as Lambruschini, Pius had then nominated all the best men of the Moderate Party, from Gizzi to Rossi, and had ended by actually entrusting his government to life-long revolutionists, such as Mamiani or Galletti, whom he himself had only lately recalled from exile or from prison. The experiment had been tried through and through and every phase of it had finally brought complete disillusionment.

In after years he seldom referred to this period, the period of his humiliation; but once, in April 1849, when receiving a Florentine commission at Gaeta, he openly expressed his feelings:

At that audience, after relating with pain the events which had compelled him to leave Rome, Pius IX spoke the following words, which should be noted in history: "What could I do more?...I had made Rossi Prime Minister and had placed Zucchi in command of the Ministry of War. They murdered one and they covered the other with insult and calumny."[24]

In fact the age-long conception of a small international state set apart for the Church, had been crushed out of existence in the conflict between imperialism and nationality; between domination and revolution.

For all the believers in a united Italy, for the men who were striving to find the right path towards unity and independence, these two years had been the period of their trial; the time when patriots of all types were pioneers gathering experience at the risk of their lives. It is impossible not to feel sympathy with each of the seekers in turn. Perhaps the chief

[24] The *Nazione* newspaper, September 13th, 1860. Extract from a long and interesting letter addressed to the Pope by "an illustrious Italian publicist and scientist".

of them were Gioberti and Pius IX, d'Azeglio and Charles Albert, Mazzini and Garibaldi. Cavour was not yet a power in the land.

Firstly, there had been the dream of Gioberti, translated into action by Pius IX: an Italian federation of free states. All chance of realising this ideal died with Rossi.

Secondly, there had been the glorious dream of Charles Albert: "Italia farà da sè." This died with Charles Albert.[25] When Cavour took up the work, he realised that Piedmont must have an ally.

Thirdly, only a few months later there was to appear the dream of Mazzini: an Italian republic; it was never more than a vision, and without Garibaldi would have been little better than a fiasco.

Yet, however hopeless, the defence of Rome was justified by results. Victory was out of the question; and this short experience proved to most people the impossibility of a republic. Nevertheless it was a triumph. It rescued the strivers for a united Italy from the depths of their humiliation, and brought to them a fresh pride in themselves and their cause. And, as a matter of history, Garibaldi's achievement was destined to go far beyond this. It was owing to his gallant defence of the old Aurelian walls, to his celebrated appeal to the volunteers, to his wonderful retreat—and the pathetic death of Anita—that his name has inspired the whole Italian people to this day. This Garibaldian story, completed by that of the Thousand, went straight to the heart of the poor workers, and undoubtedly helped more than any other influence to form the soul of the new nation.

It was very sad for Pius that all this bloodshed and needless destruction was destined inevitably to take place in Rome;

[25] It was fortunate that neither Charles Albert nor Pius were successful. If Charles Albert had set up his new kingdom he would probably have had to resign Savoy or Nice, or both of them, to France without receiving more than half of Italy. If Pellegrino Rossi had succeeded in erecting a Liberal Papal State, that would have divided Italy, at all events for many years to come.

but in no other capital could it have had so great an influence. The final scene in the tragedy was a view of the Eternal City surrounded by foreigners, but with Italians from every state defending its walls.

And, since genuine, honest, good work is never entirely wasted, we see that Pius' great effort at modernising the Papal government, though it failed, nevertheless remains the chief justification of the Papal attitude during the nineteenth century. To those who accuse the Holy See of persistent obscurantism a true answer can be made; that Pius IX tried modern, liberal, progressive measures until he found them impossible; explored the problem in every conceivable direction until it actually lost him the Temporal Power. Thus, as we now see, when he called upon the Emperor of Austria to withdraw from Italy, it was the utmost political limit to which a Pope could go; and when he revealed himself in the prayer "Benedite Gran Dio l' Italia" (O Lord God bless Italy), it was, as it were, his greeting and at the same time his supreme farewell to the newly-risen nation around him.[26]

[26] The above paragraphs are not merely the opinions of the present writers; they represent the feelings even of Pius's enemies of that day. For instance, in 1896, forty-eight years after these events, Gaspare Finale, a Bolognese revolutionist who had since then served with the Piedmontese army when it conquered the Papal State, could still express his feelings about Pius as follows: "In spite of all the diverse and contrary events which have since occurred, the men of my generation can never forget with what joyful auspices, with what faith and with what hopes his pontificate began in the year 1846. And I myself can never forget how in the beginning of 1848 I heard him bless Italy from the loggia of the Quirinal." Finale, *Le Marche: Ricordanze*, p. 44.

Appendix I

PIUS IX'S INTERVIEW WITH THE CAVALIERE BARGAGLI ON APRIL 20TH, 1848[1]

During this period we have one very valuable indication of what was passing in Pius' mind, namely an interview which he granted to Bargagli, the Florentine envoy, who was urging that the Pope should write an Encyclical to stem the flood of extreme republicanism in Italy.

On this day, April 20th, Pius seems to have talked more openly to Bargagli than he did to his own ministers, so much so that one almost wonders whether they really were all as ignorant about the coming Allocution as their Memoirs would have us believe; they were naturally anxious afterwards to avoid even the slightest responsibility in connection with it.

One thing is certain, however, namely that on April 20th, nine days before its publication, Bargagli, during an interview with the Pope, was correctly informed of its main drift and duly reported it to his government in Florence that very evening. This report of his, which seems to have lain unheeded in the Archives ever since, is surely of singular value, because it was written nine days before the event (and not like the Memoirs, several years after), and because it gives us Pius' views at that critical moment not only concerning his fateful Allocution, but also as to the whole Italian situation; and although he does not appear to have fathomed the fact that he stood actually at the parting of the ways, still his views are shrewd enough. Throughout all this period he shows a certain equanimity which surprised Bargagli;[2] in fact he seems to be acting

[1] Florence Arch. Esteri, Busta 2446.
[2] He remarks on this several times. After his interview with Pius on April 4th he wrote: "The mind of the Holy Father is not cast down at the imposing aspect of this Italian and European revolution; his trust in God seems to reassure him with the feeling that his prayers will be granted and that a happy calm will succeed the present tempest." But as the month went on and fresh movements took place, Pius evidently began to feel hurt at their being attributed to him; although he seems to have remained hopeful. On April 15th Bargagli wrote of "the state of perfect quiet and tranquillity in which the mind of His Holiness—fortunately I think— remains". Florence Arch. Esteri, Busta 2446.

in accordance with his own conscience, rather than with a view to immediate results.

Pius began, so Bargagli tells us, by showing that he fully realised the danger dreaded by the Tuscan government, namely, the torrent of demagogic and extreme ideas which was sweeping over Italy from Paris to Milan, Naples and Sicily, and might set the whole country ablaze. "In Sicily", he said, "it was extremely probable that from one moment to another they might proclaim a republic, and if that happened, God alone knew if, where and when the fire would end." But he was not without hope, because the news from Paris was good, because the war would tend to unite all Italians, and because Charles Albert would not move far from Milan until he knew the decision of the Provisional Government there, and the energy of his efforts in the cause of Italy were manifestly conditional on its not resulting in a government which would be dangerous to his own; and finally, because the Venetian republic was not a danger; its envoy had assured him that the Venetians had only adopted that form of government in order to unite all their people under one banner—the glorious banner of St Mark—that they strove only for the nationality and independence of Italy and would never depart from the advice of the Holy See in that respect.

Passing then to his proposed Encyclical, he told Bargagli that it was necessary to be very careful before opening his lips at all; and that his ministers were opposed to making an utterance, but that he intended to publish the Encyclical none the less; and that in these holy days of solitude and retirement he proposed himself to write on a few points for the people of Germany. "I am saddened", he said to me, "on account of the efforts that are being made there to turn the occasion of the present time in favour of schism. These depress (*umiliare*) my spirit.[3] I shall perhaps also

[3] In his despatch of April 17th Pareto said that papers had arrived saying that there was anger in Germany and even talk of a schism; that these would influence the Pope "who has the interests of religion very much at heart". Turin Arch. Lettere Ministri, Roma, 1848. But to Pareto on April 24th Pius merely said in general terms that he intended to address an Encyclical to "the whole Catholic world", "onde nel fare conoscere la condotta da Lui tenuta dalla sua elezione in poi, combattere le opinioni erronee che si spargono continuamente sul di Lui conto e che potrebbero recar pregiudizio alla religione Cattolica". "To make known to them the conduct which He had held ever since his election, and to fight the erroneous opinions which are constantly being spread about Him, and might

be led into speaking about Italy; but let that remain with you."
And at this juncture he did not abstain from breaking out into
vehement complaints because people tried to attribute to him not
only the commotions (*movimenti*) in Italy, but those throughout
Europe.

He said to me that certainly he had desired to make generous
grants to his subjects of the institutions that justice demanded.
But these reforms which had become the subject of such bitter re-
proofs, had they not on former occasions in 1831 been prescribed
by Austria to his predecessor? And was it then untrue, he asked,
that the bad faith shown in not carrying them out had been the
origin of the unrest in Romagna and the theme of continual
remonstrance from the European powers?

But for the example of Naples, but for the obstinacy of Austria,
both of whom had pushed matters to the extreme limits, he would
have stopped his course of reforms after the institution of the
Consulta.

Therefore it was on the governments of Naples and Austria,
and not on him, that the blame should fall for the ills that may
afflict Italy.

He ended by telling me that he had been informed by General
Durando that he could no longer restrain the enthusiasm of his
troops who wanted to cross the Po, and that he had therefore
authorised the general to do anything for the security of the state
and the tranquillity of the people. It was not the desire, but the
urgency of the circumstances, which would perhaps give rise to
the beginning of hostilities.

Finally, Pius remarked that he hoped the Grand Duke Leopold
did not suppose that Mazzini's fable about proclaiming the Papacy
as the head of an Italian republic had received any sympathy from
him. "He (Pius) was the first to perceive the poison which is
concealed beneath the veil of religion in such schemes; no one was
more certain than himself that, once the agitators of this type had
obtained their desire, the sovereignty of the Tiara would be thrown
to the earth even sooner than that of any other Monarchy, and
banished from the scene."

In this interview we have an account from Pius' own lips of
nearly all the disputed points concerning him; and in his account
of the coming Allocution he says nearly all the same things which
appeared in it nine days later, and for which he was blamed. But

prejudice the Catholic religion." *Ibid.* Lettere Ministri, Roma,
1848, 1849.

Bargagli evidently saw nothing unwise or surprising in them; and he knew already that Pius did not mean to declare a holy war,[4] though not perhaps that he would refuse to declare war at all.

Meanwhile Pareto had nearly given up hope of persuading Pius to declare war, as he wrote to the Piedmontese government after the audience of April 24th.[5]

It seems difficult to believe, therefore, that the Allocution took the ministers so completely by surprise as they afterwards asserted.

According to this evidence, then, and according to the opinions of those who knew him best, when Pius wrote his Allocution he was stampeded so to speak by his conscience into a determination to save the spiritual side of the Papacy, without quite realising perhaps that the rest of his life would be embittered by the gradual loss of the Temporal Power, until at last he ended his days a self-constituted prisoner.

[4] As early as April 11th Bargagli had written: "The noted Encyclical of the Holy Father, according to information gathered by me at the Quirinal, forms the subject of his whole thought and all his cares." It was evidently very generally known that Pius was preparing a declaration. Bargagli says that the then plan (afterwards dropped) was that it should be preceded by a circular for distribution in every parish to enable the Pope "to raise his voice against all these ideas of revolution or democratic subversion". "And", he says, "to limit Himself to this for the present. The determination to give to the war the character of a holy crusade has been suspended until more needed.

"But it is not intended to give too open a sanction to General Durando's proclamation; nor has it been thought necessary to have recourse unnecessarily to an act whose moral influence is very great, but should be reserved to the occurrence of a greater need." Esteri, Busta 2446. Bargagli does not tell us who gave him this information.

[5] Turin Arch. Lettere Ministri, Roma, April 25th, 1848.

Appendix II

KING FERDINAND II OF NAPLES

The three accusations usually made by modern historians against the King of Naples are: (1) that he was thrice-perjured; (2) that he took a pleasure in bombing his subjects; (3) that his prisons were cruel and were shown up by Mr Gladstone.

As to (1) there seems to be no room for doubt. In reality there is only one breach of his oath even alleged against him, the other two refer to his father and grandfather. But it is true, as we have seen, that he swore to the Constitution on February 10th, 1848, and that he gave up summoning Parliament after 1849. It is equally true, however, that from the very start the elected members refused all allegiance to the Constitution, so that they can hardly blame him if he no longer felt bound by his oath.

As to (2); Ferdinand II was named "Bomba" by the Sicilians, because (they say) he bombarded the town of Messina. It is perfectly true that General Filangieri shelled that city—in the opinion of the British admiral for eight hours longer than was necessary. This is a serious accusation against Filangieri, but how does it concern Ferdinand, who was not within 350 miles of the place? It is known now that on previous occasions, at Palermo and on May 15th, he had made every effort to avoid bloodshed, so that if he had been present at Messina, most probably he would have given similar orders to stop the bombardment. But in any case it is manifestly impossible to make a sovereign personally responsible for the excesses of his armies in the field.[1]

[1] If Filangieri were alive to-day (1939) he might retort that nowadays bombing defenceless cities has become the daily custom in war. On this occasion Messina was garrisoned by *squadri* from outside the town—brigands in all but name, and fairly savage in character. The fighting was bestial: no quarter on either side. Evidently there were many Royalist outrages. But it seems to be true that on the first day, September 3rd, the Sicilians killed at least 40 of their prisoners and carried round several Swiss heads on poles; it is said too by Swiss writers that the rebels paraded the arms and legs of Swiss soldiers and sold their flesh as meat in the

The third accusation concerns the years 1851 and 1852 and is therefore entirely outside the scope of this volume, which ends in 1848. Moreover, its examination would require a search of months, if not years, among original documents, for which the present writers have not as yet had time. Therefore it is impossible for them to give any opinion on the subject.

We have no views of our own; but the opinion of Signor Paladino may be of interest. His view is that by 1852 Ferdinand had passed through a campaign of slander of such unparalleled virulence that he was a good deal hardened and embittered. He was, as we know, a man aged before his time; at the age of forty-six he was said to look sixty; and he died when he was only forty-nine.

According to Paladino these last years were his worst; he was moving on a flood of reaction and he attacked members of the Liberal party in a manner unjustifiable.

Although we offer no criticism, it is necessary to say that Mr Gladstone's horrible accusations about the prisons are fully accepted by historians of the standing of Tivaroni and Masi, while in Rosi's admirable *Storia contemporanea* they are not mentioned at all. But these Italian writers, while chronicling the later accusations, do not, like some of the English, omit the provocation which Ferdinand had previously received.

Paladino evidently feels this to be necessary; he condemns the whole policy between 1849 and 1852; he speaks of a reactionary ministry containing soldiers and others who aimed at repression and "who were initiating the iniquitous proceedings which we have already mentioned". But his final verdict runs as follows:

market (Filangieri says they ate it!). This story is quoted by Tivaroni and definitely confirmed by the English chaplain at Messina, the Rev. Matthew Drake Babington, who saw the heads and arms and legs, and heard "on indubitable authority" that the flesh was sold. He adds that when boatloads of refugees implored to be taken on board the American ship on which he had found safety, the captain called out: "It serves you right for carrying the soldiers' heads about on poles the other day."

Incidentally it will be remembered that, through Lord Minto, Ferdinand had granted the Sicilians the very widest form of Home Rule, but they refused it and offered their crown to the Piedmontese Prince Ferdinand. Tivaroni, *Ital. Merid.* p. 334. Diary of the Rev. M. D. Babington, English chaplain at Messina. Rome, Reg. Ist. Vol. 662. The original is in the British Museum.

What wonder if after all this the King who had shown himself accommodating to the last extreme and had used clemency with all —that Ferdinand II who had declared himself ready to observe the Constitution even after his victory over the rebels—should have become changed in mind; should have relied for support on the reactionary and absolutist faction which had been defeated on January 29th (the day he granted his Constitution); should have shown himself intolerant and severe, and should have allowed them to inveigh even against innocent people? What wonder if he felt encouraged to take this path and proceed resolutely on it, when before all Europe he seemed to be the first sovereign to triumph over demagogy? Any other in the place of the King of Naples would have lost his head, and he lost it....At the end of July 1849 the Bourbon Monarchy was at the parting of the ways; either to continue in the path that had been pursued during the previous two years, or else to break with the constitutional party. He chose the latter.[2]

[2] Paladino, p. 487.

INDEX